THE
COMPLETE GUIDE
TO COARSE FISHING

Uniform with this volume

THE COMPLETE GUIDE TO SEA ANGLING

Compiled and edited by Alan Wrangles

THE
COMPLETE GUIDE
TO COARSE FISHING

Compiled and Edited by
ALAN WRANGLES

Illustrated by
David Carl Forbes

DAVID & CHARLES : NEWTON ABBOT

0 7153 5887 1

First published as 'Newnes Complete Guide to Coarse Fishing', 1967

This edition, revised and re-printed, 1973
for David & Charles (Publishers) Limited

Printed in Great Britain
by Redwood Press Limited, Trowbridge, Wiltshire
for David & Charles (Publishers) Limited
South Devon House   Newton Abbot   Devon

Affectionately dedicated to my father
for all his help and encouragement,
and to my son Anthony,
with the wish that his fishing years
may be many.

INTRODUCTION

EVER since recorded history began, there have been references to man's interest in catching fish. Originally the accent was on fishing as a means of obtaining food, and it is naturally impossible to say just when and where man first indulged fishing purely as a sporting pastime.

Homer made reference to a man 'casting his ox-horn lure', and the Greek poet Oppian wrote on the subject of sea fishing somewhere about 200 years after the birth of Christ. In England, most of the angling literature seems to have stemmed from a book compiled by Dame Juliana Berners in the late 1400s. That a woman should be concerned with fishing may have seemed odd in those far-off days, but in the latter half of the 20th Century many women are not only keen anglers but they take part, on equal terms, in competition fishing and in the running of clubs and associations.

It can be truly said that angling is a sport or pastime that caters equally for every age group as well as for both sexes. For me, there is a very great personal joy in seeing this development, for in an age that has seen family interests tend to grow apart it is a wonderful thing to be associated with a sport that can have an attraction for all.

To ask any group of angling enthusiasts what they individually find so attractive is to invite as many different answers as there are anglers in the group. One will probably say that it is the thrill of the having a big fish on the hook; others will talk of the many facets of angling, the beauty of the country-side, the peace and quiet of the river bank and the ever-changing scene as high summer slips into autumn, and then winter which in due course changes into spring. Not that the angler sees much of the last magical change, for with spring just around the corner, the coarse angling season comes to an end, and the next time he sees his own favourite waterside haunt the seasons have gone full circle and he is back in high summer.

The changing scene, the excitement and the mysteries of life under the surface is what this book is all about. Also, there are chapters which have been designed to give you a good background knowledge of the written as well as the unwritten laws, without which coarse angling would not be the immensely sporting pastime that it is.

The term 'coarse' is, I feel, a direct contradiction of all that freshwater angling stands for. While agreeing that from the point of view of eating, most of the fish that are so called are coarse in the extreme, neither tackle nor tactics could be so named. The same is true of the appearance of the fish. How can one term a sparkling dace, a majestic carp or a handsome perch as coarse? Even that deadly killer, the pike, has a symmetry of line that proclaims it a king of the underwater world. But so be it, coarse angling is the term by which the sport is known and loved, and through this book it is hoped that many more will come to know and love this fine and absorbing recreation.

ALAN WRANGLES

ACKNOWLEDGMENT

Except for those directly acknowledged, the photographs reproduced in this book were taken by John Mitchell, to whom I am most grateful.

A.W.

CONTENTS

CONTENTS

THE SPORT OF COARSE ANGLING

by

ALAN WRANGLES

Looking back over the years, my life seems to have been dominated by a series of angling incidents. Recalling these, I can chart the passage of time – not for me the easy method of remembering an ever-mounting score of birthdays, oh, no, pre-school days are highlighted by the gift of my first net on a cane, infant and junior schools mean a succession of cotton reels and garden canes, until that magical day arrived and I became the proud owner of my first wooden centrepin.

It may or may not have been a birthday – that doesn't really matter, what was important was the fact that at long last I could sit on the bank of the local pond and, after fixing my new reel most carefully onto my garden cane rod, could imitate my elders.

I was eleven when serious war was declared between myself and my schoolmasters. To me the choice seemed simple enough, fishing and a large slice of boyish heaven; or school, passing exams and a promise of a better life when I was older. At that time, a fish on the hook there and then seemed infinitely more exciting than the rather cloudy 'better things later on'. This, then, was my introduction to the sport of coarse angling – yours may have been similar, or perhaps you

came to know and love it through early participation with an elder brother, or a keen father.

Of course, in those days fishing was a relatively uncomplicated pastime, usually it was just a matter of asking permission, or joining a Club with fishing rights, which would cost you but a very few shillings per year. To-day, except for one or two very notable exceptions, free fishing is almost non-existent, and some Clubs have a waiting list (if joined, it will possibly take you a year or two to reach the top).

One extensive open fishery which is the mecca of tens of thousands of anglers from London and the Home Counties is that part of the River Thames which lies between the London Stone at Staines and stretches downstream to Teddington. On this reach of that glorious old river, fishing from both boat and bank is absolutely free – just so long as you respect private property.

Although some Clubs are bursting at the seams, there are many which have plenty of room for new members, and even if you do not want to join a Club there are many hundreds of miles of river, canal and lake bank which are available to the non-Club angler, just so long as he is willing to purchase a day or weekly ticket. To know where you can fish and to understand the basic rules and regulations governing coarse angling is absolutely vital.

Through the ages, many laws have been passed governing the use of rivers and the taking of fish, but for our purposes it is most convenient to start in 1923 when the Salmon and Freshwater Fisheries Act came into being. For the purposes of legislation, this Act defined a fresh water fish: 'any fish living in fresh water, exclusive of salmon and trout and of any kinds of fish which migrate to and from tidal waters, and of eels and of the fry of eels.'

In this Act provision was made for an annual close season, during which period 'no-one shall fish with a rod and line for any fresh water fish in any river, lake, pond, stream, etc.'. There are various clauses which allow the taking of fresh water fish in the interests of science and to clear salmon and trout waters of unwanted stock, etc., but from the ordinary angler's point of view it is wisest to just accept the fact that, with one or two exceptions, coarse fishing is absolutely out from the 15th of March until the 15th of June (both dates inclusive). One notable exception to this rule is Yorkshire where the close season is from the first day of March to the last day of May. Information regarding local variations is always available, upon request, from the River Authority in the Area.

It is at this point that we meet a new name – the River Authority. These are bodies which came into being on the 1st of April 1965 as a result of the 1963 Water Resources Act.

A River Authority is a Joint Board drawing a bare majority of its members from the county councils and county boroughs from whom it derives a substantial proportion of its income. Also, there are members representing fishery interests, land drainage, agriculture, public water supplies and industry. A professional technical staff carry out the day-to-day operations necessary to keep such an organisation running smoothly.

In England and Wales there are 27 River Authorities. They are Northumbrian, Yorkshire Ouse and Hull, Trent, Lincolnshire, Welland and Nene, Great Ouse, East Suffolk and Norfolk, Essex, Kent, Sussex, Hampshire, Isle of Wight, Avon and Dorset, Devon, Cornwall, Somerset, Bristol Avon, Severn, Wye, Usk, Glamorgan, South West Wales, Gwynedd and Clwyd, Dee,

Mersey and Weaver, Lancashire, and Cumberland River Authorities. The powers and duties of these bodies are many and varied in the extreme, including the conservation of water, flood control and land drainage, hydrometric surveys, the control of the abstraction of surface water by a licensing system, prevention of pollution and the administration of fisheries.

The angler is likely to have his first encounter with the River Authority when he obtains a rod licence. This can in some ways be likened to a gun licence inasmuch as it merely allows the holder to engage in the sport of coarse angling with a rod and line; it does not give him carte blanche to fish where-so-ever he pleases. In the same way, a gun licence entitles the holder to own or carry a gun, but it does not carry with it the right to go and shoot over public or private land.

Rod licences are valid only in the area administered by the issuing authority, and while costs vary from area to area, an average charge, at the time of writing, would be about five shillings. The authority to issue rod licences stems from the Salmon and Freshwater Fisheries Act of 1923, and it is a power that has been adopted by virtually every River Authority in the country. Prior to the River Authorities, there were River Boards which exercised the same rights.

In the areas where rod licences for coarse angling are necessary, the angler will also find that the River Authority has issued a set of bye-laws which are designed to protect the anglers' main interest – the fish. Fishery bye-laws include such rules as 'Prohibited Modes of Fishing' and 'Prohibited Instruments'. Also, there are often rules which forbid the retention of undersize fish in keepnets unless the angler is competing in a bona fide competition, or is keeping a specified number for use as live bait.

Fishery bye-laws are not standard throughout the country, therefore every angler is advised to make sure that he or she is absolutely familiar with all the local rules and regulations. It is always wisest to assume that licences and bye-laws are in force, so always make enquiries before starting to fish. Rod licences and copies of the bye-laws are available from the appropriate River Authority.

Normally, bailiffs and tackle dealers also carry stocks of licences, etc., but, and this I cannot emphasise too often or too strongly, the onus is on the angler to provide himself with all the necessary licences and permits, and to acquaint himself with whatever rules there may be. To be caught fishing without a licence can mean a very unpleasant trip to a Magistrates' Court.

Coarse angling is a popular sport, and so it is understandable that many waters have fallen under the control of various Clubs and Associations; the easiest way of obtaining access to these waters is by applying to join one of these bodies. Charges vary greatly, it is possible to pay as little as ten or fifteen shillings, and as much as several pounds.

Many rivers and lakes are what are known as 'ticket waters' and on these one can go fishing for a day or a week or so upon payment of a fee which may be as little as two or three shillings or as much as a pound. But no matter whether you go fishing as a Club member, or as a day ticket holder, you will almost certainly require a rod licence as well.

To go fishing on a Club or private water without permission is to go poaching, an offence which in days gone by could bring dire punishment to the offender. Transportation to the Colonies, imprisonment and heavy fines were all hazards of poaching, but these days, apart from heavy fines, the most likely penalty that you would incur is the immediate confiscation of the tackle which you are using.

Many organisations devote time and energy to improving the sport, but in my opinion among the leaders in the fight to maintain and, where possible improve coarse angling, is the Anglers' Co-operative Association. The A.C.A. seeks to improve coarse angling by tackling that vile product of the nineteenth and twentieth centuries – widespread pollution.

This is a word which constantly occurs in modern angling literature and it is most important for the angler to know something about not only the effects of pollution, but also its causes.

I am greatly indebted to the Director of the A.C.A., Mr. Charles Wade, for allowing me to use the following information from the A.C.A. Handbook:

There are several types of pollution and one of the most common is organic. This can be a discharge into a water course of a liquor containing matter which putrefies and is destroyed by bacteria. The bacteria consumes the oxygen contained in the water course which in turn results in the fish dying and the weedbeds decaying.

Another form of pollution is that which is occasioned by the discharge of hot water. The amount of oxygen contained in hot water is considerably less than that which is contained in cold. Therefore, the discharge of clean but hot water can produce the same result as a discharge of highly de-oxygenating organic effluent.

Pollution can also be caused by the discharge of water containing mineral matter. For example, if coal dust, china clay or sand is deposited in large quantities into a river it may result in the destruction of food supplies, and the ruination of spawning beds.

Occasionally fish mortality on a horrific scale is occasioned by the accidental spillage into a river of a poison, such as cyanide, arsenic or any one of many acids. Whilst occurrences such as this can have devastating results upon fish life, the effects are usually of a relatively short duration. But, of course, there is virtually nothing that one can do to rescue the fish, for as the poison sweeps downstream it kills all in its path. Eventually its action becomes less potent as it becomes diluted by the increasing volume of water.

Organic pollution has been present in rivers ever since man first began living on their banks, but the amount of pollution caused by the refuse from his small villages was relatively unimportant, and even in the Middle Ages when the River Thames was the recipient of all London's refuse, salmon thrived and annually the river had a great run of these magnificent fish.

It was not until the Industrial Revolution that rivers began to die in ever-increasing numbers, and despite the continual warnings of anglers and others interested in river life, little was done to combat the rising tide of filth.

It seems as though what legislation there was contained many loopholes through which those responsible for pollution could escape.

Eventually a stand was made and the Anglers' Co-operative Association was founded in 1948 by a London Magistrate, the late John F. Eastwood, O.B.E., K.C. He realised that under criminal law the edicts governing river pollution were hopelessly inadequate, but that it was possible to achieve much under common law. If this common law, which in simple terms is 'the right of a riparian owner to have the water passing his property in its natural state, unaltered in quality, temperature or volume' were applied, a great deal of pollution could be stopped.

You might well ask why had this not been done before? The answer comes back, as it does on so many occasions, to one of pounds, shillings and pence. To bring an action under common law can be an enormously expensive business, and even if you win, your costs will not necessarily be met. Therefore many riparian owners ignored the fact that the coarse fish in their rivers were being killed, for after all, in the years before the Second World War, rents for such waters were very small. However, salmon and trout rivers commanded high rents, and so it is understandable that the owners protected them more vigorously.

By banding together, those of like persuasion were able to finance lawsuits, and since that memorable day when the A.C.A. was born, hundreds of cases of pollution have been tackled and brought to a successful conclusion.

This does not in any way detract from the sterling work carried out by the River Authorities, Conservancy Boards, river keepers and bailiffs. The work of each is complementary to the other, but the fight against pollution is never-ending, and from the angler's point of view, and in fact from the country's point of view, the more that engage in the fight the better it is for all.

Although the A.C.A. has been eminently successful in its battle against pollution, it is not the only body concerned, nor was it the first.

In 1903 the National Federation of Anglers was formed, an organisation which has constantly been prodding Government Departments and Local Authorities, the sole intention being to safeguard and improve angling conditions.

The N.F.A. was born, as are so many organisations, of a great need to bring order, and where possible a sense of single-mindedness, to the many Clubs and Associations that were beginning to appear all over the country.

Three years after its formation, the N.F.A. organised the first National Angling Championship and in that year, 1906, the River Thames at Pangbourne was chosen as the venue. Then, a mere seven teams competed, whereas by the mid-sixties the number of teams competing had grown to more than 100, and with each team consisting of 12 anglers. It can readily be appreciated that a complex organisation is needed to operate such an enormous competition.

In a later chapter the competitive side of coarse fishing is more fully discussed, but at this point it is fair to say that it is through competitive fishing that many of our more noteworthy advances in tackle and technique have evolved.

Each year, on the second Saturday in May, delegates from all parts of the country attend the N.F.A. Annual Conference, and while the items which are discussed are varied in the extreme, uppermost in every delegate's mind is the well-being of the sport, which in broad terms returns in full cycle to the waters from which we derive our pleasure.

In the rivers, lakes and canals that criss-cross the English landscape there is a great diversity of life. Some of it is dismissed by the angler as of no account, but this is not true. The thousands of differing insects, plants and fish are all interdependent to a greater or lesser degree, for example it is upon the larvae of insects that carp feed and grow fat.

In a later chapter the fascinating chain of life which stretches under the surface is discussed at length, but here I wish to do no more than introduce you to the species of fresh water fish with which this book is concerned.

The fact that the water in a river or lake is pure enough to sustain fish life does not necessarily mean that all species of coarse fish will thrive. That which is ideal for the carp would not suit the barbel. Therefore a pattern of distribution has become established, and in it various species have fairly well-defined areas of habitat. A river which contains many different species will inevitably contain stretches which produce better fishing for one variety than another.

In this book we are concerned with the following: barbel, bleak, bream (common and silver), carp (common and crucian), chub, dace, eel, grayling, gudgeon, perch, pike, roach, rudd, ruffe and tench.

The barbel has a very limited distribution, simply because the type of river in which it will thrive is comparatively rare. They favour a well-aerated 'streamy' river with areas of hard gravel, and one which can be termed as temperate. Neither mountain streams nor the slow turgid clay-bedded type of river will suit these fish. The Thames, the Dorset Stour and the Hampshire Avon, as well as the Welland and Severn, hold good stocks of these fish, but as is to be expected, not every stretch produces good barbel fishing. These are large and powerful fish which, when hooked, will fight with all the dash and zip which one would expect from such immensely strong-looking creatures.

In complete contrast, there is the bleak. Whereas the barbel will reach 14 lb and more, the bleak on average does not exceed 2 oz. They are widely distributed throughout England and are a shoal fish usually found in sluggish waters. Being one of the smallest species caught by the coarse angler, they are rarely fished for deliberately, except when required as bait or maybe by an angler who is fishing in a competition and finds that the stretch of water in which he must fish holds nothing but bleak.

One of the most distinctive fish in our fresh waters is the bream, of which there are two species, the common and the silver. The common bream is oval-shaped, the body being compressed sideways, and individual fish weighing 5 and 6 lb are not uncommon in good bream waters. One of more than 10 lb is rare, and on many rivers fish of 2 and 3 lb are more likely to be the average size.

They are often described as a 'rather sluggardly' species, but to a large extent their fighting qualities depend upon the waters in which they live. Those from a good river such as the Thames can normally be expected to put up a far better fight than those from one of the many minor slow-flowing rivers which hold good stocks of these fish. The bream is widely distributed, being found in great shoals in the Norfolk Broads, the Cheshire Meres, some of the slower rivers in the south, and as far north as parts of Southern Scotland. They thrive in both rivers and lakes, and in flowing water will often tend to inhabit the slower deeper sections where the bed is soft.

The silver bream is a much smaller fish and is fully covered in a latter section, but in broad terms as a sporting species it is not as highly thought of as the common bream.

The real heavyweight of our fresh waters is the common carp. Every so often an individual fish weighing around 40 lb is caught, but at the time of writing, the record, 44 lb, which was set by Richard Walker in 1952 has still to be beaten. Carp is not indigenous to the British Isles, it is thought that it was first introduced into England in the 1540s, but be that as it may, from the sporting point of view, the carp is a most highly esteemed fish.

It tends to favour either still or slow-flowing waters which have a soft bed where it can root for food. Extremes of temperature rapidly affect feeding patterns, therefore the early months of the coarse angling season provide the best of the sport, but even then, unsettled weather will seriously affect carp fishing. From late October onwards, unless conditions are exceptional, serious carp fishing is out.

The crucian carp is somewhat similar in outline shape to the common bream, being completely dissimilar to the common carp, but whereas the bream has an almost triangular-shaped dorsal fin, the crucian has a long dorsal with a convex shape. In many ways its habits are complementary to the common carp, but in size it cannot be compared. One weighing more than 4 lb can be considered exceptional.

The chub are a hard-fighting species, which are widely distributed throughout England. They are gregarious, but the heaviest fish are often solitary creatures. Although they are to be caught in a wide variety of rivers, some of the best chub fishing tends to be where barbel flourish. A good average fish of 3 or 4 lb can display strength out of all proportion to its size.

One of the smaller yet most delightful of all our freshwater fish is the dace. These are a species which, although having a relatively wide distribution, thrive best of all in the rivers which suit the barbel and chub. However, the dace is not so finicky as the barbel, they will frequently grow to specimen size in rivers having a bed of sand or mud. These are a very lively fish, and for their size fight hard, giving sport throughout the whole of the season. The majority of the dace that are caught range between 4 and 12 oz, with fish approaching a pound being exceptional.

The eel is a species which needs little or no description. The majority of anglers curse them, for when an eel is hooked it will almost inevitably writhe and twist its body around the terminal tackle, liberally coating it with a sticky slime. There is hardly a water, both still and flowing, that does not hold its quota of eels, but they are rarely, if ever, caught during the winter months.

Another species which has a very limited distribution, from the coarse angler's point of view, is the grayling. I say 'from the coarse angler's point of view' because these fish are often to be found in trout waters where coarse angling is prohibited. In fact, many of the famous southern chalk streams have shoals of grayling which are hunted remorselessly. The grayling has a very beautifully-coloured dorsal fin, in fact its whole body is very handsome. It favours weed beds and streamy runs in well-aerated rivers. One of the finest grayling waters in the North of England is the Driffield Beck, Yorkshire's world famous stream.

Gudgeon are another extremely small species, the average is about 2 oz. They are quite widely distributed, but from the sporting standpoint are of little interest. However, as with other small fish they can be extremely useful to the match angler.

A species which is so distinctive as to need but very little introduction is the perch. 'A handsome fish and a bonny fighter' are words which have been used on many occasions to describe this species. It is seldom that they weigh much in excess of 3 lb, but whatever their size they fight with all the pluck that one would expect from such a bright and aggressive-looking creature. They are predators and one of the sure signs that a perch is feeding is a bomb-like burst of small fry, or the skittering of a small fish across the surface as it is actively hunted and chased.

The pike is a creature that has savaged its way into the literature of the British country scene. Feats performed by individual fish have in some cases become part of country legend, and there are many stories of great pike that lurk in dark pools ready to seize and drag down water-fowl and even swans. Many 20-lb fish are taken each year from English waters, and annually from Scotland and Ireland there come reports of fish of 30 lb and more. Legend has it that pike of 40 and 50 lb and even more have occasionally been taken from some of the great salmon waters of the British Isles.

Roach and rudd are rather similar in shape, but without doubt the roach is a far superior fighter, as well as being a species which gives sport right through the season. Rudd are normally associated with the warmer months.

A 2-lb roach is the target which most coarse anglers set for themselves, and while some achieve this many times during their angling lives there are some who never reach that magic figure. Roach are fish which seem to be equally at home in either a lake or a river, but my own experience has been that river-bred fish are far more lively than those from a lake.

I always think that rudd fishing is at its best from the beginning of the season until late July From then on they seem to become lethargic and during the winter months they are increasingly difficult to hook, particularly in shallow water.

The ruffe is almost a mini-perch, the main difference being that ruffe have one dorsal fin and the perch two. Also, the rather distinctive black stripes which slash across the perch's body are missing from the flanks of the ruffe. It is a fish of rather limited distribution, and individual fish seldom weigh more than 2 or possibly 3 oz.

Although the tench has a nature which sends it rooting and grubbing slowly through the mud when searching for its food, it is an entirely different proposition when hooked. Then it is galvanised into instant action, and there are few fresh-water species that show more pluck and dogged refusal to come to the net. They are a fish of slow-flowing rivers and lakes, but no matter whether the tench you hook be a mere half-pounder or a heavyweight of 7 or 8 lb, be sure that here you will have met an adversary worthy of your skill.

And without a doubt it is skill that, in the final analysis, makes a good angler. Inevitably, every so often a complete novice will make news by catching either an extremely rare species, or a fish of such size that it warrants great attention. But the angler who is consistently successful is not merely lucky. He is one who has made a study of the sport and considers most carefully the water in which he is fishing and the species that are there to be caught. He weighs the advantages of various methods against their probability of success under the conditions prevailing at the time, and although there is, and there always will be, an element of luck in coarse angling, it has so many facets and can tax so many varying skills that luck is but a final sharpness on your hook.

In the chapters that follow this introduction, not only are modern tackle and techniques discussed, but fishery management and fish biology are explained by men who have spent their lives in seeking knowledge, for this is all part of the sport of coarse angling.

NOTE: It is anticipated that as from 1 April 1974, ten regional water authorities will take over the duties now performed by twenty-seven river authorities. These new regional authorities will also absorb all water supply and sewage undertakings, thus bringing virtually all aspects of water control, supply and disposal under the control of these new bodies. Changes affecting anglers will doubtless occur in the future, but at the time of writing few concrete facts relating to regional water authorities are known.

THE HISTORY OF COARSE FISHING

by

Terry Thomas

The catching of fish, together with the various forms of hunting and the growing of food are as old as man, and the spear, the trap and the hook were among his oldest tools. Early man fished simply to obtain food, but, as with his other efforts to support life he found pleasure in the pursuit, and the thrills of catching a fish or hunting an animal and the pleasure of growing plants remain strong in many of us to-day. The instinct to fish is a powerful one; it is surely this inherited desire which produces so many 'born anglers'.

Historians do not agree as to which came first, the hook, the net or the fish spear. Angling however is dependent on the hook, and although most coarse anglers use both landing and keep net, and some use a bent spear in the shape of a gaff, it is with a hook that we must make our first beginnings.

THE GORGE

The earliest hook was a gorge, that is a short piece of wood or bone pointed at both ends and attached slightly off-centre to some form of line. Bait was impaled on it and when a fish had swallowed both a pull on the line caused the gorge to wedge across the fish's gullet.

The gorge was of course an inefficient instru-

ment and as soon as man (in his many stages of development in different civilisations) attained skill in the use of new materials, in particular metals, a hook was one of the first tools so fashioned.

The first outfit then consisted of a hook attached to a line of animal or vegetable matter – a handline in fact. Such an outfit has obvious limitations, in particular when fishing over vegetation, and in every civilisation at some time some man must have seen the advantage of a rod. The various stages of man's development of which we have evidence in the forms of literature or illustration all afford proof of the use of the rod. What is most strange is that in nearly every case – Assyrian, Jewish, Greek, Egyptian, the rod was always a short one of about six feet. The reasons for so short a rod are unknown but the facts of the length are substantiated and historians have satisfied themselves that the constant appearance of so limited a piece of angling equipment is fact and not artist's licence.

THE FIRST JOINTED ROD

The first rod of serviceable length appeared beyond doubt in Roman times. Nearly two thousand years ago Martial described a 'jointed' rod and although there is still some dispute about whether it was used for fishing or fowling it seems certain to me that a nation as advanced as the Romans, with many different sorts of bamboo available within the Empire, saw the advantages of a long rod and one which could be taken apart for easy conveyance. The many forms of reed and bamboo, hollow throughout, had a 'built-in' ferrule and some unknown angler must have seen how simple it was to fit lengths of different bore cane together. Two thousand years later we are doing the same thing with glass fibre.

The Roman angler then was similarly equipped to the roach-pole angler of the Thames. Using a line of horse hair or silk, with his hook attached to a single horse hair, he fished in the identical way to the way the angler in much of Europe still fishes. With this tight line method he could either float fish or leger. Strange though it may seem some Roman anglers used an artificial fly. Stranger still, the dressing of the fly, that is the materials used, were exactly the same as those used to-day in a fly we call the Brown Hackle!

Angling methods and techniques are always dependent upon the tackle available and these must have stood still from Roman times for over a thousand years. Modern angling as we know it started in 1496 with the publication of the first fishing book, the famous *Treatyse of Fysshinge with an Angle*, possibly written by Dame Juliana Berners. In this book we have a most accurate description of the tackle used and as with so many other things throughout the Dark Ages, no progress at all had been made since Roman times. As regards the rod indeed, matters had slid back, for that used in Britain at the end of the 15th Century was a vast, heavy pole in native wood 'hooped in iron'. The line and hooks were certainly no better than those used by the Romans and in consequence the methods of catching fish could not have improved. By contrast the artificial flies, as with the Roman types, were completely modern and most of the patterns mentioned are still made the same way to-day.

THE END RING

The 'fixed line' outfit with horse hair line tied to the rod's end ('dubbe the lyne and frette it fast in y toppe with a bowe to fasten on your lyne') with all its limitations in casting, effective fishing range and playing fish was to continue for another 150 years throughout one of the most dynamic

periods of discovery and invention in man's history. For several thousand years, probably many thousand years, culminating in the Renaissance and the age of global exploration, not one angler saw the obvious and simple method of extending his fishing range in every way. It was not until the first half of the 17th Century that some unknown genius thought of whipping a wire loop to the end of his rod (an end ring in fact) and taking advantage of a running line.

This great 'leap forward' is first mentioned in the 1650s when, either resulting from an increased interest in angling as a sport or conversely creating this greater interest, the books of Walton, Venables and Barker were being widely read. It was Barker who first mentions this running line in connection with some form of reel. The 26 yards of line he considered sufficient to master a salmon obviously required some form of winder to keep it tidy and away from obstacles. What form these early line containers took is subject for conjecture and the contemporary Walton, the 'father of angling' was no wiser, for in 1655 he writes of a 'wheele' about the middle of the rod or nearer the hand 'which is to be observed better by seeing one than by a large demonstration of words'.

It may seem strange that so keen an angler as Walton did not use and apparently had never seen so valuable an aid to more effective fishing. This behaviour is in fact normal and throughout the following centuries in which tackle was progressively improved, nearly every advance was initially resisted. Anglers are traditionalists and any new item of tackle has always been condemned as making fishing too easy, or as being inefficient, or with a magnificent lack of logic, for both reasons at the same time.

THE RUNNING LINE

The running line, with or without a reel, offered great opportunities to the angler of the mid-17th Century. It allowed him to cast much farther. It allowed him to trot his float downstream with the current. Above all it enabled a big fish to be played by giving and retrieving line. Hitherto a fish had to be held on the fixed line as long as possible, and when it could no longer be held, the rod was thrown into the water to be towed about until the quarry was tired, when the angler retrieved rod and fish. Catching big fish must have been a very wet affair!

Despite these obvious advantages the end ring remained the tool of the minority: most anglers continued to use the fixed line for another 150 years.

The contemporary of Walton had another great advantage. It was at this time that Charles Kirkby, a London hook maker, perfected his method of fish hook manufacture using basically the processes commonly used to-day. Not only did he revolutionise hook making; he also invented the Kirby bend of hook which is still used all over the World.

Three hundred years ago then, the angler used a long rod with or without an end ring. If he used a running line he certainly used some form of wooden spool or winder to hold it. His line was of plaited horse hair and his hook link of single hair. Good horse hair is a remarkably strong material and the writer can recall a number of North Country fishermen who in recent years preferred it to silkworm gut. Great care was taken to obtain the best hair and that of a stallion was always considered stronger than that of a mare as it was not weakened by urine. Good hair was probably hard to obtain and there was certainly experiment with other materials. Venables, for example, tried lute strings. Silkworm gut, which has been superseded by nylon only since the Second World War, was first mentioned in 1722.

On the end of his horse hair the angler of Walton's day had a sharp, well-made Kirby hook. Landing nets were certainly used in those times. One item unknown was the keep net. The catch was certainly eaten. There was no easily obtained sea fish in those days unless you lived on the coast. A pike or carp, a dish of bleak (Walton remarks that both bleak and martins are good meat) made a welcome change of diet and on Fridays for most was a religious necessity. The good Isaac even gives a recipe for chub, with which even the French do little.

The methods of fishing were the same as those used to-day. Baits were many – all sorts of worms, fruits, pastes (flavoured with honey), grubs, caddises, insects, and these would either be fished with a float or legered. Live baiting for trout, perch and pike was commonly practised. A primitive form of spinning was used and Walton tells how to make an artificial minnow. The running line must have given enormous advantages here. Fly fishing was well advanced and Walton's great friend Cotton was obviously a master. His flies were both well-made and good copies of the natural insect. Dapping with a natural insect was one of Walton's favourite pastimes. The waters in those days must have been heavily bushed along their banks and the unpolluted rivers must have run very clear. In consequence, there was plenty of cover and fish could be easily seen. Under such circumstances an impaled grasshopper or bluebottle carefully lowered from a position of cover on to the nose of chub or trout is both a deadly and exciting method of angling.

It is difficult, if not impossible, to look back three hundred years and decide whether angling had in fact always been popular or whether it suddenly burst on the British public in the mid-17th Century. Did the books of Barker, Venables and Walton spark off this popularity or result from it? Were the advances made as a result of more anglers fishing or did they lead to this state? Whichever is correct, the facts are that the 1650s were one of the golden eras of the sport.

There were also two major factors which were to have an enormous effect on the development of the sport – the Plague and the Great Fire of London in 1666.

At this time the English needle making industry with its closely allied trades of hook making and tackle making was centred in the City of London. These cottage industries were either wiped out or dispersed by the two catastrophes. After a period of wandering, and in many cases of failure, by 1730 a needle industry had established itself in the small Worcestershire town of Redditch. There is still argument about the origins of the industry there, but the presence of a Cistercian Abbey near the town must have brought skill in light metal working. At least as important, however, was the existence of water power from the River Arrow, the proximity of iron ore in the Black Country and the availability of fuel in the Forest of Arden.

Whatever were the courses of history, by 1730 Henry Milward had established a needle-making business using water power from the Arrow. The industry no doubt remained on a cottage basis for many years with individual families carrying out individual tasks. One family were pointers, another hardeners, and so on. What is remarkable is that the same families still carry out the same processes to-day, albeit of course in modern factories and not at home. The *entrepreneur* in the early days was often the publican. He organised the making of the needle and later the fish hook, took the finished article to a distributing centre, usually London by pack horse, sold it and later shared out the proceeds. Many Redditch factories are built on the sites of public houses and are still known to the locals by the name of the inn which originally stood there.

From needles to fish hooks is a logical step and by the mid-1700s a flourishing trade must have existed. By the early 1800s the World's fish hook trade was centred in Redditch. The letters of John Mills, a local needle and fish hook maker, now in the possession of the Milward family, make fascinating reading. By 1780 Mills was exporting his hooks to Jamaica and America, sending them for shipment to Bristol by ox wagon from Bromsgrove, a town a few miles from Redditch.

From fish hooks, Milwards and others, notably Samuel Allcock, who was to build up the largest tackle business in the world, progressed to other articles of tackle. The angler benefited eventually for he was able to buy articles made in well-organised factories.

It was about the time that the first Henry Milward was building his mill that rod rings began to be fitted all along the rod and not just at the end. These were 'flat rings'. That is to say they were not fixed to stand off but swung through 180 degrees. Such floppy rings were highly inefficient, yet they were to endure up to recent times!

The complete ringing of rods was, of course, the direct result of a general use of a running line and some form of reel. These early reels must have taken many forms, but the first to achieve some form of popularity was a multiplying reel, which looked remarkably like modern reels of this type. These reels were in common use by 1770, but their popularity was short-lived for they were the subject of criticism of mechanical failure.

I have one of these reels and have examined others of the same period. They are beautifully made and provided they were used sensibly, would function at least as well as reels made two centuries later. The trouble lay not in the mechanism but in the users, who were used to the pull-devil-pull-baker methods of playing fish with a fixed line. To try to winch in a fish with 4:1 gearing resulted at the best in failure to move the fish and at the worst stripped gears. It is obvious that the trouble lay here, for an 'im-

provement' was later fitted to these reels in the form of a 'stop' which in some way, usually by means of a spring-loaded lug which engaged in the drum flange, prevented the reel turning. One can only speculate whether the locked spool was intended as an aid to 'pumping' or to reduce the outfit back to fixed line but whatever the exact purpose might have been, the result was not enough. The multiplying reel lost its popularity here and it was left to the Americans to develop it and bring it to its modern standard of efficiency.

ROD IMPROVEMENTS

It is difficult to put a date on the introduction of the whole cane rod into Britain. No doubt these rods were brought back to this country by soldiers and others returning from the colonies. A rod in such material offered many advantages in weight. A top in whole cane, however, is rarely a success, being thick for its strength, clumsy and often slow. Tops were made in ash and other native woods, in imported woods, such as greenheart and also in whale bone and similar materials. It was the search for a good top joint to mount on a whole cane base which led to one of the major tackle inventions, split cane.

At about the time the multiplying reel was being produced, experiments were being made in glueing cane strips together. The idea, of course, was to reduce the diameter and improve the speed of reflex and the flexibility of the top joint. Two strips were tried at first, but these were efficient in only two directions of flex. By the beginning of the 19th Century tops made of four or more strips laminated together were in common use. Improvements in cutting and glueing led to the introduction in about 1860 and on both sides of the Atlantic of rods made throughout in 'built cane', with the Americans just beating us by a nose in producing the first ones.

Foreign woods, greenheart, degamé and lancewood, were also used a great deal at this time, both allied with whole cane for bottom rods and to make complete legering, spinning, live-baiting, sea and fly rods.

THE NOTTINGHAM REEL

The middle of the 19th Century saw another development which was to be of paramount importance to the coarse fisherman. In the Trent Valley in about 1830 an unknown angler took a wooden lace making bobbin used in the Nottingham lace industry and turned it into a fishing reel. The first Nottingham reels, as they became known, were made from wood. We do not know whether the original ones were in walnut but by the time they had been brought up to a high degree of efficiency they were invariably constructed from this beautiful material. Later they were also made in metal, ebonite and a combination of both.

The Nottingham reel had many advantages. It had single action, a wide diameter and was extremely free running. It spun fast and easily on a 'centre pin' and could be perfectly balanced by the insertion of lead in the drum flanges. On a big, fast river like the Trent such reels were perfect. Using a fine plaited silk line, waxed both as protection against damp and to prevent the line becoming waterlogged and sticking to the rod, your Trent angler could trot his float and tackle a long way down with the current. As the reels improved they allowed very light tackle to be cast from the reel, using the Nottingham cast, which is more often known as the Avon cast today. At the end of the swim the tackle could be recovered quickly by 'batting' the rim of the drum. Should a big fish be hooked, the single action gave good control and the ability to recover line without pumping. For the first time in thousands of years the angler had a reel with almost unlimited scope.

The Nottingham reel offered other advantages to other branches of angling. Given the necessary skill, a heavy spinning bait could be cast a long way, and so could a sea lead. These reels were, and still are, ideal for live-baiting. Their design in all their roles influenced the design of fly reels.

THE COARSE ANGLER IN THE 1860s

A hundred years ago then, the coarse angler used a rod we would consider heavy, with butt and joint in whole cane and with a top of lancewood or greenheart. His Nottingham reel would be filled with silk line and below his float of quill and cork would be a cast made of lengths of silkworm gut, imported from Spain and, at Redditch, drawn through jewelled dies in order to obtain the required diameter. It was then knotted together to form a 'yard bottom'. The gut cast required damping before use and, together with the silk line, careful drying at the end of the day. At the end of the cast was a Redditch made hook, fashioned by hand and file and whipped to a further length of gut. With such an outfit he could master almost any conditions and almost any fish.

THE BIRTH OF MATCH FISHING

As tackle changed, so did the habits of the coarse angler. The spreading railway network enabled him to fish much farther afield and, indeed, the same industrial progress which produced the railways polluted waters close to large towns and cities, thus forcing him to seek waters farther from home. The need to travel and the need to find and protect waters because of the poor sport close to towns, led to the formation of clubs and to the now familiar sight of large numbers of anglers leaving urban areas for the same river at the same time. Being Englishmen, and coarse fishing is essentially an English sport, there was soon wagering on the result, as well as sweeps and prizes. In the polluted rivers and canals running through industrial towns, a bet or prize added value and excitement to a netfull of stunted roach. Thus match fishing was born and the midwife was in many cases the publican with an inn close to water. Prizes offered (alarm clocks and copper kettles held pride of place) brought returns in thirsty anglers celebrating success or drowning failure.

REEL IMPROVEMENTS

The Nottingham reel, which led to such great changes in angling methods, was not an easy reel to master and its very difficulties led to other improvements. Being very free-running it was easy, when playing a fish, to allow it to over-run and cause the line to tangle. A check was therefore added, not to offer increased resistance to the hooked fish but to prevent over-run. A later refinement was the 'optional check', with a button to engage and disengage.

The same flywheel action made spinning ('casting from the reel' as it was called) difficult and ingenious mechanisms were added to take the place of skill when controlling the reel.

Despite these aids, and despite improvements in reels such as the Hardy Silex, the Allcock Aerial, the Milward Marston-Crosslé and others, the centrepin reel remained difficult to master. In an attempt to provide an easier reel to use, and in particular for salmon spinning, the Scottish firm of Malloch produced in the 1880s a reel which in its advanced form was to have greatest effect on most types of fishing all over the world. The Malloch reel was on a turntable. To cast, the drum was turned so that its end was in line with the rings, the line slipping from a drum that did not revolve. To retrieve line the drum was turned back, the reel then having a single action. As such it was limited to making heavy salmon spinning easier. Twenty years later, however, it must have influenced Illingworth in his original thinking on the fixed spool reel.

THE 1880s

Like the mid-1600s, the '80s were a period of great advance in tackle and techniques. Improvements in split cane rods benefitted all types of angling and in particular fly fishing. The extra power of these rods permitted the use of heavy oil-dressed fly lines which in turn revolutionised both trout and salmon fishing. The stand-off ring became more and more popular (although hotly opposed by advocates of flat rings) and, despite some bitter opposition, the eyed hook superseded the fly hook whipped to gut or horse hair. Through the invention by William Shakespeare of Kalamazoo in 1897 of the level wind, the multiplying reel, rejected by the English a century before, became a most sophisticated article of tackle.

THE FIXED SPOOL REEL

From the 1880s fishing tackle improved at a rate comparable with the advances in most other fields. As tackle improved, so did angling technique and in turn tackle designers and makers were stimulated to further efforts. The making of split cane was mechanised, this development improving the product and lowering its price. Tackle became lighter, fittings improved and the advent of lighter metals and alloys led to many advances in reel manufacture. Line braiding kept pace with other improved techniques in the general field of textiles. A considerable silkworm industry grew up in Murcia in Spain, both to supply the angler with his terminal tackles and the surgeon with his gut sutures. But dwarfing all these was the invention of the first fixed-spool reel in 1905 by Holden Illingworth.

Illingworth was a wealthy textile industrialist who, like the unknown fathers of the Nottingham reel before him, based his ideas on a textile bobbin. Its principle was the same as Malloch's. When casting the line slipped off the end of the drum, with no inertia to overcome. Illingworth's spool remained, however, in this fixed position. His first model, beautifully made and with a 'throw' giving a perfect crosswind, was slightly awkward to use. His second reel, produced two years later, was modern in every way. Its design included a slipping clutch, alternative right- and left-hand wind, and if required, direct drive for playing fish – everything indeed except an automatic pick up. It was above all designed for light spinning. Other similar reels followed, and light casting was born. Although the stationary drum reel was well suited to many forms of coarse fishing it took a number of years before it was universally adopted. Meanwhile many other improvements were added, notably the addition of an automatic pick up which allowed the line to be collected as the handle was wound forward, and a further improvement, the bale arm, by L. R. Hardy, became universal.

The slipping clutch was originally fitted as the only means whereby a fish could take line. Its use also encouraged fishing with fine tackle and fine lines and this in turn stimulated the use of light tackle throughout. Despite its fragile nature, Spanish Reed, a very light cane from Spain and France became more and more popular for match rods and there was considerable experiment with ferrule-less rods in this material – putting the clock right back to Roman times. Improvements in glue and in the automatic milling of split cane led to rods in hollow split cane by Hardy and Milward. Here the rod designer was able to determine exactly the taper he required and at the same time achieve the low weight so necessary for competition fishing.

The enthusiasm for match fishing grew in other ways. In 1903 a meeting was held in Birmingham which was to lead to the formation of the National Federation of Anglers and this in turn led to the organisation in 1906 of the first National Angling Championship, known more commonly as the 'All England'. This Championship, which has continued with only two breaks, during the two World Wars, now attracts some 1,200 entrants fishing both for the individual championship but also, and more importantly, in teams of 12 for the Club title.

MODERN TIMES

By the outbreak of the Second World War the British coarse angler was well armed with tackle.

His rod was usually of whole cane or reed with a split cane or greenheart top. His reel was more often than not a centrepin, for although fixed-spool reels were readily available, the lines then on the market did not match the reels in efficiency. The braided silk line, which suited the centrepin reel, was too soft to give good performance with stationary drum reels and was also easily damaged by the twist and friction imparted by the line recovery on such reels. True, a synthetic line material was available from Japan but this line, generally called Ja-gut, had too many deficiencies. On the end of the silk line the angler of the late 'thirties had a cast of silk worm gut and his hook was whipped to a length of the same material. By 1939, however, a new material was becoming available, but in short lengths only. It was a synthetic derivative of coal, air and water, called nylon. As soon as it became available in line lengths, it revolutionised fishing all over the World, for it proved the perfect match for the fixed-spool reel.

THE POST-WAR PERIOD

Not for some time after the end of hostilities did fishing and the manufacture of fishing tackle return first to a pre-War volume and then to start to advance. By 1950, however, the sport was expanding at a rapid pace in both size and thought. Influencing everything was a long period of increasing affluence based on the motor car, which gave everyone including the angler a mobility never before known.

This mobility led to wider horizons in every way. Not only did more anglers fish more widely afield, but even week-end trips to Eire became quite normal. The enthusiasm for the sport encouraged magazines and newspapers to cover these activities, and *Angling Times*, the pioneer of angling newspapers, achieved a circulation approaching 200,000 within ten years. The effect of universal education and the opportunity to write for a wide audience threw up the sort of thinkers and writers who a decade or two before lent keen minds almost exclusively to the problems of game fishing.

Typical of this new approach was the opening up of carp fishing as a popular sport. Up to the late 1940s carp were considered more or less impossible to catch. A band of keen and experienced anglers set out to catch these fish, pooling their ideas and approaching the problem in a wholly logical fashion. Much thought was given to the right type of tackle, the right conditions, the right bait and the best method of conditioning the fish to take it. This meant night fishing and the design and building of electrically operated bite alarms. It is pleasant to be able to record that in September 1952 a 44-lb carp was caught, and even more pleasant to record that it fell to the leader of the Carpcatchers, Richard Walker, who through his writings, thinking and successes has been responsible for more coarse fishing advances than any other man.

Although the basic methods of coarse fishing have not changed, they have been constantly improved, particularly during post-war years. These advances have not always been to the benefit of the sport as a whole, for example, greater specialisation has split coarse fishermen into groups, each bearing a strange title – 'Match Men', 'Specimen Hunters' and 'Pleasure Anglers'.

The design of tackle has kept pace with new thinking and, indeed, has often inspired this and made it possible. The scientist and the trained engineer now play an important part, for after nylon, now universally used, have come other synthetics such as Terylene and many other forms of plastics, and in particular glass fibre from which most bottom rods are now made; this is a material from which many reel parts will be made in the future. The coarse fishermen now wheels his kit to the riverside on a trolley, there have been great improvements in umbrellas, wind-breaks and in protective clothing.

Basically, fishing has altered but little since man first caught fish on a hook. It still remains, above all, an exercise in the imaginative application of natural history. Progress and pleasure both come from thinking out the problems, and advances in technique invariably result from advances in tackle design. The history of fishing must therefore be the history of fishing tackle. And will always be so.

TACKLE

by

Dick Orton

When writing about fishing tackle, it is easy to become deeply involved in the historical aspects of the subject, but as these are covered in a separate chapter, I propose to confine my remarks as far as possible to fishing tackle in common use during the past thirty years, with particular reference to recent developments.

It should be said at the beginning that tackle, like every other aspect of angling, is a field for endless speculation and conflicting opinion. Angling is a very personal activity; we fish for our own joy, and different people obtain their pleasures from using various equipments and techniques to achieve the same objective. There is, perhaps, too great a readiness to condemn as unsporting or absurd the chosen methods of the other man. Breadth of outlook is a thing we should all try hard to cultivate.

My point regarding the part personal taste plays in the selection of fishing tackle is borne out by the wide variety offered by any manufacturer who seeks to make his catalogue comprehensive. This variety tends to bewilder the uninitiated, and the beginner may be further mystified by the supposition that all this mass of material exists because different water and other conditions dictate a different and specific use for each item.

Rods and various other items of tackle certainly do fall into a number of clear functional categories, but it should be realised that manufacturers are also catering to individual tastes and that any of half-a-dozen rods may do the same job equally well in the hands of the men who happen to favour them. Perhaps I should say here that this firm conviction is based on thirty years experience in the tackle industry, and continual contact with anglers and tackle distributors all over the world. Like a manufacturer compiling his catalogue, I propose to treat my subject by dividing it into its basic tackle groupings, rods, reels, lines and so on. Let us start with the rod.

RODS

The last thirty years have seen a transition from natural to synthetic raw materials. In 1946 the built-cane fishing rod dominated the scene for all types of angling. Rods made from combinations of whole cane and lancewood, whole cane and greenheart, whole cane and built cane were still made in very large volume for bottom fishing. Built cane was developed first in the U.S.A. before the turn of the century, and at its best is a beautiful rod-building material. Unfortunately, only best Tonkin poles are truly suitable for the job, and these grow only in South China, now on the wrong side of the Iron Curtain. Many different bamboo canes grow in many parts of the East, and in fact some can be grown in Southern Europe and the warmer parts of Southern England. These do not, however, have the toughness and elasticity necessary for fishing rods, and all attempts to use them have resulted in failure. Only those specimens of *Arundernaria Amabilis* found in a small district in South China are entirely suitable. Analytical examination reveals that this cane consists of parallel longitudinal hard fibres set in a substance of which pectin is the vitally important ingredient. All is protected by a skin of even greater strength and hardness. Exposure to carefully controlled heat solidifies the pectin and enhances still further the natural toughness and elasticity of the material.

This is the very first process in built cane rod making, and was originally done over an open gas jet. The risk of charring and irreparably damaging the valuable surface fibres was however considerable and this heat treatment is now carried out in ovens. It is a common error to suppose that the 'baking' is done merely to drive off surplus moisture. This happens, but it is the treatment of the pectin which is the important process. It is, in a sense, akin to the jelling of jam achieved by boiling.

After heat treatment, the Tonkin pole is sawn into sections prior to tapering and cementing. All varieties of cane are harder at the surface than the centre and the cane building process is designed to take sections from only the hardest part of the pole, rejoining them to achieve great strength for minimum weight. Built cane rods are almost invariably hexagonal in section, and the hexagon is made up from six tapering triangu-

lar segments, each with the carefully preserved skin on the outside. They are planed to shape on a special-purpose machine with cutters which require frequent re-grinding – a tribute to the toughness of the material they are processing. Every 9 in or so along the cane, there is a calloused ring which forms knots in the cut material. These are ground down and in the matching of sections care is taken to avoid more than two knots coming together at any one point, knots being a potential source of weakness. The sections are bound together with twine, and are ready for cementing.

For many years, animal glue was used, and it did the job very well indeed. Now, plastic cements have taken its place and, when set, these may be even harder than the actual cane. The chief arts in cementing lie in achieving even distribution and a perfectly straight blank. When this is completed, the blanks stand for some weeks curing; when animal glue was used, the curing process took months! The blanks are then carefully scraped down to remove twine and cement without damage to the skin and are ready for further processing. As the rest of the rod making processes are quite similar, irrespective of the basic raw material, it would be as well to look now at the manufacture of glass fibre blanks.

During the Second World War, glass fibre and synthetic resins were used in aircraft construction in the United States, and the latent possibilities this material had for fishing rod manufacture were soon apparent. The tensile strength and flexibility of the material seemed promising and so experimental rods were built.

Glass fibre fishing rod blanks fall into two general categories, hollow and solid. The hollow types have many of the properties of built cane, but are a little lighter for any given strength. Solid blanks are exceptionally strong, almost indestructible in fact, but are heavier and are not at all suitable for rods where length, stiffness and lightness are important. Consequently, one does not see bottom rods over 8 ft in length made from this material.

Hollow glass fibre is made by coating woven glass cloth with synthetic resin, wrapping it round a tapered steel rod called a mandrel and then curing it in a hot oven to set the resin. The action of the rod blank produced is influenced by the gauge and taper of the mandrel, the gauge and weave of the glass fibre cloth, the form of wrapping and the type of synthetic resin used.

Solid glass fibre rod blanks are made from longitudinal glass fibres embedded in resin. Broadly speaking, the more glass fibre there is in proportion to the resin, the better will be the performance of the rod. This is the main factor influencing the different prices of superficially similar solid glass rods. So now we have advanced matters in both built cane and glass fibre to the point of the finished blanks. Both now, with reservations, receive similar treatment.

In the mid-1930s tubular steel rods made their first appearance in Britain and enjoyed a fluctuating popularity until quite recently. Also, much speculation has been occasioned by the possibilities of carbon fibres in rod production, but at present very high cost outweighs the benefit in terms of weight reduction. However, that is by no means a final judgement, and we may be at yet another turning point in fishing rod design.

Continuing the story of fishing rods in general, we come to the matter of joints. The butt, centre and top sections are joined to assemble the complete rod for use by means of suction ferrules, consisting of a socket into which a solid ferrule

is fitted by means of a push fit. And here matters become a little confused by the Redditch trade practice of terming sockets 'ferrules', and ferrules 'counter ferrules' or just 'counters'. Whatever we call them, provided they are properly made, they are the best-known method of connecting rod sections. All manner of alternatives have been tried, screw ferrules, various lock joints made with studs and keyways, and a few fishing rods are even made without ferrules at all, the sections terminating in long matching slanting planes which are positioned together and bound with tape.

The latest development is glass-to-glass jointing, either conventional fitting, (often termed 'ferruleless') or a joint in which the upper section fits over the lower. This is termed 'spigoting'.

In a built-cane or hollow glass rod, conventionally jointed with metal ferrules, one of the main points to inspect is the fitting of the socket. The highest standards of craftsmanship demand that small cane splints should be glued to the rod to provide a seating for the lower end of the socket which should have deep serrations filed to a taper. These are finally covered by a silk whipping. The cheap and easy way to attach sockets is to grind away the top of the blank until a fit is achieved, but in so doing the invaluable surface fibres are destroyed and the likelihood of a breakage at the socket or ferrule is greatly increased. Therefore, mistrust a built-cane rod on which the socket is not of a slightly greater diameter than the cane which is immediately below it.

Virtually all modern fishing rods have cork handles which are usually built by fitting a series of cork bungs on to the butt. These are cemented into place and then machined to a pleasant and convenient shape. The reel fitments are either a pair of sliding tapered rings or a more elaborate arrangement of tapered rings which are held in position by screw rings on a threaded metal body.

Handles are finished off with a metal butt cap, which is to protect the most vulnerable part of the cork, and finally a rubber button, which somehow succeeds in looking right even though it has little or no functional value.

The rings through which the line must pass are attached by silk or terylene whippings, usually in bright and cheerful colours, over which coats of varnish are applied. This gives a final waterproof protection to natural materials, but merely enhances the appearance of synthetics.

Now we come to the vexed question of intermediate whippings. These do affect the action of a rod, but they are not functionally necessary. Any extra stiffness imparted to a rod by close

whippings can be better achieved by adjusting the dimensions and tapers in the original design, so close whippings are in the main purely decorative.

In days gone by, they may have been used by third-rate makers to remedy the deficiencies of bad tapering and glueing, but the oft-repeated warnings regarding closely whipped rods are now totally obsolete. Some of the most reputable makers whip rods closely because anglers like them that way. The critics of closely whipped rods might just as logically inveigh against cars in two-tone finish, or striped shirts, or flowered wallpaper. If an angler fancies a closely whipped rod, he pays a price appropriate to the extra labour entailed, and presumably enjoys looking at his handsome property.

Let us now consider the variety of bottom fishing and spinning rods available. Bottom fishing commands the greatest numerical following, therefore we shall look at bottom rods first.

These usually are from $10\frac{1}{2}$ to 14 ft in length, although shorter special purpose legering rods are sometimes made from solid glass fibre and offered at fairly cheap prices. Bottom rods are identified by their very long cork handles, often up to 32 in., and plated wire rings of the full stand off type. The latter are used to keep the fine line as clear as possible of the actual rod. This is particularly important in rain when a line sticking to a wet rod can reduce the distance cast by as much as two-thirds.

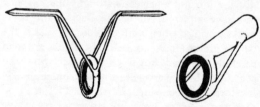

The butt and end rings on bottom rods are often lined with toughened glass, usually given some brand name, such as Agatine, Aqualite, Amber, etc.

Bottom rods are required to be light and should not normally exceed 12 drachms per foot except in the case of rods specially designed for carp, or other exceptionally large fish, where greater bulk may be needed to give increased power. In comparing rods made from the same raw material, the power, by which we mean the pressure which can safely be applied by the rod in the course of fishing, is directly proportionate to the amount of material used and therefore the weight. By adjusting the degree and position of tapers, the shape of the curve in which a rod flexes under load can be changed, and this influences its performance in casting and striking.

By absurdly unbalancing the pattern of taper, a weak point could be created, but in general terms power relates very closely to bulk. A well-made 11 ft rod, weighing 11 oz, will inevitably be more powerful than an equally well-made 11 ft rod, weighing 8 oz, when both are made from the same basic material.

Bottom rods often have to be stiff for quick striking (the need for their extreme length also relates chiefly to striking). By stiff we mean, in this context, a rod with nearly all the flexibility concentrated in the tip. With the float 30 yd or more away and a line floating on the surface of the water, subject to the effects of wind and current, considerable leverage is required to make fast contact with a fish. An 8 ft rod would not pick up the slack line sufficiently rapidly. Rods of 8 ft in length can be used for legering, because the line connects by a reasonably direct route to the hook lying on the bottom. Fishing a bait near the bottom with a fixed float in deep water also demands a long rod.

The most dramatic development in bottom fishing rods since the War has been the introduction of long, stiff, ultra-light and self-ferruled hollow glass match rods. In terms of length/weight/stiffness ratio these are literally revolutionary. They have totally supplanted the match rods made from Spanish reed, a light, rigid but not very strong cane grown in Spain and the South of France. Prior to 1960 this type of reed was used almost exclusively for this class of rod.

To explain the term 'match rod' briefly, it should be understood that match fishermen have generally concluded that matches are most frequently won by big bags of quite small fish rather than a few larger specimens. This reflects the general state of our Midland and Northern fisheries where match fishing first developed. To catch such fish, a rod must strike very quickly, but it needs a sensitive tip to correspond with the ultra-fine lines favoured. Prior to the fixed spool reel becoming very popular, match rods did not need to be strong. The rod was long (12 to 14 ft), and was used single-handed with a centre-

pin reel. The action used to cast light float tackle was gentle. Fixed spool reels naturally tempted anglers to attempt longer casts. When a fixed spool reel is used on such a long rod there is a high frictional resistance to the passage of the line through the rings. This led to double handed 'punch' casting which had disastrous results on Spanish reed. The lighter the tackle, the greater the effort that was made to punch it into the wind, and more and more reed rods came flooding back to the manufacturers, all uniformly broken about two-thirds of the way up the cork handle. The longer the rod, the more rings, the greater the frictional resistance to the line. It follows, therefore, that the shorter bottom rods, 10½ to 11 ft, all other things being equal, cast better than the longer 13 to 14 ft type.

Every fishing rod is a compromise between a number of desired attributes, and so one should select a rod carefully for the precise use for which it is required. If your fishing will mostly be in a lake or wide river, three to ten feet deep, populated by roach, chub, bream, perch, etc., of unexceptional size, a 10½ or 11 ft rod weighing 8 oz will do very nicely. Such a rod will permit light weights to be cast maximum distances and it is long enough to give good line control. You will also find that it will have sufficient power to handle lines up to 6 lb b.s. However, if the water contains big tench or specimen chub, it may pay you to go up 2 oz. If record carp are there, a rod to handle 15 lb b.s. line and 1 oz weights is recommended, most of the latter rods are to-day based on Richard Walker's famous Mark ·IV formula. These have the additional advantage of performing well when casting light weights due to the cleverly contrived tapers.

When fishing a very deep water, or one which holds relatively small but shy and quick-biting fish, then a 12 to 14 ft rod is called for, and where the fish run small the lightest rod of that length is the logical choice. Where depth of water and large fish coincide, the type of rod designed by Billy Lane, a past world champion match angler, meets the situation. Such rods are 13 ft in length, of hollow glass fibre, but have an above-average wall thickness. Although they are a little heavier than usual, the extra power thus gained is frequently more than useful.

Spinning rods may be for single or double handed use, and run from 6 to 10 ft in length. They are made in a wide range of weights, from

4 oz 7 ft trout spinners for single handed use with fixed spool reel, 2 or 4 lb test lines and 1 in Devon minnows or two drachm spoons, to double handed salmon spinners 10 ft long, weighing 16 oz, capable of imposing a 3 lb pull and casting 2 oz weights comfortably.

The coarse fish usually fished for deliberately by spinning are pike and perch. How powerful a rod is used for these species is dictated partly by the size of the bait to be cast, partly by the conditions to be encountered, and partly by personal fancy.

At this point I feel that it would be opportune to quote the formula by which one estimates the proper line for any spinning or bottom rod. It is arrived at by taking the maximum load the rod will apply, expressed in pounds, and multiplying by six. The load can be tested on a spring balance but reputable manufacturers quote the vital statistics for their spinning and bottom rods. Thus, a 16 oz salmon rod with the power to impose a 3 lb pull is lined, theoretically, with an 18 lb line. In practice it will handle 15–20 lb lines happily; use it with a 10 lb line and a savage taker may break the line; use 30 lb line and if you hold a well-hooked fish too hard you may break the rod, but usually, of course, you just tear the hooks out of the fish. Specialist fishing tackle dealers should be able to give sound advice on matching rods, lines and casting weights.

The term 'test curve' is used by some manufacturers when describing the power of a spinning or sea rod. It is calculated by fitting a line to the rod and imposing a sufficient pull to make an angle of 90 degrees between the line and the axis of the butt. This load expressed in pounds is called the test curve. As it does not of itself indicate what weight the rod may cast, or what minimum and maximum line strength it will handle, its general usefulness is open to question.

To-day spinning rods are used almost exclusively with fixed spool or multiplying reels. For the former, a tip action is usual, for the latter a slower, more even, action is desirable or 'overruns' may result. Overruns will be discussed fully in the section of this chapter which deals with reels. All spinning rods have large rings, often lined with the toughened glass which has now taken the place of the lovely but brittle German agate used in years gone by. Double handed

spinners have handles of up to 32 in but the shorter single handed patterns are likely to have handles of roughly 15 in. Screw winch fittings are almost standard equipment.

Pike rods come into a separate category, and while all spinning rods other than the very lightest are used for pike, pike fishing may also entail casting heavy live or dead baits and so something far more powerful than even the heaviest double handed spinner may be required. Here I would again emphasise that power of rod, strength of line, weight of bait, and size of hooks should all correspond logically for any type of fishing. To spin for pike with a 6 oz 7 ft rod, a 4 lb line and a 3 in. spoon armed with size 3/0 treble hooks is to ask for trouble. The hardness of the pike's mouth makes exceptionally severe demands on the tackle. A 6 oz rod may be able to drive home a size 10 treble hook on a 1 in spoon, but big spoons and plugs with their large hooks measuring that much further from point to barb require 9 or 10 ft double handed spinning rods, weighing about 16 oz. A further point to remember is that 6 oz roach are commonly used as live bait. As sea rods are often catalogued as suitable for 6 oz leads, why do we not consider such rods as dual purpose, for sea and/or pike fishing? This would seem quite rational, but we do not do so.

The rate at which the force is applied when making the cast is a factor to be reckoned with, and the shock loading commonly applied in casting a firmly attached 6 oz sea lead would tear a live bait straight off the hook. Therefore, when pike fishing with live baits the cast is made quite gently, and so we may contemplate a lighter rod. It may be heavier than the heaviest spinner, but it is less than a sea rod. Such a rod will not throw a spinner correctly, nor will it be 'comfortable' for repeated casting. The all-round pike fisher, therefore, needs at least two rods, one for spinning and one for natural baits. The latter need not be expensive, and will probably be 8 ft long made from solid glass fibre. It should be capable of imposing a 5 lb pull and should have rings large enough to allow the passage of a float stop, so that a sliding float rig may be used for live baiting when fishing in very deep water. The ferrule and socket should be stout in proportion to the strength of the rod. As even medium-sized pike are quite large fish, the comfort conferred by a long cork handle when playing a fish is a great benefit.

REELS

Manufacturers started to use synthetics for reel making some time before they had anything but natural materials for rod building, and Allcocks, as a case in point, launched a range of bakelite reels in the early 'thirties. Metal reels have been made for several hundred years, but for generations walnut was the prime material. I remember watching walnut roach reels being made as recently as 1949, but except for 7 in Scarborough sea reels, wooden reels have now passed completely out of use.

FIXED SPOOL REELS

The major trend in fishing reels during the past twenty years has been the transition to fixed spool types for nearly all types of angling. The terms Fixed Spool, Thread Line, Light Casting, and across the Atlantic, Spinning, are all used to describe the same type of reel. One of the major factors to influence this change was the enormous improvement in design achieved by the J. W. Young Company with the Ambidex series of reels which were launched in 1947 and are still going strong; then came the Continental development of larger capacity patterns and finally, the success achieved by K. P. Morritt in producing by precision die casting techniques a range of very serviceable articles at greatly reduced prices.

Bottom fishing is the field where the fixed spool reel rightly stands pre-eminent, and, together with the monofilament nylon line it casts and retrieves so well, has done more to increase the number of coarse fish caught than any other development this century.

Illingworth – a Bradford wool spinner – is usually credited with the invention of the fixed spool reel, although parallel developments were proceeding in France at about the same time. Illingworth was preoccupied with the problems presented by spinning for trout in clear shallow water in the bright sunshine of midsummer. Very small spinners and extremely fine lines were involved and even the lightest of fully tooled-out Allcock 'Aerial' reels (which had been developed for this purpose into little more than 'a lot of holes held together by wire') did not revolve freely enough to permit even a highly skilled angler to cover the water adequately when using 1 in Devons or natural minnows.

Illingworth is supposed to have been inspired by the way yarn in his mill was drawn from the bobbins over the end; thus the basic principle of the fixed spool reel was born. Previously when casting direct from the reel, the spinner, or leger weight, or shotted float tackle had to draw the line from the reel by turning the spool, which, however light and well-balanced, still offered substantial resistance. Pulling the line with the left hand in the early stages of the cast to start the drum moving, or flicking the drum into motion with the little finger of the rod hand were both partial answers to the problem but much practice was needed to achieve consistent efficiency. Many side-stepped the problem by pulling off line and coiling it on a newspaper on the ground prior to casting.

Illingworth's principle put long distance casting with light tackle within the reach of all – the dextrous and the fumblers alike. The Illingworth prototype reel was little more than a big gear wheel with a winding handle on it, meshed with a spool of line positioned in front at right angles. A simple reciprocating movement spread the line, and a slipping clutch was provided to protect the ultra fine line against sudden plunges from the fish.

In case it is not self-evident by now, I should perhaps make it clear that, all other factors being equal, the finer the line the longer is the distance which any given weight may be cast. The lighter the weight to be cast, the more critically important the fineness of line becomes.

The 'Allcock-Stanley' was the first Illingworth type reel to be mass-produced. It cast very well, and had a friction drive which was also the slipping clutch, but the actual spool revolved to retrieve line fed through a little spreader hook at right angles to the face of the spool. It was in this feature that its major drawback lay. Each and every cast made put a fresh series of twists into the line, and it was this fact that led to the development of the modern reel with its non-rotating spool and rotating 'pick-up' which lays the line evenly and solidly in position. Since then, all developments, except one, have been little more than modifications to critical dimensions, spool depth, spool width, handle and gearing, etc., to increase mechanical efficiency, give optimum performance or to render the reel more suitable for mass production and thereby reduce costs. The one exception was the development by Hardy of the full-bail pick-up. This enables the angler to focus his visual concentration on the water and trust his hands to operate the reel completely and efficiently. The full-bail pick-up has no free end (both ends being attached to the flyer) and thus the line cannot be picked up accidentally.

The first feature which the bottom fisher should seek when buying a fixed spool reel is that it should have sufficient spool capacity for the job which it will be called upon to perform. Most of the better types have at least two spools of varying line capacities and it is always possible to buy more as optional extras. If you wish to cast a large piece of paste and breadcrust for carp on a 15 lb b.s. line, the spool should hold at least 100 yards. Should you happen to be a roach and dace enthusiast and delight in using light tackle, you would probably need to put over 1,000 yd of 1½ lb b.s. monofil on a similar spool to fill it adequately. Alternately, you might use stout backing but this would entail using a knot which might become an impediment to casting. Fixed spool reels only work properly when the spool is filled correctly and the line is free from obstruction. It is to resolve these problems that manufacturers supply spools of various sizes. As the distance from the front to rear is predetermined by the reciprocating movement of the reel these capacity variations are achieved by building up the spool cores.

Next, the angler should look for reliability in the pickup mechanism. The pick-up of a fixed spool reel is by its nature fragile and should always be handled carefully. It should have a clean, sharp and utterly regular closure. Pick-ups are usually opened by hand, closing automatically as the handle is given a forward turn. Before

accepting a reel, one should open manually and close automatically at least a dozen times. Never purchase a reel which does not work perfectly twelve times out of twelve (remember that the mechanism is delicate, so never use force). Due to a uniform feature in their design, almost all fixed spool reels suffer serious and expensive damage if the handle is forced backwards while the pick-up is in the open position.

Another important feature is the geared multiplying action. All the fixed spool reels known to me are geared to speed up line recovery. The ratios vary between 5:1 in a specially designed match reel and 2:1 in a big salt water type. High gearing enables the match angler to retrieve line very quickly at the end of an unprofitable 'swim down' and any other fisherman to maintain a tight line as a hooked fish turns and runs towards him. In match fishing, time may well be money, and in any fishing, a fish which succeeds in slackening the line is very often a fish lost. On the other hand, high gearing does not help when playing a big fish, for then control is much less sensitive. There is always a slipping clutch to assist in fish control, but with even a low geared reel a fish is best played out by 'pumping'. 'Pumping' means gaining line by raising the rod tip and recovering the line gained by lowering the tip and winding the reel simultaneously.

Generally speaking, a recovery ratio of about 3:1 seems to be accepted by most manufacturers. The ratio expressed is between full revolutions of the pickup and full turns of the handle. As the diameter of the spool is also a factor, the critical question is: what length of line can be retrieved by one complete revolution of the handle. A little elementary mathematics enables one to obtain an accurate enough answer. First check how many times the pick-up revolves for one turn of the handle and then measure the diameter of the spool; multiply by three and the result by the number of spool revolutions for each full turn of the handle. For example: a pick-up revolves exactly three times per full turn of the handle, the spool diameter is $2\frac{1}{2}$ in; $2\frac{1}{2} \times 3 \times 3 = 24$ in approximately, so you retrieve about 2 ft of line with each turn of the handle.

The general shape and style of the reel is the next consideration. The bracket by which the body of the reel and the rod fitting are joined should be of a suitable length and in the right position. When the rod is gripped in the fingers (*not* the palm of the hand) the open pick-up must not foul the knuckles. Just where the rod is gripped in relation to the bracket is partly a matter of taste, but purists believe that it should be possible for the rod hand to be so positioned that the forefinger can trap the flier (the large rotating collar in which the pickup is housed) and the spool rim, the latter for increasing clutch tension manually while playing a large fish. An optional check which can be switched on to stop the handle rotating backwards is usually included in modern reels. This is brought into operation at the end of the battle when the left hand is committed to operating landing net or gaff and it ensures that a final rush by the fish must be made against the tension of the clutch. If this were not so, the fish could strip off line by rotating the entire mechanism in reserve and gain sufficient slack line to throw the hook.

On many reels the handle can be fitted on either the left or right; often, too, folding handles are available (this helps stowage). The former feature is of importance to the manufacturer and distributor as one pattern thereby serves a wider market; whether it offers any advantage to the individual angler is doubtful. There is no objection to a folding handle provided the mechanism does not include an obstruction on which line may catch.

There is little to be said about body shape except that a pronounced neck between body and spool housing is a potential line trap. Helical gearing provides the most efficient movement for fixed spool reels. As dealers are not likely to encourage the use of screwdrivers by potential purchasers the angler usually has to assess the quality of the action by winding the handle. A smooth and easy movement, free from irregularities, coupled with a reputable trade mark, usually guarantees the reliability of the mechanism. Flaws are more likely to be discovered by winding slowly; it is of course unreasonable to expect parts to be machined to tolerances of ·0001 in when the entire article is unlikely to cost more than £10, and there is another factor which must be considered – a reel built to such fine limits throughout might seize up if one grain of river sand entered the mechanism. Even in the hands of careful anglers fishing tackle takes some pretty severe punishment and this fact is never forgotten by experienced designers.

Mistakenly, many anglers uncover the mechanism of a new fixed spool reel and pack it with a thick grease. They have an idea that this will be beneficial, but, if it were, the reel would be lubricated in this manner by the maker. I do not know a quicker way of incurring a fat repair bill. Thorough drying after use, the removal of visible grit and sand, plus a regular lubrication with light cycle or sewing machine oil, will usually keep a reel in first-class order for years.

Finally, a fixed spool reel is not a winch; it is in fact a particularly inefficient machine for winding up heavy weights, so big fish *must* be played by 'pumping'. There are reels which, in the hands of a capable angler, will kill a 30 lb salmon, yet if one attempted to winch up a 1 lb weight with one of them, the mechanism could be seriously damaged.

The closed face reel is a recent variation on the fixed spool theme. It was originally developed specially for the American angler, and is an adaptation of the standard open faced British fixed spool reel. The American traditionally fishes with his spinning reel on top of the rod and controls it with the thumb on his rod hand. All the features of the closed face reel stem back to those two vital necessities, which are prerequisite to successful marketing in the United States. To re-adapt a pre-adapted reel so that British anglers can mount them beneath the rod does not on the face of it make the soundest technological commonsense, and the closed face reels I have so far examined offer very little that is new or to my mind of any practical benefit. I would not, however, care to predict what the future may hold in this field – it could be very interesting indeed.

CENTREPIN REELS

Some years ago, a fierce controversy raged between those who favoured the fixed spool and the traditionalists who stuck to the centrepin reel for orthodox bottom fishing. Happily the controversy is now dead and while anglers have their legitimate preferences, none would aspire to be considered an all rounder unless he were proficient in the use of both types.

'Centrepin', a term which once had a more precise meaning, is now used to describe a reel of simple design comprising a large diameter drum rotating on a spindle mounted in a back plate, which also houses the 'scoop' or 'anchor' by which the reel is attached to the rod. Two plain balancing handles are fixed opposite each other near the periphery of the drum.

Paradoxically, the centrepin range embraces the very crudest fishing reels and the most sophisticated. At one end of the range are small reels

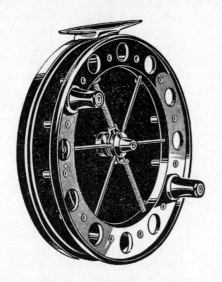

made from two cheap pressed metal flanges which sell for less than 5s; at the other there is the 'Aerial' type of centrepin reel which is known to match fishermen wherever the sport is practised. In this category precision machining and balancing have produced a reel which, after a little use to run it in, will spin for fully 60 seconds before slowing almost imperceptibly to halt.

That precision-built centre pin reels are popular and becoming more so is a fact which cannot be disputed; in my opinion this type of reel cannot be equalled for making a measured cast and trotting the baited hook exactly down the path taken by the ground bait, and to repeat it exactly again and again.

When playing a fish on a centrepin reel the onus of decision lies with the angler – there is no slipping clutch to compensate his errors of judgement, and for the purist this is an added joy. The other important advantage given by the centrepin reel is the direct and positive contact with the float which is maintained at all times. Also, there is the high speed of retrieve, which it is possible to achieve by flicking the rim of the drum with stiffened and bunched fingers. Tackle can be drawn back upstream in this manner very

much faster than it can be retrieved even with a 5:1 ratio fixed spool reel.

For à centrepin reel to be acceptable to an angler of experience it should have a circle of fine pins mounted between the flanges of the drum. These should be spaced $\frac{1}{2}$ in or less from the rim. This avoids the hundreds of yards of heavy backing line which would otherwise be needed to bring the final coils reasonably near the rim. It is only when the reel is correctly filled that full advantage of the large diameter may be taken, for it is this that helps the angler to achieve a rapid recovery. A diameter of $4\frac{1}{2}$ in enables an angler with hands of normal size to control the reel comfortably. The front flange must be tooled out as fully as possible for lightness. Adjustable spokes at the hub are an indication of precision balancing, but the angler should not interfere with this adjustment. There is usually a quick release device, and also a spring-tensioned screw drag which will reduce the free running properties of the reel to that which the user requires or the conditions of the day dictate.

An optional ratchet check is virtually a standard fitting on all centrepin reels; it should be light and smooth and should not sound in the least like a football fan's rattle!

The best centrepin reels have only a very small clearance between the rear flange of the drum and the rim of the back plate – less than ·003 in so that 1 lb test nylon line cannot possibly enter. The distance between the flanges need not exceed $\frac{3}{4}$ in so that a $4\frac{1}{2}$ in reel with pins spaced $\frac{1}{4}$ in from the rim and flanges $\frac{5}{8}$ in apart will hold 200 yd of 8 lb b.s. monofilament; this is about four times the capacity most bottom fishers actually need.

Cheap centrepin reels, like all cheap fishing tackle, should be scrutinised very carefully before purchase. Metal reels of non-British origins should be viewed with special caution. A 'Bakelite' reel is often a good cheap buy. As the basic material is inexpensive there is something left over to finance a precision ground spindle and bush, a decently hardened check pawl and check wheel, as well as an element of craftsmanship. Although I would not recommend owners of bakelite reels to bounce them on the ground, the modern material is infinitely tougher than the earlier form. A blow sufficient to crack a 1967 bakelite reel would also do drastic damage to its metal equivalent.

A hot day in summer and the water in this stretch of the Kennet and Avon Canal was as clear as glass. Fortunately there were weeds and rushes close to the edge and the angler here took full advantage of the cover. He caught roach to the 2 lb mark on a No 20 hook baited with wheat.

The bream is safely
in the landing net
and a smile of
satisfaction comes to
the face of the angler.
But there are more
bream in that swim,
so the fish is put in
the keep net and the
tackle cast out to the
spot again. . . .

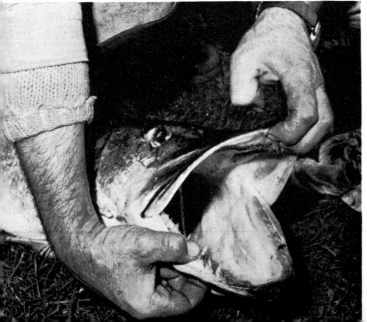

Photo: Alan Wrangles

*Portrait
of a
killer*

SPINNING REELS

The reels most commonly used for spinning to-day are of the fixed spool type; level wind multipliers come second in popularity while only the rare devotee spins with the centrepin reel. Almost all I have said about fixed spool reels in connection with bottom fishing applies here, and there is not in fact a lot more to be said. Always remember that fixed spool reels were originally devised for light line fishing, and so when spinning for pike it is imperative to play the fish by 'pumping' – any attempt to winch in a big pike is to simply beg for a mechanical breakdown. It is most important that all anglers should grasp this simple but essential fact.

For heavy spinning the level wind multiplier is also used. In its most modern form, it is by no means so difficult to use as many suspect. While it may be strictly true that the multiplying reel was invented in Great Britain several hundred years ago, few would deny that almost all the important developments of this reel have taken place in the United States of America. The names 'Shakespeare', 'Pflueger', 'Bronson' and 'Penn' are significant in this field. In their early attempts to achieve extreme freedom of rotation coupled with adequate line capacity, the designers opted for a long-barrelled spool with relatively small diameter flanges. Spreading the line by hand evenly on such a spool was extremely awkward and uncomfortable, so the automatic level wind mechanism was evolved. This is a wire loop through which the line is fed and driven from end to end of the spool by a long specially cut gear which is virtually a channelled rotating bar. This in turn is geared to the winding mechanism. With the small diameter spool, to achieve an adequate rate of retrieve a 4:1 gear ratio was necessary; hence, the term 'Multiplying Reel'.

So long a spool obviously needs extra support, so a rigid mounting was devised, and the well-known double-ended frame housing of the classical multiplying reel has not changed its silhouette significantly for 200 years.

The traditional American way of using the reel is to mount it on top of a 5 ft single-handed rod. An overhead cast is employed, the thumb of the rod hand controlling the reel by 'thumbing the spool', to use the conventional term. This method has been adopted generally in Western and Northern Europe. But in Britain the tendency has been to mount the reel high on a long double-handed spinning rod where it is controlled with the thumb of the forward hand, the cast being made with a sweeping lofted side swing. I think this is due chiefly to the fact that there is relatively little lake spinning from boats in Britain but a great deal of spinning from the river bank. The longer rod casts further and affords more sensitive fish control, a fact which is not quite so critical when fishing from a boat, where long spinning rods are sometimes more hindrance than help. If two anglers are sharing a boat and spinning, short rods and overhead casts are much to be preferred, if from no other aspect than that of safety.

The main drawback to the level wind multiplier is the 4:1 ratio which tends to operate against the angler playing a large fish. There is the optional ratchet check, but significant braking is done only by thumbing the spool. This may be perfectly all right when playing relatively small fresh water bass in the U.S.A. or comparatively small pike, it may even have been feasible to play a salmon that way in the days of soft silk spinning lines; but with the hard abrasive synthetic lines of to-day the thumb soon becomes seared, blistered, raw and bleeding when a big fish makes a long fast run. A stout thumb stall, or better still a button-operated friction brake on the spool rim is greatly to be desired. I do not care for a star drag slipping clutch and one way wind, although reels so designed certainly have their adherents.

One other contentious point is whether or not governors should be fitted. If too much force is used when making the cast, and the angler fails to brake the reel as the bait begins to fall or the casting action is jerky, an over-run results. This calamity can also be caused by other factors, for example the bait can flick an obstruction as it flies through the air, for it must be remembered that the spool rotates during the run off of line at something approaching forty revolutions per second, and a sudden stoppage during the cast will cause the coils of line to pile one on top of the other in a hideous bird's-nest. A tangle of this sort can easily take an hour or more to unravel.

The very instant the angler senses that something has gone wrong, he should dab his thumb down onto the spool; this usually reduces the overrun to a problem that can be solved in a few minutes. With practice it is surprising how nearly instantaneous human reaction can be. Governors slow down the acceleration of the spool and thereby reduce the risks of overruns but they also limit the maximum distance the angler can cast. I dislike governors for this reason and believe that an adjustable friction drag gives the reasonably dexterous angler all the help that he really needs for either playing safe or living dangerously. In my opinion, governors, star drags and handle locks leave the angler dependant on mechanical aids. In the long run greater pleasure is derived from learning to develop and co-ordinate skills of eye, hand and judgment. To many, these give the deepest satisfaction of all.

So few anglers spin with the centrepin reel that the models specially designed for this may well disappear from the market altogether within the next few years. They are however so ideally right for pike live or dead baiting that a few words are well justified.

The high grade centrepin is, in my view, the nicest and most efficient reel with which to play a fish. What leverage there is favours the angler, and the transition from yield to retrieve and vice versa is instantaneous and positive. With fingertips on the rim of the drum the angler can exercise the most sensitive control of all. It is difficult to cast light weights with the centrepin reel, a fact which must limit its popularity, but when casting 2 to 6 oz natural baits for pike the problem does not arise.

When selecting a pike reel, choose one that has a reasonably large capacity (200 yd 20 lb b.s. line), has a good solid construction, and revolves freely. Fairly large handles are also important, these help to give the angler a good grip in cold weather. The centrepin reel is fitted in the conventional manner beneath a double handed rod, and the cast is controlled by the forefinger operating on the inside of the rim of the flange. There are a number of pike reels on the market, all of which are free running and decently put together and are offered at quite reasonable prices. Some of the cheapest have very stiff ratchet checks which is a bad feature. When pike fishing, one frequently leaves the check on, and a fish may well reject the bait if it finds that it has to pull against the resistance of a stiff check during the critical phase at the beginning of a take.

LINES

A fishing line is a textile with certain critical attributes and to assess which textiles make acceptable fishing lines, a question must be answered – what do anglers seek from a fishing line?

First, it must be strong for its gauge; secondly, it should not be unduly susceptible to damage by immersion in water; thirdly, its resistance to shock loading must be reasonably high; fourthly, its surface must resist abrasion. It is an added advantage if the material is transparent or translucent and therefore not readily visible in water. Finally it should not stretch under load more than 10 per cent or so before breaking.

The story of the post-War years is one of almost total conversion from natural materials to synthetics. In 1946 silk was pre-eminent for fly lines, for spinning and for fine lines for the bottom fisher. The gut from which casts were made, and to which the bottom fisher's hooks were mounted, was another product of the silk trade. To produce this gut, the entire silk worm cocoon was immersed in acid and then stretched into a filament 6–10 in. long.

The production of silk worm gut was an advanced technology in its own right, the trade being carried on in Southern Spain in and around Murcia. The value of the exports was large, for not only anglers but surgeons used the material. In its natural form gut could be obtained as fine as ·008 in, this was known as 'refinucha' but supplies were very limited. As the demand for fine tackle grew, the practice of drawing gut through tiny jewelled holes in a draw plate was adopted. By this method the surface was removed and the diameter reduced. Gut was drawn as fine as ·004 in; out of this came the present gut terminology which has been inherited somewhat irrationally by nylon.

The finest undrawn gut which was in regular supply was termed by the tackle makers as 'fine'. The code of 1X, 2X, 3X, 4X, etc., was derived from terming the successive sizes of drawn gut, as extra fine (X), or (1X), two extra fine (2X) and so on, down to 8X and even 10X. As even a 2 lb b.s. opaque silk line was highly visible in the water, the bottom fisher of the pre-nylon era used a drawn gut cast of 1, 2 or 3 yd in length, between line and hook link.

Today for all purposes except fly fishing monofilament nylon line stands pre-eminent in popular demand. It can be obtained with breaking strains of from less than 1 lb to 150 lb, although for angling 60 lbs b.s. is the usual upper limit (lines of this order are for sea angling). Monofilament lines are supplied in a wide variety of packs for the convenience of the angler who may wish to buy anything from 25 yd to 300 yd in one continuous length. Polymers vary considerably, some making better textiles than fishing lines. Those polymers made primarily for further manufacture into fishing lines make the best lines – which is obvious but not universally understood.

Much of the strength of a monofilament lies in its surface skin and if this is ruptured a drastic reduction in strength may occur. An important but little-known fact about nylon monofilament is that stretching it to near its breaking point temporarily weakens it. The strength recovers as the molecules resume their normal pattern. Therefore, to quote a practical example, if when pike spinning the line is strained hard whilst trying to free a lure that has lodged behind a stone, it is prudent to let the line have a five minute rest before one resumes fishing.

Freedom from undue extensibility is a desirable feature in monofilament line, that is to say that a 10 per cent minimum is much to be preferred to the 30 per cent maximum encountered in some brands. Consistent diameter is not in itself very important, but it is a good guide to consistent strength. The advantages of relative stiffness or flexibility are a matter for debate and vary with intended use and the actual gauge of the material, for example, 6 lb b.s. nylon of marked suppleness makes good fly casts. The same brand in a 2 lb b.s. used for bottom fishing on a fixed spool reel may not cast quite so far or give so smooth a pay-off when long-trotting, but a stiffer type will tend to spring off the spool of its own accord. However, the former brand in 15 lb b.s. may make a reasonably serviceable line for use with a level wind multiplier, whereas the 15 lb b.s. size of the stiffer line might well be completely unusable on the multiplier, due to its tendency to spring loose and thereby cause overruns.

As a general guide I would always recommend supple lines because my own experience indicates that while the occasional benefits derived from a stiffer line are only marginal (used in the wrong place at the wrong time it can cause devilish trouble), the disadvantages of supple line are generally speaking of a minor nature.

Nylon lines are made with polished or matt finished surfaces. The polished lines tend to be a little stronger, gauge for gauge, but they glint and shine to such a degree that I would always sacrifice that benefit for a soft, dull, non-glinting surface.

Colour is the next point. There has been some rather gimmicky advertising in this highly competitive market over the years but I say without hesitation that I have never heard of any scientific experiment which proved conclusively that nylon of any one specific colour was less visible to fish, under all conditions of light and water-opacity, than any other colour. Frankly, I think the question is so complex that I believe it beyond the scope of any angler to equip himself with line in colours calculated to give him any worthwhile advantage when related to the water and sky conditions he may meet. After all, as one fishes, the light intensity is probably varying from minute to minute, even when fishing at night.

Common sense suggests the selection of a pale colour and I think that off-white shading to blue, green, sorrel, grey or even mauve are all equally sound. Remember though that several hundred coils of a blue tinted line, which in the individual strand may be almost transparent, may look a pretty positive pale blue on the spool; it will not just look off-white.

The big disadvantage of all monofilament nylon is that in gauges above a 10 lb b.s. or so even the most supple of lines are in truth pretty stiff and therefore do not lie passively on the reel. In heavier sizes one is usually better off with a plaited line (often termed 'braided' these days) of either nylon or terylene. These kindred synthetics can be produced in a very fine denier form which braids up into a very supple line however stout it may be. Braided terylene is very free from extensibility, and is to be had from 2 lb test up to 120 lb shark line. Sizes from 15 lb to 25 lb test are usually used for pike spinning, the heavier lines by sea anglers. It should be realised though, that superior though the braided line in the heavier gauges may be, monofilament nylon is nevertheless used in very much greater volume. Price is certainly the key to this paradox.

HOOKS

Rod, reel and line follow in logical order; the other essential common to all angling is the hook.

Fish hooks are made from steel wire, of high carbon content, and recently from stainless steel wire. No other material is used and rumours to the contrary are founded in the various protective finishes which may be applied. The 'brass' hooks one hears of are actually gold plated steel.

The first process in hook making after cutting the wire into suitable lengths is pointing. Done at one time by hand-filing, this process is nowadays mechanised and one manufacturer, at least, achieves by machine a hollow ground point, a feat which was thought to be impossible for many years after the introduction of machine pointing. After pointing, the barb is cut with a chisel and then the hook is bent into shape. Next the end of the shank is formed into either a ring, a turned-down eye, or a flat (spade end), or marks are formed for line attachment. After this

the barb is cut is naturally the weakest spot, and care has to be taken during manufacture to avoid cutting too deep and thereby creating a weakness. A combination of a deeply cut barb and over-brittleness is of course fatal.

After heat treatment, hooks are scoured bright, and in the case of those which are made from ordinary steel wire, a protective finish is applied. This may be gilding, silvering, chrome or nickel plating, tin plating, japanning, lacquering bronze, or simple heat blueing. Different markets call for varying finishes. I would not suggest that it is rational they do so; inherited purchasing habits and prejudice seem the only feasible explanation for this massive variety in fish hooks, of shape as well as colour.

The names given to fish hook bends (by 'bend' the trade means 'shape') often suggest their

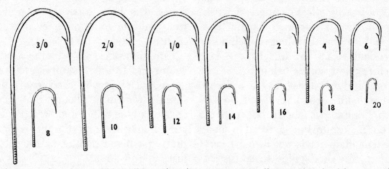

Hooks, reproduced actual sizes (Nos 3/0–1/0 are more usually associated with sea angling)

come the processes which make or mar – hardening and tempering.

The soft wire hooks go into an electric furnace through which coal gas flows to make a purely chemical contribution. The temperature and time factors are closely controlled and when the hooks emerge and have been quenched, they are as hard and almost as brittle as glass. A big conger hook can be snapped between the fingers. Hooks must be not only hard but resilient, and so they are now tempered in a slower, cooler furnace from which they emerge covered with scale but slightly softened and with just the right degree of springiness.

In the trade we judge that the point of a perfectly made hook should open to an angle of 30 degrees to the shank without breaking or distortion. Some go further, but ultimately there is a point at which every hook, if strained sufficiently, will either break or distort. The point at which

geographical origins, and sometimes their designer. 'Limerick', 'Dublin', 'Kendal', 'Carlisle', 'Aberdeen', 'Cincinnatti Bass', 'Dutch Eel', 'Old Italian' and 'Exeter' are examples of the former; 'Kirby', 'McKenzie', 'Pennel-shaped Limerick' and 'O'Shaughnessy' of the latter. The most widely known hook is called a 'Model Perfect' which while being a manufacturer's trade name, also denotes a specific shape. Other terms such as 'Round Bend', 'Standard Roach', 'Whiting' or 'Sneck' are literal descriptions of shape or the original function for which the hook was designed.

To denote hook sizes, there is the Redditch fresh water scale, in which the hooks run from about 10/0, a hook which has an overall length of approximately $3\frac{1}{4}$ in., down to a size 22, which has an overall length of a little over $\frac{1}{4}$ in. Presumably because this was a little too simple to be interesting, H. Cholmondeley Pennel, a 19th Century angling writer, devised the Pennel or 'New' scale for fly hooks. He took the Redditch size 14, called it size 1 and progressed his numbers upwards 2, 3, 4, etc. to denote increased size and used 0, 00, 000, and 0000 to denote Redditch sizes 15, 16, 17 and 18, respectively.

Bottom fishers often use 'Crystal Bend' hooks which are extra fine wire versions of the 'Limerick' bend, or the 'McKenzie' which has a widened round bend. The 'Model Perfect' is a 'Forged Reversed' hook, patented by Allcocks in 1900, with a shape somewhere between 'Limerick' and

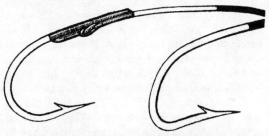

'Model Perfect' bend (left) and Crystal bend

'Round Bend'. Forging means slightly flattening the wire throughout for extra strength and 'reversed' is the trade term for an off-set point, one which cocks upwards when the hook is laid flat, with the point laid to the left of the shank. The opposite is termed 'kirbed'.

Bottom fishing hooks are usually gilt or silvered, although in Lancashire a very fine, very long shanked hook called a 'Wigan Round Bend' is finished blue.

Double and treble hooks are made primarily for arming artificial spinning baits. When used in conjunction with natural baits they do so much damage if swallowed that I cannot see justification for their use.

Anglers are often puzzled by manufacturers' descriptive terms, such as 2X Fine, 3X Long, 1X Stout and so on. To understand these, one must first visualise a standard range of fish hooks, so let us suppose a manufacturer called Smith devised a new shape of hook and called it 'Smiths Super Perfect'. He might make the hook in 16 sizes from a 4/0 down through 3/0, 2/0, 1/0, 1, 2, 3, 4, 6, 8, 10, 12, 14, 16, 18, 20. The dimensions of sizes 1 might be overall length 2 in., width across the gape $\frac{5}{8}$ in., the other sizes being larger and smaller in proportion. The gauge of wire used for each hook would be in proportion to the size; size 1 would be made from stouter wire than size 2 and so on.

After marketing the hook for a sufficient time for the brand to become well known, Mr. Smith would certainly hear from a distributor somewhere in the world asking him to make a quantity of 'Super Perfects' but with the stipulation that the shanks must be slightly longer than the standard lengths to meet some special local requirement. On ascertaining just how long the hooks had to be, Smith might make the size 2 the same length as a standard size 1, and so on, in which case they would be termed 1X Long. If he made the size 2 as long as a standard 3/0 they would be termed 4X Long.

Next, he would probably be asked to make hooks similar to his standard 'Super Perfects', but shorter. If the size 2 hooks are required to be as short as the standard size 6, for example, the range would be termed 4X Short. I have known hook ranges from 7X Short to 10X Long, and from 3X Fine to 3X Stout. A range could be 6X Long 2X Stout, or, 3X Short 1X Fine. The combinations and permutations are almost endless, and when one realises that all these gauge and length variations may be called for in all the various colour finishes available one begins to understand the problems facing hook manufacturers. Remember one fact, though. To identify hooks described in trade terms you must always refer to the 'standard range'.

The subject of fish hook types is vast and could be treated exhaustively only if an encyclopaedia was wholly devoted to it, but in this survey I should not omit to point out that some names like 'Wigan Round Bend', 'Carlisle Kirby', or 'Rohu Carp' actually imply a special degree of length, fineness, or stoutness in gauge.

Finally, let us consider the painful question of hooks that break or open while in use, thus losing a good fish. Anglers want their hooks to be as fine as possible, but consistent with a minimum degree of tensile strength. This gives the manufacturer virtually no margin of safety, a fact which is equally true of rods and lines. Traditionally, most anglers expect to buy small hooks for a penny or less. When mounted to nylon they naturally cost more but it is rare for the actual hook to represent more than the penny mentioned. In the face of this limitation, it is remarkable that manufacturers produce hooks to such a high standard that a failure is so rare that it usually provokes a strong letter of complaint from an angler.

Hooks which would never break or open in fishing can be made, and have been made, but they have to be constructed from wire so stout that anglers will not buy them. Why does a hook fail? It is almost invariably due to an unfortunate hooking. Hooks very rarely fail when a roach, bream, chub, tench, or other fish with rubbery or leathery mouth is hooked. The point penetrates, and often emerges, the fish being held by a pinch of skin and flesh which is bearing against the centre of the bend of the hook. A hook so positioned will survive any stress that can be imposed by a fishing rod – but whether the tissue of the fish's mouth will stand it is another question.

Carp, trout, pike and perch have hard mouths in which bone, gristle and/or teeth are plentiful. Here the hook all too often penetrates only just past the barb and lodges as though in a vice, held by the hard tissues surrounding it. Every plunge, every shake of the head, every change of direction, places flexing and opening strains on the hook. Metal fatigue builds up, and if the fish doesn't surrender first, failure is only a matter of time. Naturally a well-made hook will take the strain longer than a poor one and so it behoves anglers never to economise on hooks. Bearing in mind that an angler may well hook and land a 4 lb bream on a size 18 hook which consists of only a few milligrammes of wire, it is as well to appreciate what a miracle of craftsmanship a small fish hook is, and also to accept the inescapable hazards of the sport in the right spirit.

Hooks may be mounted to nylon for fresh water angling, but the standard mounting is a whipping of waxed silk. Nylon is so smooth that a safety knot in the nylon just where the whipping covers it is an important safeguard. At the far end the nylon link is looped, and either knotted or silk whipped. Flatted or spade end hooks are snooded (i.e., a knotted whipping is formed from the end of the actual nylon link). Hooks are usually mounted singly but for certain types of worm fishing some anglers favour two or three hooks mounted in tandem. The former are termed 'Pennel' or 'Thompson' tackles, the latter 'Stewart' tackles.

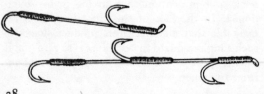

Before 1945 hooks to a yard of silk worm gut, known as 'one-yard Bottoms', were the connoisseur's choice, but now top grade hooks are usually whipped to 18 in lengths of nylon. Experience suggests that a loop 18 in away from the hook will not deter fish from biting even in very clear water (but the degree to which problem is visual is another subject for speculation). Cheaper hooks are whipped to 10 or 12 in of nylon which terminates in a knotted loop.

TRACES AND TERMINAL TACKLES

When bottom fishing with fine monofilament nylon it is quite often the practice to tie the hook direct to the main fishing line. However, it is not usual for anglers to attach hooks, spinning baits, and so on direct to the actual fishing line when hunting predatory fish such as pike or perch.

When spinning, the bait is separated from the reel line for various reasons. Most so-called spinning baits do in fact rotate as they are drawn through the water, for this action contributes to their attraction for the fish. Certain lures such as the Devon Minnow spin very fast indeed, and so it can be readily understood that as excessive line twist leads to appalling tangles there is a constant problem in preventing the bait from imparting a twist to the line.

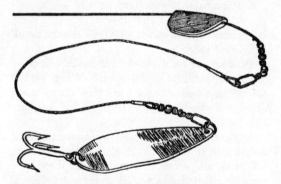

A combination of swivel and anti-kink devices is used to overcome this problem, and this dictates the use of a trace. This usually has a link-spring swivel at the bait end and a loop at the other, while use of intermediate swivels is optional. It is usual to tie another swivel at the end of the line, and attach the trace loop to this. An anti-kink vane attached a short distance above the trace may help, but my experience has been that a ball bearing swivel between line and trace is the best anti-kink device of all. These are much dearer than ordinary box or barrel swivels, but they are vastly more efficient.

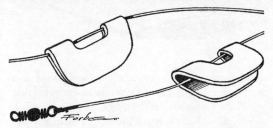

When spinning deep with heavy baits, a big anti-kink lead solves the problem cheaply and completely, but these are not suitable for spinning in clear shallow water. Wire is the standard spinning trace for pike – due to the belief that a pike may bite through anything less tough, for these fish are notorious for their numerous teeth, some with sharp edges.

Bronzed twisted brass wire is the usual material and it is supplied in strengths from 8 to 48 lb test, the angler making the choice according to his optimism. The pike fisher's special live baiting hooks are called Jardine Snap Tackles, these are also mounted on this type of wire. The Jardine consists of a large double hook with a small lip hook to the rear, fixed to the bottom of eight inches or so of wire; there is also a specially shaped treble hook with an extra eye on the shank. This is designed so that the angler may slide it up or down the wire to the correct position. One point of the movable hook is passed beneath the dorsal fin of the bait, the lip hook of the bottom double is fixed into the bait in the mouth, the gill, the root of the pectoral fin, or the root of the ventral fin according to taste. Natural baits differ in size, of course, and this dictates the need for a sliding hook. The Jardine tackle was preceded by other designs, now so obsolete that there is no point in discussing them.

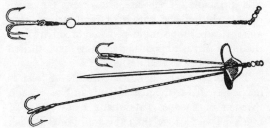

Various tackles employing multiple treble hooks have been designed for the angler wishing to fish a dead roach for pike, by either spinning or sink and draw, and a selection are illustrated. Millward's 'Archer' dead bait spinner, with the adjustable clips at the head, holds the bait more securely than any other I know. I would not, however, give a very high efficiency rating to any of these tackles, and this is no reflection on the designers. The problems presented by the weight and softness of the bait, combined with the shocks associated with continuous long distance casting, never have been solved, and probably never will be. The simpler tackles usually tear clean out of the bait, and fitting the more elaborate ones is a messy and intricate task, particularly so with cold fingers on a winter's morning. It is small wonder that the great majority of pike anglers use artificial spinners or live bait tackle.

ARTIFICIAL BAITS

A golden rule to follow when selecting artificial baits is to ignore those which look most lifelike, for that which appears realistic to the angler often fails to interest the fish. The appearance of a bait as it revolves six feet beneath the surface of slightly coloured water can differ enormously from the appearance of the same bait when held in the hand for inspection. The plain simple spoon bait for pike, with a design based on the bowl of an ordinary dessert spoon, is the classical example of this important fact. The coarse fish we catch regularly on artificial baits in Great Britain are pike, perch and, to a lesser degree, chub. The last-named seem to take spinning baits during the late spring and summer, but at this time they are usually caught accidentally – and, of course, out-of-season – by salmon fishermen. The most exotic bait I ever saw taken by a chub was a yellow and orange Pflueger plug the size of half a banana. The Irfon chub to whose downfall it led weighed two pounds, six ounces.

The essence of an artificial bait is that it shall either spin on its axis, wobble, undulate, dive or dart, or perhaps do all these things simultaneously as it is drawn through the water. It is fished by continual casting and retrieving, and a fish, on seizing it, will very quickly be aware of its artificiality; it must therefore be armed for instantaneous hooking.

Usually, the more water which can be covered, the better the chance of attracting fish, so the bait must lend itself to long distance casting and therefore should not be too light. It must not on the other hand too readily fall to the river or lake

bed and there lodge among the boulders or other obstructions. It must spin, wobble, etc., so the shape is critical, it must also be bright enough for a fish to see from some distance, but not so bright that its unnaturalness is immediately apparent.

Bearing in mind the limitless variations in light intensity, water depth, rate of flow and colour, it is not surprising that one leading tackle maker finds it necessary to offer no less than 350 different artificial baits for fresh water fishing alone. Tastes find very free expression in this field, and I would not suggest that an angler needs all 350 to be comprehensively equipped.

Baits are made from metal, wood, plastic and rubber. Metal baits include Devon Minnows and a host of variously shaped 'spoons'. Semi-buoyant Devon Minnows made of wood are now very popular; plug baits may be made of wood or hard plastic. There are soft flexible plastic Devon Minnows on the market, but most of the soft plastic and rubber baits are non-spinning variations on the plug bait theme.

The basic Devon Minnow is a slender tapered bait which is spun by large pectoral fins, the pitch of these determining the rate of spin. They usually have large eyes painted on them, and in general appearance resemble exotically coloured gudgeon or stone loach rather than minnows. Devons are made in all sizes from ¾ in. to 3 in., the common colours being plain gilt, silver, dark blue above with silver below, brown above and gilt below, black above and gilt below, or dark green above with a yellow belly. They may also have red spots or scale markings.

The vice of all orthodox Devon baits is the way in which they kink line, this is due to their ultra-fast uni-directional spin. The problem is particularly acute when using the smaller Devons in clear shallow water, as any object on the line, lead, swivel, anti-kink vane or what-have-you seems to deter the fish from taking. Various attempts have been made to overcome this by designing Devons with reversible fins, or even by selling them in pairs, one to spin clockwise and one anti-clockwise. Setting the pitch of the fins to slow down the spin to the point where a single swivel in the nose prevents line twist has proved successful, but it seems that ultra-fast spin is a vital factor in attracting the fish.

Devons have a separate and removable mount, which now carries one treble hook only. Twenty years ago, Devons had up to four treble hooks,

these were placed above, below, amidships and at the rear. The modern Devon is so designed that the body may shoot up the line as soon as a fish is hooked. This prevents the fish from using the body of the Devon to lever out the hook.

The earliest spoon baits were shaped more or less like the bowl of a dessert spoon. Such a spoon, fished narrow end foremost and mounted with a swivel at the front and a treble hook at the rear, spins with a slow flashing movement. The appearance is oddly lifelike. These spoons are usually finished copper on the convex side, and with nickel on the concave side; nickel throughout, or nickel outside with the inside painted bright red. An elongated form of this bait, called a 'Geneva' spoon, is also very effective. Some are made in the classical proportions, but with scales stamped on. These are termed 'Norwich' spoons.

Big pike rarely chase a fast moving bait, and so most of the basic developments in spoon bait design have been calculated to improve the free spinning properties at the slowest possible rate of retrieval. One of the first attempts was the 'Colorado' spoon. Here, the old plain spoon was modified by the addition of fins, by deepening the bowl, and by adding a bar to which a swivel and hook were attached. The next step was to add a lead to the mounting bar. Another interesting variation was to mount a kidney shaped blade, by one end only, to a Colorado type bar. Gradually, bar mounted spoons have superseded the earlier models and the majority of the modern patterns, which are made in France, are based on this principle. They are, however, far more elaborately finished with spots and stripes, etc., and instead of the simple lead weighted bars as in the older British spoons, they now have turned brass bodies of special designs.

The deep rivers and fast currents of Scandinavia have led to the manufacture in Norway and Sweden of spoons baits made from metal of much heavier gauge than the traditional British pike spoons. Basically they are designed for salmon and sea trout, are usually long and slender, and often have scales etched on the convex surface. Provided they are used in the right type of British water, they can be most effective. Their weight makes them unsuitable for slow spinning in lakes or slow flowing rivers, and perhaps I should add at this point that there is nothing new in heavy gauge spoons; they have been made in Canada, and to a lesser extent in Great Britain, for many years.

Imparting a twist or a fluting to the blade during manufacture provides a spoon which will lurch and wobble, or flutter during retrieve. A blade shaped like a shoe-horn also wobbles nicely. The more closely the action of a spoon imitates the predator's moving prey, the better.

Over much of the United States there are two very fine sporting fish, the large-mouth and small-mouth black bass. These fish thrive in weedy lakes where they haunt the lily pads, moving out to attack anything swimming on or near the surface. Consequently, a bait had to be devised which would cast well, lie dormant on the surface if necessary, and work either on or just below the surface during the retrieve.

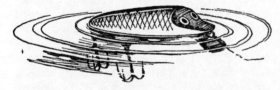

And so we come to the plug bait, and it was found that British pike also respond very well to this particular bait form, especially so in shallow lakes and rivers. As the name suggests, plug baits were originally little more than painted wooden plugs; they have now evolved into something of much greater sophistication. Use of various timbers and plastics, balanced dimensions, scalloping out the face and fitting shaped metal vanes in just the right position enables the manufacturer to offer a range of plugs with most varied and elaborate actions. The best of them wriggle so hard as they are retrieved that the rod tip is felt to vibrate. Some float when stationary and dive to varying depths depending on the rate of retrieve; others sink slowly when at rest, and climb towards the surface on retrieve; some splash and pop along the top of the water, while others undulate and writhe like a sick or wounded perch. Some do nothing except absorb water, swell, and burst off their paint. These, I need hardly point out, are the ones to avoid.

Plastic plugs, with their tinted, translucent ghost-like appearance attract both anglers and pike, but wooden plugs should not be discounted, provided they are made very carefully and are sealed completely against the entry of water. However, a good wooden plug bait can never be cheap.

In all plugs, especially jointed plugs, the positioning of the hooks is very critical. They must be positioned so that they cannot possibly link together whatever position the bait assumes in flight.

I know that pike are sometimes caught on exotically coloured plugs, but I have found that consistent success comes from using plugs coloured to imitate the fish on which they actually feed. Blue, silver and white with a flush of red; dark green, yellow and white with grey or brown bars; shaded yellow and brown with red and black spots, these are the colours that I favour. The addition of eyes is important, for I believe that it is the eyes of the fish that show them up distinctly to their underwater enemies. They seem to completely break up any camouflage pattern which may otherwise exist.

Before leaving fresh water baits, a word on artificial baits made from actual fish and other creatures is necessary. Allcocks first introduced these in the late thirties. They were called 'Nevison' baits, and were produced by applying preservative to freshly killed minnows, sprats and boiled prawns. They were tubed in a manner similar to Devon minnows, so that they could be mounted, and then they were encased in layers of hard plastic. They are truly durable, and although they are expensive, many salmon and sea trout fishers swear by them. They have been copied, usually by using a flexible plastic coating which has the advantage of being ejected less readily by the salmon or pike, but is more vulnerable to damage.

FLOATS AND LEADS

Floats can be described as floating bite indicators, and they are used by anglers who are fishing with natural baits for coarse fish, and with live bait for pike.

The object of the float is to give visible indication of a bite and it may also serve to suspend the bait at a predetermined depth above the bed of a stream or lake. It may have to be buoyant enough to suspend a considerable amount of lead (usually in the form of split shot) which has been added to the terminal tackle. Shot is added either to hold the bait down in fast water or to weight it so that it may be cast well away from the bank. Sometimes the lead is added for both reasons, but it should be remembered that the ideal to be aimed at is the smallest float, coupled with the smallest amount of lead necessary to achieve these purposes.

To register the bite, fish have to overcome the residual buoyancy of the semi-submerged float. This resistance, if at all pronounced, usually leads them to take fright and reject the bait. The basic problem in designing a float, therefore, is to achieve sufficient buoyancy to carry the weight but to retain minimum residual buoyancy so that a bite is clearly registered. The more shyly the fish bites, the more important this becomes.

The effect of turbulence on float behaviour also has to be considered. Obviously, the buoyancy of an exceptional sensitive float may be overcome quite easily by the effect of the complicated cross currents and vortexes found in fast running water. In such conditions an exceptionally sensitive float is a handicap, but in fact there is not a major conflict of requirements here. Still water fish often bite shyly, fish living in fast turbulent water usually bite very boldly, and therefore give a strong indication of a take. If they don't flash up and snatch their food, the current whisks it out of sight in a second.

Buoyancy is influenced by both shape and specific gravity, and so floats which have to be sensitive are always slender and tapered. The stems of feathers combine these critical features, and so swan, pelican, goose, turkey and crow quills have been used for many years. Pelican and swan quills are very buoyant, and have an enormous capacity for carrying shot, but crow quills have so little buoyancy that unless a small cork body is added they are unlikely to carry more than one or two dust shot.

The most popular, and in my view, the most generally useful quill for float making is that which comes from the porcupine. These are durable, they do not perforate easily, and they combine weight carrying qualities with sensitivity in a very satisfactory way. They are available in all lengths from 3 to 12 in but the supply of lengths greater than $8\frac{1}{2}$ in is strictly limited by nature. A mature Indian porcupine is clothed with quills of various lengths, but not all in equal proportions.

Cork has been used for float making in Redditch for well over a hundred years. Samuel Allcock was actually apprenticed to this craft as a child in the 1840s.

Nowadays, the practice of fitting cork bodies to quill floats is dying out, wooden stems having become almost universal. Balsa wood is sometimes used for bodies as an alternative to cork, but its tendency to split can be a nuisance. Injection-moulded plastic floats are now on the market, but I have yet to use one that I could recommend as equal to floats made from natural materials. Time of course may change this. Floats made of other synthetics, for example celluloid, have been available for many years, and some of them, particularly the antenna types, are very good. The antenna float is the ultimate in sensitivity, as it is fished with the buoyant body completely submerged and only the tip of an exceptionally slender stem (the 'antenna') shows above water. The least touch registers boldly, and were it not for the passionate determination of so many inexpert anglers to have some bold flourescent object cocked up out of the water I think antenna floats would be universally used in still and slow-flowing waters. As it is, they are all too seldom used, and when they are it is often

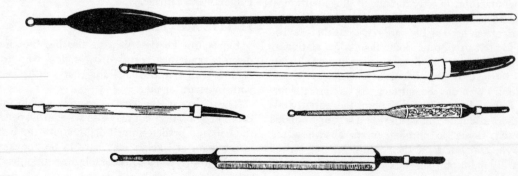

with about half the amount of shot for which they were designed. When half the body stands clear of the water, they are useless to register anything less than a violent pull from a very hungry and strong fish. The smaller or shyer ones just steal the bait off the hook unbeknown to the angler.

A few anglers favour luminous floats for use at dusk, but I do not think they show up any better than those with their tips painted fluorescent, which is now standard.

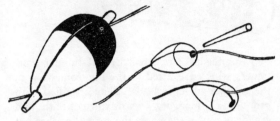

Pike floats have a considerable weight to suspend, and in consequence are large and bulky. They may be designed as sliders, so that very deep water may be fished. The most popular type of pike float is the *Fishing Gazette* egg-shaped cork float; these are split so that the stem may be removed and the float attached or detached without disturbing the bait.

Floats may legitimately bear a bright colour at the tip, to enhance identification in poor light, but brilliant overall colouring is not calculated to appeal to the angler's most mature instincts.

Leads for float fishing usually take the form of split shot, these range in size from S.S.G. through AAA, AA, BB 1, 2, 3, 4, 5 and 6 to No. 8 dust shot. The approximate diameter of S.S.G. is $\frac{9}{32}$ in and for No. 8, $\frac{3}{32}$ in. The softer the lead, the better the shot. Sharp cutting to a good depth also helps shot to close and reopen easily. Re-opening is necessary to move shot up and down the line.

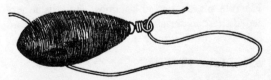

Legering is the method of fishing by which the bait is anchored to the bottom by means of a drilled lead arrested by a split shot. A fish pulling the bait does not feel resistance until contact with the rod tip is made. For many years drilled bullets and flat lozenge-shaped leads up to an ounce or so in weight were standard, but the disadvantage of these was the tendency to tangle in flight and thus impede the free passage of the line when a fish picked up the bait. In the early 1950s Richard Walker developed a new leger lead by inserting a swivel into the neck of a pear-shaped freshwater paternoster lead, and by passing the line through the eye of the swivel. Maximum force can be used when casting, a pull on the rod tip frees any tangles there might be. These weights are called 'Arlesey Bombs'. A more recent development still has been the 'Capta' lead. In this a swivel inserted into the top of a lead which is shaped rather like a flat iron, and whereas the bomb lead may roll with the current, the Capta stays put. For use when spinning, fold-over leads, spiral leads, swivel incorporating Wye leads, and bullets with a clip to attach to the

eye of a swivel all have their adherents. The ideal spinning lead should be very easy to attach and detach so that adjustments can be made to the tackle as the angler moves over water of different depths and varying currents. Leads should not, however, be self-detaching when in use! All these patterns that I have mentioned run from about $\frac{1}{4}$ oz to 2 oz in weight.

LANDING GEAR

Fish of respectable size are usually landed by means of a net or gaff. A landing net is self-explanatory, and these are available in various sizes. A four-foot cane or alloy handle, a detachable, collapsible steel or alloy frame, either circular or triangular, and a cotton or nylon net from 22 to 36 in. in depth are the most usual styles. When choosing a landing net, make sure that it is large enough. The chances of the individual catching a 40-lb carp, a 14-lb barbel, or an 8-lb chub may not be great, but most of us have our dreams, and how stupid to prevent your dream from coming true by penny pinching when choosing a landing net!

Gaffs are basically large hooks on long handles,

and are used to land pike too large for any normal landing net. Provided their use is followed by instant despatch, I do not think we need object to them on humanitarian grounds. The simplest form of gaff is a large sea hook, lashed to an ash staff; at their most elaborate they are constructed from alloy, rubber and stainless steel, and open telescopically from about 15 in. to 36 in. The best known are made by Sharpes of Aberdeen.

Match anglers and many other bottom fishers retain their catch in a keepnet, usually a long circular tube of netting, reinforced by metal or plastic rings. These are designed to collapse into a thick disc for easy carriage. Twenty years ago they were made of waterproof cotton and were from 3 to 5 ft in length, 12 in. or less in diameter, and had galvanised iron rings. They used to wear out very quickly, but modern nets, 18-in. diameter nets, 8 ft long and made from soft nylon mesh with flexible polythene rings, wear almost indefinitely and are much kinder to the fish.

SUNDRIES

Bottom fishers' tackle boxes contain many necessary sundries including disgorgers (tools for removing deeply-embedded hooks); spring gags to hold the jaws of pike open while hooks are removed; priests, small weighted bludgeons for killing fish by stunning (the name presumably derives from the fact that they perform the 'last offices' for the fish).

Baiting needles and rod rests almost conclude the topic of pure fishing tackle. The former are special needles, 6–10 in long with springy loop eyes which can be opened to accommodate the loop of a mounted hook. For baiting with dead fish, black slugs, cray fish or other large baits, they are essential.

Rod rests come in a variety of shapes and styles starting with a simple V-ended stick. Line floatant (grease) used to be an important part of the fisherman's kit, but to-day the almost universal use of monofilament nylon, it is almost a thing of the past.

Finally, bite indicators and swim feeders. The former are used primarily for night fishing and are fairly elaborate mechanical or electronic devices which give a sonic alarm when a fish bites. They are operated by a pull on the line, and in this connection the swing tip should also be mentioned. This is a visual bite indicator, for

leger fishing, and consists of a short extra tip whipped on to the top point and hangs beyond the end ring. This extra tip also has an end ring through which the line is passed, and as the fish bites, so the tip lifts and registers the take.

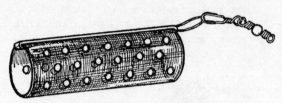

Swim feeders are small drilled tubular containers which are fitted to the line somewhat in the manner of leger leads. They are filled with ground bait, maggots, or a mixture of both, and are for use in rivers where the current washes out the particles, thus attracting the fish to the baited hook. Their purpose is to facilitate exact ground baiting, as it is so dreadfully easy to throw the ground bait in one place and fish the baited hook elsewhere. An error of only a foot or two can make the difference between the occasional bite and a big bag of fish.

Tackle Carriers include seat baskets, rod holdalls, sophisticated canvas bags with elaborate pockets and compartments, float and hook wallets, and the boxes with perforated lids in which one carries worms and maggots. Seat baskets are to be had in various sizes, and are usually made of osier. As their name implies, they both seat the angler and provide a receptacle for his tackle.

Rod holdalls are for the man who is equipped with several rods. These should be made of durable cloth, incorporate a good zip fastener and a leather or PVC-reinforced base with metal studs for protection. Boxes for natural baits were, until recently, made from tin plate or aluminium. Flexible plastic has now almost entirely superseded these materials, for plastics do not dent and bait lives much longer in these boxes.

ANGLERS' CLOTHING

One of the biggest changes in my lifetime on the fishing scene has been the vast growth of protective clothing purpose-built for anglers. Just after the Second World War all save the wealthiest anglers did the best they could with old weather-beaten mackintoshes, ex-army gas capes and Wellington boots. Now anglers' waterproofs are generally available at very reasonable prices, some good, some absolutely excellent. The development of PVC and waterproof nylon have been critical factors. Inexpensive and completely waterproof coats are made of the former, the latter can also be completely waterproof provided nylon of a sufficient stout gauge is used. They are rather more comfortable to wear, but they are also somewhat dearer. At the top of the range, Messrs. Barbours are still supplying their magnificent tear-proof, waterproof clothing in a heavyweight oiled fabric which is lined against the harsh winds of winter and early spring. While PVC is made into good, cheap, totally waterproof garment, its resistance to splitting and tearing is not quite so high as the other materials mentioned. Waterproof nylon of a sufficiently heavy gauge is comfortable, fairly light, waterproof, quite durable, but not exactly cheap. Barbour type clothing is beyond reproach for wear and protection, but is rather warm for summer use, and although the value is extremely high, the price is not within the reach of every pocket.

Fishermen also require waders, and the rubber thigh-length patterns are the most usual. Thigh boots with plain rubber soles, such as firemen wear, are not to be recommended, even if the soles are cleated. Underwater rocks and reservoir dams are liable to be coated with slippery algae and unless waders have metal studs, painful and dangerous falls are likely.

On anglers' tweed hats, I will not comment at length. Let it suffice to say that I love and revere them as the insignia of our religion.

FRESH WATER LIFE AND FISHERY MANAGEMENT

by

ERIC BIRCH

To many anglers the medium in which they fish is just water where fish swim, nothing more. There is, however, a great deal more to it than this. Angling water is teeming with life of all sorts, both plant and animal, each organism playing an important part in the pattern of life under water.

A volume of water as a whole is called an environment and each environment consists of many habitats and sub-habitats, each providing a home for a different kind of animal. These homes provide all that the animals they harbour require in terms of food, shelter and breeding facilities.

STILL WATERS

The surface of the water provides a home for several frequently seen animals, some of which are classified under the order *Hemiptera*, or bugs. These are the water crickets and pond skaters. They can be seen moving about on the surface in search of food. The water crickets are about $\frac{1}{4}$ in long and blackish in colour on the back. The underside, however, is a bright orange. Water crickets are found in ponds and corners of large still waters but they also occur in slow-flowing streams in eddies and sections where the current is not too strong. They feed on small insects and breed in floating vegetation.

The pond skaters are seen more readily as they are larger. There are ten species altogether and are confined to still water. When disturbed, these insects dart quickly across the surface. Pond skaters grow to about 1 in. in length and feed on other insects that fall on to the surface of the water. They breed on submerged plants.

Among the other important surface dwellers are the whirligig beetles, which can be seen on still waters gyrating rapidly about on the surface in large swarms. Whirligig beetles have shiny black wing cases which glisten in the sun, and although they live on the surface they are able to disappear beneath it when alarmed. The eggs are attached to submerged water plants in spring and the larvae, when fully grown, attain a length of about 1 in. Despite the fact that the larvae are comparatively large, the adult beetles are only about $\frac{1}{4}$ in long. When ready for pupation, the larvae crawl out of the water up plant stems and spin cocoons in which to pupate.

These then are a few of the relatively small number of animals that are specially adapted for life on the surface.

There is much activity at the surface, for many of the insects living beneath the surface either breathe or use air for buoyancy and therefore are compelled to come to the surface to take in fresh supplies. If you watch closely you will see many of these activities; most are fascinating, and some incredible.

Among those adult animals that take in air at the surface are various water bugs and beetles. The water boatmen store their air supply in a space between the body and wings and either swim or float to the surface to renew their supply, remaining motionless as they do so. The majority of the water beetles cannot obtain oxygen from the water, and so must replenish their storage spaces from the atmosphere through tubes which are situated along their bodies. Air is stored under the wing cases in a manner similar to that of the water boatmen.

Among the larger animals in fresh water, newts must also take air from the atmosphere and they do this so quickly that they are very difficult to spot. The eye can hardly catch them, all one sees is a slight dimple on the surface which could have been made by anything.

The larvae of some aquatic animals take in air in a manner similar to the adults and one of the most likely to be encountered is that of the great diving beetle. This is a fearsome-looking, greyish larva with prominent pincer-shaped mandibles. It appears to hang from the surface while taking in air through tubes in its tail-end. It grabs its prey between the strong mandibles and sucks all the juices from it (a large larva can consume up to a dozen tadpoles during one feeding cycle).

Certain species of water-bred flies also have air-breathing larvae, one of which is the familiar mosquito. These are often seen in water butts where they appear to be suspended from the surface, staying motionless for long periods unless disturbed, but if they do move, they do so rapidly with a jerking movement. Although very common, these flies are quite fascinating and well worth study. The eggs are cylindrical with pointed ends and are laid in masses on the surface, where they float about like little rafts and are quite unsinkable. An interesting feature about these eggs is that they are placed on end and packed closely together.

The egg platforms have a slightly convex form which helps to distinguish them from bits of flotsam which accumulate on the surface. I have never found these eggs on weedy waters – the adults seem to prefer a clear surface on which to oviposit. After hatching, the larvae feed by taking in minute particles of food brought to them in a water flow created by vibrating hairs on their body. After about three weeks or so the larvae gradually thicken at the head end and change into pupae. At this stage they appear to be all head, the body being about the size it was at the larval stage, but perhaps a little thicker. The pupae take in air from the atmosphere through two small projections on the head. At this stage they do not feed but seem to gambol about.

In due course the pupae can be seen at the surface making wriggling movements and are much agitated. This is a sign that the fly is about to emerge and eventually the pupal skin splits where the head touches the surface and out crawls the perfect insect. It is amazing how quickly this transposition takes place.

The larvae and pupae of all species in this group of insects are an important source of food for many coarse fish, particularly those that feed at the surface, for example the rudd. These insects only inhabit still waters and by sitting beside a pond during the summer you will be able to see these insects in all stages of their development. Many hatch in the evening, this is why many anglers who fish during the evening or night smear the exposed parts of their bodies with an insect repellent cream. The insects' piercing, blood-sucking organs can inflict painful wounds; it is generally the females that do the biting.

Before considering certain aspects of life beneath the surface, there are the water plants to be considered. Some live at the surface of still waters and do not root in the lake bed; these derive their nourishment purely from the water, and the oft-seen varieties include the duckweeds, frogbit, hornwort and water soldier. Duckweeds can multiply very quickly, completely covering the surface of a pond to the extent that all light is excluded. Plants of this type are able to survive when conditions below are very poor indeed, and the more they are removed the more rapidly those that are left seem to multiply.

Hornwort is a feathery-leaved plant that harbours many forms of life and is most useful in any still-water fishery. In the autumn the main body of the plant rots after sinking to the bottom, leaving only the tips of the shoots alive. These tips remain on the bottom all winter, but under the warming influence of the spring sun they rise to the surface and develop quickly. These shoots are known as winter buds.

Life beneath the surface is so varied that it is impossible to cover all aspects in one chapter, and those interested should seek further knowledge from the many excellent books devoted to the subject. However, we will look at some of the more interesting organisms and plants and see how they are integrated into the environment as a whole, before taking a closer look at the intriguing world at the bottom of pool and stream. Since they are so different in make-up, still waters and running waters must be dealt with separately, and this particularly applies when considering these in terms of fishery improvement and management.

In the shallows at the edge of the pool one can see that the taller plants growing on the surrounding land have gradually given way to smaller plants that are actually growing in the water. If a patch of bottom has no plants growing on it and is gravelly in nature, pick up a stone and take a careful look – in a good water it will be covered with a slimy green substance. This is algae, the staple diet of many of the underwater creatures, and it is able to thrive because the water is both clear and warm in these shallows. Under a larger, irregular-shaped stone it will be noticed that creatures are moving about in the indentations formed by the stone's irregular outline. These will probably be fresh water shrimps which feed on the algae and on decaying vegetation.

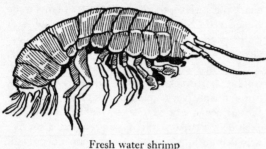

Fresh water shrimp

Fresh water shrimps are crustaceans and not true shrimps. They are greyish in colour and grow to about ½ in. in length. When disturbed they swim away rapidly and smoothly either on their sides, or on an even keel. Shrimps will often be found in pairs, one clasped firmly by the other. The larger males carry the females about with them, the female carrying the eggs underneath her. After hatching from the eggs, the young are carried in a similar way for quite a while. Shrimps are found in both still and running water and as they are eaten by most species of fish, make a fine natural bait.

The water hog louse may also be found under the same stone, but will more often be found among rotting vegetation in the shallows. This animal has probably been named 'louse' because it resembles the familiar wood louse. Neither is a louse, and the name water slater given to the water hog louse seems more fitting. A good place to find slaters is under the bark of a rotting tree branch – in fact, they are found in situations similar to those favoured by wood lice, only under water. Water slaters are scavengers and eat most types of rotting organic matter, plus a certain amount of algae. The females carry the eggs under their bodies after the manner of shrimps. There are several species living in this country, the only differences between them are size and colour.

One of the most interesting animals found in both still and running water is the caddis; a familiar insect to most anglers. Who has not at some time or other searched for caddis grubs under stones on a stream bed? Caddis are the larvae of sedge flies and there are over 180 known species inhabiting the waters of this country.

Caddis larvae are found almost everywhere in fresh water. There are species adapted for living in every conceivable type of habitat, and their life history is fascinating. The eggs are laid in a mass which is protected by a covering of jelly, and is either deposited on the surface or fixed to the leaf of a water plant. While some species lay their eggs above the surface of the water, the females of others crawl into the water via some projecting object and lay their eggs on stones and submerged branches, etc. When the little larvae emerge from the eggs they immediately set about making a case where they can live and which will protect their soft bodies. An interesting feature of this stage is that the various species can be identified by the shape and composition of the cases.

Some larvae make a case of tiny grains of sand and pieces of grit, others construct them from flat pieces cut from the leaves of water plants, and yet another species make cases out of small snail shells. Weed stems all cut to the same length, pieces of stick, watercress leaves, and stones are all materials which are found to be turned into cases. Some of the tiniest species make a case of gelatinous matter which is manufactured by the larva itself.

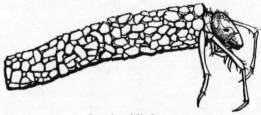

Cased caddis larvae

In rivers, caddis larvae make cases out of small stones, this helps them to prevent being washed away. Some caddis attach a long twig to their cases more for camouflage than security, and there are species of caddis that do not make a case. These free-living species spin a small net in which they catch small particles of food brought along by the current.

As the larvae grow, so they extend their cases

accordingly, often making one larger than they need, and when this happens they cut off the extra tail-end. Some types are extremely ferocious, and if kept in an aquarium will devour each other. I have hatched caddis eggs collected from a lake, and as soon as the grubs grew a little they could be seen lifting small green algal growths from the sides of the tank and devouring them. They would prize the circular patches from the glass with their powerful jaws, and on being transferred to another tank to cut down losses through predation, they soon set about the small water snails in their new home, eating two at a sitting. They deftly cut away the fragile shell with their powerful jaws until they could get at the snail's body. However, as the snails grew bigger the shells proved to be too tough for the caddis and they had to find other foods.

After twelve months or so in the larval stage the caddis grubs, like butterflies, pupate for a spell. When they are ready they seal up the ends of their case and usually attach it to an immovable object, particularly in running water. Whilst the pupation is being undergone, water flows through the case via gratings constructed in both ends. Some river species encase themselves in a tough gelatinous case until the time comes for them to emerge.

The emergence of the insect is fascinating. The pupa cuts open the end of the case with its jaws and emerges, to either swim to the surface or crawl up a plant stem or other protruding object. When in the air the abdomen of the pupa splits open and out crawls the perfect insect. I have had caddis flies emerge from their pupal skin whilst lying on my hand. It all happens very quickly, unlike the emergence of some of the other flies.

After emergence the wings are dried and the adult caddis flies away to mate, and the cycle begins again.

The adult sedge flies are very moth-like in appearance having four wings and a very floppy and awkward flight motion. Most fish take the larvae and pupae of the sedge fly, and, unlike anglers when using caddis for bait, do not divest the larvae of their cases but swallow the lot, their powerful throat teeth making short work of the cases. Adult caddis flies vary in size from $\frac{1}{4}$ in to nearly $1\frac{3}{4}$ in, and are harmless.

One other interesting group of insects which

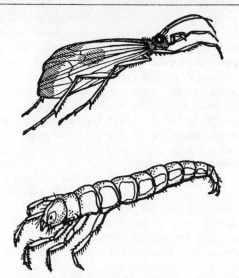

Sedgefly (top) and free-living caddis larvae (bottom)

are found among the water plants in the shallows are the dragonflies. These familiar insects are well-known to anyone who spends time by the waterside. However, the larvae are not often met with in the course of a day's fishing. There are many species in this group of insects, some being large and colourful, and are termed 'horse stingers' in many parts of the country, despite the fact that they are quite harmless. There are two types, those with short fat bodies usually blue in colour, and those with long, thin bodies which are predominantly brown in colour. If you take a close look at the latter type you will see that their very beautiful bodies have red, yellow and green colouring.

The eggs are generally laid on a submerged object, but sometimes shed at random over the surface of the water. Some species deposit their eggs in a slit made in a plant stem. As the larvae grow, they shed their skins from time to time to allow for body growth as their skin does not expand as they grow. Before the new skin hardens, after the manner of a crustacean, they have a short time in which the body can enlarge. Before the larvae are fully grown, the skin is shed possibly a dozen times. The larvae of some species propel themselves through the water in a most curious manner. Briefly, the body cavity contains a store of water which is exuded by the contraction of strong muscles; this 'jet reaction' propels the creature rapidly through the water. Whilst the water is within the body of the larva, oxygen is extracted from it by special gills and the deoxygenated water exuded. Normally the water is ejected slowly, but if the larva is alarmed it can be shot out very quickly indeed.

These larvae are extremely ferocious and will devour anything that ventures near. They are equipped with a pair of claspers fitted to an extension (called a mask), and when their prey comes near to their hiding place this mask shoots out and secures the prey which is then transferred to the mouth.

The larvae always crawl out of the water to emerge from their skins for the last time prior to becoming an adult insect. They usually use a plant stem or protruding branch, etc. for this purpose. Emergence takes place slowly when compared to the caddis flies, the long body being pulled very gradually from the larval skin after the thorax, head and legs are free. At this stage the wings are merely lumps on their backs, but if you watch carefully you will see them gradually expand until they are the full size. When the wings are dry, the dragonfly flies away to feed on other, smaller insects. The larger types can be seen well away from water but the smaller ones, called damselflies, never leave the waterside, and are brilliantly coloured, either red, green, blue, yellow or orange. Their bodies have a single colour only.

The plant life in the shallows is both interesting and varied. Plants are essential to the well-being of most aquatic organisms, for they provide both shelter and food. Another important function is the absorption of carbon dioxide during the daylight hours when the light is bright enough and the production of oxygen. This is achieved by a process known as photosynthesis. The green plants utilise solar energy, combining carbon dioxide and water to make carbohydrates in the form of sugars. The oxygen is released as a waste product during this process and it can be seen that plants are, in fact, water purifiers. At night the process is put into reverse. Plants make far more carbohydrate than they need immediately, therefore this is changed into starch and stored. Insects are quick to take advantage of this fact, they soon find the supply and feed on it.

Plants to be found in the shallows are: water crowfoot, water milfoil, starwort, water cress, fennel pondweed, water celery and parsnip, Canadian pondweed and dense pondweed. There

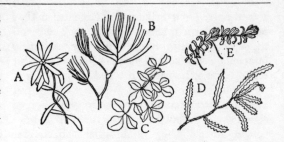

A. Starwort; B. Crowfort; C. Watercress; D. Curly pondweed; E. Canadian pondweed

are several species of some of these, their main variants being adaptations to differing habitats.

Although there are several species of crowfoot, some liking still water with a muddy bottom and others fast water, they all have one thing in common: the flower. This is a five-petalled white blossom with a yellow centre, masses of which can be seen in early summer on rivers and pools throughout the country. Crowfoots have two kinds of leaf, one is submerged and finely-divided, not unlike a crow's foot, but the other is similar to the common field buttercup, which is of the same family. Crowfoot, or water buttercup, is one of the best plants to have growing in a fishery, for it harbours the larvae of many types of insect. It is also a good oxygenator.

Water milfoil is a stringy type of plant with leaves running in whorls around the stem. One identifying feature is its mauve coloured stem – the leaves are similar to the underwater leaves of crowfoot. The flowers are insignificant. This plant is apt to spread extensively in still waters and can choke the shallows if care is not taken. It is a very good spawning weed in still and slow-flowing waters.

Water starwort is a bright green plant that usually grows in clumps favouring a muddy bottom. There are no flowers that are readily recognisable as such and the whole plant is very tender. The leaves are narrow and about $\frac{1}{2}$ in long except when they reach the surface, where they form a star-shaped cluster. This is a good plant for insect larvae and water snails and it is probable that some fish eat the plant itself – goldfish and crucian carp in aquariums feed on it quite readily. Starwort grows in most waters and rarely gets out of hand except in shallow rivers where large quantities of mud have been allowed to collect on the bed. It is best confined to margins where it will form into large cushion-like growths along the edges of mud banks, thus forming good cover for fish.

The plants growing in the deeper waters are mainly pondweeds and lilies. The common, or broad-leaved, pondweed is a most useful plant for all coarse fisheries, for it will grow on a muddy bottom, thrusting its leaves up through 6 ft of water, and I have seen it growing in 8 ft of water where the clarity is exceptionally good. The leaves are about 2 in across and float on the surface like a lily.

If you examine a bed of these plants you will see that they harbour a great deal of life. The broad leaves provide a feeding-ground for many insect larvae, some of which burrow into the leaf while others feed on algal growths on the under surface. Turn one or two leaves over and examine them carefully, and you will probably find one or more strips of jelly; these are the eggs of water snails and the jelly is there to protect the eggs which appear as clear blobs in the centre of the coating. Similar deposits, but with a softer jelly, appear to be just jelly, but if you examine them with a glass you will see that they also contain eggs placed in lines similar to that of a magnetic field. These are the eggs of sedge, or caddis flies. There are many other collections of tiny eggs to be found, some will be water beetles of various kinds, and the tiny worm-like ribbons of mud will be the homes of the larvae of a species of midge.

Water boatmen will be found scurrying from leaf to leaf searching for food; these small bugs have a liking for this type of plant and derive much of their nourishment from what they find on the undersides of the leaves. Carp, particularly crucians, love to feed on the snail spawn jellies, finding them most nutritious. Large carp and occasionally tench will feed in this manner, especially if a pool has extensive beds of these plants. Similar foods are found also on lily leaves but in greater quantity.

Let us now take a look at the open water. Run a fine-mesh hand net through the water, and you will be amazed at the 'life' that is caught. Sometimes a quantity of silt-like matter is left in the corner of the net, and if a glass is used it can be seen that the substance is, in fact, zooplankton. This is composed of planktonic crustaceans, such as Daphnia, the water flea, Cyclops and other tiny animals. Other almost transparent objects not unlike small fish about $\frac{1}{4}$ in long may be seen,

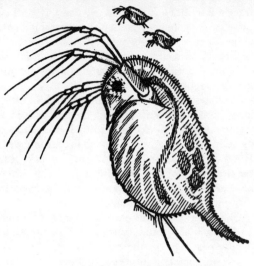

Daphnia (the water flea)

these are phantom larvae which will eventually hatch into phantom midges. The small organism called Cyclops has what appears to be two tails, one on either side of the body. These are egg sacs which are carried by the females.

Zooplankton is the staple diet of most small fishes and is an invaluable food for the fry of the larger species. Large bream also have a great liking for these organisms. During the day these clouds of plankton will alternate between the surface and the bottom, and occasionally they will be found at mid-water. Often they will be found in the vicinity of weed beds and in places where vegetation overhangs the water.

The bottom of a typical small pond will be of deep black mud that is rich in organic matter, and if the pond is deep and dark-looking it is quite likely that the oxygen content of the water is low. Certain organisms are adapted to living in such conditions and among these are the larvae of several species of midge. One of the most common is the bloodworm, familiar to many anglers as a killing bait.

Bloodworms live in little mud tubes on the bottom and care not whether there is oxygen or not, for they carry their own supplies with them. The red colour that gives them their name is haemoglobin, the red pigment that is found in blood cells. This substance combines with oxygen to form oxyhaemoglobin which is able to rapidly give up its oxygen to any part of the body requiring it. Therefore if the larvae need oxygen from water which is temporarily short of it, they can extract sufficient from their own pigment. Other species of midge larvae that live in a similar way are either yellow, green or a mixture of both, for they inhabit water which contains more oxygen.

All these larvae feed on matter which is sifted from the muddy bottom and they pupate in a manner similar to the mosquito larvae already mentioned earlier; they also hatch in the same way. However, the eggs are laid in 'ropes' near the water's surface, and the adults can often be seen flying about with the eggs attached to them, looking like a fine hair.

One other important item in the diet of bottom feeding fish are pea mussels. These are no larger than a pea, live on the mud bed and have an interesting method of reproduction. They are hermaphrodite and the young are fully formed within the shell of the adult, which ejects them when ready.

Larger pools and lakes have a more interesting fauna due to the varying habitats provided by the many different kinds of bottom they contain: mud, sand, gravel and marl, with areas covered by thickly-growing fine-leaved plants called stoneworts, for example. The muddy regions will harbour the same kinds of animals as muddy ponds, but in the other areas there are creatures which are specially adapted for living in such habitats.

The main types in this group are the nymphs of a species of water-bred fly called *Caenis* and a species of caddis fly. The former live on the bottom and are perpetually covered with silt, an existence that would be fatal to many other creatures. The silt grains which adhere to them serve as an effective camouflage. They feed on decaying plants and animal remains that have fallen to the bottom. These flies hatch out in their thousands at certain times of the year, mainly in the late evening or very early morning in late spring. In favourable conditions, prodigious numbers will hatch almost simultaneously, and if you go down to the water's edge they will settle all over you and will shed their skins by crawling out, leaving the old one behind on your jacket. Eventually all that remain are dozens of cast white skins which look like grotesque headless husks.

The caddis that lives on the sandy bottom of certain lakes makes a very unusual case. Apart from the cylindrical part in which the insect lives, it has a wide flange all around it which is made from tiny sand grains. This flange is pear-shaped and when the caddis lies motionless on the bottom it is almost invisible. Few fish feed on it, and it is amusing to see these small pear-shaped accumulations of sand moving about.

Parts of the lake bed that are silty rather than muddy will contain some of the larger molluscs, the freshwater mussels. There are several species of these, the smaller specimens providing food for tench and carp, particularly the former. These creatures are found on firm muddy bottoms. Very soft muds, particularly if deep, allow the mussels to sink too deeply. They live half in and half out of the mud and in order to live must have part of their bodies exposed to water.

Fresh water mussel

Freshwater mussels have an interesting life-history. The shell is in two halves, and hinged along one edge. Propulsion is achieved by a foot which protrudes between the two halves of the shell when these are slightly apart. The foot is often buried in the mud together with part of the shell.

In order to breathe, the mussel is equipped with two organs known as siphons. These protrude from between the shell halves on the opposite end to that which is buried in the mud. Water is drawn into one of the siphons, passed round the mantle, or the body of the mussel, and is then ejected through the other siphon. A continuous flow of water is thus passed through its body, the syphonic action being kept going by organs called cilia. These are tiny hair-like projections which are continuously flexing and it is this movement that causes the current. The cilia are situated on the special gills of the mussel which are unlike fish gills, being spongy in texture. These so-called gills have another function to perform as well as that of respiration. They arrest tiny particles of food in the flow of water; these are passed into the mouth (which is situated near the mussel's foot).

It can thus be seen that this continual flow of water through the body of the mussel is a most important feature, for it provides not only the necessary oxygen required by the animal but its food as well. Waste products are passed out of the mussel in this flow. The inlet siphon also sucks in fertilising fluid for the eggs which has been given off into the water by the male mollusc (some species are, however, hermaphrodite, the male and female organs being contained within one shell). Fresh water mussels are able to control the flow of water entering their bodies to some extent, for if matter injurious to them comes near the inlet siphon, they can eject a spurt of water in an attempt to drive it away.

The method of reproduction of the fresh water mussel is also of interest and most unusual. When the eggs are formed in the ovaries they pass from these into special brood pouches in the gills which are swollen greatly above their normal size. This takes place in the autumn and winter. The young mussels hatch in the pouches, but at this stage do not at all resemble their parents, being roughly triangular in shape. Eventually the tiny mussels are ejected by the adult and swim about freely searching for a fish to which to attach themselves, or they drop down among the plants until a fish happens along.

At this stage in their development they become parasites on fish. After attaching themselves they are able to feed, obtaining their nourishment from the host fish. Eventually, the skin of the fish grows over the tiny mussel, thus forming a cyst, in which situation they remain for about three months. During this time they change their form, finally bursting out of the cyst as fully-formed mussels. It is interesting to speculate on the harm these parasites cause their hosts.

The gravelly parts of a lake bed support a different kind of fauna. There are not many plants growing in such areas and those animals that live on gravel are mainly algae eaters, or they feed on the bodies of dead creatures. Snails of many kinds can be found feeding on the algae that grow on the stones, and freshwater shrimps and water slaters may also be present. Some species of caddis are sure to be there, and lesser water boatmen favour this type of bottom, obtaining good feeding from the detritus. Leeches may be found in good numbers as well as several species of flatworm.

RIVERS AND STREAMS

The rapid, rocky rivers of mountainous districts do not hold coarse fish and therefore will not be discussed here. It is with the slower-flowing, lowland streams that we are mainly concerned. These do, of course, have fast-flowing and shallow stretches but these are usually situated between pools and deep glides.

The fast shallows are often ignored by anglers when hunting coarse fish, but it is in these reaches that the better part of a river's food supply is grown. Some parts of a shallow, or indeed a whole shallow reach, may be devoid of all plant life, having only a gravelly bed, whilst others will be thickly carpeted with water plants such as celery and crowfoot. Fish know all about these 'larders' and will move up into them at nightfall from the pools where they have been lying 'doggo' all day.

Lift a large flat stone from such a shallow and see what a wealth of life it has on it. There will be caddis larvae, caddis in pupal form, betrayed by the little mounds of stones, and shrimps and slaters that scurry away when exposed. There will be freshwater limpets that stay put whatever efforts are made to detach them, and if the bottom is composed of larger stones – and the water not polluted to any degree – there may be a crayfish or two hiding under them.

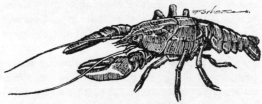

Fresh water crayfish

Freshwater crayfish are most interesting creatures as they are the largest animals, other than fish and some species of mussels, to be found in our rivers and streams. During the day they remain in hiding under stones and in holes in the banks but at night they emerge and start feeding. They will take almost anything, water plants, snails, other crayfish – they are great fighters – insect larvae, and dead fish, etc.

If you lift a stone and finding a crayfish, wish to capture it, do not try to grasp it, for if you do, it will either give you a strong nip with its powerful claws, or will retreat rapidly backwards, being propelled by a flip of its broad tail. Place a net or other receptacle behind the crayfish and then chivvy it with a stick, usually it will dart backwards into your net.

Crayfish are remarkable in that they can grow 'replacement' legs and claws, for they frequently lose a limb when fighting. The eggs, when laid, become permanently attached to the parent and remain there until they hatch. Eggs are laid in the autumn and remain with the female until spring, when they hatch into tiny crayfish which are exact replicas of the adults. Crayfish cast their shells in order to grow and reach about $1\frac{1}{2}$ in during the first year and add perhaps $\frac{3}{4}$ in during each of their remaining growing years.

When crayfish have shed their shells in order to grow rapidly until the new shell hardens, they are vulnerable to attack and at this time many fall victim to foraging fish. These crustaceans are a great favourite of chub which will take quite large ones, while the smaller ones are no doubt taken by many kinds of bottom-feeding fish.

Since the faster-flowing, shallower reaches of a river are more highly oxygenated than the more sluggish parts, there will be certain insect larvae that require highly-oxygenated conditions to survive living among the stones and plants. These belong to a family of water-bed flies known as the *Ephemeroptera*. These are more familiar to trout fishermen, but they do play a very important part in the food supply of such fish as chub, dace, perch and roach since these fish live at certain times almost exclusively on a diet of insects in one form or another.

Of the groups that live in fast-flowing water, some crawl about on stones, feeding on algae, others cling to the leaves of plants, and a third type live in the silt at the edges of the main current flow. If you pick up a stone from the river bed and see black, fearsome-looking beasts, appearing to be all head and legs, crawling rapidly away, you will be looking at the larvae of the first group of these flies. These nymphs are adapted to living on stones and their undersides are concave so that they can cling to the rounded surfaces by suction. Fish can pick these nymphs off the stones if they are quick. However, they take most of the nymphs as they rise to the surface to hatch into flies.

The life history of this group of flies is most interesting. The group includes the large mayfly that appears on many rivers between mid-May and mid-June. It is true that coarse fish anglers will not be at the waterside fishing at this time of year but the appearance of the large mayflies and the smaller species is important to all fish, as they feed greedily on both nymphs and adults which sometimes hatch in prolific numbers. The large mayflies appear just as many coarse fish have finished spawning and need food which takes but little effort to obtain. A walk along your favourite stream during this period of the year will tell you a lot about the water and its fish.

These flies live for one, two and sometimes three years in the larval and nymphal stages before hatching into flies. There is no pupal stage as in the caddis flies; the larvae gradually change into nymphs as they mature, shedding their skins as they do so. When the nymphs are ready to hatch they either swim or float to the surface or crawl up a plant stem. After a short time, the skins split and out come the flies. They are very delicate creatures and not at all like the flies one is accustomed to seeing about the garden.

These insects have a pair of upright, semi-transparent wings, which resemble small sails, and they float along on the water like ships while drying their wings after hatching. Some species have a second pair of wings, but these are so tiny that they can hardly be seen unless especially looked for. The flies in this stage are called duns, and after drying their wings they fly off to nearby trees and bushes. They are able to feed at this stage in their lives, but probably take only a little dew or moisture from the undergrowth.

After a period which may vary from a few hours to several days, according to the prevailing weather conditions, the flies go through yet another stage in their transformation to the perfect insect. The skin between the wings splits and out crawls the mature fly, in exactly the same manner as the Caenis flies which are of the same family and were described earlier. These flies have no mouth parts in this their final and perfect state, their only function being to mate and lay eggs.

After mating, which takes place high in the air, the females come down to the water to lay their eggs. This they do by either dipping onto the surface of the water, extruding a few eggs at each dip; dropping the eggs in a little ball on to the surface; or by crawling down something protruding from the water and then depositing the eggs on an underwater object in little irregular-shaped masses. Some are buff in colour, some yellowish and some darkish purple. If you see a branch sticking out of the water pull it out and examine the part that was under the water, you may find one of these egg patches (but remember the stick must come from fast water). These egg deposits can be found during the summer months and even into early November in a warm season. Sometimes when standing in the water in waders, the flies will land on your legs and immediately crawl down into the water and begin egg-laying.

If the weather conditions are bad and the water temperature remains low these eggs will remain unhatched until the following spring. I have over-wintered eggs in tanks and they hatched successfully during the following April, but unfortunately the larvae did not survive because they were a type that needed swift water. Still-water types do not go down into the water to lay their eggs but shed them on the surface.

Another interesting and valuable insect that inhabits faster-flowing water is the reed smut. This is a house-fly type but has more slender wings and a black body. According to the species, the eggs are laid in a mass either under the water or on the leaf of a water plant. A feature of the larvae of these flies is they are able to spin a thread from their salivary glands. As soon as the tiny larvae emerge from the eggs they spin a thread which is attached to the egg mass and this gives them a sort of safe conduct to some water plant where they stay. It would appear that many of the larvae may stay on the host plant, so to speak, as great numbers may be found on one plant.

If you see either a celery or crowfoot or any stringy type of plant that appears to have a woolly covering, as if mud has settled on the leaves, take a close look at them. If reed smut larvae are present shake the plant gently and you will see all the larvae leave the plant and become suspended on their silken threads. These larvae are quite unmistakable, they have a thick fore-end and are similar in form to a marrow which has a bulbous end. When they are ready to pupate the larvae spin conical cocoons which are attached to the leaves of the plants on which they are living. Many dozens of pupal cases can be seen on each leaf all clustered together like little huts.

The pupation period varies from a few days to about two weeks, the exact length of time depending upon the water temperature. The pupae are surrounded by a bubble of gas within the pupal skin, and this remains after the pupae have emerged from their cocoons and it helps to carry them to the surface, where the bubble bursts and the fully-formed adults fly away. These insects are so numerous that they are an important source of food for coarse fish. The smaller varieties no doubt take the larvae, but larger fish will take the pupae as they rise to the surface to hatch.

MANAGEMENT

The basis of a good coarse fishery differs little from the requirements of any good fishery whether it be in still or flowing water. Naturally, the water must be of a sufficiently high standard of purity to allow fish and other organisms to live and breed successfully.

Apart from water quality there must be ample space; a sufficient and continuous food supply sufficiently varied enough to provide for the needs of both mature and immature fish of all species; an adequate variety of water plants to provide cover for the fish, and a breeding and feeding ground for the fresh water animals that are the main food of fish; and, finally, suitable areas where fish can successfully spawn. Many coarse fisheries fall down on one or more of these requirements and, in attempts to put matters right, the measures taken often aggravate an already serious situation. Taking the basic requirements one by one, let us examine how these apply to fisheries.

SPACE

It is probable that the majority of coarse fisheries in this country are overstocked with fish, allowing insufficient space for their populations to grow to the maximum size. Thus, while the spawning facilities are satisfactory, the numbers of the various species may multiply so much so that individual fish become stunted.

When fishing deteriorates in quality, those responsible add more fish of good size, and at no small expense, in the hope that they will improve the strain. This misguided action achieves the exact opposite. The good fish spawn, and since they are of large size, produce more eggs than the stunted ones, the situation then progresses from bad to almost impossible.

FOOD

It may be argued that in order to make more space available to the fish, drastic weed cutting operations should be carried out. Many coarse fish anglers seem to have an inherent hatred of water plants of any kind, but to cut or up-root large areas of plants is to severely reduce the available supply of natural foods, since many creatures will be living in, and on, the plants and will be removed from the water when the cut is carried out.

Actions of this kind make it almost impossible for the natural supply of insects, molluscs, crustaceans, etc. to survive, because they will have nowhere to feed and breed, and future supplies of these creatures are thus put in jeopardy. The fish now have more space, but they will be starving, and therefore the reduction of plants has done nothing to alleviate the situation.

COVER AND SPAWNING REQUIREMENTS

The removal of the plant beds will also cause two other upsets. There will be a deficiency of cover, and there will be no spawning facilities. The result is that fish will, if possible, leave the environment altogether and return only when the plant beds and food supplies are what they require.

It can thus be seen that life in fresh water is complex and that a balance between all requirements must be maintained at all times. However, very often nature does not allow things to develop in a way that suits fishery interests.

The weeds grow rampant, the fish overbreed and perhaps interbreed, the natural food supplies become scarce and the quality of the fishing goes into a decline.

What brings about this state of affairs and why did it not take place in the time of our forefathers? This is a question that is often posed; the answer is to be found in the very development of this country. The growing population, coupled with the industrial revolution, has brought about an unprecedented demand for water which has strained the water resources of the whole country. The result has been a diminished flow in rivers and widespread pollution. The water demands of a dense population must be met, and to this end the head waters of many rivers, as well as the vast underground natural reservoirs that feed them,

have been tapped to a disastrous degree so that often there is but a trickle left in the watercourses.

The lack of flow, coupled with the high organic content in sewage effluents, has encouraged the coarser varieties of weed to grow to such an extent that they have, in some cases, completely blocked watercourses from bank to bank. This is often the root of the trouble where rivers have, from the sporting standpoint, gone into a decline.

The deterioration of lakes and pools poses different problems. Here it is a gradual and natural process which scientists call 'ageing'. Pools and lakes gradually become richer and richer as time goes by, until they are completely silted, there being little water over a basin of deep, evil-smelling mud. Where lakes have a feeder stream, this ageing process is often accelerated by the silt from the stream being deposited on the lake bed. If the stream becomes polluted, even though it may not be drastic enough to be noticed, the enriching effect of this on the lake bed will give rise to a rapid increase in the growth of coarse weeds which in time may completely colonise the inflow end of the lake.

This area gradually increases, taking in more and more of the lake bed until there is only a small area of deep water left. This reduction in the volume of water available to the fish is bad enough on its own, but the fish population will be increasing to an extent that a really stunted population results.

In smaller pools and ponds this process may take place more slowly, particularly so if sewage is not present, but take place it does. Year after year prolific growths of weed appear and die down, and coupled with this, some pools collect large amount of leaves from surrounding trees. Gradually the pond becomes very shallow, sometimes many feet of deep mud is covered by only a few inches of water. The dressing of surrounding farmland with fertilisers also has an enriching effect on small pools which is similar to that caused by sewage, then the ageing process is greatly speeded up.

In the case of the smaller waters the lack of a management policy has allowed the deterioration to proceed unhampered. Whereas if a sound preservation policy has been put into effect the deterioration could have been slowed down considerably. Likewise with rivers and streams.

What, then, can be done to improve our coarse fisheries? The first thing is look and think, have a good look at your fishery and size up the situation. Try to decide what the fish population is like, and take stock of how many different species of fish are present, and to what size they grow. Are there species present that you do not particularly wish to catch? Is the average size of the fish small? Are the anglers plagued with small roach or perch? Are the weeds dense? Is there much life in the weeds and are they growing so quickly that the upper leaves are shading the lower ones? Are the shallows overgrown with coarse reeds and rushes?

These are some of the questions that should be asked, and if they cannot be satisfactorily answered, then try to find out why. The numerical position of the fish stocks is all-important, and to get an idea of what there is in the water, ask every club member to make a note of the vital statistics of a proportion of the fish they catch. Specimens of all species inhabiting the water should be accurately measured and weighed so that over a period a list of the largest and average sizes of all varieties can be compiled. Scales from a few fish should be examined by an expert so that the age and growth rate can be determined and be compared with known standards.

Weighing up the consequences of taking any of the actions mentioned earlier, it becomes obvious that the most effective and that least likely to upset the natural balance of the water is the removal of part of the fish population. This will allow the remainder more space, more food and a chance of growing to a good size. This will eventually lead to a better class of fish, and the bigger ones will tend to breed a larger type. It will take time, probably as long as it took the stock to become stunted, but if circumstances are favourable, it may happen surprisingly quickly.

When compared with fisheries in warmer climes, those in this country are only capable of supporting a comparatively small head of fish, when quoted in pounds per acre of water. The best regulated fisheries in this country will only support about 300 lb per acre, and so, bearing this fact in mind, consider just how many fish are placed in some small, enclosed waters and stretches of canal. Often they can be counted in tens of thousands. A ten acre lake in first-class condition will support 3,000 1 lb fish. A lake of the same size but in poor condition will only

support 150 lb of fish per acre, i.e., 1,500 fish of 1 lb. Therefore, for each fish of 2 or 3 lb that is present, there must be 2 lb less of smaller fish.

What likelihood is there of quality fishing if 50,000 2 oz fish inhabit a water that will only support 24,000 fish of this size? There is some flexibility in these figures when a water is carefully stocked with species that do not directly compete with each other for whatever food is available. However, space requirements remain the same, although with careful attention to the needs of certain species the population figures can be raised somewhat. Obviously one can have a greater number of fish if the stocks are divided between bottom and surface/mid-water feeding varieties.

If you suspect that your fishery is overstocked make every effort to remove as many fish under 6 in as you can. If by compiling records of weight and length measurements you find that certain species do not appear to be doing well and are perhaps declining in condition, have no hesitation in removing them from the water by all possible methods, either by netting, trapping or rod fishing. Better fishing can be produced by culling out all the poor specimens, nothing is quite so important as the regulation of fish populations. It is little use trying to introduce new fish into an environment that is both unsuitable and already overcrowded; if you wish to restock, then do so by all means, but not before you have removed a very large proportion of the smaller fish.

Once you embark upon an improvement policy of this kind, it is essential that the netting, etc. to remove a proportion of the small fish is carried out each year. This is most important, for by removing many of the smaller fish those that remain will be given a far better chance to grow, and when the spawning season comes round the fish will not only produce a better class of fish, but they will spawn more heavily.

Pike are a species which always cause a great deal of discussion when fish populations are being settled. They can do a certain amount of good until they attain a length of about 18 in; after this they become a menace, especially in small waters. Pike of 20 lb have no place in a fishery of less than 150 acres in extent or a deep, weedy river where there is adequate cover for the fish upon which they prey. Have pike by all means if you prefer pike fishing, you may get some fine specimens of other species, even some fit for glass cases, but they will be few in number.

Once you have control of the fish population, the numbers of aquatic animals will automatically adjust themselves accordingly.

Before turning to problems associated with weed removal it may be useful to say something about the management of newly-flooded gravel pits, for these waters are becoming more and more important, and in fact the time may arrive when they become the coarse angler's mainstay.

Wet gravel pits have special problems – some seem to start off well and some remain poor for years. When gravel has been removed, the bottom of a pit may consist of either clay, or clay under a thin layer of sand and gravel, or in some cases mainly sand. The different types of bottoms contain varying amounts of mineral salts, therefore some will sustain plant growth and some will not. The plants may grow for a time in some and then die down prematurely; in others, they never grow at all.

A fishery without plants is never very special, and remember, plants need clear shallow water in which to grow. Many of the gravel pits that are used as coarse fisheries have steeply-shelving sides, and in consequence there are no shallows at all. In such waters food supplies are very scarce, and the fishing never very good. Nor is it likely to be until plant beds are provided, for algal blooms alone rarely grow good heads of fish in this country.

It may sound ridiculous, but in such cases plants can be planted in skips, tubs or baskets, and suspended from the sides on strong wires. Alternatively, if there is space, bays can be excavated in the surrounding land and joined to the main lake. These make good spawning and food producing areas.

If plants do not grow after two or three years from the time the pit is filled, they should be introduced into all available shallows. Well-rotted stable manure should be spread over all shallow areas in the vicinity of the plants, but take care not to smother the plants. Good manure about two years old is far better than inorganic fertilizers. If you ever have the chance of renting a newly worked-out gravel pit, do not stock it with fish for at least twelve months, and only then at a rate of 200 young fish per acre.

The first year should be spent in manuring and establishing plant beds. See how the fish grow,

and then if they are doing really well, more can be added. It is a mistake to introduce too varied a population at the start. Confine the species to carp or tench, roach or rudd and possibly chub if you have deep water. Never mix roach with rudd and rudd with bream, and experience has shown that carp and tench are best kept apart to begin with. Bream do not fare particularly well in some gravel pits and therefore are best kept out for a start. When the bottom has a layer of mud on it, perhaps a few can be put in as a trial. Pike and perch should not be introduced in the early days of the creation of a new fishery.

When a new fishery is being set up, supplies of freshwater snails, shrimps and Daphnia should be introduced as nuclei of future populations. During the twelve months in which the lake is left to mature these will give rise to dense populations of food suitable for future fish stocks.

If the water is stocked at the correct ratio of fish per acre of water good fishing should be forthcoming within two or three years. However, a close watch must be kept on the fish and if it is found that one or more species finds the environment particularly suitable for spawning, steps should be taken to reduce the stocks of fry. Netting, trapping and the removal of spawn are the answers, not the introduction of pike or other predators. This latter action would be folly indeed.

You cannot take over a worked-out gravel pit, stock it with fish and leave it at that. A water must be managed in the same way that farmland is. Imagine what would happen if a farmer left a flock of sheep for a period of years to breed uncontrolled. He would soon have a disease-ridden, starving flock on his hands. A similar situation can occur when dealing with fish and water. Overcrowding soon brings disease, hydridism, or severe stunting.

The stocking of rivers is also a many-sided problem, often fish are bought and introduced into club waters without a thought for their future well-being. The attitude would seem to be, they are fish and fish live in water, we have put them into water so all must be well. Stocking should always be carried out to a definite plan and never in a haphazard fashion.

Several things can happen when fish are released into a particular reach of a river. If the environment is suitable they may stay, unless driven away by the resident fish. However, if conditions are not suitable, they will immediately leave the stretch for which they were intended, for if they do stay they may well die of starvation. If there are obstructions preventing their migration, many of them will certainly die. Selective stocking is the only way of building up a stock of specimen fish, it is far better to set aside certain reaches for a particular species and manage these accordingly.

If the environment is complete in all respects, i.e., provides an adequate food supply, plenty of cover, ample spawning sites and is not already overstocked, newly introduced fish will remain in the locality. For instance, roach are found in many types of water: canals, ponds, lakes and most rivers. But, in how many waters do they grow to specimen size? Environments in which fish will live, and those in which they will thrive and grow to their maximum size, are vastly different in make-up.

When acquiring fish for restocking always find out from where they originate. Those that are bred in highly oxygenated water will not thrive in one which is low in oxygen, the reverse also applies. Never accept a consignment of fish that look sickly or have any outward signs of disease, examine them carefully for external parasites. If your restocking programme is complete, vigorously resist all offers of free fish from all sources, you do not need them, so why have them just because they are free? Your fishery will be far better off without them.

Many anglers have an aversion to water plants of all descriptions and consider them a hindrance to fishing. They tear them out and toss them carelessly on the banks to rot. Those responsible for this treatment then set to and fish the water feverishly in the firm hope that there is nothing to prevent the fish giving themselves up. When they catch nothing but a few small ones they are genuinely disappointed. The fact is that there are probably no fish of any consequence in the whole of the cleared water, because the whole environment has suffered a shock which has upset the balance of life and has therefore had far-reaching consequences. Some water plants do not take kindly to being severely mauled and cut down, and may well take seasons to recuperate from such treatment, but on the other hand some plants grow quickly after being cut and therefore become a greater hazard to the angler who prefers a clear swim.

With the removal of the plants, a large part of the food on which the fish subsist also goes, and along with the plants it dies, in the rotting heaps on the bank. If this kind of clearance has been carried out on a small water, for example an enclosed pond, the fish will still be there of course, but as their cover has gone they will become extremely shy, so that the slightest shadow or footfall will put them down immediately.

Water plants, or weeds as they are usually termed by the angler, are the very essence of a good coarse fishery. They oxygenate and purify the water during the daylight hours, taking out carbon dioxide and giving off oxygen. They provide good feeding and sanctuary for the many kinds of organism on which fish feed, they also give cover and shade for fish. Nevertheless, when introducing new water plants it pays to remember that some species tend to grow very vigorously and therefore need controlling.

In pools and ponds, milfoil, crowfoot, starwort and broad-leaved pondweed tend to colonise the shallows. The broad-leaved pondweed can, however, grow in 4 or 5 ft of water. Water lilies and the small double yellow lily do become a nuisance at times and should this happen these plants should only be thinned out with a drag made of rake heads fixed together, or specially made tined drags. Cutting is effective, especially with lilies. Generally speaking, these plants do not like being cut and if it is done selectively the method can be most effective in controlling them, but never cut out a whole bed of plants. Keep certain fishing areas clear and keep them free from spreading shoots by persistent trimming. Beds that are getting too thick can be thinned out, and never trample down the marginal plants, as these provide egg-laying sites for many insects as well as cover for anglers. By having a screen of rushes or reeds in front of him, an angler can greatly improve his chances of making a good catch. Fish like to nose about close to such plants for it is here that they find snails, etc.

The water plants that grow in river and stream present differing problems to the angler, but here again, they should never be drastically cut down to the level of the river bed for the whole width of the watercourse. The marginal weeds in rivers and streams should never be cut or thinned, they should be left absolutely alone. Any cutting that is necessary should be confined to the centre of the river. The only exception is where the marginal beds are so wide that a cast cannot be made over them or a fish easily handled. Where heavy growth has to be contended with, then circular swims should be created or narrow channels cut at right angles to the bank. On no account should the tall marginal growth be cut down.

Where lilies or other plants have heavily colonised a watercourse, then obviously attention is essential. Those that grow in the main channel should be cut out as they do little but hold up silt and mud to such an extent that the centre of the stream can become completely blocked. When growth is so thick that light is prevented from penetrating to the river bed it often becomes barren and completely de-oxygenated. The upper leaves of the plants tend to shade the lower ones thus rendering them useless for oxygenation, no algae will grow and no animals be found on them.

If the marginal plants are encroaching into deepish water and are very thick, then some thinning can be carried out, the aim should be to let the light penetrate to the lower leaves and, where possible, to the bottom. Shallows seldom seem to be given much attention by coarse fish

anglers, many think of them as useless stretches of water. Far from it – these reaches are the food producing areas, and therefore should be kept free of coarse growth such as rushes and reeds.

Rushes will tend to completely overrun shallow stretches of water, eventually to the exclusion of all other plants. The river's flow is nullified and oxygenation reduced. Eventually, if action is not taken, whole shallows become one vast rush bed and so badly silted that the flow of the river can hardly percolate between the rush stems, a situation which can lead to the flooding of adjacent farmland.

Shallows should always be kept free of emergent plants. If they have lush growths of celery and crowfoot these should only be thinned out so that the main flow continues un-hampered along defined channels. If silt is allowed to collect, the whole shallow will eventually turn into a mud bank, which finally forms an island. From then on, the flow will be restricted to a narrow channel under each bank and the fishery will decline.

Attention to the points covered in this chapter will mean a cleaner water which in turn will mean more food, and in consequence, bigger and better fish to catch.

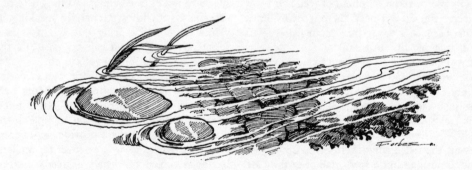

FRESH WATER SPECIES, AND FISH BIOLOGY

by

James A. Gilmour, B.Sc., M.I.Biol.

Although the modern scientist can reduce life to the elementary particles of which it is ultimately composed and in a few cases, even re-synthesise these back into some of the more complicated compounds of the body, he cannot yet reverse the entire process to produce living protoplasm. We are, therefore, still uncertain as to how life first arose. It seems most probable on the little evidence we do possess, that it originated in the mud and pools of the seashore. From the first primaeval forms, a long slow process of evolution lasting over two billion years, and still continuing today, has gradually given rise to the twenty thousand different species of fish we now know.

Of this estimated total, some six thousand species are truly fresh water fish in that they cannot survive in salt water. How this change-over from a saline environment to a fresh water one came about is not fully understood. Some perhaps, like the powan of Wales and Loch Lomond, were cut off from the sea by upheavals in the earth's crust; others may have adapted first to the brackish water of estuarine reaches and later evolved to meet the requirements of fresh water conditions. However it actually happened, the adaptations were restricting. Some species, for example, carp, roach and tench, can withstand brackish conditions but only a very few such as the eel, sturgeon and salmon appear equally at home in both fresh and salt water.

To write of fresh water in such general terms is, of course, to over-simplify the concept. By fresh water we mean a very wide diversity of habitat ranging from deep or shallow lakes and reservoirs to ponds, canals, streams and rivers. Each of these presents opportunities for very different modes of life and offers its own advantages and difficulties to the fish which live in them. An understanding of the physical construction of a fish and the limitations which this, as well as the environment, imposes on it, provides some, at least, of the answers to the questions asked by the thoughtful, practical angler.

STRUCTURE AND FUNCTION

Four parts are usually distinguished in a typical fish – the head, the body, the tail and the fins. The limit of the head is determined by the gill opening and that of the body by the vent. The actual shape of the body bears a definite relationship to the kind of life for which the fish is adapted. Fish found in the faster-running water – such as grayling, dace and chub – vary little from a basic spindle-shaped form which reduces drag and offers the minimum frictional resistance to water. In general, the more active a fish is, the more its body must approach a streamlined shape. On the other hand, bottom feeding fish of slow streams and sluggish waters, such as carp and bream, show a hump-backed, laterally compressed outline well suited to movement amongst growing plants.

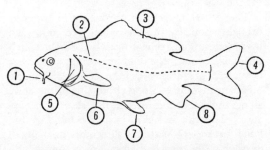

A typical fish: 1. Barbel; 2. Lateral line; 3. Dorsal fin; 4. Tail fin; 5. Gill flaps; 6. Pectoral fins; 7. Pelvic fins; 8. Anal fin

FINS

In a typical fish, there are two sets of paired fins, the pectorals and the pelvics, and three or four single fins, the first dorsal, the second dorsal (often absent), the caudal (or tail fin) and the anal fin. The fins themselves are supported by fin-rays which are joined together by fin membrane. Each fin-ray is a bony process which may be either jointed or unjointed. If it is jointed, it is called a soft ray: soft rays are usually divided at their distal ends to become branched rays as, for example, in the dorsal fin of carp. If the fin-ray is unjointed it is known as a spiny ray and good examples of these are to be found in the dorsal fins of perch and sticklebacks. In general, the numbers and types of fin-rays are constant, within limits, for a particular species of fish and this feature can serve as an aid to identification.

SWIMMING

Water is both heavier and 'thicker' than air (in fact, some eight hundred times as dense) and it is through this medium that fish must push their way. They are considerably assisted in the majority of species by the fact that they possess an internal air or swimbladder which is filled with gas. This organ reduces the overall weight of the fish by increasing its buoyancy and so prevents it from sinking to the bottom. The fish is thus enabled to maintain its position in midwater with a minimum of fin movement and expenditure of energy. The swimbladder also permits fish to detect changes in external pressure and for this reason their behaviour may differ under varying atmospheric conditions. When the young larval fish hatches from the egg, no gas is present in the swimbladder and it swallows air from the surface in order to fill it for the first time.

The actual movement through the water is brought about by the fins which are controlled by muscles. The skeletal muscles of fish, which form, of course, the edible portion, are very large and are arranged in a series of muscle blocks or myotomes along either side of the body along the backbone. When the skin is peeled away, they can be seen as a peculiar 'herring bone' or zig-zag pattern. The individual fibres of which the muscle blocks are composed lie parallel to the backbone and their arrangement is such that as the muscles on one side contract and shorten, those on the opposite side relax and lengthen. This has the effect of pulling the tail through the water in a side-to-side sweeping movement. Water resists this movement. As it is displaced backwards and sideways, it exerts an equal and opposite force to the body of the fish. This serves to drive it forward. The actual speed

reached is dependent on the number of tail beats per second and the distance of the tail sweeps. Speeds of 4·6 m.p.h. have been recorded for pike and 3·9 m.p.h. for dace. More important than the top speed which can be reached, however, is the degree of acceleration possible – either to obtain a meal or to avoid being taken as one. Experiments have shown that carp, rudd, dace and pike, starting from rest, can accelerate at over 40 yards per second per second over short distances. They cannot sustain high speeds for long periods but these are, in any case, unnecessary, as short, sharp darts and turns are more characteristic of life in the water.

Each muscle fibre contains a special sensory organ which records the degree of contraction and this information is conveyed back to the brain. There is, therefore, a double stream of messages constantly being sent forwards and backwards from the brain to the muscles – outgoing messages which inform the muscles of when and how much to contract and incoming messages from the sensory receptors. In this way, co-ordinated action and graded responses are possible. Under 'normal' conditions, only a small proportion of the total muscle is being used at any one time. Graded responses varying from a slight flicker of the tail, designed to maintain position, to a full power sweep can thus be obtained.

BALANCE

As well as straightforward, purposive movement, balance and postural control are just as necessary in the water as they are on land; fish achieve this by adjusting the position of their fins. The fin-rays each have individual muscles of their own. Thus a dorsal fin can be raised or lowered and individual movements are possible in the pectoral or pelvic fins. These movements are necessary to counteract the rolling, pitching and yawing tendencies which result from sweeps of the tail or from the effects of the river current. When a fish turns, banks or dives, the fins are set and used as manoeuvring organs in much the same manner as the rudder and flaps on an aircraft. The pectoral fins, for example, are used as brakes both when a fish pulls up sharply and also when it is hovering since there is a constant tendency to move forward when water is expelled from the gills. If a fish requires to maintain its station in a school or keep its position in a bank of weeds, precise, adjusting movements are continually required from all its fins.

The shape of the body and the position and movement of the fins show modifications which assist individual species in their mode of life. Take the pike, for example. The body is spindle shaped for speed; the dorsal and anal fins are situated well back towards the posterior end of the body. This particular positioning potentiates the effect of a sudden stroke of the powerful tail and helps to keep the fish on a straight course during sharp, short, bursts of speed.

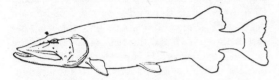

The streamlined body of the pike, and the placing of the dorsal and anal fins well back near the tail, enable it to achieve bursts of high speed and to maintain a straight course

In perch and sticklebacks, the spiny rays of the dorsal fin can be raised as a protective measure against predators. Pike have been seen to spit out young perch and sticklebacks which had their dorsal fins raised in this manner.

SKIN

A fish is covered with skin in which are embedded bony scales which are protective in function. Skin, which is rich in collagen – a protein from which some glues are manufactured – consists of two layers, an outer epidermis and an inner dermis which is attached by connective tissue to underlying structures. Unlike the skin of humans, where the outermost layers of the epidermis are 'dead', no such horny, keratinised layer exists in most fish and the epidermis presents a 'living' structure to the outside world.

The epidermis contains large numbers of special mucus-secreting cells which produce the slimy, slippery secretion familiar to all anglers. The eel and tench are covered with a particularly thick layer of this slime. Its presence protects the underlying cells from invasion by bacteria and fungi present in the water. At one time it was believed that mucus also reduced the effects of friction and so enabled the fish to slip more easily through the water. Recent research, however, throws doubt on this idea and suggests that a more likely function is to lubricate and ease the movement of the scales when the body flexes and curves.

Of special interest to the angler is the connection between mucus and the effects of pollution. Chemically polluted water often contains metallic salts as a waste product of industrial processes. These salts form a chemical combination with mucus and cover the body and gill surfaces with an impervious layer. When this happens, oxygen cannot be absorbed and the fish may literally die of suffocation.

ALARM REACTION

Another interesting feature is that the skin of some fish has been shown to contain a special substance which when released into the water arouses alarm or fright reactions in other fish of the same or related species. When skin is damaged, and only then, this alarm substance is freed from injured cells, diffuses through the water and is picked up by the olfactory organs of other fish in the area. The particular form in which the alarm reaction is manifested varies in different species. Minnows, for example, retreat from the feeding ground and seek hiding places; tench and carp swim with their heads knocking against the bottom in a manner likely to stir up mud and debris which might help to conceal them. Other species become motionless, relying on their camouflage to save them from danger. It is thought that this alarm substance is a biological mechanism which protects schools of young fish from attack by predators. Whilst it cannot help the individual fish which was captured and which released the alarm substance it can warn the group of impending danger. The capture of a single minnow, for example, by a pike, creates sufficient damage to the skin to release the alarm substance and initiate the alarm reaction for the rest of the shoal. This special chemical does not appear to be present in all fish and, in research work carried out so far, it has not been demonstrated in perch, pike or members of the salmonid family.

COLOUR

The beautiful iridescent sheens and the varieties of colour found in our British freshwater fish are due to the presence of coloured pigments – yellow, orange, brown, black, white and red – contained in special cells in the dermis called chromatophores and also to crystals which reflect light contained in cells called iridocytes.

To some extent, the colouration depends on the natural background of the fish. For example, vegetal colouration, that is brownish, greenish or yellowish, on the back and stripes or blotches on the sides of the body, is adopted by fish inhabiting weeds, such as pike and perch. Demersal colouration – dark back and sides with a lighter belly and frequently with spots or stripes along the flanks as in young grayling and minnows – renders the fish less conspicuous against a background of stones in clear, running water. Fish of the same species from different areas and sometimes from the same one, however, show very wide variations in colour.

Alterations in colour to suit a particular background are believed to be initiated through vision. The chromatophores have five branching processes. The pattern can be altered to some degree by the pigments migrating out into these processes in which case, the skin appears darker. On the other hand, if the pigments are concentrated in the central part of the cell, the skin appears paler. Thus a fish may change in colour as it moves from one habitat to another, as often happens during development. Other colour changes are cyclical in nature and are related to the breeding season. At such times, the pituitary gland at the base of the brain releases a chemical messenger or hormone into the bloodstream. This brings about the nuptial colour changes seen during courtship and mating.

The iridocytes contain elongated crystals of a substance called guanin which has the property of reflecting and refracting light. This produces the iridescent, silvery sheen so commonly seen on the belly. The actual colour of an individual fish at any given time depends on the number and distribution of chromatophores and iridocytes. The source of the pigments is apparently from the diet. For example, fish which have been deprived of certain foodstuffs tend to lose some of their red and yellow pigmentation.

Apart from the breeding season when the adoption of a silvery sheen or bright hues may be necessary to stimulate and attract the opposite sex, the main purpose of colouration is the protection it affords from many enemies. Camouflage, of course, is not a monopoly of the hunted. Predators like pike also adopt cryptic colours and the yellowish hue of this fish with its yellow

spots and dark vertical bands blends beautifully with the rushes and reeds in which it lurks to await a passing quarry.

A most effective device found in many species and seen, for example, in members of the *Cyprinidae* – carp, tench, bream, roach and barbel – is that of countershading. Here the back is much darker than the underparts. As fish swim about in pond, lake or stream, daylight normally falls on them from above. This tends to make the back look lighter in colour. At the same time, shadows cast by the body on the undersurface would tend to make this look darker than it really is. But because the underparts are lighter to begin with, light from above and the shadows cast below now make the fish appear much the same shade all over. This produces an illusion of flatness which, when coupled with colouration, blends with the background of the environment and makes the fish very hard to spot.

If a fish is in distress for any reason, it may be unable to swim on an even keel and the erratic, fluttering movements it makes causes the silver underparts to flash in an unusual way. This attracts the attention of predators who are always eager to pick up an easy meal. The success of many spoons and spinning Devons as baits is partially due to the fact that they flash in the water rather like an injured fish.

SCALES

The young larval fish hatches from the egg without scales and these protective coverings are gradually produced from the inner skin until they eventually overlap each other like the tiles of a roof. Each scale starts off as a small growth which pushes upwards and expands until it stretches the overlying epidermis. The epidermis is often thin and transparent but although it may not be immediately obvious, it is always present and forms an unbroken cover over the scales of healthy fish.

Once the scales have developed in the young fish, no more are normally formed. They simply grow in size as the body of the individual becomes larger. In short, the number of scales remains constant. This fact can be used to identify a particular species. Freshwater fish bear a longitudinal row of scales along the mid-line of the body. These are easily picked out from the remainder by the presence of a light or dark dot or streak. These scales mark the position of the

At the end of the day the catch is counted and weighed. This catch – all bream measuring over twelve inches each – added up to 30 lb and gave the angler first place in a match.

Always use a big keep net to hold large numbers of fish. Crowded together in a small keep net the fish could die. A long bank stick is also helpful in keeping the net in deeper water so that the captured fish have water in which to swim around.

lateral line, a special sensory organ. Scale counts are taken along the lateral line and also upwards to the origin of the dorsal fin or downwards to that of the ventral fin. When these counts are considered along with certain other anatomical features, identification becomes fairly certain. For example, dace, roach and rudd are somewhat similar in appearance but they can be distinguished by using the techniques we have discussed above:

A. *Dorsal fin in line with the ventral fin*
   Dace: 47–54 scales along the lateral line;
   7–8 branched rays in the dorsal fin.
   Roach: 40–45 scales along the lateral line;
   9–11 branched rays in the dorsal fin.
B. *Dorsal fin originating behind the ventral fin*
   Rudd: 40–43 scales along the lateral line;
   8–9 branched rays in the dorsal fin.

The scales, as we have seen, are living structures growing continuously throughout the life of the fish. The scale itself consists of two distinct layers – an inner or lower layer composed of fibrous connective tissue and an upper or outer layer composed of hyalo-dentine, a substance similar to the dentine found in our own teeth. This hyalo-dentine is laid down in the form of ridges and, as growth continues, more of these ridges are formed. A characteristic feature of fish growth, however, is that it is periodic and uneven. In times of quick growth, as, for example, when food is plentiful in spring and summer, these ridges are widely separated. In winter, when the water is colder, food scarcer and growth slower, they lie much closer together. Bands thus appear with each successive summer and winter not unlike the annual rings found in trees. These bands indicate the age of the fish. At spawning time, the outer edge of the scale may show rings and marks which are the result of the cessation of feeding before breeding and the exhaustion which may follow it. These rings or eroded areas on the scale mark the fact that an individual has passed through a reproductive period. Scale reading, often taken in conjunction with the rings which appear on certain bones, and also in the otoliths or ear stones which lie within the inner ear, can yield a considerable amount of useful information about the age of a particular fish, its rate of growth and how often it has spawned. The relationships between the size of fish, their rates of growth and their ages are obviously of the greatest value in the management of fisheries and the study of available food supplies.

RESPIRATION AND THE NEED FOR OXYGEN

In its simplest terms, respiration is the taking in of oxygen and the giving out of the waste product, carbon dioxide. This statement, however, gives no indication of the elaborate and complicated processes involved in extracting sufficient oxygen from the water, transporting it round the body, off-loading it to tissues which require it, and its final use in oxidising foodstuffs to release energy. It is this question of energy which is the key to understanding the importance of oxygen.

All tissues require energy in order to carry out their specific functions. Basically, this energy is obtained by 'burning' glucose, a simple sugar, with the aid of oxygen. Glucose circulates in the bloodstream in a definite amount which is controlled by the hormone insulin. Some tissues, for example, the brain, use glucose directly. In humans, if there is insufficient glucose in the bloodstream, symptoms of fatigue and disturbances of brain function soon occur – or if there is plenty of glucose but insufficient oxygen to 'burn' it, unconsciousness can occur in a matter of minutes.

The release of energy from glucose is a complex, step-by-step process which is controlled at each stage by a series of chemical catalysts known as respiratory enzymes. These ensure that the available energy is not released as a sudden burst of heat but is set free bit by bit and paid out slowly in a manner which the cells can use. If one of these enzymes stops working, the whole process collapses. For example, one of the respiratory enzymes is carbonic anhydrase, a substance which is inhibited completely by cyanide. If water is polluted with 'Cymag' used for gassing rats and rabbits, cyanide is released and may be carried a considerable distance downstream. Should even a small amount be absorbed through the gills of a fish, the action of carbonic anhydrase is stopped and glucose cannot be 'burned' by the brain. The fish becomes unconscious, floats to the surface belly up and death follows through asphyxiation, i.e. through a blockage of essential respiratory processes.

Research work in the field of biochemistry has shown that in other tissues, such as muscle, energy can be obtained for a short time without the use of oxygen at all. In muscle, the immediate source of energy is a 'high energy' chemical compound, adenine triphosphate or ATP for short. When a fish moves its tail, for example, it can only obtain the energy necessary to contract the muscles by breaking up ATP. No oxygen is required for this purpose but the ATP in yielding energy is broken down to a second substance, ADP, adenine diphosphate. Before ADP can be used again, it must be converted back to ATP – and this reconversion process requires energy. This reconversion energy is obtained by using oxygen to 'burn' the glucose stored in the muscle. The whole process has certain biological advantages. It permits an individual to be very active for short periods and to run up an 'oxygen debt'. For example, a man may run a hundred yards in under ten seconds – but he cannot possibly take in enough oxygen to supply the energy that this effort requires. He is only able to do so by virtue of the energy stored in ATP and by the fact that this permits him to accumulate an 'oxygen debt'. After the race, this debt must be repaid by gulping in extra oxygen which is then used to 'burn' glucose and reconvert ADP back to ATP. In much the same manner, fish may undertake sharp bursts of activity and recover later by passing more water over their gill surfaces and extracting additional oxygen from it.

Man can obtain his oxygen relatively easily since the air contains about 20 per cent of this gas; fish on the other hand, must extract dissolved oxygen from water which holds at best, only about 10 cc of the gas per litre. Further, water obeys certain physical laws for the solution of gases and as the temperature of the water rises less and less oxygen can be held in solution. Fish vary in their oxygen requirements and this determines which species can live in certain environments. Very active species such as grayling require some 5-7 cc per litre; other species such as roach can survive at concentrations around 4 cc per litre; while still others such as carp and tench which are relatively inactive species, can continue to live even when the oxygen content drops to as low as 1 cc per litre.

Water may lose part of its oxygen content in several ways. As we have noted, a rise in temperature of the water means that less oxygen can be held in solution; in summer, aquatic vegetation releases oxygen during the daylight process of photosynthesis in which plant foods are manufactured but uses it up rapidly at night, and decomposing organic materials and debris use oxygen as they disintegrate. Various forms of pollution too may prevent water from absorbing oxygen from the atmosphere; in winter, the presence of a coat of ice stops air from reaching the surface of the water. In short, a large number of factors determine whether or not a particular water can hold sufficient oxygen for the survival of a particular species.

Natural waters vary in their temperature and their oxygen content from point to point. Even in the comparatively short British rivers, it is possible to divide them into stretches or 'reaches' suitable for various types of fish. The upper reaches where the water is faster, colder and with a much higher oxygen content is the natural home of trout and grayling; as the river slows down and the current moderates, the water warms up in summer and the oxygen content drops. These stretches are the habitat of barbel, bream, roach, all those species whose demands for oxygen are less high.

GILLS

Water containing dissolved oxygen is first taken in when the fish opens its mouth. When the mouth is closed, water is forced over the gill surfaces and out through the gill flaps. As the gill flaps close, the mouth opens again and this alternating cycle of events ensures that a virtually continuous stream of water is passed over the gills. The frequency of these respiratory movements is related to body size and activity. In resting tench, for example, the rate is about one per second. In smaller fish such as sticklebacks, the rate may be as high as one hundred and fifty a minute.

In conditions of low oxygen supply or after bursts of activity, the rate and depth of the respiratory movements are speeded up so that more water is passed over the gill surfaces. The triggering factors for the increase of the respiratory rate are the lack of oxygen and the accumulation of carbon dioxide in the bloodstream. When the level of carbon dioxide which is produced as a by-product of the 'burning' of glucose rises, it stimulates a 'respiratory centre' in the brain. This centre responds by sending out more nervous impulses to the muscles controlling the respiratory movements. These increase in rate and more water is moved over the gill surfaces. This promotes the intake of oxygen and the removal of carbon dioxide. As the level of carbon dioxide in the bloodstream falls, the respiratory movements slow down.

The gills themselves consist of a series of folds, the gill filaments, each of which has numerous subdivisions. Along the edges of these is a very rich network of thin walled blood vessels, the capillaries. It is in this region that oxygen diffuses from the water to the bloodstream through the exquisitely thin membranes of these tiny blood vessels. The oxygen is first dissolved in the liquid portion of the blood, the plasma. It then passes into the red blood cells to form a loose chemical combination, oxyhaemoglobin, with the respiratory pigment, haemoglobin, which is only present inside the red blood cells.

From the capillary network of the gills, the blood, now containing a small quantity of oxygen in physical solution in the plasma and a much larger quantity in the form of oxyhaemoglobin inside the red blood cells, is recollected into a series of arteries which ramify throughout the tissues. At the level of the tissues, the arteries redivide to form capillary networks and oxygen is released to the cells.

The actual release of oxygen depends primarily on the fact that a gas will tend to flow from a region of high concentration to one of low concentration. In regions of the body which have been most active, for example, the large skeletal muscles, the oxygen content is low since the cells have been using it to provide energy by 'burning' glucose. Under these conditions, oxygen readily dissociates from oxyhaemoglobin and passes from the plasma into the tissue fluids and finally enters the muscle cells. The dissociation of oxygen from haemoglobin has been studied and it has been shown that a rise in temperature and an accumulation of acid waste products in the area increase the rate at which it is released. Since actively respiring tissues produce lactic acid as an intermediate product in the 'burning' of glucose and since some of the energy is produced in the form of heat, these conditions help to ensure that an adequate oxygen supply is delivered to the tissues which most require it.

After giving up its oxygen, the blood, with its oxyhaemoglobin now reduced to haemoglobin, is recollected into veins the largest of which, the sinus venosus enters the heart. The heart is a muscular pump and the contraction of its walls forces the blood back under pressure to the gills where it picks up a fresh load of oxygen. In the gills, carbon dioxide accumulated from the tissues, diffuses back into the outside, watery environment.

TEMPERATURE, RESPIRATION AND HEART BEAT

Fish are poikilothermic animals, that is, their body temperature varies with that of the environment. In winter, as temperatures approach freezing, bodily activity is reduced, less oxygen is required and the heart rate and thus the speed of blood flow through the gills, drops. This fall in metabolic rate (i.e. the rate at which the body uses energy) enables the fish to survive through disadvantageous times when food is less readily available. To satisfy their basic energy requirements (i.e. the minimal amount just required to keep them alive) even when they are inactive, they may be forced back on the fat and oil reserves built up in times of plenty during the summer. As a result, they 'go back in condition' and may become thin after the winter.

During warm weather, fish face a different set of problems. As the water temperature rises, the tissues of the body warm up and become active. This creates a demand for more oxygen. In order to satisfy it, they must pass a larger volume of oxygen through their gills. This, in turn, requires a faster respiratory rate and a faster heart beat. Under such conditions, fish, depending on their specific oxygen requirements, may tend to move to areas where the oxygen content is adequate for their needs. The requirements of grayling and perch are relatively high, those of pike moderate, while those of carp, tench and bream remain fairly low.

Fish are able to detect areas of water which are unfavourable to them from the point of view of oxygen content. Experiments with perch and minnows show that the immediate reaction is one of increased activity. They become restless and swim about seeking more favourable conditions. As we have seen, natural waters vary in oxygen content from area to area, being richest where the water is white and broken near weirs or where there are many natural obstacles interrupting the flow of water. Fish with high oxygen requirements tend to move into such areas during times of high temperatures.

THE DIGESTIVE TRACT

The digestive tract, or alimentary canal, is a hollow tube with an opening at the mouth and an exit at the vent. Since each species of fish is adapted to utilising certain foodstuffs, a good deal of variation is found in the structure of the digestive tract. Teeth, for example, may or may not be present on the bones which border the mouth. Pike and perch have the pointed and somewhat recurved teeth one might expect in predators; the cyprinids are toothless but have tooth-like structures in the lower bones of the fifth gill bars which are called pharyngeal teeth. In bream, these pharyngeal teeth form a single row and are adapted for crushing food; in chub, the pharyngeal teeth are sharp and are arranged in two rows, a suitable way for dealing with the small fish which form part of its diet; in barbel, the pharyngeal teeth are arranged in three rows and are intermediate in shape. This provides yet another means of identifying different species.

A well developed, highly distensible stomach is present in predatory fish; both the stomach and the oesophagus (gullet) can expand to accommodate large meals. In cyprinids, on the other hand, there is no stomach and fish such as carp grind their food with the pharyngeal teeth until it is finally divided before swallowing it.

Although the living materials which it eats are made up of proteins, fats and carbohydrates, an individual fish cannot assimilate these materials directly. It must first break them down chemically into the common building stones – amino acids which are obtained from proteins; fatty acids and glycerol which come from fats; and simple sugars (such as glucose) which form carbohydrates. This breakdown process – or digestion – takes place in the digestive tract where digestive enzymes are released from cells in the wall of the stomach (when present) and the small intestine.

The food material is gradually softened and reduced to a semi-fluid mass and this chyme, as it is called, is moved along the alimentary canal by means of waves of contraction in the muscular walls. As the digestive enzymes complete their work, the food is converted into amino acids, fatty acids, glycerol and glucose. Finally these materials along with vitamins, minerals and water are absorbed into the bloodstream through small, fingerlike projections called villi which stud the lining of the small intestine. Undigested and indigestible remains are periodically excreted through the vent.

Once in the bloodstream, the basic food materials circulate throughout the body. The amino acids may now be rebuilt into the specific fish protein and used to repair normal wear and tear processes in the adult, or during growth, to form completely new tissues. Amino acids are also essential constituents of enzymes and hormones. Fatty acids and glycerol may be reformed into oil and stored in the liver and fatty tissues of the body or 'burnt' along with glucose to provide energy.

The time taken to complete the digestive processes varies considerably. The digestion of a large prey in a pike may take from three to five days, while the passage of food through carp may vary from 14–18 hours depending on the temperature. A rise in temperature speeds up the rate at which food is passed along the digestive tract, digested and absorbed.

Whilst a good deal is known of the chemical processes involved in digestion, it is very much less easy to understand why fish may feed at particular times. In some experiments using perch left to their own devices and with an unlimited food supply, the fish did not eat continuously but appeared to fill up during one or two feeding periods each day. Although they could be tempted into feeding oftener than twice a day, an analysis indicated that the total amount consumed daily over a period of several weeks was no greater than if the fish had been fed only once daily.

Although a great deal of research work remains to be done, it appears that fish in general show a periodicity in their feeding rhythms and that this periodicity is not the same for all species. Roach, for example, consumed food about every four hours while pike may feed at intervals of one to two days or even longer. This periodicity depends to some extent on the rate of passage of food through the gut, a factor which is affected by temperature.

The actual factors which trigger fish into feeding responses are uncertain. It has been shown in humans that the empty stomach produces waves of contraction which we recognise as hunger pangs. In experiments with animals, activity usually increases after a few hours without food. Under wild conditions, this activity would be translated into purposeful movements in search of food. After food is discovered and eaten, a quiescent period may follow while digestion proceeds. In one laboratory pike, this pattern was closely followed. After taking about five minnows within a few minutes of each other, it retired to lurk almost motionless in a corner of the tank from which it could not be tempted – even by the flutterings of a small damaged fish – for about 48 hours.

Some fish, such as carp, seem to start feeding with the onset of dawn but changes in the light intensity during the day do not seem to affect the rate of feeding to any great extent. Light, of course, favours the predator which hunts by sight but equally it helps the prey to observe the predator. Fish too may often be selective in what they choose to eat but whether this selectivity is based on smell, taste or visual attraction is largely unknown. In short, scientific knowledge on the whole subject is limited and inducing fish to accept a particular bait at a particular time still remains largely an art.

FOOD SUPPLY

The range of foodstuffs taken by freshwater fish is extremely wide. The young larval fish not long hatched from the egg may feed at first on microscopic plants and animals. As it grows, insect larvae, worms, shrimps, snails, water fleas, weeds, other fish – indeed, every aquatic organism – may form part of the diet. The study of the relationships between one species of fish, the other kinds present, and the plant and animal inhabitants of a particular water, is called ecology.

These natural patterns of life are complicated and although there is a close correlation between population density, the average size of fish, their growth rate and the amount of food available, it is not always easy to discover how the relationships can be altered in such a manner as to favour the most desirable types of fish. In most British water, there is competition for available food both amongst members of one species and also amongst different species. This situation arises since many species utilise the same general types of foodstuff.

The most important basis of foodstuff is plant life. Plants exist in two principal forms – the minute single-celled diatoms and algae and the higher forms growing in the mud. Both of these vegetable materials may provide food directly for fish or indirectly by sustaining the other small animals – shrimps, waterfleas and insect larvae – on which fish also feed. The picture is usually complex. If these small animals are favoured by a heavy growth of weed, the cover may become too dense for fish to get at them. If weeds and mud are removed, then both the fertility of the area and a potential source of fish food is reduced. The improvement of fisheries, therefore, requires great skill and understanding.

EXCRETION AND OSMOREGULATION

In order to function properly, the cells of the body require stable conditions in which to work. This relatively constant medium is provided by the blood and by the tissue fluids which surround the cells. During metabolic processes waste products are constantly being formed – and since some of these are toxic, they must be removed. Some, like carbon dioxide, are carried in the blood to the gills where they are excreted; others such as certain excretory products contained in bile, are passed through the gut. The largest proportion, however, are eliminated through the kidneys.

Fish have special problems in excretion, problems which arise from the fact that the gills and membranes of the mouth over which water is constantly passing, are permeable to both water and salts – i.e. they allow not only water but substances dissolved in it to pass through into the blood stream. The amount of salts dissolved in fresh water, however, is less than that contained in the body fluids of freshwater fish. Since there is always a tendency for water to move through permeable membranes from a region of low salt concentration to one of higher salt concentration, there is a risk that the blood and tissue fluids might become too diluted by water 'sucked' in through the gill membranes. The kidneys must cope with this problem by ridding the body of large amounts of dilute urine and at the same time by controlling the concentration of salts in the bloodstream.

The kidneys themselves can be seen as two dark, red masses lying next to the backbone. When these are examined under the microscope, they are seen to consist of a large number of individual units, the nephrons. Each nephron consists of a small tuft of capillary blood vessels, the glomerulus, which is inserted into the blind, expanded end of a coiled tube. This tube eventually joins up with the others to form collecting ducts which pass the formed urine into the vent, the common external opening for the intestine, the excretory and the reproductive systems.

The process of urine formation consists of two distinct phases, filtration and reabsorption. Blood passes into the kidney and reaches the filtering tuft, the glomerulus. The diameter of the blood vessel entering the glomerulus is larger than that leaving it. Consequently, the pressure of the blood inside the tuft is raised rather like squeezing a rubber hose. This higher pressure forces water and substances dissolved in it (such as glucose and amino acids and waste products such as urea and uric acid) through the wall of the blood vessel from the bloodstream into the cavity of the blind ending tubule.

If all of this material filtered from the blood were permitted to leave the body, the fish would be deprived of essential water, foodstuffs and salts. The task of the tubule, therefore, is to reabsorb some of the water and all of the vital materials and pass them back into the bloodstream. As the filtrate passes along the tubule, these materials are reabsorbed back into the bloodstream while the waste materials and the unwanted portion of water are allowed to pass onwards to be finally expelled as urine. In order to cope with the large amount of water passing through the gill surfaces, the filtering tufts of freshwater fish are large and the amount of urine passed is copious but dilute. The reabsorption of water by the cells lining the tubule is controlled by a hormone released by the posterior part of the pituitary gland at the base of the brain. The selective reabsorption of salts is controlled by a hormone from the suprarenal glands which lie just above the kidneys.

The whole mechanism is delicately balanced to control the excretion of various substances so that the 'internal environment', (i.e., the composition and quantity of the fluids bathing all the tissues) is kept reasonably constant in spite of what may be widely varying external conditions. This is of enormous, biological advantage. It permits metabolic processes to go on for most of the time in what amounts to optimum internal conditions.

The kidney of fresh water fish, of course, shows considerable structural modifications from that of a salt water fish where the problem is exactly the opposite – i.e. water, the 'external' environment, has a higher concentration of salts than that of the 'internal' fluids. In these circumstances, water would tend to be 'sucked' out of the tissues of the fish and it would tend to become dehydrated. In salt water fish, the kidney has a more highly developed tubular system to reabsorb much larger quantities of water from the filtrate. Small quantities of highly concentrated urine are excreted.

THE NERVOUS SYSTEM

In order to survive, animals must be able to make advantageous responses to changes in the environment. Even the amoeba, a lowly creature consisting of a single cell, is able to advance towards foodstuffs and retreat from unfavourable chemical stimuli. In higher organisms, composed of millions of individual cells, differentiation occurs and some cells – the receptors – specialise in the reception of sensations; others – the effectors – specialise in making the appropriate response. In vertebrates, a dominant co-ordinating centre, the brain, has also been developed together with the spinal cord which runs backwards along the body within the spinal column. Running outwards from the brain and the spinal cord are paired nerves which supply connections to the tissues. These nervous connections, although they may run in the same nerve trunk, are of two different kinds – those taking sensory messages concerning changes in the environment inwards from the receptors, and those taking messages outwards from the co-ordinating and controlling centres in the brain and spinal cord to the organs which can produce effective responses.

The structural unit of the nervous system is the nerve cell or neurone which is too small to be seen by the naked eye. Each neurone consists of a nerve cell and several slender processes, the 'ingoing' dendrites and the 'outgoing' axon. The neurones are linked together at meeting places or synapses where the nerve processes of one cell almost touch the cell processes or body of another. Microscopic examination has revealed that the two processes never quite meet and there is always a tiny gap between them.

Messages are passed throughout the nervous system by means of the nerve impulse which is basically a very small electrical current. When the nerve impulse reaches a synapse, it brings about the release of a small quantity of a chemical substance which bridges the gap between neurones and permits the onward conduction of the nerve impulse to the next nerve cell. A most interesting feature of the nerve impulse is that it is self-propagating. Since any one neurone is usually linked up with a great many others which may be widely scattered in different parts of the brain and spinal cord, intricate pathways for both incoming and outgoing information can be built up within the central nervous system.

REFLEX ACTION

While the neurone is the structural unit of the nervous system, reflex action is the functional unit on which all nervous activity is finally built up. In its simplest form, a reflex arc consists of a receptor, a sense organ which receives the stimulus from the environment; an ingoing nerve fibre which conveys impulses to its cell body in a reflex centre in the brain or spinal cord; and an outgoing neurone whose nerve fibre transmits the impulse to an effector organ. To see this in action, let us take, for example, the knee jerk, a well-known reflex in man. Here the sensory receptors are present in the muscle attached to the knee cap. When the knee is tapped, stretch receptors are stimulated and nerve impulses are transmitted along ingoing nerve fibres to the nerve cell body situated in a reflex centre in the spinal cord. Here a synapse occurs with a neurone whose outgoing fibre now transmits the impulse to the muscle. The muscle now contracts in the familiar jerk. In the same way, reflex swimming movements of the fins and tail can be induced in fish by touching the right spots.

Reflexes appear to form the basis of all central nervous system activity and occur at all levels of the brain and spinal cord. In man, some reflexes rise into the level of consciousness. Links are present between reflex centres concerned and higher centres of the brain where we are made aware what is happening. Many reflexes, however, occur without our conscious knowledge. For example, alterations in the size of the pupil of the eye and many movements of the gut are in this category.

A distinction must be made between unconditioned and conditioned reflexes. For example, when food is placed in the mouth it stimulates nerve endings in the tongue. Nerve messages are sent inwards to a controlling salivary centre in the brain and outgoing messages are transmitted to excite or stimulate the secretion of the salivary glands. This is an inborn reflex. It

occurs when food is placed in the mouth of an infant. It does not depend on experience.

A conditioned reflex, on the other hand, depends on experience. The sight of food becomes associated with the taste of food. Association pathways are established between visual and taste centres in the brain so that eventually the sight of food alone can evoke salivary secretion. This type of reflex probably forms the basis of all 'learning' and it becomes difficult to say where reflex or involuntary behaviour ends and purely voluntary behaviour begins.

Difficulty arises when we attempt to separate inborn reflex actions and conditioned reflexes from intelligence. Man's superiority over other animals is due to the development of the uppermost part of his brain, the cerebral cortex. It is from the activity of the cells in this area that we obtain our ability for relational, constructive thought directed towards the attainment of some specific aim. Here too, we are able to break the bonds of the present and to project our minds forwards into the future and backwards into the past.

Since there is little development of the cerebral cortex in fish, we cannot rate them very highly in the intelligence plane. While it is true that fish can produce a complex series of actions in a variety of situations, most of these are stereotyped and reflex in character. This does not mean that fish cannot 'learn'. Conditioned reflexes do become established and fish can be 'taught' to master mazes and to discriminate between colours. They are, however, slow to do so and require many 'trial and error' attempts. In the present state of knowledge, it is not, therefore, meaningful to attribute qualities of cunning or foresight to fish in general.

THE SENSORY RECEPTORS

Like ourselves, fish can only respond to those forms of stimuli from the environment for which special receiving organs have been developed. This is perhaps made clearer if we consider first, in the case of man, electromagnetic radiation which comes from the sun. At one end of the scale are the very short waves – cosmic, gamma and X-rays – of which we are unaware even though they may damage cells or even kill the body; at the other end are very long radio and television waves which we can only see or hear when they are adapted by receiving sets to suit our eyes and ears. In the middle range of the electromagnetic band is the visible spectrum to which our eyes are able to respond. Although sunlight is made up of several different wavelengths of light – red, orange, yellow, green, blue and violet – we see it as 'white' light. It is only when sunlight is passed through a prism or broken up in a rainbow that we can appreciate the range of spectral colours.

The actual visual receptors are of two types, rods and cones, both of which contain photochemical pigments of different composition. Rods permit vision in dim light but see only in black, white and grey. Cones react in bright light and according to one theory, are of three kinds – those which respond to red wavelengths, those activated by green wavelengths and those stimulated by violet wavelengths. The wide variety of colours which we perceive is believed to be due to the varying proportions of these three types of cones being stimulated at any one time. This can be demonstrated experimentally by the use of coloured lights. At the present time, however, no one theory completely covers all the known perceptual phenomena of colour vision. We do know that cones permit colour vision and that they are also responsible for acute vision, i.e. sharp detail. Not every animal possesses cones – dogs and cattle have none and see therefore in black and white by means of rods.

When we turn to freshwater fish, we find that they possess both rods and cones. In short, they can see colours and react to them. In the stickleback, for example, the normal colour is a silvery or greenish hue but in the breeding season during spring and summer, the male acquires a bright red chest and a green and blue metallic lustre on the sides of the body. If a male stickleback is presented with a model fish at this time of the year, his reactions depend very largely on the way in which the model is coloured. If it has a red patch painted on the underside, greenish blue on the upper side with a blue eye, attack is the response. On the other hand, if the model is painted with a silvery colouration, then a 'courting' reaction is produced and this is enhanced if the model has a thickened underbelly like a female ripe with eggs. There is thus some evidence that colour produces certain reflex responses, yet there is a great deal still to be learned in this field. Fish can be trained to respond to certain colours and associate them

with food but the value of colouring baits to attract fish remains largely speculative. The one exception is the silver flash of the underbelly which is known to draw the attention of predators.

In brief, the various parts of the fish eye are the clear, outer cornea and the spherical lens with the attached retractor muscle suspended behind the aperture in the pigmented iris. The lens brings the light rays to focus on the light sensitive retina or 'screen' in the cells of which photochemical changes take place in response to light. Leaving the back of the eye is the optic nerve which transmits impulses to visual centres in the brain. The geometrical optics of the eye are interesting. The transparent lens, unlike that of man which is biconvex or 'acid-drop' in shape, is accurately spherical in form with a focal length about two-and-a-half times the radius.

In man, the function of accommodation is to maintain an exactly focused image of an object on a special area of the retina, the fovea, no matter what distance the object is from our eye. When we wish to transfer our gaze from a distant object to something close at hand, we must alter the curvature of the lens by 'bulging' it in order to bring it into focus. In other words, we must make it a 'stronger' lens to keep a sharp image on the retina.

In fish, however, where there is generally no fovea, there are reasons for believing that the unaccommodated eye, at rest, has adequate vision for large objects at all distances, provided they are behind or to one side of the eye. Since the retina is semi-ellipsoid, however, the fish tends to be myopic or shortsighted in front. It can, therefore, see small objects clearly if they are a short distance ahead. Large objects are blurred and only seen clearly if they are placed to one side or behind the eye. When the fish accommodates, it contracts the focussing muscle and brings the lens nearer to the retina. Distant objects ahead can now be seen clearly.

Just how clearly fish can see in terms of exact appreciation of structure depends on the 'fineness of grain' or the degree of concentration of the visual cells of the retina. Whilst there are differences between species, the retina, at its best, is of such quality as to approach that of land animals. In clear water, pike are believed capable of picking up movement up to fifty feet ahead of them.

Since the lens bulges through the pupil and

A gag can be used on a pike to keep its mouth open while the hook is removed. Note that in this picture the angler has left the clamping bar on the gag in order that the mouth is not opened too wide to cause damage to the fish.

Take care when removing hooks from a fish. This No 8 hook could have caused a nasty wound if accidentally run into a finger while the tench was being unhooked.

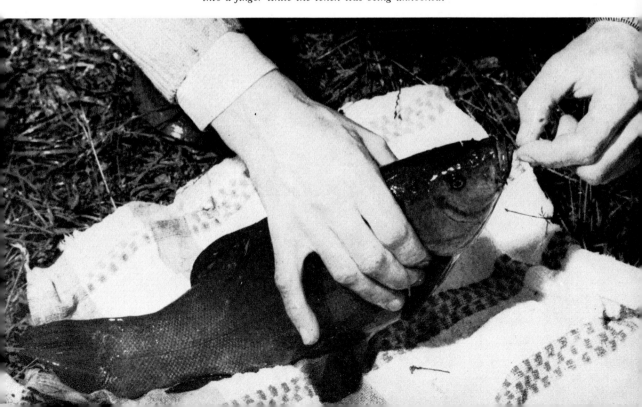

*Tench feed close to weedy swims and this fish was taken only a few feet away from the edge of the water
life – and the bait – near the bed of rushes.*

The rod is held well up to take the strain exerted by the fish and the landing net is ready and waiting in position for the fish to be safely landed.

Boating and sailing interests do not always conflict with those of angling. In this case the sailing dingies did not worry the fish at all for they were quite used to boats sailing over their homes. In fact, if the usual boats were not present the fish could be frightened by the lack of surface movement!

Fishing from a deep bank, both a long landing net handle and a long keep net are really essential items of tackle. The long rod rest is also useful while fishing such a swim!

since the eye projects from the surface of the body, fish can receive light from above and below as well as from the front and sides and this affords the eye some of the properties of a periscope. Further, the eye can see behind except where the fish's own body blocks out the visual field.

In our own vision, we enjoy a fairly large degree of binocular vision (about 140 degrees). In other words, the field seen by one eye overlaps that seen by the other. This affords us considerable assistance in our judgment of depth and distance. In predatory fish such as perch and pike, there is a relatively large binocular field of vision – about 30 to 40 degrees in the horizontal plane. The pike has also two 'sighting' ridges down the snout and undoubted these factors contribute to the accuracy with which they can strike.

The development of the eye is linked to the development of special areas of the brain. A good example of this is found in pike which hunt by day. The eye is well developed and possesses both rods and cones. The brain has large optic lobes but relatively small olfactory lobes. This means that smell is very much less important to pike than vision when it hunts down its prey. In contradistinction, the burbot has large olfactory lobes and smallish eyes and hunts food at night largely by smell.

THE LATERAL LINE

Sound is transmitted as a series of alternating waves of compression and rarefaction which can, perhaps, be imagined best by thinking about the prongs of a tuning fork as they vibrate to and fro in the elastic medium of air. These sound waves can also be passed through water and fish possess well developed organs for detecting such vibrations. The basic sense organs for 'hearing' in fish consist of the inner ear which lies in a capsule within the head; and the lateral line organs which form a special sensory system unknown in land animals.

Although fish lack the outer ear flap and the middle ear of humans, sound vibrations are picked up through the head and conducted through the bone to the inner ear which contains hair cells. These hair cells are arranged rather like the strings of a harp and are set in motion by sounds of particular frequencies.

The lateral line organs consist of two long canals which run down either side of the body and also extend forwards into the head region. This canal system is sunk below the head and beneath the scales but opens at intervals to the surface. The sensory receptors are called neuromasts and each bears a projecting, hairlike structure. The tips of the hairs are usually embedded in a gelatinous material in a dome shaped structure, the cupula, which is free to move in the surrounding water. The purpose of the neuromasts is to respond to waves, disturbances or vibrations in the water. These bend the cupula and the hair processes and trigger off nervous impulses thus informing fish of nearby moving objects. In this way, they serve as an aid to vision and convey information concerning water movement and current flow. In a series of experiments with blinded fresh water fish, it was shown that these lateral line organs were used to find food. For example, characteristic food searching reactions were aroused in minnows by creating a small mechanical disturbance in the water. Even though they had no eyes, the fish would move in the right direction in response to tiny jets of water ejected from fine nozzles. In short, the lateral line organs are concerned with what has been termed 'touch at a distance'. During darkness, or if the water is muddy, they may help by acting rather like echo sounders where the time interval between the waves caused by the swimming movements of the fish itself and reflected water waves may reveal the presence of a nearby obstacle. Shoaling fish may use them to maintain their position at night.

The precise structure of the lateral line organs varies from species to species. In pike and other predacious fish, such as perch and eels, large well developed grooves or pores containing neuromasts are present on the head, whilst in the carp family they appear only as fine dots. The high degree of development on the head doubtless aids predators to pinpoint the exact position of the prey.

Sounds are produced by a number of fish, for example, chub, carp, barbel, minnows, loaches and eels. They do so by releasing gas bubbles from the swimbladder but the exact biological purpose is undetermined. They may serve as warning noises or be implicated in the defence of territory or in breeding behaviour. As far as the practical fishermen is concerned, the most important aspect of fish hearing is the fact that they can pick up vibrations through the earth of the river bank or from the bottom of a boat. Atmospheric noises made by talking are reflected off the surface of the water and are unlikely to be detected by fish.

BANKING, DIVING AND TURNING

The twists and turns of chub and perch, the sudden manoeuvres of pike and roach, indeed, all the darts and plunges of a hooked fish are the essence of the sport of playing. All these moves, as we have seen, can only be carried out in an organised manner if the brain is receiving information as to the exact position of the body and the degree of contraction of each group of muscles. Many systems are involved in keeping the brain aware of what is happening. The eyes, the ears, the lateral line and the nervous connections to the muscle fibres are all in action. Yet another important contributor is that portion of the ear which is concerned with the maintenance of balance and which helps to bring about righting reflexes by keeping the brain informed of the position of the body in space. This is achieved by means of the semi-circular canals, the utriculus and the sacculus which form the labyrinth of the inner ear.

There are three semi-circular canals in each inner ear, one in each of the three planes of space. Each canal is a membranous, fluid-filled tube with a small swelling (or ampulla) at one end of each semi-circle. In each swelling, a cupula with its embedded hair processes is present. These receptors are stimulated mechanically by the starting and stopping of rotatory movements of the head. For example, when the head starts to move, the fluid in the semi-circular canal which lies at right angles to the axis of rotation, tends to lag behind the movements of the head. As a result, the cupula is displaced. Its hair cells are stimulated and ingoing impulses inform the brain. If necessary, correcting action can be taken to prevent the head turning further in that particular direction by adjustment of the fins. On the other hand, if the fish continues to turn in that direction, adjustments are made to the eyes. When a fish turns to the left or right, reflex messages are sent out from the brain to the eye muscles which cause the eye to be pulled round in the opposite direction. These eye movements can easily be observed in aquarium fish.

Similar cupula receptors are present in the utriculus and sacculus. These are designed to respond to gravity and to register the static position of the head in space at any one moment. If the head is pointed upwards or downwards, the sensory hair processes are bent and again messages are sent to the brain indicating the position. This constant stream of information about its position in the water and concerning any yawing, pitching or rolling movements while it is swimming, enables the fish to 'balance' precisely and to carry out with accuracy all the complicated manoeuvres of its daily life. The utriculus contains an earstone which rests above the sensory hairs and it is this which responds to gravity and bends the hairs. It is composed of calcium carbonate which is laid down in layers as the fish grows. This earstone (or otolith) can be used to assess the age of the fish.

THE CHEMICAL SENSES

The chemical senses are those of taste and smell. Although man tends to make a sharp distinction between them, they are, in fact, closely related, a fact which soon becomes obvious when one suffers from a bad cold in the head. The end result of tasting and smelling is achieved by the response of special cells called chemoreceptors situated in humans in the nose and on the tongue. Chemoreceptors, as the name suggests, are stimulated by very small amounts of chemical substances in solution. Even when we smell gaseous particles in the air, they must first go into a watery solution inside the nose before the smell receptors can respond to them. This dependence on solutions in water make these two senses even more difficult to distinguish in fish.

In land vertebrates, the nose with its internal opening has evolved in association with the lungs as a means of obtaining oxygen. The primitive function, however, is that of smell and in fish there is no opening into the mouth. The nasal structures usually consist of a pair of pits placed well forward on the head. Each pit has two apertures – an entrance and an exit through which water enters and leaves in a continuous stream. Inside each pit, the epithelium is folded into ridges in order to increase the surface area. Within the epithelium lie the olfactory cells each with a brush of short, sensitive hair processes. Substances in solution are brought in by currents of water to the nasal pits where they make contact with the hair processes of the olfactory cells. Each cell has its own nerve fibre extending directly to the olfactory lobe of the brain. The efficiency of the sense varies with different species of fresh water fish. It is particularly well developed, for example, in eels. If chopped food is placed in a bag in the water, eels will begin to hunt after a very short period. On the other hand, pike, which hunt largely by sight, show little response even when hungry.

The sense of smell not only serves some fish in finding their food but it appears to enable them to recognise their own species and members of other species as well. Minnows, for example, have been shown to possess the ability to distinguish between some 15 different species of fish as well as several different kinds of aquatic vegetation. The reactions of minnows to pike odour are particularly interesting. When subjected to it, they reacted either by fleeing or by becoming motionless. This 'freezing' action in minnows to odour is obviously a defence mechanism since it is to moving fish that predators are principally attracted.

TASTE

In humans, the taste cells are limited to the taste buds on the tongue and a few cells at the back of the throat. In fish, however, taste buds may be developed not only on the tongue but on the lips, barbels, gill rakers and over the surface of the body. Carp, for example, have a large pad of taste cells on the upper part of the mouth and taste buds on the barbels and body. Fish have, therefore, great possibilities for 'tasting' substances before and after they take them into their mouths.

The four basic taste sensations are sweet, sour, acid and bitter. Carp, at least, can discriminate between these four. In addition, 'ordinary' touch organs respond to the feel of food in the mouth and differentiate between hardness and softness. In finding, selecting and eating suitable foodstuffs, taste, smell and touch combine, but our knowledge on this subject is limited.

REPRODUCTION

Amongst individual species of freshwater fish, there is a wide variation in the time during which breeding takes place. This extends, for example, from as early as February for pike to as late as November for trout. The actual spawning season is associated with the needs and habits of a given species and has been evolved to afford the maximum advantage to the young at the early and most vulnerable period of their growth. In order to achieve this, there must clearly be a built-in 'biological clock' which ensures that both sexes of a particular species are in the right condition to breed at the same time.

Part of the answer to the difficult questions involved in the understanding of the mechanisms which bring about this synchronisation lies in the endocrine glands and in the natural cyclical changes of light and temperature. The endocrine or ductless glands release a number of chemical compounds into the bloodstream. These compounds are called hormones, a word derived from Greek and meaning to arouse or stimulate. The master gland, sometimes called 'the leader of the endocrine orchestra' is the pituitary body, a tiny pea-shaped gland attached to the base of the brain by means of nervous tissue. In response to a gradual increase in the number of daylight hours registered through the eyes and to an increase in the temperature of the water which heats up the blood, the pituitary gland, in spring and summer breeders, begins to increase the amount of hormones it produces. These pituitary hormones affect many tissues of the body and they also stimulate the other endocrine organs such as the thyroid, the suprarenals, the ovaries and the testes to produce hormones of their own. When these endocrine organs become active, their hormonal secretions in turn, exert profound influences on growth, development, sexual characteristics and reproductive activity.

For example, under the influence of one of the pituitary gonadotrophic hormones, the ovary of the female produces female sex hormones or oestrogens. The combined effect of these is to promote the growth and production of eggs from the ovaries and to evoke female sex characteristics and behaviour. In the male, the pituitary stimulates the production of the male sex hormone, testosterone, from the testes. This hormone is concerned with the development of the male reproductive tract, the formation of sperm and evokes male sex characteristics and behaviour. Striking colour changes may be hormonally induced. For example, the male stickleback assumes his scarlet, green and blue coat as spawning time approaches. The evidence for such changes being hormonal in nature and initiated by light and temperature has been obtained from a variety of experimental work. Premature spawning can be induced in sticklebacks and other fish by manipulating the temperature and lighting conditions under which they are kept. In other instances, the injection of male hormone into the female induced male sexual behaviour. It would seem from such evidence that physical factors initiate the process by bringing about the release of hormones. These hormones cause the eggs to ripen, mature the sperm and trigger off specific, instinctive patterns of behaviour which have been evolved to ensure the survival of the species.

DEVELOPMENT AND HEREDITY

Fish, like ourselves, can only start their existence as a result of the fertilisation of an egg by a sperm. In order to achieve this, the sperm must penetrate the egg. The eggs, containing the germ cell from the female and the nutritive yolk, are produced in the ovaries in large numbers. The female carp, for example, may produce as many as 100,000 eggs per pound of body weight and the pike about 15,000 eggs per pound of body weight. Each individual egg is surrounded by a soft shell in which there is a minute opening, the micropyle. Through this tiny gap, a single microscopic sperm gains entry to the egg. When the egg is shed at spawning, however, the micropyle remains open for only a very short period. In pike eggs, for example, this lasts for about 30 to 60 seconds and unless one of the sperms which are produced in astronomical numbers by the male testes succeeds in reaching the aperture in time, the egg will remain infertile.

After fertilisation, water is drawn into the egg and it swells. The outer shell now becomes hard and rigid. The embryo within begins a complicated course of development starting from the division of the single, fertilised cell. As more and more cells arise from the division process (mitosis) they become specialised for the job they will ultimately perform. The energy for the process of growing is supplied by the rich yolk which contains albumen and fat supplied by the female parent.

While a few fresh water fish such as trout and grayling bury their eggs in redds in the gravelly bottom of the spawning bed, most species lay them in masses in the vegetation of the shallows and leave them to their fate. Since they are subject to predators of many kinds, the eggs are laid in very large numbers but less than 1 per cent. are likely to live to maturity in the wild.

The time taken for incubation varies with the temperature of the water. Perch hatch in some 8–10 days at 61 degrees Fahrenheit; pike, which may spawn when the water is colder, may take as long as four weeks to incubate. Since the egg shell is rigid, some means of escape must be provided when the young fish is ready to leave. A special chemical or hatching enzyme is produced within the egg and this dissolves away part of the outer covering and allows the young fish or alevin to work itself free.

At this stage, the alevin is only about $\frac{1}{4}$ in long and it is equipped with a yolk sac containing food material on which it depends while it continues to develop over the next few days. Its behaviour at this time depends on the species. Young perch alevins are active as soon as they are out of the egg. The reason for this is the fact that the swimbladder is empty of gas and must be inflated by the swallowing of air. Since the connection between the swimbladder and the oesophagus closes after the first few days, they must start the struggle upwards to the surface almost as soon as they are born. Pike and carp alevins on the other hand, are quiescent during the first few days of life and attach themselves to the leaves of water plants by means of adhesive organs on the top of their heads. After about two days, the young carp too must make the long journey to the surface where it swallows bubbles of air.

As the yolk sac is gradually absorbed, the body increases in size and the dorsal and anal fins become apparent. Eventually, when all the food reserve is gone, the young fish must fend for themselves. Their mode of life, however, is instinctive. Young perch form schools and feed on waterfleas and insect larvae in the shallow water; pike at $\frac{1}{2}$ in long are already cannibals eating weaker and smaller members of their own kind as well as any other small fish, crustaceans, worms and insect larvae with which they can deal; carp hunt for the tiny algae and microscopic animals which make up their early diet.

Provided it continues to escape its enemies, the continued growth and development of the young fish depends upon the interaction of heredity and environment. The hereditary factors are carried as messages or 'genes' on the chromosomes in every cell of the body. During the formation of the reproductive cells, eggs or sperm, a special reduction division occurs (meiosis) which reduces the number of chromosomes in these cells to one half of the total normally found in all other cells of the body. When fertilisation occurs and the sperm unites with the eggs, these two halves bring the chromosomes back to the full number. In this way, one half of the hereditary material is derived from the male parent and one half from the female.

The messages carried on the chromosomes – the 'genetic code' – are now known to consist of nucleic acids called DNA and this chemical material is at work from the moment of fertilisation. It is believed to set the potential limits of fish (as well as humans) in all directions including the pattern and rate of growth. Normally no set of messages is ever precisely and exactly like that of another so that every individual is unique in itself. In one interesting experiment with the same male parent but different female parents, the offspring of one female grew rapidly during the first few weeks and then tended to slow down. The offspring of the other female grew more steadily and eventually were significantly larger at the age of eight months. Since the environmental factors were similar, this difference in growth pattern was inherited. Hereditary factors have also been shown to influence the age at which fish mature and this plasticity helps to explain the other differences in shape, colour and the number of fin-rays and scales found in different individuals of the same species.

The sex of an individual fish is determined by two special sex chromosomes, the X and Y chromosomes. If a fertilised egg has two X chromosomes, it will develop into a female; if it contains an X and a Y chromosome, it will become a male. As we have already noted, the chromosomes are reduced to half the total number in the reproductive cells. Female fish, therefore, can only produce eggs containing an X chromosome; male fish can produce sperms of two kinds, those carrying an X chromosome and those carrying a Y chromosome. It is the male therefore which determines the sex of the offspring but which particular sperm fertilises a particular egg is a matter of chance and nature has so arranged matters that the sexes come out about equally.

MUTATIONS

Occasionally there may be a chemical change in the nucleic acids which form the genes of the chromosomes. Such changes are normally unfavourable and affect the development of the individual in an adverse manner. If it lives, it may become a monstrosity with a 'bull nose' or some other deformity affecting its body or fins. Now and then, however, mutations are produced which gives rise to new varieties – carp are well known for the number of mutations they produce and the mirror carp and the leather carp are examples of varieties produced in this way. Mutations provide a means for change and since the chromosomes themselves are directly affected, favourable changes are hereditable.

While hereditary factors may set the limits which are possible, the environment plays an equally important part in determining how close to the maximum an individual will attain. Growth in fish depends on the conditions existing during its active growth phases. Temperature, light, space and competition for food all appear as interwoven strands. The 'survival of the fittest' is no idle phase under wild conditions. Occasionally an individual may receive a particularly favourable set of genes from both parents and develop under suitable conditions. Such well endowed fish may live to become the 'specimen' fish which form the targets for the specimen hunters and which, from time to time, add fresh entries to the record books.

Man, of course, can 'interfere' with natural conditions by reducing populations, providing protection from enemies or by selecting from his stock the 'right' kinds of parents which have shown the characteristics he wishes to perpetuate. On the other hand, pollution of the water with chemicals from industrial sources or from herbicides and insecticides used in agriculture may produce an environment which is unfavourable and even lethal to fish life.

SOME COMMON PARASITES AND DISEASES OF FISH

Like all other animals, fish are subject to normal ageing processes about which very little is known. In the wild, of course, their longevity depends on the maintenance of good health, freedom from disease, their ability to find sufficient food of the right kind and their luck in escaping enemies. Provided they do so, they may enjoy a comparatively long life span of some 12–20 years. Generally, those species with the larger individuals live longer. Carp, for example, may reach around the 50 year mark – and even possibly 100 in a few exceptional instances. Pike have been recorded as approaching 25 years in the wild and have reached an authenticated 75 in captivity. Eels, on the other hand, usually die after migration and spawning at the age of 11 or 12. Various deteriorative changes occur as the ageing process develops. There is a slowing in the rate of growth, a gradual loss of reproductive capacity and a drop in the metabolic rate. Male fish show such changes sooner than females and usually die of senescence at an earlier age.

As well as old age, fish may die or be seriously affected by a number of organic disorders or the effects caused by the invasion of their tissues by a wide range of disease-causing organisms. Such fish show a variety of signs. In extreme cases, they may be unable to swim properly; they may move around in circles, swim jerkily, sink to the bottom or even float belly upwards. A generalised loss of colour is often indicative of circulatory or metabolic disorders and this may be accompanied by degeneration of the fin tissue which looks worn and torn. Dark or black patches and ulcerated areas on the skin are often signs of infection with skin parasites; local swellings may be a manifestation of internal infection with certain stages of tapeworms. Although an exact diagnosis of the particular condition usually requires specialist observations and tests, the general appearance and behaviour of any individual fish which makes no attempt to escape usually alerts the angler to the fact that all is not well. A few of the commoner conditions are discussed in more detail below.

SKIN PARASITES

The 'Gill-Tail', Carp or Fish Louse (*Argulus foliaceus*) is one of the better known skin parasites attacking not only carp but roach, tench, bream, pike, perch, eels and even tadpoles. The greenish brown body has a diameter of about $\frac{1}{4}$ in, is flattened and leaf-like in shape; on the undersurface two small sucking discs have been developed as well as claws and these enable the parasites to scuttle across a wet skin with surprising speed. A small, fish-like tail containing

both respiratory and reproductive organs protrudes and it is from this that the name 'gill-tail' has been derived. They suck blood from their host through a piercing hollow stylet and are usually found around the base of the fins or sometimes in the head region. The damage inflicted by a few of these parasites may not be particularly serious in itself but they cause irritation and fish may rub themselves against stones in an attempt to dislodge them. There is always a danger that other organisms, aquatic bacteria or fungi, may thus gain entry. Lice are also suspected of being implicated in the transmission of other fish diseases.

LEECHES

The Fish Leech (*Piscicola geometra*), which grows to about an inch in length, can be recognised by the wormlike body with its series of rings. Suckers are present at both ends of the body. It sucks the blood of its victims and may cause considerable damage to young fish. In common with many other blood suckers, it injects anti-coagulant into the bloodstream of its prey. This prevents the blood from clotting and the wound may continue to bleed for some time after the leech itself is fully engorged. Most species of fish are attacked and young fish may even be killed. Since they are able to survive for very long periods without a blood meal their eradication from ponds is extremely difficult.

ANCHOR WORMS

These parasites (*Lernaediae*) are found on minnows, tench, Crucian carp, pike, perch and sticklebacks. The females have a long worm-like body about $\frac{1}{4}$ in long. The name 'anchor worm' is derived from the fact that the female penetrates the flesh of the host fish and proceeds to grow long processes like the flukes of an anchor which hook into the underlying muscle tissue of the fish. During the summer, the young stages are not easily noticed but by the following May when the female is ripe with eggs, they are large enough to attract attention. After egg-laying, the female anchor worm dies leaving an entrance hole in the skin of the fish through which bacteria may enter.

SPOROZOAN PARASITES

The Sporozoa are single-celled organisms belonging to the *Phylum Protozoa* which includes such species as those causing the devastating diseases of malaria and sleeping sickness in man. Where fish are concerned, one of the most important groups is the *Myxosporidia*. They appear to gain entry into the intestine along with the food. Once in the gut of the fish, they pass through the intestinal wall into the bloodstream where they are carried to a variety of organs. Frequently they produce large boils or 'knots' in the skin as, for example, in Boil disease of barbels, or the smallish, greenish-white knots in 'Knot' disease of carp. Affected fish lose weight and the skin becomes dull and lustreless. Some species affect the gills or rudd and roach where they form white cysts; others again are found in spleen, kidneys and liver of carp and tench. One species of parasite is found in the nervous system of young salmonid fish where it causes a condition known descriptively as 'staggers'. The young fish is unable to maintain its balance in the water and literally 'falls' about.

BACTERIAL DISEASES

Bacteria or 'germs' are microscopic organisms of a very small size. Fish suffer from their attacks in numerous ways. In some instances it is far from easy to separate them from virus conditions. Well known examples are furunculosis in salmon where the furuncles or boils may swell and burst to discharge their pus and blood into the water. Pox diease of carp and sometimes of tench, rudd and bream are caused by other species of bacteria. Here the symptoms are the appearance of small, milky white spots like candlewax which gradually grow in size until the whole body of the fish may be covered.

Other examples are Red Pest of carp and tench in which the lower parts of the belly, along with the ventral and anal fins, may become dark red in colour due to the occurrence of haemorrhages in the skin. A similar condition causes Red Pest of eels.

Bacteria belonging to the genus *Mycobacterium* attack many kinds of freshwater fish causing a form of tuberculosis which is not transmissible to man. Infected fish lose weight, retire to out-of-the-way spots and often show ulcerated conditions of the skin. Any tissue may be attacked, however, including the bones where the disease may manifest itself in deformation of the jaws and spine.

FUNGAL DISEASES

Dermatomycosis, a skin condition caused by attack from fungi, does not normally occur on healthy, undamaged fish but since these moulds are present in the water, there is always the risk that they may gain entry into the skin where it has been damaged by wounds or by the attacks of other parasites or bacteria. Once the barrier of the skin has been penetrated, the moulds may ramify throughout the cells and grow into muscle tissue. Infection is usually characterised by tufts of fungus, rather like cottonwool, which appear on the skin or on the fins.

Other lethal fungi, notably *Ichthyosporidium hoferi*, invade the intestines and may spread to many different organs including the heart, liver, brain and reproductive organs. Small whitish cysts forming hard granules can be felt or seen in the infected parts. If a vital organ is heavily attacked, death may follow rapidly. Infection is spread when other fish eat contaminated material.

PARASITIC WORMS

Whilst the diseases of fish and the many kinds of parasitic worms which infest them are, in general, specific to them and not communicable to man, it is, perhaps, worthwhile finishing this brief summary of fish parasites and disorders by dealing with one instance in which man and fish are intricately bound together in the life-history of a parasite which is common to both of them. Fortunately, the condition is not usually serious in man but a fairly recent survey (1958) revealed that 10,000,000 people in Europe, Scandinavia, the U.S.A. and Canada were infected with the adult stage of a tapeworm which utilises freshwater fish such as pike, perch, ruffe, salmon and trout during its complicated transmission from man to man. This Fish or Broad Tapeworm (*Diphyllobothrium latum*) has been reported in Ireland and since the larval stages do occur in fish in Great Britain, it is potentially dangerous.

The adult tapeworm, broad, flat and ribbon shaped, lives in the intestines of man or other carnivorous animals, dogs, cats, foxes, where it may attain a length of many feet. The head of worm serves to attach the adult individual to the wall of the intestine and the neck region buds off an endless succession of segments. Each of these segments contains both male and female sex organs and as they ripen, each segment becomes filled with innumerable eggs which are eventually discharged to the exterior along with the faeces. Nourishment is obtained from the host and anaemia, digestive upsets and abdominal discomfort may result from the presence of the tapeworm.

If the eggs reach water, they hatch into a tiny embryo which must be ingested by a waterflea or similar crustacean. In the body cavity of this initial host, the tapeworm embryo turns into a more solid form. In turn, as chance will have it, the waterflea may be eaten by a perch or a minnow or a trout. In this second 'home', the larval tapeworm continues to develop in the muscles or body cavity of its host. The minnows or trout may themselves be eaten by a pike but no further larva development is believed to occur and the existing larval form simply transfers to the new carrier. The final chapter of the story now awaits the arrival of man or other suitable carnivore who become infected by eating raw or undercooked fish. In the intestine, the head becomes attached to the wall of the gut and in a short time, fresh segments are being budded off and new eggs produced. It is a wise precaution therefore to cook fish well before eating them

since this will definitely kill off any larvae in the fish muscle.

Man, of course, has been living in intimate association with this parasite for a very long time and in the general scheme of nature, parasitism is not an abnormal way of life even though it is prone to arouse feelings of revulsion. Host and parasite usually dwell together in a state of equanimity and it is in the interest of the parasite that the host remains in good condition. In studies of tapeworms in Loch Lomond, light or moderate infections of the larval stage in trout and powan did not interfere with the condition of the fish.

There are many other species of tapeworms which inhabit the intestines of freshwater fish in the adult or ribbon-like form. The larval forms of these pass through a variety of hosts from shrimps to worms but they cannot and do not infect man. Others again reach the adult stage in fish eating birds of many types.

In large numbers, the worms may cause intestinal obstruction and block the passage of food but fish and other animals which suffer from tapeworms can withstand a moderate infection without showing untoward effects.

SOME BRITISH FRESH WATER SPECIES

THE CARP FAMILY (*Cyprinidae*)

The *Cyprinidae*, which includes the Common Carp with its two varieties, the Mirror Carp and the Leather Carp, the Crucian Carp, tench, barbel, rudd, roach, bream, silver bream, dace, chub, gudgeon, bleak, minnow and goldfish, is one of the most important and widespread families of bony fish. Common family features are the naked head and scaly body, the toothless mouth – though pharyngeal teeth are present in the back of the throat which bite upwards against a hard plate – and flexible fin-rays. The diet is usually a mixture of decomposing vegetable material and some members feed on bottom fauna such as snails, insects, and crustacea as well. Interbreeding between some species is not uncommon and hybrids between rudd and bream and between roach and bream are known.

THE COMMON CARP (*Cyprinus carpio*)

The original home of the carp is believed to have been the Black Sea, the Caspian Sea and

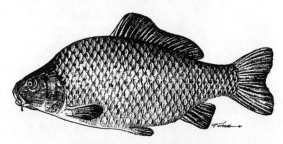

eastwards into Asia. It possesses a peculiar ability to stay alive in very small quantities of water – indeed, it can be kept alive for several hours if packed in damp moss – and probably for this reason, it was easily introduced into Britain several centuries ago by monks who cultivated it in stew ponds. Today, it is widespread.

Identifying Features: The carp can easily be distinguished from other members of the family by the presence of four barbels on the upper lip. There is some variation in form and colour but the body is heavily built, laterally compressed and completely covered with scales.

Fin-rays and Scales: 17–22 branched rays on a long dorsal fin; lateral line scale count 35–39.

Habitat: The common carp is a fish of lakes, ponds and slow, sluggish rivers where the bottom is muddy. It is principally a bottom feeder but it will take weed or insects from the surface or from under the edges of aquatic plant leaves. There is a large pad on the roof of the mouth which is covered with taste buds and this appears to aid it in discriminating between detritus and food material. By nature, the carp is a shy fish in the wild state, quick to take alarm at anything unusual in its surroundings. It possesses a relatively large brain and is difficult to take on the rod and line. Dawn, dusk and night fishing offer the best chance of sport but carp do feed also during the daytime. In winter, it lies dormant and can survive very low temperatures.

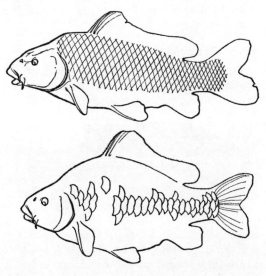

Varieties: Both the Mirror Carp and the Leather Carp are examples of mutations which have arisen from changes in the genes on the chromosomes. The Mirror Carp is easily recognised by the one or two rows of large gleaming scales along the lateral line; the rarer Leather Carp by the thick, leathery skin and the absence of scales.

Spawning: Breeding time is May and June when the fish move into shallow water where the female lays large numbers of small eggs among water plants. The young larvae hatch out in about 3–4 days.

CRUCIAN CARP (*Carassius carassius*)

Although a close relative, the Crucian Carp is a separate species from the Common, Leather and

Mirror Carp. The body is smaller in size, deeper in shape and the tail more forked and the absence of barbels makes it easily distinguishable. Its general habits and mode of life are very similar to those of the Common Carp.

TENCH (*Tinca tinca*)

Tench, which are found over most of the country except North Scotland, have the reputa-

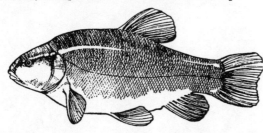

tion of being 'lazy', somewhat inactive fish except during the breeding season. The flesh is edible and highly praised on the Continent and it is believed that tench as well as carp were cultivated in the stew-ponds of the monks. The mucous cells in the skin are numerous and secrete a thick layer of slime which covers the body. An old belief was that this slime had curative properties for sick or wounded fish and for this reason, tench were once known as 'Doctor' fish.

82

Identifying Features: Two barbels are present, one on each side of the mouth and the numerous small, yellowish scales covered with slime make the tench an easy fish to identify.

Fin-rays and Scales: 8–9 branched rays on the dorsal fin; lateral line scale count 95–100.

Habitat: The tench is a fish of still waters, weedy lakes, canals and slow running rivers. It prefers a muddy bottom in which it lies dormant during the winter. Rooting round the bottom, it stirs up sand and mud to find the small bottom animals and vegetable matter which form the basis of the diet. It usually feeds well in morning and evening and yields good sport to rod and line.

Spawning: In May and June, tench spawn gregariously in weeds. The eggs are very small, about 1·2 millimetres only in diameter and are laid in large numbers.

ROACH (*Rutilus rutilus*)

The roach is one of the commonest fresh water fish, widespread in England and Wales but not so frequent in Scotland north of Loch Lomond.

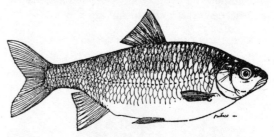

Identifying Features: A laterally compressed, somewhat hump-backed fish, it may be distinguished from the rudd by the dorsal fin which originates just behind the pelvic fins in the roach and a considerable distance behind it in the rudd. The iris of the eye is a deep red.

Fin-rays and Scale Counts: 9–11 branched rays in the dorsal fin; lateral line scale count 42–45.

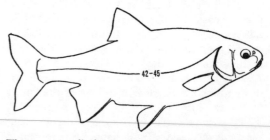

42–45

There are usually between 42 and 45 scales along the lateral lines in roach

Habitat: The roach is to be found in most rivers and canals and it is also present in many still waters. In rivers, it prefers a steady flow where the current is not too rapid and in suitable habitats, it forms schools. In winter, it retires to deeper, slower waters away from the main current. Principally a bottom feeder, the diet includes worms, shrimps and insect larvae.

Spawning: The roach spawns in April and May amidst the vegetation of shallow water. The eggs are small, numerous and transparent.

RUDD (*Scardinius erythrophthalmus*)

Closely resembling the roach in appearance, the rudd is not quite so widely distributed and it

tends to appear only locally in certain waters. A quieter, less active fish than roach, it is well known in the Norfolk Broads but elsewhere, is not so widely fished. The name is interesting as it is derived from the Anglo-Saxon word 'rudu' which means red.

Identifying Features: It may be distinguished from the roach by the dorsal fin which starts well behind the pelvic fins; the iris of the eye is yellower in colour and fins of a deeper red colouration.

Fin-rays and Scale Counts: 8–9 branched rays in the dorsal fin; lateral line scale count 40–43.

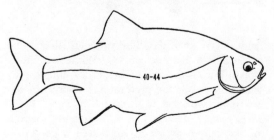

The rudd may be distinguished from the roach by the position of the dorsal fin, the yellower iris of the eye and the lateral line scales, which usually number 40–44. Hybrids, however, do occur

Habitat: A fish characteristic or lakes and sluggish rivers where it prefers weedy situations. The diet resembles that of roach and it will take flies from the surface. It may mix with shoals of roach or bream and even interbreed with the latter. Hybrids usually look like a deep-bodied rudd.

Spawning: Rudd breed in April and May and in habits are very similar to roach.

BARBEL (*Barbus barbus*)

The name barbel comes from the Latin *barbellus* which means a small beard and like the

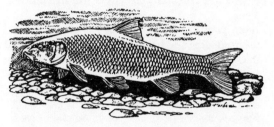

carp, this fish has four barbels. It is easily recognised, however, by the long, curved snout and the projecting upper lip. The barbel is a fish indigenous to the Thames, Trent and a few Yorkshire rivers and it was introduced into the Avon and Stour where it has successfully established itself.

Identifying Features: The body is long and somewhat cylindrical in shape. The snout, large and almost equal barbels and short dorsal fin separate it from carp and other fish. There is considerable colour variation but greenish olive predominates.

Fin-rays and Scale Counts: 8–9 branched rays on the dorsal fin; lateral line scale count 58–60.

Habitat: Unlike carp and tench, barbel avoid warm, sluggish stretches of the river and prefer faster running waters where the temperature is moderate and the bottom pebbly. A gregarious fish, it is usually to be found in shoals, often in deeper water during the daytime. At dusk, it feeds mainly on worms, shrimps and insect larvae and occasionally on weeds.

Spawning: The eggs are laid in gravel redds which are covered over by the parent fish. Breeding takes place in May and June.

CHUB (*Leuciscus cephalus*)

Chub are generally distributed over most rivers in England but is not found in West Wales, Devon and Cornwall. It is primarily a fish of

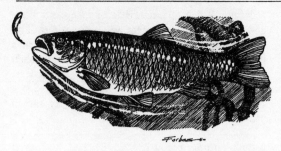

more rapidly running waters, but it is also found in lakes. The young fish form shoals but the older and particularly the larger fish live on their own.

Identifying Features: The body is elongated and the head large and broad. The scales are large and thick. The colour is somewhat variable, the smaller individuals being silvery while those of a larger size may be greenish-brown with a yellowish tinge along the sides.

Fin-rays and Scale Counts: 8–9 branched rays on the dorsal fin; lateral line scale count 44–46.

Habitat: A good, sporting fish, chub are practically omnivorous in their diet eating both vegetable and animal material. It will take young fish, frogs, insect larvae and worms as well as freshwater plants. The diet appears to consist more and more of young fish, however, as the individual becomes older.

Spawning: Chub spawn in April, May and the early part of June, gathering together in large numbers in the shallows where the current is moderately strong. The eggs are sticky and adhere to stones and water plants.

DACE (*Leuciscus leuciscus*)

The dace, like the chub which it resembles, is a widespread fish in England but is not found in

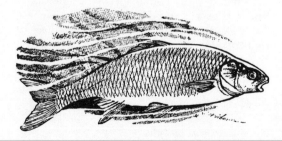

Scotland. A small species, rarely exceeding a foot in length, it will also rise to an artificial fly and it thus affords sport to both fly fisher and coarse

angler alike. The name is derived from the old English word 'darce' which means to dart.

Identifying Features: The body is more slender than that of the chub with a narrower head and a more markedly forked tail fin. The colour is silvery with a greenish tinge to the back and dorsal fin. The pectoral, pelvic and concave anal fins are tinged with red.

Fin-rays and Scale Counts: 7–8 branched rays in the dorsal fin; lateral line scale count 47–54.

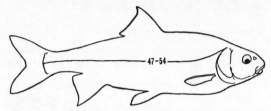

The slender body of the dace, together with its markedly forked tail, concave anal fin and lateral line count of 47–54 scales, distinguishes it from the chub

Habitat: The dace is a fish of clear streams where the water flow is fairly rapid. It prefers a diet of shrimps, insects and worms though it will occasionally take vegetable matter.

Spawning: Dace breed in April, May and June in the shallows of the river where the eggs are laid on the river bed.

BREAM (*Abramis brama*)

Bream are found chiefly in the east and south of the country and are absent from North Scot-

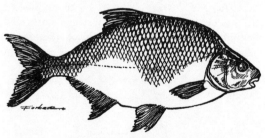

land and West Wales. The younger fish may be confused with those of the White or Silver Bream but all the fins of bream are bluish-grey whilst the pelvic and pectoral fins of silver bream are tinged with red or orange.

Identifying Features: The body is hump-backed and laterally compressed but there is a good deal of variation. The colour an olive brown with a metallic sheen on the sides and a whitish belly. The dorsal fin is short and pointed.

Fin-rays and Scale Counts: 9 branched rays in the dorsal fin; lateral line scale count 50–57.

In addition, there are 23–28 branched rays in the anal fin; this distinguishes it from the silver bream which has 19–21 branched rays in the anal fin.

Habitat: Bream congregate in shoals, preferring still water or sluggish streams. They are bottom feeders including worms, molluscs and crustacea in their diet. When attempting to escape from enemies, they have a habit of stirring up mud and debris from the bottom with their projecting snouts and this helps to conceal them. In late summer they tend to gather in shoals in deeper water where they lie up during the winter.

Spawning: Bream are noisy spawners, rushing about in shallow waters near weeds during May and June. The eggs are adhesive and are laid on water weeds. The older fish often spawn first and are followed at intervals by the smaller individuals.

WHITE OR SILVER BREAM (*Blicca bjoerkna*)

The silver bream is confined to the eastern rivers and is therefore a much more locally distributed fish. Its general habits and mode of life closely resembles that of bream but they are very much smaller in size and of less sporting value.

Identifying Features

Fin-rays and Lateral Line Count: 8 branched rays in the dorsal fin; 19–23 branched rays in the anal fin; lateral line scale count 44–50.

THE PERCH FAMILY (*Percidae*)
THE COMMON PERCH (*Perca fluviatilis*)

Although somewhat variable in shape and colour, perch are easily identifiable and hand-

some fish widely distributed throughout the country with the exception of North Scotland.

Identifying Features: The body is slightly hump-backed, the upper parts being dark olive, the flanks yellowish and the underbelly white. Five vertical bars are usually found on the flanks

though the degree of development depends on the environment. The mouth is large, the teeth are pointed and the gill cover ends in a spine.

Fin-rays and Scale Counts: There are two dorsal fins, the first or anterior having 13–15 spiny rays. The anal fin has two spiny rays.

Lateral line scale count 58–68.

Habitat: One of our commonest fish, perch are found in most rivers and lakes. In rivers, it prefers regions where the current is not too strong; in lakes, it frequents the slightly deeper water close to the shallows. It is a gregarious species swimming in shoals though frequently, the larger the shoal, the smaller the individuals which compose it. Larger perch tend to keep to themselves. In winter, the fish retire to deeper waters where they are much less active. They are voracious feeders and include small fish, fish spawn, worms and insect larvae in their varied bill of fare.

Spawning: Perch spawn from about mid-March to early June in shallow water where there is ample weed. The eggs are laid in long ribbons attached to the weed. Shoals of young perch are ruthlessly harried by other fish, notably trout.

THE PIKE FAMILY (*Esocidae*)
THE COMMON PIKE (*Esox lucius*)

The common pike is the only member of this family found in Britain. Along with salmon, it

shares the honour of being the largest fish of our fresh waters. Its predatory habits, however, make it very unwelcome in trout rivers.

Identifying Features: The body is elongated and the snout flattened. Both jaws are armed with strong, sharp, recurved teeth and the lower jaw projects beyond the upper. The colour is greenish with dark vertical bands and the scales are small. The single dorsal fin is set far back on the body.

Fin-rays and Scale Counts: 13–15 branched rays on the dorsal fin; lateral line scale count 105–130.

Habitat: Pike are found in most rivers and lakes. They are solitary fish except during the breeding season and the larger specimens tend to keep to deeper water. Small pike are often called 'jacks'. Ferocious feeders and predators from the moment they are hatched from the egg, pike will attack almost any animal smaller than themselves and fish of all sizes including their own kind; frogs, small mammals and even birds are included in the diet. For the most part, pike are somewhat sedentary fish, lurking idly in the reeds and darting suddenly when the opportunity of a meal presents itself. Once established, they are extremely difficult to eradicate from a particular water.

Spawning: The breeding season extends from February to May. The eggs are laid in quiet shallows and stick at first to stones from which they break away later and float to the surface.

THE SALMON FAMILY (*Salmonidae*)
THE GRAYLING (*Thymallus vulgaris*)

The grayling, which belongs to the same family as salmon, trout, sea trout and char, is

usually included in the list of coarse fish. There is some difference of opinion as to its value in trout streams where it competes with trout for food supply but where, as a spring breeder, it can extend the fishing season over the winter.

Identifying Features: There are two dorsal fins, the second or posterior being reduced as in trout and salmon to a small adipose fin. The first dorsal fin, however, is very long. The body colouration varies but an iridescent greenish-gold sheen is characteristic and longitudinal stripes and small spots are usually present. The name is derived from the greyish foundation of colour but this belies the fact that grayling are one of our most beautiful fish.

Fin-rays and Scale Counts: 14–17 branched rays on the dorsal fin; second dorsal fin present as an adipose fin; lateral line scale count 80–88.

Habitat: The grayling is a fish of faster flowing streams where the oxygen content is high and the bottom stony. A gregarious species, it forms shoals. The food consists of insects, insect larvae, snails and worms and it will take an artificial fly from the surface very much in the manner of trout.

Spawning: Grayling, unlike trout, are spring breeders and the eggs are laid in April and May in redds on stony or gravel bottoms in the river. The parents cover the eggs over with gravel after laying.

THE EEL FAMILY (*Anguillidae*)
THE EEL (*Anguilla vulgaris*)

Although there is only one species of eel inhabiting British waters, the difference in size

between the large females which may grow to 3–5 ft long and the much smaller male which is usually only about 20 in long, and the marked difference in colouration between the 'Yellow Eel' and the 'Silver Eel', which is only the former at breeding time, has led to the adoption of several different local names.

Identifying Features: The body is elongated and snake-like. Pelvic fins are absent and the dorsal and tail fin appear as one. The scales are small and embedded in the skin.

Habitat: The eel is widespread throughout the country in rivers, lakes and ponds. It possesses the ability to leave the water and cross stretches of country by travelling at night over damp grass. The smaller eels feed on worms and crustaceans but the larger ones will take frogs, mice and water-voles.

Spawning: Until the turn of the Century, it was known that young eels or elvers migrated upstream from the sea in spring and large or silver eels moved downstream in autumn. Where the fish went in the intervening period, however, remained a mystery for the silver eels were soon lost in the sea. About 1926, it was finally discovered that the main breeding grounds were in the Sargasso Sea and it is in this direction and over hundreds of miles that the silver eels travel. After breeding, the eels are believed to die. The eggs which are tiny, contain a drop of oil and they float until the larvae hatch. At first they are slim in shape but later become broad and leaf-like and during the next three years drift back towards the coast of Europe. Eventually they change shape again to form the slim, cylindrical 'glass eel' or elvers which migrate upstream in our rivers in spring.

COARSE ANGLING METHODS

by

DAVID CARL FORBES

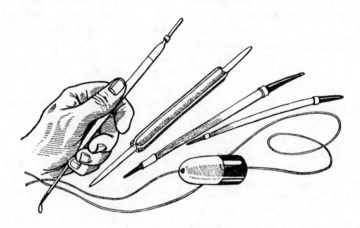

Fishing tackle is merely a means to an end but, perhaps unfortunately, it can also develop an intrinsic value out of all proportion. One tends to amass highly-coloured floats, spoons and plugs, and sometimes even the number of fishing rods grows beyond reason. It is an understandable fascination, and there *is* a place for this in our angling. It is the study, the den, store-room, and perhaps even the attic; it is never, never the waterside. Fishing suffers as you lose time wondering which combination will serve best – fishing is a simple pastime and it should be kept so.

At one time I planned my fishing trips well in advance. Thinking of, shall we say, chub, I would whip a large hook on to a 4-ft length of line on to which would go a large float, which after tests in the bathroom, would be suitably weighted with shot. This ready-use tackle length was then laid around a piece of cardboard and, come hell or high water, I was ready for my chub fishing. I caught very few chub.

It was a long time before I discovered that, basically, it is not the fish we set out to catch which determines the tackle to be used, but rather the condition of the water we are to fish.

Now I believe that there is no such thing as standard roach tackle, or standard roach technique, or for that matter a standard tackle and technique for any fish. The ultra-fine tackle so effective in the near still water canals of the North will lose its effectiveness in the rushing waters of a chalk stream, or the coloured deeps of a major river. But it is not even a particular river or lake which controls our methods and tackle, although there are extremes, it is the condition of the water in the swim we are to fish on the day we are to fish which should control our choice of method or methods. I never decide how I am going to fish until I have had time to study the water.

I do not own, neither do I believe that it is necessary to possess, a multitude of rods to be successful. I have found that most conditions can be tackled if two rods, one of 10 ft with a supple action and lots of power, and one of 14 ft with a faster action, are carried. These should suffice for anything we are likely to encounter in English fresh waters. The water conditions can usually be successfully overcome by the careful use of terminal tackle, plus the right approach to your fishing.

The float is traditionally part of the angler's equipment, and because of this many are loath to discard it. It might be as well to bear in mind that line and hook are the basic essentials on which we can catch fish. A rod and reel makes the task easier, and any additions are mere refinements; some are even unnecessary refinements.

The most basic, yet perhaps one of the most recently publicised methods is called *free-lining*, and while it was undoubtedly one of the earliest of angling techniques, its effectiveness is still not appreciated by the majority of anglers.

The terminal tackle consists of a hook whipped direct to the line, nothing more. In moving water it can prove first class for chub and barbel, large perch, and even roach. The bait, by necessity, is large; it can be a chunk of bread, a lob worm, or a slug. The angler moves along the river bank picking the spots that seem likely to hold fish, and to these he casts. When chub are present bites are likely to come almost immediately after the bait hits the water, or as it is sinking; there is little finesse about a chub bite, the rod top will be whipped round as if the line were being pulled by the hand of an unseen giant.

Should the bites fail to materialise, allow the bait to swing in the current. Keep the line straight between rod tip and bait, but hold a loop of line (between the butt-ring and the reel) in your hand. The line will transmit the feel of a bite which will often register as a definite pluck or possibly a series of tremors. As these are felt, release the loop of line between rod-ring and reel, the next indication should be a definite pull; this is the time to strike.

This rig, or terminal tackle arrangement, can be used in still water, and is extremely effective when fishing for carp, tench, bream and roach. When used in this situation it is called free-line legering. When carp fishing, the bait can be a large piece of bread crust, presented on the surface, and this is where a 10 ft rod with a supple but powerful action can be used. Before casting, dip the crust into the water, for the added weight will greatly improve the distance you are able to cast. Much practice is needed before you will be able to long-cast a bait such as this, for if the action is at all jerky then the crust will fly from the hook. As alternative baits, try a lob worm or a ball of bread paste – these provide sufficient weight for casting. Where small worms or maggots are used, it will be necessary to encase the bait in either ground bait or lake-side mud, this will provide the weight necessary for casting. Once in the water the casing will fall away.

When the cast has been made, the rod is placed upon two rod rests, as illustrated, and then a bight pulled down. A bite indicator can consist of many things, from a small ball of bread paste or a piece of tinfoil, to an electronic device. But whichever method is chosen, make sure that the resistance to a taking fish is cut down to a minimum. It is essential that neither the rod rests nor the method of bite indication obstruct the line in any way.

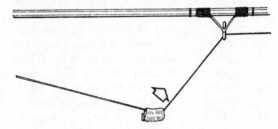

The most important aspect of float fishing is a thorough understanding of the purpose and function of this fascinating piece of equipment. It controls the depth at which the bait is fished, and in moving water it can take the bait to where we believe the fish to be. Not only does it indicate bites, but it helps to provide the weight which is necessary for efficient casting.

Sometimes our fishing could be improved

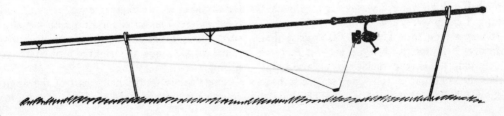

immensely if we paused to consider whether or not we could accomplish these tasks without the use of a float. But, on balance, the float methods are probably the most versatile, lending themselves to many alternatives. By adjustments to float and shot we can present a bait in a variety of ways, from just tripping along the river bed to one which sinks slowly through the water. The bait can be left just resting on the bottom, or it can be suspended at any depth.

Fish do not react well to great disturbances in the water, nor to indications of our presence. Both these deterrents can be eliminated by getting well upstream of the fish and lowering the tackle into the water and allowing the stream to carry it down to the fish. This is known as trotting, or trotting down.

On the smaller rivers one most productive method is to trot the tackle downstream close to the bank, the float moving at the same speed as the current. Make sure that the line runs smoothly from the reel, for a jerky action will have fatal results to the bait. On larger rivers, where bankside disturbances or excessive shallows obstruct the even flow or trot down, the angler will be forced to cast and fish possibly many yards out, and a new problem will arise. Unless great care is taken, fishing in this manner will inevitably produce loops of slack line between float and angler. This drags across the current, causing the float to deviate from its downstream course and, worst of all, it renders striking ineffective. The power that should go through to the hook is absorbed in lifting slack line from the water. For the best results the angler must be in a position where a 'striking' movement is immediately transferred to float and hook. This can be achieved only if slack line is picked up as soon as it starts to appear. As long as the line is kept following the path of the float this problem is kept to a minimum.

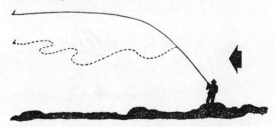

When trotting a considerable distance, a very buoyant float, one capable of supporting a good weight of shot, is often essential, as the terminal tackle will have to draw the line from the reel as it goes downstream. It does not necessarily follow that the float must be bulky – these days the tackle trade produces fluted floats constructed of balsa and quill which are ideal for the task. On small rivers, when trotting short distances, one can perform adequately with a quill, but invariably the reel must be aided to give line at a sufficient rate.

In rivers having a good flow, but containing swims which are of a limited size or possibly constricted, for example by boat moorings or weeds beds, a method known as 'stret-pegging' is called for. This method is unlimited in its effectiveness, but is designed to be limited in range.

The float is set to give 12 in more between float and shot than the depth of the swim. The cast is made so that as the tackle settles in the water there is virtually no slack line. As the bait sinks down, watch for a bite as the float swings to the pull of the current, and once the bait has come to rest there should be an almost straight line between lead shot and rod tip, with the float showing half-cocked on the surface. Bites are invariably indicated by sharp tugs, but one should strike when the normal position of the float alters. In my experience, this method is most effective when small baits are used.

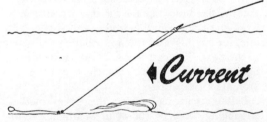

Float legering can be employed in very rough conditions, and is merely a variation of stret-pegging. The split-shot weight is replaced by a drilled bullet, or a barrel lead, which is stopped 12 in from the hook by a split shot. As the fish takes the bait, so the line is drawn through the lead and consequently the float indicates a bite.

The lift method is obscure in its origin, but it was developed and brought to popularity in recent years by Fred J. Taylor, who employed it to make some magnificent catches of tench. As the name of the method implies, the float rises or lifts in the water instead of dipping as the fish takes the bait. It is a method developed for still water fishing for tench, but it is equally effective for any of the more cautious species.

The modus operandi is quite simple. Carefully gauge the depth of the swim, and place the split shot on the line 1 in from the hook, then adjust

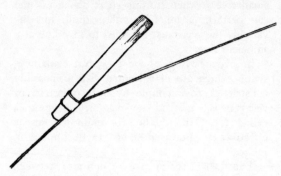

the float so that the distance between shot and float tip is approximately 4 in more than the depth of the swim. As the fish picks up the bait it takes the weight from the float, causing it to rise. The strike is made instantly a bite is indicated. For this method it is essential to have two rod rests and these should be positioned as for free-line legering. However, it is not necessary to have the rod tip pointing at the water. As the strike is made the rod must come straight from the rod rests in one smooth upward swing. It can be seen that the rests must be sited conveniently so that the hand can pick the rod up without fumbling. One cannot hold the rod in anticipation of a bite, for any movement is immediately imparted to the float. The cast is made, the tackle drawn tight, and then left untouched until a lift prompts a clean strike.

Before discussing legering, the general method of gauging the depth of water in which one intends to fish must be mentioned. It is most important that the angler is aware of the depth of water, for this knowledge is essential to the correct assembling of certain types of tackle.

In my opinion, the conventional lead plumb is a shocking device. Generally it is a cumbersome piece of lead weighing approximately 1 oz and conical in shape. At one end there is a wire ring, and at the other an inset cork section. The hook is passed through the wire ring and is set into the cork. By casting in, it will be seen whether or not the float is set correctly. If it is too low, then the lead plummet will drag it down, if too high then it will lie flat on the surface. Although this

method is feasible close to a bank, when one tries to gauge the depth at a distance of 30 or 40 ft damage is done. What is the point of a cautious approach if one immediately ruins all by the great commotion that is caused by the impact of a 1 oz lead?

I prefer to overload a slim porcupine quill with leadshot, and adjust the float until it shows at the surface. This rig make take a little longer to put together, but there is compensation in its comparatively quiet entry into the water. There seems little point in frightening away the fish before we have even commenced.

At one time legering was considered a rather crude method of angling, and in the manner it was practised it generally was. To-day, legering has many variations; leads have definite purposes, as opposed to being merely weights to get the bait 'out in the middle', and legering rods are no longer short, stiff pokers. The advances in leger techniques and tackle over the past 15 years can be attributed to anglers such as Peter Stone, of Oxford, whose remarkably large catches of bream from the Thames brought a glamour to legering that it had never previously known.

This can be a very sensitive method of fishing, and in the main its success stems from the correct use of weight, which must suit the prevailing water conditions. Failure lies with the thought that the leger weight is merely an anchor.

Choose a swim that is not too heavily weeded, and without a major obstruction in the centre of it. Cast across the river, and let your bait roll with the current until it comes to rest under your own bank. This is one extremely effective method despite the fact that the bait is moving unnaturally across the current for the majority of the time. Should it encounter a snag before it can complete its arc, then the purpose of the *Rolling Leger* will be defeated.

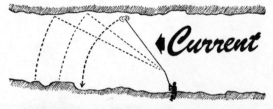

It is unlikely that you will gauge the correct amount of lead the first time, usually trial and error attempts will be necessary before the right action is achieved. Ideally, the bait should travel slowly, inch by inch across the current, all the time being held on a tight line. Drilled bullets and barrel leads give the right movement, but these leads cannot be changed easily, therefore to solve the problem use a short length of nylon and a number of swan shot. The short length is bent over the reel line and a swan shot nipped lightly on to it, thus forming a small loop. A smaller split shot is placed on the reel line to prevent the loop sliding down and masking the bait. Swan shot are added, or taken away, until one has exactly the amount of weight that is needed. Should the line become snagged it can invariably be pulled free with only the loss of the nylon loop and a few swan shot. This attachment is now widely known as the *Link Leger*.

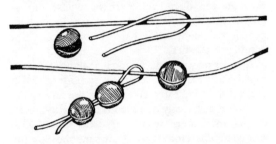

This method is ideal for winter chub fishing, and for bait a piece of cheese or bread paste large enough to cover a size 6 or size 4 hook should be ideal. Stop the link leger about 18 in from the hook. This last 18 in is known as the *Trail*.

After casting wait for the line to tighten as the current pulls on the bait. For bite indication either watch the rod tip or hold the line between your thumb and forefinger. The bite might be indicated by a series of sharp tugs, the tip pulling forward some 5 or 6 in, or possibly a continuous tremor. Allow the fish a little more time if using worms, but strike immediately when using bread or cheese.

When fishing for barbel it is generally advisable to shorten the trail to 12 in, and in waters with an excessive weed a trail of 6 in is sufficient.

My own belief is that broadly speaking it is not the species that displays a certain characteristic when taking a bait so much as the indication which is the direct result of the method used. When the line is tight between hook and rod tip one can expect fast, snatching bites, but given an amount of slack line between hook and rod tip, and the bites become progressively slower. This is a general rule which I have found applies to most

fish, but it is one that is confounded by the barbel. Their bites show the most amazing variations, ranging from tremors which vibrate, as though one was attempting to saw the rod in half, to savage tugs which are capable of pulling the rod from your hands. On other occasions the rod may pull forward slowly, ease back and then pull forward again. Exactly when to strike at these bites is a matter for conjecture – members of the Barbel Catchers Club have spent much time fruitlessly trying to find the answer.

In the main, legering is carried out by presenting the bait down or across stream. However, sometimes good fish may be taken by a method called *Upstream Legering*.

Once again the link leger can serve as terminal tackle, but on the smaller streams it is often unnecessary to add more than one swan shot direct to the reel line for an efficient set-up. This method is really no more than the free-lining method I outlined earlier, merely with the addition of a small amount of lead.

The cast is made upstream, and as soon as the bait enters the water, begin taking up the slack line and continue retrieving it, keeping pace with the current. Do not be tempted into retrieving line by hand, for this slack line will become a problem when a fish takes. Once the bait has moved downstream (relative to yourself), allow it to swing round and come to rest close into your own bank. These final stages are really no more than the rolling leger technique.

Whilst the bait is upstream of your position you will find it very difficult to detect bites – if there is anything definite about this form of fishing it is that bites are seldom as decisive as those encountered in other forms of legering. At first, without realising it, you will miss many, but as you get the feel of the current you will appreciate that sudden stoppages, tremors, or a sudden slackness in the line are in fact bites. Bear in mind that the current must do the work of moving the bait and never reel in line faster than the speed of the current, but merely take up the slack and keep in contact with the bait.

Bite indicators for use on both moving and still waters are available in many shapes and forms; many have had their moment of glory only to disappear from the angling scene. One commercially-made indicator – the battery-operated type used when night fishing – has proved to have lasting interest, and in very recent years, an entirely different type of indicator has found much favour. I refer to the *Swing Tip*.

In very basic terms a 'swing tip' is a short, jointed 'extra 'tip which is fixed to the top of the rod, hanging down at an angle. As a fish takes the bait so the bites are indicated by the tip swinging up in line with the rod. When this method is used in fast water, lead wire is wound around the tip so that it maintains a sufficiently acute angle to allow bites to register.

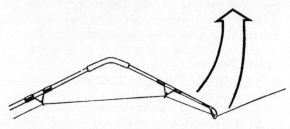

The advantages claimed for the swing tip are that it does not have to be adjusted and that it may be used quickly and easily. However, there are those who maintain that the addition of this tip is detrimental to both accuracy and distance when casting.

Most bite indicators are claimed to be improvements upon the old-fashioned dough bobbin, but whatever type of indicator is used, in my opinion the most efficient of all is the angler's sensitive fingertips. These are the best indicator that the leger-fisherman can have.

In popular thought the angler's bait is worm. However, in practice, more often than not it is maggot, but variations in bait can often improve our chances of catching fish, and sometimes larger ones. Anglers should beware of adopting a particular bait as a general purpose one, for no single bait is sufficient. As with fishing methods, conditions and seasons should control the type of bait we use.

In summer months plant life is at its highest, also countless food forms are to be found in the vicinity of plants, for these are holding areas for plankton and larger aquatic insects. The water level in rivers and lakes is often low, and invariably clear, and when, at this time of year, still waters are clouded with plankton the fish are never short of food.

In winter the plants are at their lowest ebb. They have died back and in rivers the food larders, at least what remains of them, are exposed to faster, deeper waters. Flood waters in rivers

and the excessive cold in most levels of still water makes the task of finding food somewhat harder for the fish. The easy pickings of summer have gone, and the angler's bait may appear to the fish as a bonus.

These are the extremes of our climate, and call for separate angling treatments, but there are gradual changes throughout the year, apart from the freak alterations brought about by rain, and these changes are reflected in the habits of the fish. Seldom does one experience identical conditions on separate fishing trips.

The effectiveness of certain baits may change from river to river, and on some waters the effectiveness may last only for a short period. Quite often a bait may lose its effectiveness half way through the day, even perhaps whilst one is taking fish from a shoal (then an immediate change to a contrasting bait will often keep fish coming to the net).

Anglers may introduce sufficient amounts of one type of bait for it to become accepted by the fish as a natural food form. As maggots are an acceptable food and easily obtained this situation often occurs on waters which are hard-fished with maggots. Therefore most of the time they are the only bait worth using, but on 'off' days a contrasting bait, such as lob worms, will sometimes produce large bags of fish.

While I believe that an excess of tackle can be detrimental to your fishing, one can never have too many types of bait. One tackle combination and a range of contrasting baits will produce more fish than half the contents of a tackle shop and one large tin of maggots.

Never restrict yourself to the use of one bait, and remember that you are attempting to induce a fish to take food, and therefore your bait should be more attractive than what is naturally available to it at the time; why else should it deviate from its natural food?

The correct bait is vital because it is the initial and thus important contact between fish and tackle, but regardless of what bait you are using, only results can show whether or not it is the correct bait presented in the correct manner. Although certain fish are attracted to a particular bait form, success stems from the angler's ability, or luck in choosing the bait to suit the fish and the occasion.

The angler with a full keep net is often asked 'What bait are you using?' but remember the right bait is right only because it is being presented in the correct manner. Give four anglers a loaf of bread for bait, and their varying catches will indicate the way in which they have used it. For one it may be merely a white substance that sometimes catches fish, but for another it could offer four contrasting types of bait.

Bread, a most readily available commodity, is at its best, a deadly bait. However, incorrectly mixed or used, it is virtually useless.

Every part of the loaf has its use, and for some aspects it is essential that the loaf be the freshest you can obtain; for crust fishing the loaf can never be too fresh.

Tear the crust from a new loaf – do not cut it off – so that a small amount of white is left on the underside. Lengths of crust should be left complete for if it is broken into small pieces it will quickly dry out and lose its effectiveness. The best way to keep the crust in its most efficient state is to wrap it in a damp cloth – dip the cloth in water and then wring it out thoroughly before covering the crust.

It is sometimes difficult to convince anglers that this is a bait that will stay on the hook, but once confidence is gained it is soon discovered that crust is good for large roach and dace. Possibly the answer is in it's buoyant qualities – as it travels through the water it 'floats' just off the bottom.

Mounting the bait is a relatively simple task but, as always, there are one or two points which deserve extra consideration.

Use a round bend hook for crust fishing. It will swing into the crust nicely, forming only a small hole as it goes in, and it will afford a better purchase than a crystal bend hook. Do not cut the crust into neat cubes, for while it will still work, it will not do so with the same effect as that which has a ragged, less artificial appearance.

The white part, more commonly known as flake, should also be kept covered to avoid drying out. Once again, pieces to be used as bait are best torn, not cut with a knife. A flake about half as long again as the hook is ideal, but remember handle the bait as little as possible, for it must retain its open, flakey appearance. Mounted on the hook correctly it will stay on well whilst both trotting and legering and although it comes off the hook whilst retrieving the little extra work, rebaiting on each cast, is more than worthwhile. At the beginning of the season, when still-water fishing

for tench, roach and bream, bread flake can be ideal, and in the winter it is an excellent bait for chub, roach, and really large dace in rivers. Often the largest dace recorded each season in the angling press have been caught on flake.

The commonest bread form used by anglers is paste. Forget the fresh loaf, and instead work with bread which is between one and three days old. Paste made from new bread tends to become hard and rubbery and form a ball which is too hard for the hook to penetrate easily as the strike is made. Should one miss a fish and the hook be retrieved with the paste still intact, it is a sure sign that it is too hard for effective fishing.

I like to dampen the bread at the waterside, and pinch off pieces to knead to the correct consistency as I require them. One could dampen all the bread – removing the crust first – and knead it up into a large ball. The crust from a suitable loaf will be of no use, for if it can be used for crust fishing then the flake will be too fresh to make suitable paste. Conversely, if your paste is right, then the crust will be too dry for effective crust fishing.

There is no set formula to describe the mixing of paste. One adds just sufficient water to the bread to arrive at a consistency which will stay on the hook when casting, trot down in fast water without coming off the hook, yet still be soft enough to allow the hook to pass through the bait into the fish's mouth immediately the strike is made. If it is mixed too stiffly it remains on the hook after a strike is made.

Paste may also be made from flour and water, and at one time it often was, but I do not think it is so efficient. It tends to be very rubbery, and it hardens rapidly during the course of the day's fishing. To be really effective it must be very soft, and then it requires an additive such as cotton wool to keep it on the hook. It is a comparatively messy bait, and one which is pointless to make when a much better product can be more easily arrived at with bread.

Carp fishing has greatly increased in popularity over the past fifteen years, and with this growing interest many new baits have developed. One such bait is the *Balanced Crust*.

This bait combines the weight of paste with the buoyancy of crust which is sometimes needed to overcome the problems associated with fishing in waters with thickly-weeded, or soft, muddy bottoms. Sufficient paste is added to the crust to to make it sink through the water very, very slowly, but if it is correctly balanced this bait will not sink into the weed or mud.

Crust, as I have already noted, is sometimes an excellent bait for carp. Larger pieces, possibly match-box size, are floated upon the surface. The crust is cast out on a completely free line, and is taken from the surface by the carp. Quite often a bait will drift across the surface and there is no harm in this, but where weed causes restrictions, a running leger set on the line at the depth of the water prevents the crust drifting too far.

Sometimes the crust is lowered from the end of the rod so that it just touches the water, and only sufficient line is given to allow the fish to take in the bait without pulling it from the hook. With the rod on two rests the angler sits quietly back to wait for his close-range carp – it can be very exciting.

Possibly these methods have led to the popularity of crust as it is used to-day. The latter method is known as *Margin Fishing*. Look carefully at the illustration on page 129, in his chapter on Carp Fishing, Eric Taylor discusses at some length fishing with crust, and offers several good ideas.

When crust is being used for roach and dace it should be borne in mind that this bait expands in water, and allowance made for this when breaking the bait. For barbel, chub, and carp it will not matter.

These are the basic methods and the baits which stem from a loaf of bread. It has been shown that there is more in the correct use of bread than first meets the eye. Used incorrectly it can cause frustrations, but correctly used it can bring many fish to your net. Particular care is required to keep crust and flake suitable for use. An old maxim for naval gunners was 'keep your powder dry'. For anglers it could well read: 'keep your bread from drying out'.

In his chapter on the subject of bait, Bill Howes details many types and their preparation. Knowing Bill, I do not doubt that our ideas on various aspects will differ, and this is a good thing. Whatever school of thought you choose, I hope it will serve you well.

[Editor's note: Spinning techniques are covered in the chapter on Species (Perch and Pike)]

The hook of a spring balance should never go under the gill of a fish for weighing. Use a wide-mesh net or polythene bag

CASTING AND LINE CONTROL
(FIXED SPOOL REEL)

by

BARRIE WELHAM

The fixed spool or threadline is often called the 'everyman's reel' because it is so easy to use. Certainly fixed spool casting can be quickly learnt and in addition it has such versatility that it can be used in places so cramped and confined by natural obstacles that fishing with any other type of reel would be impossible.

Before going further, perhaps a word or two about the reel itself would not be out of place for the stationary drum type reel has quite a long history.

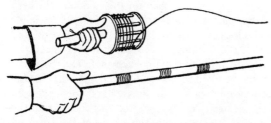

For some hundreds of years people have been fishing with various contrivances where the line slipped over the edge of a drum but it was not until early in the present Century that an Englishman designed the first true fixed spool reel where line was rewound on to the spool by means of a rotating flyer. Immediately this happened a new era of simplicity opened for spinning, and all other forms of bait casting; but because it made bait fishing so much easier there also followed a wave of feeling that considered the new reel took much of the skill out of angling and that it was now too easy for the beginner to catch fish. Some even refused to use the new reel for this very reason, but it was really the price that limited its wider appeal. This high cost situation lasted almost until the outbreak of the Second World War, but during the post-War era the pattern has changed dramatically. To-day, anglers can choose from a multitude of reels at varying prices, some actually costing less than the cheapest offered in pre-War days.

Coinciding with this greater choice came the fishing boom and some maintain that it was the fixed spool that accentuated it. Their reasoning may well be right for certainly a novice angler using a fixed spool can soon cast well enough to catch fish whereas before the difficulties of even getting the bait into the water were enough to dishearten many a would-be fisher.

This is now history, but it will perhaps have emphasised the simplicity of the fixed spool. Even so, this does not mean there are not still standards of good and bad, and even though the bait always seems to go out – somewhere – the more you learn to control your cast the more satisfying it becomes.

THE REEL

Much can be learnt by studying the reel, its parts and their functions. There are certain features which are desirable and there are certain parts which must be honestly made and properly located if they are to give satisfaction.

Casting is important but that is a later step and one which will come more naturally if we have first learnt a little about the mechanical features.

The principal parts of a fixed spool reel, which are annotated A-H in the drawing on page 96, are as follows:

Reel Foot (A). This part holds the reel to the rod. It should be slim and streamlined so it will go easily under the rod fittings, but not too thin or too steeply tapered, or the rod fittings will never lock on it properly.

Reel Stem (B). This should be slender enough to go comfortably between your fingers.

Rotating head (C). This is the only revolving part and it should be perfectly balanced.

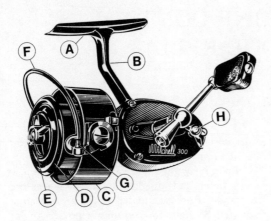

made of tungsten carbide. Some reels are fitted with line rollers and while this seems a good idea they often seize-up when they get dirty. To make a roller that will really work needs accurate machining and, as this is expensive, beware of rollers on very cheap reels. They rarely work for long and, being soft, they groove very quickly and they stick.

Anti-Reverse Switch (H). This serves only to keep the handle from turning backwards, so enabling the angler to have his left hand free for netting his catch. It is an aid in fighting the fish; it does nothing during the cast. It is also a useful refinement when walking from one swim to another with rod made up.

FILLING THE SPOOL

Good, smooth and trouble-free casting can be affected by a number of different causes, but there is one common source of trouble. It happens when the line is put on to the reel incorrectly – loading the spool is most important and with the fixed spool reel is more critical than with any other type. The reason for this is due to the very principle on which the reel works, a principle which relies on the line slipping smoothly and with the minimum of resistance over the lip of the drum. For the line to run freely the spool must be filled as near as is practical to the lip, and although the actual distance will vary depending on the dexterity of the user and the thickness of the line, if it comes to within $\frac{1}{16}$ in of the front lip it will be about right. With very thick line, which can be somewhat springy, this measurement may need to be revised slightly if you are not to suffer from the line flowing off at inconvenient moments. Conversely an expert angler using a very light float in conjunction with a correspondingly fine line, might fill his spool until the line was level with the lip and not experience any trouble.

Many fixed spool reels which are seen in use are so badly underfilled that one gets the impression that the line has been wound on to the reel with little if any backing and with no thought of the finished height.

Assuming that a new 100-yd line is to be run on to the spool, the quickest way to judge the amount of backing needed for correct loading is to wind the new line straight on. How much of the spool it will fill depends on the gauge and the size of the spool, but almost certainly it will not reach to the rim. Allowing then that it has only

Spool (D). The spool must have sufficient line capacity for the particular fishing you have in mind. If your requirements are for more than that amount of line, then you need a larger reel. If you are in doubt it is always better to get one with a larger capacity since the extra space can always be filled with backing whereas if you buy a reel that is too small there is nothing that can be done. As a rule most reels will hold more than sufficient line for general coarse fishing but you do need to be sure about this if carp, barbel or pike are your quarry.

Tension Nut (E). This is the adjustment for the slipping clutch – the safety valve that can save a fine line being broken by a strong fish. The slipping clutch works only while fighting a fish and has nothing to do with casting or retrieving. Because it may be necessary to adjust the setting even while the fish is running, the tension nut should have 'star-like' spokes so that it can be easily gripped if the hands are cold and wet.

Bale Arm or Pick-up (F). This part is swung out of the way while casting and is held there by its own catch. It does nothing while the cast is made. Directly the handle is turned the bale flips across the front of the spool picking up the line on its way. The line runs along the bale and on to the line guide (G).

The Hard Line Guide (G). The line runs here during the retrieve and because of the wear caused by friction, the very best reels have guides

Note the positions of the mouth and the eyes on this tench. This fish will have to stand almost on its head in order to feed – the reason why tench bites normally react on the float as a 'lift'!

Man wins clay from the earth

Nature reclaims her own

The angler creates a fishery

Photos: Alan Wrangles

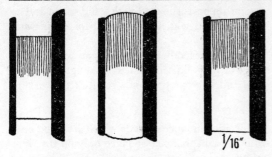

1/16"

A reel under-filled (left), over-filled (centre) and correctly filled (right)

come to approximately halfway, tie on the backing and carry on winding until the total level is to within the $\frac{1}{16}$ in mentioned earlier. Now with the aid of a couple of line winders or another spool of equal size, reverse the lot so the backing now goes on first, followed by the line. You finish with a perfectly loaded spool.

LINE

The type and size of line is dictated by the method of fishing. Good monofilament is smoother and finer for equal strength than any other and is therefore the most popular material.

The number of brands of monofilament are legion and ever changing, so it is difficult to recommend any particular one. The only general advice can be – buy a branded product of known origin, treat it with care and discard it when it shows signs of wear. Remember, the line is the link between you and the fish and it is very false economy to skimp on the line and so risk losing the fish of a lifetime.

One factor which should be considered when buying line is the relationship between its diameter and breaking strain. Some brands are stronger than others of equal thickness and if all other things such as uniformity and suppleness are equal, it is worth taking advantage of this smaller calibration because, although it might seem to be a very marginal advantage, the finer the line, the less rapidly does the lip friction over the edge of the spool increase.

The circumference of an average fixed spool drum is only about 6 in when the spool is brim full. On a short cast of only 25 yd therefore, more than 150 turns of line must slip from the spool. The amount the line has dropped below the lip is considerable and it is by minimising

this drop that the amount of drag which builds up as the coils slip away is minimised.

This is why the very best reels have spools that are wider than average, as the wider the spool the less the line drops for any given cast.

To illustrate how a small increase in diameter can affect casting distance, the following are a few actual distances that were achieved with the same rod, reel and weight all under identical conditions. The averages of a number of casts were as follows:

·008 in dia.	5 lb b.s.	193 ft
·010 in dia.	8 lb b.s.	171 ft
·012 in dia.	10 lb b.s.	146 ft

The test distances themselves are not important, they are neither long nor short. The comparison is the significant thing for it will be seen that from 5 lb to 10 lb b.s., with an increase in thickness of only ·004 in, the distance dropped by 47 ft.

These figures prove that it pays to be highly selective, but there is something more than just better casting to be gained from using the finest possible line. The finer the line the less resistance it offers to the water current, therefore it follows that a much smaller lead will hold bottom. This in itself is important as no one wants to fish with more lead than is absolutely necessary. This is why a piece of heavier gauge nylon is often used to take the strain of the cast while the spool is filled with lighter running line. This 'bumper leader' is just long enough to reach from the bait, down the rod and around the reel three or four times; the strain and shock load of casting is then taken from the main line.

SPECIAL SPOOL LOADING FOR LONG CASTING

Just occasionally – only very occasionally, in fact – there comes in a full fishing career a certain set of conditions that requires casting a greater distance than is normal. We have already dealt with correct spool filling, the use of the finest possible line commensurate with the actual fishing and the advantages of a bumper leader in conjunction with a slightly finer running line. In addition there is the matter of the right choice of rod, and the correct and best disposition of the rod rings, but these will be dealt with later. There is also considerable advantage to be gained in the use of properly streamlined terminal tackle when reaching out for distance. But even

97

then, and after all these foregoing points have been covered there is still one last factor which can give you a few additional yards which on those rare and special occasions might just be sufficient for your needs.

For these occasions a specially prepared spool, on which the level of the line at the back is higher than that at the front, is worthwhile. This can be devised by removing the spool and jamming it on to a pencil or a wooden skewer which is in turn held in a small hand brace or drill. Wind the last of the backing on to the spool by hand so that it comes quite steeply to the back. Replace the spool on the reel and wind on the main line in the normal way. Make sure that the last few turns of line do not come above the back flange and in so doing rub on the inside of the rotating head. The piling of the line to the rear of the spool will reduce the amount of friction as it leaves the spool and will allow you to actually over-fill the drum while still avoiding the nuisance of the line spilling over the lip.

RODS

The fixed spool reel is suitable for nearly every type of coarse fishing, and therefore it is not possible to lay down a strict guide to the rods that lend themselves to this type of reel. The only things on which comment can be made concern the rod action and the positioning of the rings.

ROD ACTION

Fixed spool reels can be used to the greatest advantage with rods which have a fast snappy action; in general these should be more 'tippy' than those used with revolving drum reels. With no drum inertia to overcome, the bait is clear and away from the very instant the line is released.

It is important that the rod should have 'action' – many on the market, particularly some of the short single-handed spinning rods, are little more than poles and although often light in weight they can be completely lacking in throw.

At this point it should be made clear that there is no such thing as an 'all-round' or 'all-purpose rod', and this applies even to the sub-sections of fishing. For example there just is not one rod that will be perfect for all and every type of spinning – a rod that behaves well with a small spinner weighing 4 drm cannot be expected to

give of its best if loaded with a big spoon and an up trace lead which is intended for deep water pike fishing.

To be perfectly equipped you will need a range of rods differing in length, weight and purpose and in some cases in strength (test curve).

RING STRATEGY

Specific guidance on rods which are to be used with a fixed spool can be given only on the rings or guides.

Firstly, there must be enough of them, for wide spacing leads to stress points, and these at the least mean a loss of strength, at the worst a badly strained or broken rod.

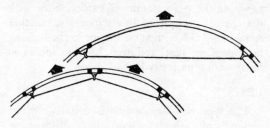

To amplify this let us consider a 7-ft spinning rod. Now it it may be thought that the fewer the rings the lower will be the friction, and therefore long casts will result with correspondingly little line wear. Actually the reverse is the case, for as the line spirals from the spool it balloons out and tends to flap along the rod causing the lure to rapidly lose speed. The question of friction is important as the exact placing of the rings can be finally decided only when the curvature of the rod under a maximum load has also been taken into account. For perfection the line would have to run in a tube to make it follow the bend of the rod, but as this is not practical, a compromise is made by having just sufficient rings to eliminate any sharp and sudden bends. Since the action, or bend, in a rod varies from one to another, it follows that the number and position of the rings varies from rod to rod. For instance a rod with a pronounced tip action will need most of the guides towards the top end as most of the bend will be there. Conversely a through-action rod needs rings spaced almost equally along its whole length. Irrespective of length, type or material from which the rod is made, the rings must be placed so that they strengthen it.

In addition, the first or butt ring has also to perform a second function which makes its positioning doubly important. Because the line leaves the reel in a spiral form, the butt ring has to collect or gather it and break down some of the 'flap' before passing it on. To help in this the first ring must be large. The actual placing of this guide is theoretically tied to the construction of the reel, for the centre axis of a fixed spool should not be parallel but slightly inclined into the rod, so that at some point, the two axes (rod

and reel) will join. As it happens, this position must remain a theoretical one as far as the ring whipper is concerned, for the point of intersection will alter with reels of different make and will also be affected by the position of the reel on the rod handle. On your own rod you can decide the position and move the butt ring to suit. The size of this first large ring has also to be a compromise, for it has to be large enough to gather the line but not so large that it fails in its other purpose, i.e. to funnel the line into the next and subsequently smaller ring.

The remaining guides between the butt and the tip can, with advantage, all be on the large side and stand rather high from the rod. If the rings are spaced carefully, and selected correctly, it should be possible to look through from butt to tip and see an elongated cone. If this cone is of the right size and taper the line which whirls from the reel in a fast spiral will be settled, controlled and flowing straight by the time it leaves the rod tip.

Before closing this section on rods, I will offer some further advice. If you are limited to buying just one rod and are in fact purchasing your first one, take great care. Choose one that will be perfect for the style and type of fishing you will do most frequently. You will then have a rod which you will really enjoy using on the majority of your outings. However, if you try to buy one that will perform every task you will finish up with a 'something' that will not do anything perfectly. What is more, it will confuse you, for instead of having a decided need for another rod for a particular type of fishing, this 'general purpose' thing will be straddling all your requirements and obscuring your exact need.

CASTING

Having discussed the varying items of tackle we now come to the mechanics of casting.

Right at the onset it might be as well to just repeat that the very principle on which the fixed spool reel works makes casting so easy that you only have to wave the rod, release the line, and the bait literally hurls itself out. This is so true that the newcomer to this type of reel can learn to cast proficiently in a matter of minutes.

BASIC METHOD

The question of how to hold the rod when the reel is mounted is not one with only two answers – one right and one wrong. In fact there are several variations, all of which are equally right but conversely there are also several other popular styles which are so awkward in themselves that they must be wrong, even if they were practical, which often they are not.

THE GRIP

The proper grip when using a fixed spool is around the stem of the reel. The variations which are acceptable on the grounds of comfort are whether the stem lays between your second and third fingers (see drawing) or between the first and second. The choice is dictated by personal preference, the size of your hand, and the diameter of the rod butt. Whichever method is chosen, the hold must be comfortable and relaxed with the thumb resting on top of the rod ready to squeeze down as power is applied.

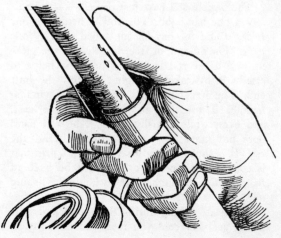

TO CAST

The first operation is to disengage the line from the pick-up of the reel, this action will quickly become slick and almost automatic. The reel handle is turned until the line guide is uppermost, and the first finger of the casting hand (see drawings on pages 99 and 101) reaches down and takes the line across the ball of the index finger (*not* in the first joint) and lifts it clear of the line guide. The free hand now reaches across to turn the pick-up backwards for a quarter turn, and then snaps it open to be held by its catch. As the cast is made and the rod moves forward, the index finger straightens and releases the line. This finger now drops to a position alongside and just clear of the spool lip ready to trap the flowing line if the bait goes too far. Just before the bait splashes down, check the line so that contact with the bait is never lost. The index finger is the key to 'bait contact'. By touching the lip of the spool with the tip of this finger the flow of line is immediately stopped or retarded. The bait can therefore be 'smoothed' down and dropped into the water on a relatively tight line.

Meanwhile, the free hand has moved to the handle of the reel, which at the first forward turn releases the pick-up catch so that the bale arm passes across the face of the spool, snaps closed, and takes control of the line once more. If the rod tip is slightly raised at the same instant no slack line can possibly be left lying on the surface of the water.

FURTHER THOUGHTS ON CASTING

The basic cast I have just described is essentially a one-hand job. The rod is held, the line released and the pay-off controlled – all by one hand. The off-rod, or free, hand opens the pick-up and if the rod is long or heavy it helps to steady it by taking a light hold on the butt end. The free hand also operates the winding handle. Throughout the whole of the cast, and even while actually fishing, the rod hand does not move its position from around the reel. It is thus essential that you find a grip that is comfortable, for your hand will be fixed in that position throughout the whole of a fishing day.

If you are fishing during the winter and your hands get very cold you may find difficulty in keeping a positive hold on the line when casting. Occasionally it may slip away prematurely, resulting in a bad cast; in these circumstances you will find it helps if the index finger is pulled right up against the rod butt. It releases just as smoothly, but when it is very cold and you can hardly feel the line this position is more positive than the one afforded by the more usual, half-extended finger position.

In the last method the line is disengaged from the pick-up in the normal way, and then trapped by a finger at the side of the spool. As the cast is made the finger is lifted sideways and the line slips away. This method has certain advantages for short casts, or where great accuracy is called for, as the finger is already hovering just off the spool lip and so is well situated to check the line if need be. The main disadantage is that when powerful casts have to be made the finger has to exert considerable pressure on the spool lip if a few turns of line are not to escape prematurely.

One can cast with a fixed spool reel in any number of ways, for it is not only very simple, but also very versatile. You can cast with one hand or two, underhand, overhead, side, and in variations on these basic ways. You can learn to cast with pin-point accuracy as well as to achieve great distances. You can also make perfectly adequate casts from small spaces cramped between trees and bushes – in fact you can comfortably fish from places where it would be quite impossible to even cast with any other type of equipment. For instance, in very cramped conditions the cast can be made by pulling back on the bait and flexing the rod and then shooting it out rather like a bow and arrow.

In ordinary circumstances, when there is ample room, some anglers cast with the rod held sideways

The bow and arrow cast

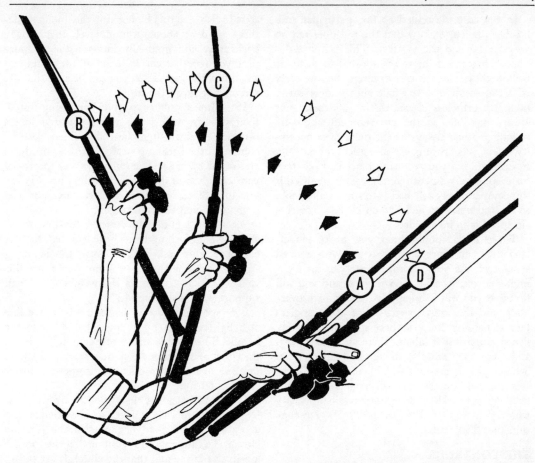

and almost parallel to the ground. I very rarely do this myself for not only is it difficult to control the direction of the cast, but I am also conscious that it can be dangerous – with the rod held low and the baited hook swinging in a wide circle at face level it is very easy to hook a neighbouring angler or even a passer by. For this reason I nearly always cast overhead; the bait will fly straight, and what is more, safely.

The diagram sequence, above, shows the overhead cast. Position A shows the rod and bait stationary, and it is at this point that the pick-up is opened. Now with a slow up and backward movement, the rod is taken to a position just past the vertical (B). Pause momentarily while the bait swings behind and up, and then chop forward smoothly through position (C) and stop at (D) while at the same time releasing the line by straightening the index finger.

This casting style is particularly useful when the weight of the bait does not marry with the rod. If the lure is rather too heavy, it can be cast with much less strain on the rod by this method than by any other overhead style. Conversely if the bait is barely sufficient to flex the rod, casting by this method will be easier and more satisfactorily executed. For heavy baits use a short overhang from the rod point, while for very light weights a long overhang will give the best results.

The wrist does most of the work with just the smallest amount of forearm action but it is rigidly controlled for the action should be 'snappy' – with the rod making most of the effort. In single handed overhead casting the rod is moved in the vertical plane, but for double-handed casting you will find it more comfortable, and the amount of power available will be increased, if you lay the rod out to the right very slightly. This is because the left hand will come more easy to the bottom of the butt, whereas if you attempt to cast with the rod held straight up, the left hand has to reach across the body.

In the casts described so far, particular care has been taken to show that the rod does not go very far beyond the vertical. This is quite deliberate because if the rod is allowed to go to far back there is a tendency to release the line early with the result that the bait goes unnecessarily high. Nevertheless classic casting styles are not always possible, as the environment and surroundings must always be the dictates of necessity. The type of fishing can also affect the casting. For example, if you are using parboiled potatoes for carp, a very smooth gentle cast is required if this comparatively soft bait is to stay on the hook, so the rod needs to be laid well back if excessive tip speed is to be avoided.

These hints should help you make longer, smoother and more accurate casts with a fixed spool reel. As you improve your casting techniques so your confidence will grow and you will find that you will fish happily, in confined, overhung and overgrown spaces that other anglers tend to pass by. Because these spots are so rarely fished, the fish that inhabit them are not so wary, and often they are also of better quality. What is more, when you do have a blank day it will not seem so bad because you will have enjoyed controlling your tackle and putting your bait exactly where you want it. This in itself will give considerable satisfaction.

THE CONTROLS

The Slipping Clutch has already been mentioned, but this should not be taken to mean that low breaking strain lines can be used under all conditions. In fact the term 'threadline', once much used in fixed spool circles, is in my view unfortunate and it has been given undue emphasis over the years. I can see nothing sporting in using lines of a low breaking strain in conditions where natural snags could mean the loss of a good fish.

The line should be related to the strength of the rod, for then a break, even under maximum power, is almost impossible. But you cannot just guess at it – you must make sure; when you are sure you will gain greater confidence. Many anglers are confident before they hook a big strong fish, but when the moment finally comes they lose all confidence and are reluctant to put any real strain on the rod.

You will avoid this if you get to know your outfit by putting it to the test before you ever

start to fish. Do this by hooking the line to something solid at about ground level, then slowly back away and gradually increase the pressure until you feel that you have put all the strain you should on the rod. Then you can be sure that the rod cannot break the line.

If the line should snap while it is being tested, then you are using one which has too low a breaking strain. Often the rod builders will recommend the breaking strain that their products are meant to carry. The only safe way to pre-set your clutch is to do so after tackling up. Fix the line to a fence or tree and exert maximum rod pressure. Then set your clutch.

As a broad guide the starting tension of the slipping clutch should be a little less than the test curve of your rod, and, in turn, the breaking strain of the line should be about four times this value. (The test curve is the weight a rod will support when fully flexed.)

The spool can always be induced to give line at a lighter strain by giving a half turn to the handle. This may seem a contradiction, but it has the effect of breaking the static tension and allows the line to be drawn off at the somewhat lower slipping tension.

It should be noted that when recovering line by winding, the weight which can be lifted is only a fraction of the holding power of the slipping clutch. To illustrate this, assume that the rod has a 2-lb test curve and that the clutch is set to slip at just below this weight. It would then be possible to suspend a $1\frac{1}{2}$-lb weight on it. A movement of the bale arm will start the spool slipping and the tension will be reduced to about 1 lb. The retrieving power of the reel however, would be only a fraction of a pound (when the reel is taking the strain it is being assisted by the friction of the line on the bale arm and on all the rod rings). On the other hand when the reel is attempting to wind in, this same strain is increased by the friction of all the rod rings plus the bale arm which is now working against the reel. Therefore, when retrieving line against a strong fish a special 'pumping' technique is called for. Raise the rod as far back as possible so that the fish is literally dragged towards you, then slowly lower the rod but maintain the pressure by winding at the same time. This process is repeated over and over again until the fish is brought to your side.

When line is being stripped from your reel via

the clutch, it upsets the otherwise perfect balance between the twists that are imparted when the line is cast out and those which are removed when the line is wound in. Line lost when the spool revolves upsets the balance of give and take and line twist will therefore result. Take care not to continue winding when the spool is slipping. To help you in this most reels have an audible line loss clicker at the back of the spool. Although in the form of a light click check, it is not a check in the accepted sense. In fact the reel would work just as well without this little refinement, but by audible indication you know when the spool is slipping without ever taking your eyes off the line.

One final point on slipping clutches, and this particularly applies if you choose to pre-set them. Do not forget that the tension increases as the line goes out. Line stripping from a full spool has greater torque, or leverage, than line coming from a spool that is half empty. Consequently the resistance becomes greater as the core gets smaller. Failure to remember this can mean a broken line and a lost fish. Because of this it is necessary to have a clutch with an easily gripped and readily accessible tension nut that can be quickly re-set even while the fish is still running.

The secret of efficient casting with the fixed spool reel – just as with any other tackle – is practised familiarity. But familiarity can only be achieved if each cast of differing type is carried out with a basic similarity of execution. With this in mind, careful, attention should be paid to the line overhang from the point of the rod. Substantial variations in overhang lead to widely varied castings.

A light weight will call for a greater overhang than a heavy one, since the longer the overhang the longer the arc of the cast and therefore the greater the ultimate forward impetus. Try to cast similarly weighted tackle, allowing something for 'streamlining' and therefore wind resistance, with the same overhang.

It is upon this ability to judge consistency of overhang and casting swing that precision depends. In any angling method that is based on precision, the most precise angler is the most successful in terms of fish caught.

CASTING AND LINE CONTROL (CENTREPIN REEL)

by

Terry Thomas

The centrepin reel (see pages 20-21) consists of a drum with a relatively heavy rim which is fitted into or onto a cage, or to a plain back. It has no gears but a single action and the drum revolves on a centrepin. In consequence it spins very freely and is therefore particularly suitable for heavy spinning and certain types of float fishing, in particular live baiting and long trotting.

The centrepin reel, often still called the Nottingham reel, is now little used for the casting of heavy baits because the fixed spool reel and the multiplier are so much easier to master. The main virtue of the single action reel is the direct control it gives when playing fish in heavy water or in heavily weeded areas. There are still occasions when these reels are the best weapons to choose.

Casting difficulties stem from the fact that initially a high degree of inertia has to be overcome to start the drum spinning. Once it starts, however, it spins at high speed and skilful and delicate hand control is required to prevent overruns. Mechanical means are available to assist control but even when the reel is governed in this way split second timing in the release is needed.

HEAVY CASTING

When casting a heavy bait, that is one ounce and upwards, a long rod (9–10 ft) and a long swing are required. The rod tip needs to pass through some 270 degrees in order to overcome inertia and cast smoothly.

The reel position is a matter of personal choice but it is best to mount the centrepin reel low down on the handle. The reel is controlled throughout the cast by pressure from either the forefinger or the middle finger of the left hand.

The moment of release, that is the moment when the drum is allowed to start spinning, is

always most difficult to describe in words. With the Nottingham reel release depends to a great degree on the weight being cast, but the drum must be allowed to revolve almost as soon as the forward cast is started. As previously explained, pressure is applied to the drum throughout the cast, although, as experience is obtained, it can at times be allowed to run quite freely. When the bait hits the water the drum is stopped completely.

FLOAT FISHING

The main modern use for the centrepin reel is for float fishing. There is still much argument as to which is the better, the Nottingham or the fixed spool reel, but I believe that 'there is a time and a place for both'. It is generally conceded that casting, particularly long casting, is easier with the latter while the former gives greater control.

FLOAT CASTING

There are three methods of casting with a centrepin reel, loop casting, casting from the reel and 'slip' casting. With all three methods the reel is mounted according to personal choice but with the hand generally above the reel.

When using the first style the loops of line lying between the rod rings are plucked out by the fingers of the left hand and stretched back and away from the body. As the loops are gathered the rotation of the drum is controlled by finger pressure from the right hand. On the forward cast the loops are released and the line 'shot' in this way. Long casts can be made with this style and speed and control achieved with use and practice. The loop cast gives a high degree of accuracy and, most important, allows repeated casts of the same length to be made.

When casting from the reel, the Avon, Wallis or Nottingham cast is used. This cast originated on the Trent, was brought to perfection by the late F. W. Wallis and is now used particularly on the Hampshire Avon. It is a most difficult cast and far harder to master than any other type of casting, fly, spinning, float or sea. It is best used with heavy terminal tackle.

The problem in casting float tackle directly off a centrepin reel is to overcome inertia and start the spool revolving. Float tackle is too light to do this without assistance, so the left hand is used early in the cast and pulls line off the reel to the rear in order to start the drum spinning. The line is held firmly in the left hand but as soon as the float starts to fly forward it is released and allowed to flow through the fingers. Throughout the cast the reel is controlled by pressure from the right hand.

The sequence of the cast is as follows: The angler starts with both hands close together and opposite his chin. As the right hand moves forward to swing out the float, the left hand which holds the line pulls back to start the reel spinning and then, still retaining the flowing line, moves back to the reel. All through the cast the reel is under finger control. With the typical heavy terminal tackle used on the Avon casts of over 25 yd plus can be made.

THE SLIP CAST

The third and most simple method of casting with a centrepin is my own invention and is called the Slip cast. A cageless reel is required and the principle of the cast is to cause the line to fly off the rim of the drum as off a fixed spool reel but to the side. To do this the non-casting hand is held opposite the centre of the reel on the open side of the drum.

To take a simple case, the reel is mounted with the handles to the left. The left hand holds the line firmly about a foot to the left of the centre of the reel with a slight loop of line hanging from reel to hand. The left hand must remain in this position during the whole of the cast. As the cast is made and the float flies forward, the left hand opens and allows the line to slip off the edge of the reel through a circle formed by the thumb and middle finger and thus on through the rod rings and forward.

This is a simple cast to learn and a simple way of making a long cast. While learning, it will be found best to look at the hands all the time the cast is being made. Control of the line throughout with the disengaged hand gives considerable accuracy. Should the reel be used with the handles to the right, the cast should be made with the rod turned so that rings and reel are on top. After the cast, of course, the rod is turned back to the normal 'rings down' position. Thus there are four alternative positions to suit both right hand and left hand use in casting and in retrieving.

There is one snag with the Slip cast. Used too often it causes line kink. It is therefore not suitable for repeated long casting.

TROTTING CONTROL

As mentioned at the beginning of this chapter, the Nottingham reel is best used in a long-trotting role. The line can be fed off the reel by the left hand so that the float moves unchecked down with the current, and the retrieve can be made at high speed by 'batting' the rim of the drum with the disengaged hand, causing the reel to spin to the rear and collect the line in this way. ('Batting' is the name given to the act of striking the rim of the drum with the palm of disengaged hand.)

PLAYING FISH

The centrepin is, in my opinion, the best of the three types of reel for playing fish, and particularly big ones. Due to its absence of gearing, line can be recovered with a minimum of 'pumping'. Extra control over a running fish can be exercised by finger pressure on the rim of the drum. The centrepin reel takes a little time to master, but it is time well spent. No float angler can consider himself 'complete' until he can manage both fixed spool and Nottingham reel.

HOOK BAIT AND GROUND BAIT

by

BILL HOWES

MAGGOTS

Maggots are used as bait by the vast majority of anglers for a number of reasons, but the two prime motives are that they are easily handled and readily obtained in any quantity required. Literally thousands of gallons are used throughout the country every weekend, and with such huge amounts put into the water during the course of a season it is not surprising that fish have come to accept maggots as a natural food form.

sand. In time the maggots will wriggle down leaving the extraneous matter, sawdust and chrysalids, etc. on top. This should be removed, and the maggots left in the sand for a day or so to continue cleaning themselves. If the maggots are not inclined to burrow, leave the container in the sun or a bright light – this will encourage them to move down into the sand.

This cleaning process helps to remove grease from the maggots and so minimises the risk of them floating when they are used as ground bait.

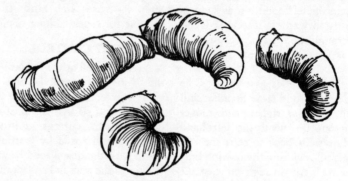

Maggots, the most popular bait, can be improved with conditioning. The hook point is usually nicked into the skin at the thick end

The perfectionist, invariably the top-flight match angler, breeds his own maggots, but generally it is much simpler to buy them from the local tackle shop. The quality of the maggots may vary from shop to shop, depending upon whether they have been fed on fish or meat, but there are ways for the angler to coach his bait on to maximum size and generally improve its condition.

Towards this end it is as well to buy the maggots a few days before the fishing trip is planned, for this will provide time for conditioning and preparing.

Fill a large container with slightly damp sand, and distribute the maggots over the top of the

106

If maggots do not quickly sink to an effective depth, they are liable to take the fish out of your swim as they float downstream.

Use a sieve to separate the maggots from the sand, but should the sand adhere to them you will have to wash the maggots in water and dry them off with a large piece of old towelling. This should be done prior to sorting out the larger maggots which will be used as hook bait (these can be placed in a tin of bran, with a little added Demerara sugar, and left alone for at least one day in a cool place). Place the smaller maggots in a separate tin of bran, these can be used as groundbait.

Finally, the maggots intended for the hook are

transferred to clean bran, bread crumbs or saw-dust, a medium which, by their constant wriggling, will cleanse and polish them.

Always remember that it is absolutely essential to keep maggots in a sawdust type material as without it the maggots will sweat and die. Ensure that the tins containing maggots are well venti-lated and kept in a cool place. If cold enough, but not freezing, the maggots will keep a long time without becoming chrysalids.

Clean, and natural coloured maggots will normally prove a good bait, but occasionally when the fish are shy, it may prove advantageous to dye them a brilliant green, yellow or orange. Coloured maggots can usually be purchased from a tackle dealer but a wider selection of colours can be produced if you dye your own. Colour more than you need for the hook, and add them to the feeders and ground bait.

The best colour results can be obtained by colour feeding. This is achieved by sprinkling the colouring powder onto the base on which maggots are being reared. An internal colouring is created which shows attractively through the maggot's transparent skin, and which long immersion in the water will not fade.

One method of adding colour to the maggots, after they have been cleaned and scoured, is to add two teaspoonsful of the dye solution to each handful of maggots, and then leave for about 15 minutes. Sprinkle a little powdered dye onto the maggots, stir with a float or stick to distribute the colour, and leave them for three or four hours to reach the required colour. Finally, clean them in sawdust and transfer to bran or bread-crumbs.

Ground baiting with maggots and/or chrysalids is a practice which must be carried out with extreme care. There are several methods by which these creatures can be introduced into the swim: they can be thrown in by hand, lowered to the bottom and released from a bait-dropper, they may be packed into a swim-feeder, or con-tained in balls of ground bait.

Whichever of these methods is used, the floating maggot or chrysalid should be avoided, for it will only tend to draw the fish up off the bottom and away from where you are presenting your baited hook.

The vast majority of maggots are in first-class condition when bought, but the angler should not retain them too long, for they become empty and will then tend to float more readily than they will sink.

If using maggots in a swim-feeder, either plug the ends with dampened bread-crumb, the centre of the feeder being packed with loose maggots, or mix the maggots with a crumb ground bait, then fill the swim-feeder with this mixture. The flow of water and the movement of the maggots will discharge the contents.

When ground baiting a swim with maggot, remember that it is always best to feed little and often. (See Editor's note, p. 117.)

CHRYSALIDS

Chrysalids, which are also known as casters, rapidly grew more and more popular as a bait during the sixties. The man largely responsible for their success is that great Lancashire match fisherman, Benny Ashurst.

Chrysalids, or casters, are a small and effective bait for the match angler

On many occasions the caster has proved itself to be the most efficient of all baits, although it is not the easiest of baits to use.

A long-shanked hook is essential to success when fishing with casters, so that the hook tip is well down in the bait. Frequently, and most particularly when they are shy, fish will merely crunch or nip the bottom off the caster and avoid being hooked (this is described as 'shelled'). A short shank hook will enable roach to shell many casters without being caught; a long shank hook makes this far more difficult.

When using casters for hook bait, feed the swim very sparingly, and above all make sure that those you loose-cast are sinkers.

Maggots will rapidly turn into chrysalids if left in a warm place. Freshly evolved chrysalids are orange in colour, but soon change to dark red.

Most fish will take this bait, but it is especially attractive to roach, dace and rudd, as well as to barbel and chub.

Floating chrysalids can be effectively used as bait when lake fishing for rudd. Scatter a few on the surface to attract the fish, and cast to them with very light unshotted tackle. Surface fishing with floating chrysalids is also a method for taking dace from shallow streams, but to keep the shoal interested a steady supply of loose cast chrysalids is essential.

When legering, and baiting a size 10 or 12 hook with three or four maggots, the bait will often be taken more readily if the hook tip is masked with a chrysalid.

One of the great charms of angling is that the individual has so much freedom of choice, and nowhere is this freedom more apparent than when selecting bait. Good anglers frequently owe their success to their ingenuity in applying varying baits and techniques to different forms of fishing.

It therefore follows that there is seldom a set rule for the use or preparation of baits, and many anglers derive great pleasure from using their own interpretation of a popular method – particularly if it is successful. This is all well and good for the experienced angler who understands the form, for he knows how to extract and apply what he has read, but what of the beginner? He might well be forgiven for thinking that seasoned anglers do little but contradict each other – but then these anglers are writing of their own experiences, based on methods which have brought consistent success. It should be apparent that a bait, or a method of preparing that bait, would soon be discarded if it gave poor results. Do not recognise anything in angling as being cut-and-dried, and be very grateful that it is so.

You will read in the chapter on methods by David Carl Forbes that in some instances his preparation of baits, particularly bread, differs from mine. We both have confidence in our methods and we both catch fish.

Eventually you will develop your own ways and preferences – as David and I have done – and you will be confident in them, and you will find yourself adapting our methods and the ways of many others to your own requirements.

BREAD

Bread paste is prepared by removing the crust from a white loaf, placing the remaining white crumb in a piece of clean cloth and holding it in water long enough for it to soak. Squeeze the

surplus water out and knead the bread to the right consistency whilst still wrapped in the cloth.

It is difficult to determine exactly how one achieves the right consistency, for only actual use can prove whether or not the paste is right. It should be only just firm enough to stay on the hook in fast water, and if a vigorous cast throws the paste from the hook it is an indication that it is kneaded to the right consistency.

Fickle fish may be attracted to the paste by the addition of any one of many flavouring commodities, e.g. custard powder, honey or crushed hemp – here there is great scope for the angler to be ingenious.

When bread and bran are used for groundbaiting, it is as well to mix a little bran into the paste used for hook bait, or to rub the plain paste into bran so that particles break off in the water and attract fish.

Legering or laying-on tactics for the larger species is sometimes more effective if large pieces of paste are used, but when trotting with float tackle for roach and dace, a hook bait no larger than a garden pea will usually be large enough.

I have found that coloured waters usually produce more fish if a larger bait is used, and in clear waters the smaller baits are attractive. But one must not be too dogmatic, for the size of the quarry and the size of the hook must be taken into consideration.

If your paste is correctly mixed you will be able to hook fish without effort, but do not be afraid to leave the hook point exposed. In fact, if your paste is rather stiff it will be to your advantage to leave the hook exposed so that penetration is more easily achieved.

The size of both hook and bait should correspond – it is pointless to put a tiny hook into the centre of a large piece of paste. Apart from the fact that such a large bait very easily flies from the hook when cast, it completely masks the hook point.

Bread crust can be a difficult bait form both to prepare and use. One well-tried method which is used in the preparation of crust is that which calls for two clean pieces of board and a heavy weight. Place a slice of dampened crust between the boards, put the weight on top and leave it overnight. The crust is then cut into strips and then into cubes. After removing the crust the remainder of the loaf can be used for paste making.

A variation of this method and one which is extremely popular is that which calls for the use

Cubes of bread crust have accounted for many specimen fish. To be effective this bait must be used carefully

of a small metal press. The crust is placed in this small vice-like instrument, the wing nut at the top screwed down, and within a few minutes a most efficient piece of cube is ready for the angler's hook.

This press has one added advantage. On the metal pressing plate there are two small spikes. As the baits are made, the spikes hole the crust so that the hook can be slipped through easily.

Obviously, large cubes should be used when fishing for barbel, chub, or carp but remember that all cubes swell quickly in water.

Using bread cube, I would suggest the following hooks: for roach, size 10; for bream, size 8; for chub, size 6; and for carp size 4. Insert the hook point into the crust and bring it out through the white crumb. Presented in this way the crust will not impede the penetration of the hook.

There are several ways in which bread cube can be kept for some time, e.g., packed in salt in a screw top jar and plastic airtight containers, but my preference is for fresh cube made at the time of fishing.

Crust floating on the water is a hook bait which must be presented naturally if a big fish is to be tempted to rise and take it

Small unpressed pieces of crust may be torn from a loaf and used; these will float and prove

most attractive to carp, and sometimes even to dace.

Floating crust is generally more effective at night when fishing for carp, although many good size fish are taken during the day from both lakes and rivers. During the summer months chub, too, frequently respond to this bait.

A platform of crust onto which is built a mound of paste can often be used to great advantage when fishing over a soft bottom of mud or a thick blanket of weed. The crust adds buoyancy to an otherwise heavy bait. This method is fully detailed in the chapter dealing with methods.

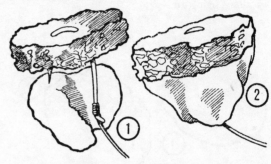

A piece of crust on the bend of a hook (1), with paste covering the shank (2), is a combined and balanced bait which will rest lightly on the soft bottom of a lake

A small flake of white crumb from the inside of a new loaf gently squeezed around a hook to completely cover it (2)

CHEESE

Cheese in many forms is another much favoured bait. Chub, barbel and roach will take it at any time of the year, and although I believe that the cheese is more effective when fresh, many anglers swear by cheese that is 'high', claiming that in this state it is especially good for chub.

Most varieties of cheese can be used, but certain types lend themselves to particular bait forms more readily than others. When adding cheese to a bread paste I favour the softer cream cheeses or grated stale Cheddar, although I have on occasions used the more exotic types such as Camembert and Brie. Gorgonzola blends well with bread. The harder varieties of Cheddar can be cut into small cubes and used as a hook bait, whereas the softer processed cheeses can be kneaded into a putty-like mass that makes an excellent bait form.

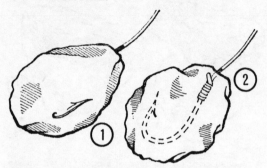

Cheese must be well kneaded to mould around a hook. If the cheese is of a firm consistency the hook point should be exposed (1); a softer cheese can cover the hook completely (2)

When using this last-mentioned bait the angler can experience difficulty during the winter months when the water temperature may be almost at freezing point. Then the cheese tends to become very hard and unattractive, and it is then that I would add a very soft paste in almost equal quanties. But in any case change the bait fairly often – this keeps your offering more attractive to the fish.

In slower water, cream cheeses can be used direct from the wrapping paper, but during the summer months care must be taken for then cream cheese straight from the wrapping can be too soft.

When using paste baits, whether they be based on bread or cheese, always remember that a hard bait will frequently be ignored by a fish that will freely take one which is softer.

WORMS

Earth worms are a fish's natural food, and therefore are an excellent bait. There are many types of worm, from the threadlike creatures which live in the mud at the bottom of lake and river to the solid rounded snakelike creatures which abound in well-manured soil. Fresh water fish will at one time or another accept worm most readily – indeed, there are occasions when worm is the only effective bait.

However, worm fishing has its disadvantages, and particularly so during the summer months. From June until late September and sometimes even later, to use a worm as bait is almost certainly to invite the attentions of an eel. This would not be too bad if the eels were always large, but unfortunately more often than not the eel is likely to be of bootlace proportions.

The most efficient part of a lobworm is in my opinion its tail. It looks attractive, moves well in the water and has a deadly fascination for many species. The red worm is smaller but is used very successfully, as is the brandling which is distinguished by the yellow rings around its body.

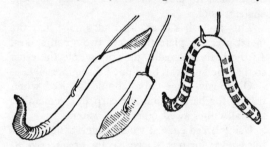

All earthworms make good bait for many species

Most patches of soil will yield their quota of worms, but the richer the soil is in humus, the more worms it is likely to contain. Old compost heaps often yield good quantities, and stones and logs of wood are always worth turning over. If you are fortunate enough to be able to create a 'wormery' in your garden, fork in plenty of garden refuse and empty tea-leaves on to the patch during the driest months of the year. Remember to keep the area moist and cover with a damp sack during the summer.

Worms can be kept for a considerable period in plain wooden boxes which have been filled with old leaves and moss. A whole winter's supply can be gathered and so long as the box is reasonably well protected and is not allowed to freeze, the inhabitants will remain lively and in good condition.

Lobworms can be collected from a lawn after

dark, and especially when the grass is wet. Move stealthily when gathering them for they are most sensitive to vibration and to light – the bright beam from a torch will cause them to withdraw into their holes, so use a diffused light. You will still need to be quick to seize a worm which is lying partly out of its hole.

Whether or not worms are better hook baits after a week's preparation of scouring and toughening in damp moss is a matter for conjecture. I believe that they are. However, there is a school of thought which expresses an opposite opinion.

Place some sphagnum moss in a container and put the worms in on top. Keep turning the container and the worms will continually work through the moss, which will clean and toughen their skins. After this treatment they do not tear off the hook when cast a great distance. Freshly dug worms are soft, and vigorous casting easily flicks them from the hook.

Earthworms remain in good condition if taken to the water in fresh clean moss in a cloth bag or wooden box. Tin boxes and glass jars will quickly kill the bait.

Both Stewart and Pennell tackles were originally developed for use with large worms. Today many are of the opinion that these tackles are cumbersome and they obtain better results with a single hook baited with a worm's tail. When using only the tail end, the hook point is pushed into the broken end and brought out of the side.

Another method that may be employed when using a single hook and a full-length worm is that in which the worm is hooked twice through its middle, thus leaving the head and tail to wriggle attractively.

Baiting with worm can be a slippery procedure, and therefore some find it easier to accomplish if the worm is first dipped in fine sand (an old boot-polish tin that has been thoroughly cleaned and filled with fine sand is thus a useful accessory).

HEMP

Hempseed is a bait which has caused much controversy and on some fisheries its use is banned. Contrary to the belief held by some, hempseed is not a drug nor can it be converted into a drug when it is prepared for bait. It is banned simply because it is thought that excessive use of hemp creates in the fish a desire for this bait only. Hempseed is cheap and frequently

Hempseed, a quick reaction bait, must be cooked until the seed splits. The bend of the hook is pressed into the split and the white kernal allowed to protrude

anglers will take large quantities of it to the river and that which is not used is thrown in. It lies on the bottom, the fish gorge themselves upon it and become so accustomed to a grain which has a very high food content that a fishery can become a 'one-bait water'.

To be successful when using hemp, the angler must have a very quick reaction. Fish such as roach become expert at taking the seed from the hook. Instant reaction is necessary to stand any chance of hooking fish; the angler who reacts slowly will not succeed with this bait.

This is possibly an over-simplification of a very involved subject; so much controversy exists over this bait that here one can but discuss its efficiency and use as a bait.

Hempseed is a small grain requiring a small fine wire hook and ultra light tackle. It is generally used when fishing for roach or dace.

Ground baiting with hempseed can very easily be overdone, so use only small amounts, throwing in a few grains at a time at well-spaced intervals throughout the day. Hempseed usually produces the best results in waters that have a steady flow; when fishing sluggish water use even less as ground bait.

Bread paste mixed with crushed hemp makes a good bait for barbel and big roach, but it must be used in a swim that is often fished with hemp.

Prepare the seed by soaking about a pint of hemp in water overnight, then bring it to boiling point and simmer until the seeds begin to split and the white kernel protrudes. This is the part of the seed the fish like best. Regular hempseed anglers often paint the shank of their special hemp hook white to disguise it. Add soda to the water in which the bait is cooked; this will darken the husks and improve its presentation.

Hooks which are flattened at the bend are easily pressed into the split in the seed, and remember that when hemp fishing, fish bite at split shot by mistake, so regular hemp anglers use a coil of thin wire on the cast. One dust or size 8 shot prevents the wire from slipping down onto the hook.

GRAIN

Stewed wheat is another first-class grain bait that attracts big roach. To prepare wheat for the hook, wash the grain thoroughly and place it in a saucepan with water and put on a low heat and raise to boiling point slowly. Simmer gently for about an hour, or perhaps a little more, until the wheat has turned a golden-brown colour. As soon as the grain swells, splits and shows the white kernel, it is ready for use.

An alternative is to put the wheat in a vacuum flask and then pour in boiling water to within a couple of inches of the top. The space is needed for the expansion of the wheat. By morning the wheat grains should be soft and ready to use on a No. 12 or No. 14 hook. Push the point of the hook through the kernel, but for vigorous casting the hook will be more secure if inserted through the husk.

Wheat is fished on float tackle, and a few grains thrown in as ground bait at intervals helps to keep the fish in your swim. Do not ground bait too heavily.

Pearl Barley is another grain which is prepared in a similar manner. The liquid is drained off as soon as the bait is cooked. It is a good bait for roach and dace and is used on a No. 14 or No. 16 hook.

Rice may also be used as a hook bait, and it can also be used as a ground bait in conjunction with pearl barley on the hook. The larger 'Patna' rice is best as hook bait. To prepare, soak the rice overnight and treat as wheat.

Macaroni has also to be cooked before use. Boil for a while to soften, and if using long sticks break them before cooking. Drain the liquid and allow to cool slowly.

Half-inch pieces of macaroni can be used on a small hook, insert the point at the middle of the bait. Alternatively, take the hook down through the hole in the centre.

When preparing macaroni for chub fishing, add a cheese flavour by cooking it with grated cheddar.

BERRIES

Many berries find favour with anglers, and at one time or another almost all fruits of this nature have taken fish in varying numbers. Cherries, snowberries, blackberries, etc. are a few of the many that could be listed.

The most popular is the elderberry, and this is a fruit that can be used quite efficiently in conjunction with hempseed. The elderberry can be placed on the hook, and the hemp used as a feed or vice versa.

The ripe berry is used on a 12, 14 or 16 hook which should merely nick the skin. On occasions the fish will take more readily if the hook is buried inside, but care must be taken not to completely mask the hook tip with a hard piece of skin. One of the difficulties of using this fruit as a bait is that if it is over-ripe it will burst, so it is best always to use a very sharp thin wire hook.

Ripe elderberries should be handled carefully when nicking a sharp hook under the skin

Elderberries can be preserved quite easily and they often prove to be a most efficient bait 'out of season'. I favour a berry that has been preserved in syrup, although they can be kept for a considerable period in a solution of one part of formalin to ten parts of water. Before attempting to preserve, thoroughly clean the fruit and remove all stems and pieces of twig and other extraneous matter.

No list of fruit baits would be complete without banana, although this is not so widely used as it might be (for chub and carp it is to be particularly recommended). The banana should be firm and sliced into a size that suits the hook that is being used. Care must be taken in casting this bait, as it can easily be thrown from the hook by a too vigorous action.

VEGETABLES

Potato is one of the most successful of all the many baits that are used by the carp fisherman because a potato being a completely alien commodity in water, and one that seems to appeal to the carp, it allows the fisherman to be extremely

Photos: Roy Shaw

A pool on the Driffield Beck, where a convenient backwater provides some fine sport with grayling.

The huge dorsal fin of a freshly caught grayling reflects a most unusual tortoiseshell mixture of chestnut and purple.

This is a well organised match stretch – note how the anglers blend in with the trees.

selective in his choice of fish. The smaller species in a lake, for example small roach, perch, etc., will seldom attempt to take a parboiled potato the size of a golf-ball.

On many occasions when deliberately fishing for carp the fry of other fish and in fact many of the smaller species will attack large pieces of dough, bread crust, or bread flake, their attentions gradually reducing the size of the bait until the hook is left completely bare. Whilst this is going on the carp fisher is faced with all manner of indications that a fish is at his bait, but not one of them giving the tell-tale long steady pull and first run of the fish he is seeking.

While it can be argued that bread is in fact just as alien as a potato, fish become accustomed on many waters to feeding on bread which has been thrown to swans and ducks, etc. A water that contains a stock of carp can be fed in a similar manner, the carp becoming accustomed to this feed until eventually they will accept potato on a hook. In waters where carp seldom, if ever, encounter a potato then it will be no more effective than a parboiled golf-ball. In short, the fish must be educated to this particular bait form.

To prepare potato as a bait, select a number all roughly the size of a golf-ball, and certainly not much larger than a hen's egg, and boil them in their jackets. They must not be overcooked so that they break up very easily, nor must they be so hard that the fish reject them. It is impossible to indicate the number of minutes a potato should boil as there are so many factors which have to be taken into consideration.

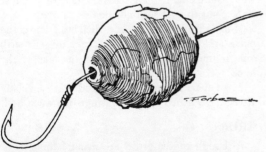

When baiting with a parboiled potato, it should be pushed down and onto the hook before the skin is peeled

The potato provides its own weight for casting. A baiting needle, or a slim porcupine quill, is pushed through the potato to make a channel for the line which is passed along the hole. Finally, the hook, a size 2, is tied onto the line. The potato is now pushed down onto the hook and the skin is peeled so that the bait shows white on the lake bed.

This bait should be preceded by the use of potato-based ground bait, and it does not matter how soft this is because it will be widely broadcast into the area to be fished.

Carrot is another vegetable bait for which fish can acquire a taste. The raw vegetables can be cooked lightly and diced to a size to suit the hook you plan to use. Tinned carrots have a softness that is hard to equal.

Haricot beans and garden peas may sometimes prove to be exceptionally good baits, but generally only in areas where the occupants of houseboats are continually tipping into the water. Good roach are quite often taken on garden peas presented on size 10 or 12 hooks, but if fresh peas are used they must be cooked until they are soft. Once again, it is much easier to use tinned vegetables.

MEAT

Sausage is used extensively when barbel fishing. For use as hook bait the sausages should be lightly cooked, and then cut into pieces large enough to accommodate a No. 6 or No. 4 hook. An uncooked sausage may be used, in which case the hook, a No. 2, can be pushed inside the meaty content.

A small beef sausage often stays on the hook more firmly when cast.

Sausage meat mashed with bread can be used for both hook and ground bait.

Lightly fried small chipolata sausages, cut in half, with the point of a No. 4 hook inserted in the round or unbroken end and pushed well into the sausage, make a good bait. By careful manipulation, the point of the hook can be just exposed through the outer skin; the sausage will then stay on the hook well, and offer a better chance of penetrating a taking fish.

On smaller hooks use smaller baits, for there are other species which take this 'meaty' bait.

SILKWEED

Silkweed, a soft cottonwool-like substance which grows on submerged stone and woodwork, is included in the natural diet of fish, particularly roach and dace. It is a good bait for summer and autumn use when the rivers are running clear.

Silkweed bait can be successfully fished by the free-line style, as well as on more orthodox float tackle.

Soft silkweed should be wrapped as naturally as possible around a hook

Bait the hook by lowering it amongst a thick growth and then drag the hook through it. Sometimes it is easier to gather silkweed by hand and keep it in a water-filled bait tin. Wrap a sufficient quantity around the hook, and if the loose ends are left straggly it will appear more natural. Use hook sizes No. 10 to No. 14. If a larger hook is used, cover it completely.

The soft weed will not stop the hook-point from penetrating when a strike is made.

CRAYFISH

Crayfish are a natural food for the larger species of fish, but they can be found in only a few rivers and streams. Where they can be caught, a drop-net baited with a piece of fish should be tried. Tie the bait securely to the net to prevent the flow of water from washing it away, or the crayfish dragging it off. Lower the baited net into the water until it rests on the bottom, and tie spare line to a peg in the bank. Several nets may be used, and a piece of white cloth tied to each line will help you to find them in the dark.

Leave the nets in position for at least an hour before inspecting them. Then, raise each net quickly, taking care to keep it level. To avoid a nip, pick off the captured crayfish with a forefinger and thumb placed across the back.

The drop-net method is most successful from dusk onwards because the crayfish feed mainly at night.

During daylight hours crayfish are found under large stones and among weed, in fact almost anywhere they can find cover.

They may be kept alive for a day or so in a domestic bath, but the tap must be kept running steadily, and they can be carried in a container holding a quantity of wet moss.

Crayfish that are intended for preserving should be killed, washed and placed in a strong formalin solution (two tablespoons of formalin to one pint of water). After a few days when the solution has become discoloured remove and wash the crayfish in fresh water before adding a fresh, but weaker, solution of formalin in which the baits can be stored until required. Keep the preserved crayfish in a flat container, they lie in a natural position and are thus more attractive to fish. Layers of paper will prevent the crayfish becoming damaged whilst carrying to the river.

Live crayfish make the best bait, either on float or leger tackle, although legering is to be preferred. Use a hook size No. 6 or No. 4, and hook the creature through its tail.

When legering keep the trace between the bait and the weight relatively short, for if given too long a rein the crayfish will move into a weedbed or similar cover.

Crayfish make a particularly good bait for chub.

SHRIMPS

Fresh water shrimps are less than an inch long, and form a normal part of a fish's diet, so are well worth the trouble involved in collecting them. Shrimps are to be found in most rivers and streams, but the soft weeds in the shallows and backwaters are their most likely home. The thick, green weed commonly known as blanket-weed offers them much good cover, and if dragged from the water with a garden fork or rake the shrimps can be collected as they fall out onto the bank.

Keep the shrimps alive in a container that is well padded with their native weed, or in river water, but they should not be overcrowded.

Hook through the crusty shell and leave the point and barb exposed. Whether you bait with one or more is dependent upon the size of the hook.

Most species take this bait, and it is especially attractive if fished along the fringe of a weed bed.

GRUBS

Although caddis grubs are usually thought of as 'food for trout', most freshwater fish devour them eagerly. They can be found amongst weeds and under stones.

At first glance the caddis appears to be a small piece of stick, but movement discloses their identity. If a branch of gorse is sunk in the water for several hours a few caddis grubs should be seen crawling on it when it is withdrawn. However, it may be quicker to search the water for a thick bunch of weed, where a few caddis are almost certain to be found on the fronds and leaves. Stones in shallows often cover a goodly supply of these creatures.

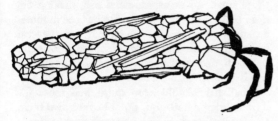

A caddis grub complete with case. To remove it, the closed end should be squeezed to encourage the grub to protrude far enough to be gripped

Leave the grubs in their cases until they are needed for bait (if kept in a fairly large container of water with some weeds on which they can feed, the grubs will live for several days). When required as bait, carry in damp moss.

Before hooking, the grub is removed from its case by squeezing the closed end, and as the grub shows at the other, take hold of it carefully and withdraw. Hooked through the skin of the back, or tail, the caddis attracts most species of fresh water fish.

Beetle grubs or meal worm thrive in flour as used in bakeries and similar establishments, and can be used as bait to catch roach, dace and other like species. Few anglers have the opportunity to collect meal worms but they can be purchased from pet food suppliers. Unfortunately, they are expensive and usually priced by the ounce.

Meal worms resemble caddis grubs without their cases, and may be fished in a similar manner, using one or two on the hook. The meal worm has a hard skin which is an aid to keeping it quite firmly attached to a No. 14 or No. 16 hook.

Blood worms have recently acquired the reputation of being a deadly bait, particularly in match fishing circles. They are very thin and about an inch long and are the larvae of Chironomids, tiny flies and midges. Because of their size it is difficult, if not impossible, to impale one on a hook larger than an 18 or 22. Also, the hook must be extremely sharp.

Bloodworms live in the bottom mud of ponds and rivers and thus are another natural bait.

Gathering these worms is a messy process, but aquarist suppliers sometimes have them for sale in small quantities.

Slugs are used as bait for chub, tench and carp. The small white slugs which are common among bankside vegetation, as well as the much larger black slugs, are especially attractive. They may be used alive on No. 8 and No. 6 hooks.

Swan Mussels can be raked fairly easily from most waters. They lie close in to the bank and with a long-handled garden rake a good supply can be gathered. Use any size mussel, but before it can be used as bait the shell has to be prised open with a strong blade of a knife. Remove the fleshy portion from the shell, and use it on a large hook, possibly a No. 6. Mussel bait is not usually worried by small fish. Some mussels may be chopped and loose cast as ground bait.

Wood lice are an efficient bait for roach and dace, and can be kept alive for a long period in a bait tin packed with moss. Use small hooks, e.g. Nos. 12 to 16, and fish this bait on float tackle.

Wherever there are overhanging bushes and trees, you may be sure that many insects fall into the water. These swims can be very rewarding to the angler who presents a natural bait by dapping. This is a particularly good method for taking chub. Grasshoppers, caterpillar, moths and beetles are just a few of the many creatures that can be used.

These natural baits are sometimes difficult to obtain, but they can be imitated with silk and feather, and plastic artificials are always worth carrying.

Wasp grubs are a soft and juicy delicacy to many fish, and are larger than blow-fly maggots. Being very soft they have to be handled with extreme care, and the hook must be extremely sharp if the bait is not to burst. Some tackle shops do sell wasp grubs, although this is exceptional and generally speaking the angler must collect them for himself.

Wasps construct an underground nest and the normal course is for the collector to pour a solution of cyanide of potassium into the entrance. The nest is then dug out, all the grubs removed from the cells and placed into a tin containing bran.

To toughen the grubs, the complete nest can be put into a large saucepan and boiled, or alternatively, the grubs may be removed from the nest and baked in an oven. After this treatment the skins should be tough enough to stand up to casting or the pull of really fast water.

Roach, dace, chub and grayling accept this bait quite readily.

Greaves, the fatty refuse from tallow candle manufacture, was once used most successfully for barbel, chub and bream, but to-day it is a scarce and rarely used bait.

Pith from a bullock's spine can be skinned, washed and cut into baits that will suit the size of hook being used. Bullock brains, when boiled and mashed, are excellent ground bait, but are not of a suitable consistency for hook bait.

FISH

Minnows and many other small fish are used as live or dead baits when fishing for pike, perch and chub. Minnows are often considered the most important bait fish because they form a basic natural food for bigger fish. Some waters contain huge shoals of minnows, which when fully grown are about 3 in long. They can be caught in a minnow trap baited with bread.

Two types of trap can be used. A celluloid one purchased from a tackle dealer, or a clear glass wine bottle with a funnel-shaped base can be used. A hole is punched in the base to make an entry for the minnows to reach the bait, and the cork hole is covered with a cloth or muslin. Tie a length of string to the baited trap and lower it gently to the bed of the stream, with the funnel opening pointing up or downstream.

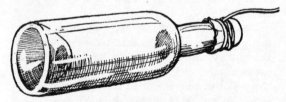

A useful minnow trap bottle, with a funnel-shaped base, rests on its side on the river bed

A live minnow bait can be fished either on leger or float tackle.

When legering hook the minnow through the top lip, but when trotting the bait on float tackle slip the hook through the base of the dorsal fin.

Remember to pass the hook through the top lip only; if both lips are caught on the hook the bait is prevented from breathing correctly and will therefore soon die.

Other useful bait fish are gudgeon, bleak, loach, small dace, roach and rudd. As small perch are preyed upon by the big perch, a small one makes an excellent live bait for its larger relations!

Gudgeon are excellent live bait, and bleak, those small, silvery sprat-sized fish, make a fine dead bait for eels. They can also be used mounted on spinning tackle, for which purpose they can be used fresh or after being preserved in formalin.

Roach, dace and small rudd are mostly used as live bait for pike.

Small fish should keep quite well for a few days in a large bath, but do not overcrowd them, and if possible maintain a flow of fresh water.

Although expensive, goldfish bought from a pet shop can be used for spinning or live baiting. The brilliant colour of the goldfish makes it a very attractive bait.

Both sprat and herring are used as bait by the coarse angler, and every season hundreds of pike and large eels are taken on them. Sprats can be mounted and used as a spinning bait for pike, or legered for eels. For pike spinning mount the sprat on a tackle fitted with a body pin which is inserted right into the mouth of the fish. Secure the treble hooks to the sides of the sprat with several turns of thread.

Herrings are best used on either leger or sink-and-draw tackles.

To give sprats and bleak an attractive golden look, add a small amount of powdered acriflavine to fish that are stored in formalin. To dye fresh-caught fish first remove the scales, and then immerse it in a household brand of yellow-tint dye. When coloured sufficiently, rinse in fresh water.

Preserved fish baits will keep in good condition for months, and as natural baits are often not available when most needed, it pays to 'bottle' a few during the summer. Once caught, minnows should be killed at the waterside and kept straight while carrying them home. Wash them thoroughly and place in a preserving solution of one tablespoon of formalin to one pint of water.

After a few days remove the fish and rinse in clean water before re-bottling in a fresh, but slightly weaker solution. Add glycerine to this final mixture to keep the baits pliable. If preferred, the baits may be preserved in glycerine only.

Insert the baits head first into the jars, to

prevent them sagging and bending. Remember to grease the thread to prevent the lid from corroding.

Wash the baits thoroughly before using to remove the formalin taint, and dip in pilchard oil to enhance their appearance.

A mixed supply of bait fishes which is to be preserved should be sorted into size groups, and bottled accordingly.

GROUND BAIT

Ground bait is used to attract and hold fish in the swim. Its use is essential on many waters if a good bag of fish is to be taken.

Bread forms the basis of most ground bait mixtures, the consistency of which depends largely upon the type of water being fished. Fast flowing rivers and streams indicate the use of a ground bait that sinks quickly to the bottom, while in a slow stream a cloud bait is often best.

Ground bait can be prepared by soaking stale bread in water, draining, and kneading the mixture into a pulp. To dry off and create a substance that can be formed into small balls, butchers' rusk or similar dry crumb can be added.

In a fast stream ground bait may travel a long way before reaching the bottom, so judge the strength of the current and put the bait in as far upstream as is necessary to get it to the river bed where your hook bait is lying. When the river is deep and fast-flowing, mix the bread with bran, chicken meal or mashed potatoes. This will give it added weight to get it down to the bottom. When maggots are being used as a hook bait add a few to the ground bait.

Cloud ground bait is made from bread which has been dried in an oven or a warm room. The dry, crisp slices are ground into a fine powder which is dampened at the waterside and squeezed into small balls. Once in the river it will cloud the water as it sinks. To increase the cloud effect mix the bait with milk. Cloud bait is most effective in slow-flowing rivers, and it is a useful ground bait to use in conjunction with loose cast feeder maggots.

Chopped worms and even small pieces of liver can be added to a heavy mix of pulped bread, bran and chicken meal. When fishing the turbulent waters in a weir pool one might try moulding clay from the bank into a cup and filling it with maggots or worms. After closing the top with a flat piece of clay, cast into the pool where the water will soon break it up and release the enticing contents.

A shoal of feeding bream, or barbel, will consume an enormous amount of worms, maggots and the various ground bait mixtures. For this reason ground baiting was done in the past on a grand scale, with anything up to four or five thousand lobworms being tipped into a swim for several days before a fishing trip. Such large-scale ground baiting is virtually impossible these days. Nevertheless, without ground baiting, big catches of bream can hardly be expected. A bucketful of bread, chicken meal, bran, boiled potatoes, crushed wheat, or biscuits, etc. is the minimum amount required for a day's good sport, and in this mixture samples of the hook bait should be included.

The various dyes which are used for colouring maggots may also be used for colouring ground bait and should be added during mixing. Oil flavourings such as oil of rhodium, aniseed, or verbena may be added (but there is much disagreement as to their efficiency).

The correct presentation of both hook and ground bait is an art which once mastered will bring great rewards, not only in the number of fish caught, but through the sense of satisfaction which comes through mastery of a craft.

EDITOR'S NOTE: From the opening of the 1972/73 coarse-fishing season, maggots became a prohibited bait on the Royalty Fishery on the River Avon at Christchurch, in Hampshire.

SPECIES

BARBEL

by

PETER STONE

Of all coarse fish none excites me more than barbel. The first one fell to my rod when I was a boy and now, many hundreds of barbel later, even a small one still fills me with the excitement I first knew all those years ago.

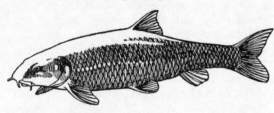

Unfortunately, these fish are not very widely distributed, and so few have the opportunity of really concentrating on their capture, but for all that if you know what you are doing they are not too difficult to hook. However, the specialist inevitably catches the greatest number, for to be consistently successful, one must concentrate upon barbel to the exclusion of all other species.

It is not generally realised that although barbel may inhabit a particular stretch of river they may only feed in one very confined area, a fact confirmed by experience. For example, I have located a shoal of barbel in a reach which was completely uniform in character, but quickly learned that the bait had to be placed accurately for they appeared to feed in a particular area, no more than a square yard – and this has been confirmed in other rivers that I fish. On one occasion on which I went fishing I found the swim which I would have chosen already occupied by an angler who was casting to the exact spot. He hooked four fish while my bait remained untouched. Eventually I was able to cast into their feeding area, and within minutes had a five pounder on the bank. This story indicates the importance of accurate casting.

Barbel are found over various types of river

beds, and the adage that they feed only over gravel is not in my opinion wholly true. In one reach of the Thames the bottom is so littered that to move the bait only a few feet results in the hook becoming snagged – yet this is one of the finest barbel areas that I know.

Barbel often congregate in weirpools to recover from spawning, and although some remain there throughout the year, many others search for quieter water. In my opinion weirpools are over-rated; most – if not all – of my best fish have been taken well away from the weirs, often in completely slack water.

Large beds of lily or streamer weed are two areas that can usually be expected to harbour barbel; places where underwater roots claw their way out of clay banks, and boulder strewn river beds, make good holding areas. But one feature must always be present; a good supply of food.

Barbel frequently give away their presence by rolling on the surface or even leaping clear of the water. These are the signs by which I know that I am fishing a swim which contains these fish, as often this is a far more reliable guide to a 'barbel swim' than what is sometimes called a 'known swim'.

When a barbel rolls, all you are likely to see is its big red tail as it waves idly in the air for a moment or two before the fish goes down. However, when it leaps, it is as if all the demons of the river are trying to grasp its tail, the water erupts as the fish claws skywards, but its tail is hardly clear of the water before it slumps back like a spent rocket. I have seen barbel behave like this during most summer months, but it is most likely to be seen in June and July, and especially so if the weather is very warm.

There are many opinions regarding the times that barbel feed. In my experience it depends to a large extent upon the river. For example, on one particular reach of the Kennet, an area which I know extremely well, the most profitable period is the hour before dark, but sometimes during overcast days the afternoon will also provide good sport. On this river I cannot recollect ever catching a barbel in the period from dawn to breakfast. However, there are many other waters on which the mornings have proved most productive.

During one recent season I regularly caught barbel from a swim in the hour before sunset, and where dawn too was a good period. Yet some three miles away, and still on the same river, there was a swim which yielded fish during the early post meridian hours, but all other times was far less productive. Therefore, one should remember that conditions which apply to one river may not necessarily apply to another, and that even the various reaches of the same river have different characteristics. The time at which the fish feed may last for a comparatively short period or may extend for several hours. Time of year and often purely local weather conditions can play such an important part in deciding 'zero hour'.

Fortunately, barbel accept a wide variety of baits; even so, what is a killing bait on one water may be far less effective on another. One bait that has made an impact by its attraction to barbel is sausage. This can be either in the form of a paste made with bread and sausage meat, or on occasion a whole sausage. It is several years now since I first heard about sausage, and in recent times it has become not only a well-established bait for barbel but it frequently lures other species.

In the chapter dealing with bait there is much good advice regarding the preparation of sausage and sausage meat for use as a hook bait. Here I will do no more than explain my own method for preparation and use.

I always boil the sausage for I have found that at times the fat will cause the bait to float. However, when I use sausage meat the bread or rusk stiffens it and it then makes an extremely good hook bait. Although the sausage paste is an excellent bait, I have found that in waters where there are many small fish they tend to worry the paste and in so doing reduce it to an insignificant size, finally stripping the hook of bait. To overcome this problem I use either a whole sausage or a part of one. When using a whole sausage I always remove the skin from the small area where the hook protrudes slightly.

Lobworms, brandlings, cheese, bread, maggot and small fish are all excellent baits, and during the early part of the season my experience has been that small fish are often the most attractive. There is one other bait which must be mentioned, although it has been the centre of a controversy on one of our premier fisheries. The bait is hemp. That hemp has taken a lot of barbel is a fact that cannot be denied, and to some extent a certain mystique has surrounded the use of this grain. It is utter nonsense to suggest that it is in any way a drug; it is merely a grain that fish find palatable. In my opinion the big danger that hemp fishing brings in its wake is that any water which is subjected to continuous and heavy ground baiting with it soon becomes a water in which the fish are difficult to tempt to any other bait. My own preference is for the more conventional baits.

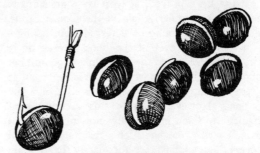

A grain of hemp on a No. 6 hook. The seed has been cooked until it has just split

Barbel are quickly educated to accept a bait that they see regularly; thus it is inevitable that certain baits will appear to be more successful than others.

In days gone by our forefathers carried out vast ground baiting schemes before fishing for barbel. To-day there are far too many anglers to make preparations of this kind worthwhile, for it is more than likely that the ground bait that you put in would do no more than serve as an attractor for a nearby fisherman.

The tackle and tactics used for barbel fishing are to a large extent decided for you by the type of swim you intend to fish. First, ask yourself how fine, or in other words how light, can you fish. Take into consideration all the relevant details, for example the average size of fish in the water, the possible snags around which the fish can take your line, or whether an area is relatively free from obstruction. If you consider that an 8 lb b.s. line is necessary to cope with the situation, then use one, but if you think that you can use a 5 lb b.s. line with equal success, then choose the lighter.

There is, I think, very little doubt that barbel are suspicious of heavy lines – a conclusion reached after some twenty years of angling for this particular species. Generally speaking, I choose a 6 lb b.s. line, and only in very exceptional circumstances would I go to a line having a breaking strain of less than 5 lb.

Regarding hooks, the main point to remember is choose one of a size that matches the bait. For example, I would suggest a No. 6 for lobworm, a No. 8 for brandlings, and when fishing large pieces of sausage or cheese, a No. 4 should be adequate. If maggots are the chosen bait, then sizes 10 and 12 will accept three or four of these creatures and not be overloaded.

It has been proved, at least by a great many anglers who regularly fish on the Dorset Stour, that barbel are not to be deterred from taking a bait they fancy even if the hook is excessively large when related to the bait. On a large number of occasions I have known them to accept a single grain of hemp which has been presented on a No. 6 hook. However, despite this seeming contradiction, I am still firmly convinced that in overall terms one has better results if the bait covers the hook far more adequately than a grain of hemp would a No. 6. But always remember not to mask the hook point with a material that would prevent the tip and barb from penetrating the fish's mouth.

The rod on which the angler must depend is extremely important, but with the vast majority of British manufacturers producing equipment which is second to none, there is inevitably a very wide choice. I would recommend that any rod used for barbel fishing must have a really efficient all-through action. In my opinion a tip action rod is absolutely unsuitable.

The method which the angler finally chooses, i.e. legering or float fishing, will almost be decided for him by the nature of the swim.

Some of the areas which I fish are virtually no more than small spaces between weed beds, and here I would choose leger tackle with just sufficient lead weight to hold my bait in position. Under these conditions I would hold my rod high with the line taut between rod tip and lead, the bites being registered on the rod tip.

Where the fish are lying downstream of a boulder or similar underwater obstruction then one successful method is as follows: position yourself approximately ten yards upstream of the mark to be fished and set the lead so that there is about three feet of trail. Cast slightly upstream and away from the boulder, so that the current brings the weight to rest against it and the long trail swinging round behind it. When fishing in this manner strike at the first indication of a bite.

Weed beds offer a really stimulating challenge to the angler, and here again I have found the leger method to be most efficient. The angler should position himself well downstream of the weed, and cast to the clear water alongside it. If there is a channel running through the centre of the bed, then this may also be fished in the following manner: simple leger tackle with an Arlesey bomb weight and a trail of approximately three feet should be cast into the clear run, and the rod should again be held high so that as little line as possible is in the water. By tightening the line the bait can be moved slightly, in fact the current will frequently do this without help from the angler. When the barbel picks up the bait it will inevitably move the lead, this will result in the line falling slack. When this happens, strike immediately. Experience will soon teach you the difference between bait movement caused by current or by a fish taking it. Upstream legering for barbel is usually successful in most rivers.

Where the river bed is more open, then legering in the normal manner, downstream and across, is the method to choose. The amount of weight that is used should be just sufficient to hold bottom, but not so much that the current is unable to move it. In other words, as the weight settles downstream and across from where the angler is casting, so the current should be able to move the bait across the river bed to end up under the bank on the same side as the angler.

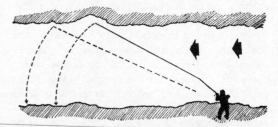

Rolling a leger. The cast is made towards the far bank, then allowed to roll under the angler's own bank. Subsequent casts are made slightly lower downstream, until the fish are found

The rod is held well up and the landing net is slipped under the fish (in this case a bream). In the centre of the picture another fish is fighting and in the far background yet another bream has just taken the bait and is being 'struck'.

A fine carp taken by Eric Taylor.

Peter Stone with a catch of 120 lb of bream.

Photo: Peter Ston

There were 40 lb of bream, weighing up to 4 lb each in the net being re-positioned and the angler in our picture made sure that they were comfortable before he put another bream into his second net.

The boat in this picture is anchored well away from the bank where the other fishermen are enjoying their sport. Boat anglers have the advantage of greater mobility.

Each cast should be sent just slightly further downstream so that the whole of the river bed is searched for fish, and once the barbel are located then continue casting to the same spot.

When fishing in this manner I prefer to hold the rod and I would strike at any bite that moved the rod top confidently, if only a little.

During June and July I have often found that a lip-hooked minnow, which can be either dead or alive, is a particularly deadly bait when presented on float tackle. Use a No. 8 hook which is slipped through the top lip, and about a foot above the bait add one or two swan shot (the exact number is dependent upon the current). The float, a piece of ordinary cork about an inch in diameter is threaded on to the line and held in position with a piece of stick. The distance between cork and bait should be equal to the depth of the water and

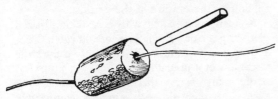

Cork float – a rough piece of cork plugged with a stick

the bait should trail along the bottom. This method is particularly effective when fishing in weir pools or in the fast glides close to the bank or alongside weed beds. When the fish takes, the cork will react by either appearing to bounce along the surface or will just disappear. In either event, strike immediately and firmly.

Long trotting is a well-established method by which barbel are taken, particularly on rivers such as the Avon. I would choose a fluted float, one which carries two or possibly three swan shot, which I would bunch approximately two feet up from the bait.

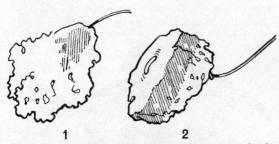

1   2

Baits. 1. A piece of flake pinched lightly onto a hook shank. 2. Crust. The hook is passed through the crumb, out of the crust and then back through the crumb

Maggot, crust and flake are all effective, but when using crust I would make an adjustment to the positioning of my shot. Crust will tend to lift as it is buoyant and I would therefore bring my weight down to within a few inches of the hook. Remember, whichever bait you use, to continually loose cast a few pieces into the swim to attract the fish, and always make sure that the line is kept under strict control (as little as possible lying on the water, and that floating).

The 'stret-pegging' method can be used when fishing an open stretch of water which might be immediately behind a weed bed. You will find that occasionally barbel drop back from under the weed and if a bait were fished in this manner right in their path, then it might prove attractive.

Set the float so that it lies at half-cock and hold the float back very close to the weed. On one occasion I caught nine barbel in this manner, and every time a fish took, the bite was extremely sharp, the float dipping out of sight. All these fish were taken on maggot bait, a few of which I introduced at intervals via a bait dropper.

Despite the fact that barbel are an extremely active fish and when hooked will frequently display great sporting tendencies, do not be lured into thinking that the indication of a bite will be violent, indeed nothing could be further from the truth.

Waiting for the rod tip to be snatched into a violent arc is not the recommended method. Frequently the most insignificant-looking indication will, if struck, result in a good-sized barbel being hooked. Learning to differentiate between the various rod tip movements is something which cannot be achieved by reading; time and experience are the best tutors.

Barbel will occasionally pick up a bait, turn and swim downstream to take up a position at the rear of the shoal. When this happens, that enormously exciting flexing of the rod tip is a joy to behold, but when the fish merely mouths the bait and then lies in the same position the only indication is a tremble on the rod tip which is accompanied by what can only be described as a sandpapering sensation on the line – in fact many of my friends term this a 'sandpaper bite'. With experience you will find that you rarely miss one.

Sometimes the rod will ease gently forward; possibly only two inches, and often less than that. It may give a sharp 'knock', which seconds later is followed by a pull of anything between six feet and six inches. The rod may 'kick back', or it may pull forward slowly but confidently; all these are indications of good barbel bites.

Earlier in this chapter I mentioned the difficulty that can be experienced by anglers when smaller species attack the bait. One of the worst offenders is the dace. These can give a sharp reaction on rod tip, and a shoal of small to medium-sized dace can drive one almost to distraction, with their continual 'knock', 'knock',

'knock'. Even so, strike at these indications, for barbel too will produce these 'knocks' and barbel and dace often share the same swim.

Barbel are fish which offer a great challenge, for not only are they a hard-fighting species but they are one which seems to possess a highly-developed sense of cunning. I am sure that once you have caught your first one you will be well and truly 'hooked', and you will tend to seek them whenever and wherever possible.

BLEAK

Most English rivers and streams hold bleak in varying quantities. By disposition it is a gregarious creature, spending its life in shoals that are often seen close to the surface, just downstream of a bridge support. They will wander, seemingly aimlessly, through the shallows of a river but at the slightest sign of danger they will flash as one into deeper water, their bright silver flanks and greenish backs disappearing like ghosts into the depths.

The bleak is not a species which is actively

hunted by the sport fishermen, although small boys frequently absorb some of the charms of angling by the capture of these fish.

A small hook baited with a matchhead-sized piece of paste or a single maggot will catch them, and as live bait they will frequently attract the attentions of a predator.

In many ways these fish resemble the dace, but they do not attain a comparable size – a bleak of 2 oz can be considered a fair weight.

BREAM

by

PETER STONE

Bream are one of the most heavily fished species, and this is certainly true so far as the match-angling fraternity are concerned. However bream have their critics – some say they lack fight and others point to the thick coating of slime which these fish possess. In my opinion bream, particularly those from a river such as the Thames, can and do fight well. I will admit that many still water bream are lethargic, but I have also taken many pike from lakes and pits that have offered only token resistance. Hundreds of the bream which I have caught have fought as hard as any tench, and I well remember one particular shoal which provided fish which fought as hard as any barbel of equal weight. My

experience has been that it depends to a large extent where you catch them.

I fully admit too that bream are slimy creatures, but then so on occasion are roach and tench – the slime from the latter gets everywhere, nets,

hands and clothes are smothered, yet no-one considers this a drawback when discussing tench.

One of the delights of bream fishing is that a feeding shoal can provide you with a hundred-weight of fish, and on many occasions I have had some really wonderful days of sport. There have also been many, many blank days, but this is bream fishing.

Blank days or occasions when the fish are shy and difficult to tempt I accept as a very great challenge. It could well be that my technique and/or bait needs changing, or it could be that the fish have reacted to weather conditions in such a manner that no matter what you do they will just refuse to take.

Basically there are two methods which I use for bream fishing, legering and float fishing. Both are effective but if one is used in the wrong place at the wrong time then all your efforts will be wasted.

To illustrate the two methods of fishing and locations and times best suited, I will describe two separate adventures.

Weather has a considerable influence on bream fishing, as indeed it does with most forms of angling. On this particular occasion dawn had not long broken and the sky was overcast, and a warm breeze ruffled the surface. An ideal weather combination. Had the sky been very clear, so that shortly after dawn a bright sun would have glared on the surface, then I feel that my chances of success would have been greatly diminished.

The first job was to find the fish, and so not knowing just where they would be feeding, I made for a section where there was plenty of underwater growth, and lilies in particular. Even if they were not feeding there, I felt very confident that a shoal would not be far away.

This was a swim where I felt that legering would bring most results. At this point the river is about 70 yd wide, the majority of the weed growth way out in midstream; with an upstream wind ruffling the water, float fishing would have been extremely difficult.

My leger rod had a very fine tip, for it is in the tip that much of the success in this type of fishing lies. I rarely use a swim feeder or a bite indicator; my preference is for the hand-held rod, and by holding the line between thumb and forefinger in a loop which has been drawn downwards between the reel and first ring, a bite can be instantly detected and struck. While there

are occasions when bream will bite so freely that the rod tip is whipped round in a half-circle, it is more usual for them to display a more timid approach, the rod tip or line moving no more than an inch or so. Under these conditions a 5 or 6 lb b.s. line would be ideal, for not only could there be 4 or 5 lb bream in the swim, but the profusion of underwater growth added many hazards. Remember, to hold a feeding shoal, one must remove each hooked fish speedily and efficiently.

For a weight I chose a sliding link on to which two swan shot had been pressed. This method, which is really quite simple, consists of a split ring to which a 4 in length of nylon is tied, the shot being pressed on to the 4 in length. The main line is passed through the split ring and by adding a split shot to the main line the split ring can be stopped from running down to the hook.

This is a method which I have used since about 1950, and one of its biggest attractions is the fact that additional weight can be added to the link or removed from it, very easily. It is not necessary to unship your terminal tackle to change weights.

The link was stopped approximately 15 in from the hook, which in this case was a No. 10 baited with two brandlings. Although brandlings are my favourite bream bait, they are not always as successful as I would like them to be. Therefore, lobworms, paste and a loaf of bread were in the tackle basket.

The ground bait, a mixture of sausage rusk and bread crumbs, was quickly mixed and three heavy balls about the size of bread rolls were soon despatched into mid-stream. My theory regarding ground baiting is quite simple: a fairly steady supply and all into one spot. Haphazard ground baiting can completely ruin your sport. For despite the fact that a shoal of bream may number several hundred, they usually feed in a fairly concentrated area. A reasonably heavy concentration of a fairly stiff mixture in a relatively confined area helps to keep the bream well shoaled, and by casting to the ground baited area one should take fish fairly regularly.

On this occasion my first cast was accurately placed, and within seconds of the bait hitting bottom and the line being tightened, the rod tip flicked round some two inches, I struck and the fish was 'on'. I kept the rod well up, drew the fish away from the shoal, played it out, and it was soon in the keep net.

Almost before I could re-bait and cast again, a bream swirled and rolled on the surface over the area which I was ground baiting. Another ball of feed was cast in, followed immediately by a hook baited with two lively brandlings.

It wasn't long before the rod top moved again, but on this occasion my strike failed to hook the fish. This happened several times, so I realised that a change of bait was called for. I believe that occasionally bream will become suspicious of a certain bait, and when this happens they will be extremely wary and only mouth rather than take. When this occurs, ring the changes. On this occasion I changed to a soft paste.

Within a minute of the bait striking bottom, another fish was 'on'. As soon as it was in the keep net, it was time for more ground bait, and another cast to again exactly the same spot. I have found that on many occasions it is the smaller fish, for example the two and three-pounders, which feed more freely at the beginning of a good spell of bream fishing. Frequently the bigger fish are preceded by a distinct lull in the sport. And so it was on this occasion. After a lull of almost ten minutes a five-pounder took the bait.

As soon as the larger fish begin to come, feed slightly more heavily. On this particular day I introduced one large handful after each fish was caught. If the shoal is not taking as quickly as they sometimes can, then I would put in a similar amount every three to five minutes. I do not believe that ground bait will hold the shoal, it merely ensures that they will feed in a particular spot, but to encourage them to do this, one must ground bait accurately.

When fishing with a companion, there are several points which I consider of great importance, and of these, priority must be given to ground baiting. I think that it is a mistake for two separate anglers to ground bait two separate spots, for this will tend to disperse the feeding fish. It is much better for them to come together and share the same swim and fish one patch. I cannot repeat too often how important it is that ground bait should be concentrated in a relatively small area. Once it is in the water, the current will tend to spread it, and the disturbance caused by the feeding fish will move it even more.

Two anglers fishing side by side can present certain problems, and probably the biggest of these is having sufficient room to strike. I have found that just so long as you are separated by a distance which will allow your rod tip to miss your companion's head by about a foot, the remaining difficulties are insignificant. You can both cast into the same swim, and providing there is a little give-and-take, both can fish quite happily, and there are not nearly as many tangles as one might imagine.

On this golden day I used 30 lb of dry ground bait in four hours of almost continuous sport, but at the end of this period the shoal had decided to move, and for the following hour only a very occasional fish was landed.

Eventually the catch was weighed and photographed and it totalled 146 lb. I do not claim credit for this whole catch, as for most of the time my swim was being shared by a very old friend, but the tactics we adopted were identical.

This catch confirmed several things that I already knew. The importance of ground baiting was once more underlined – I am firmly convinced that without ground bait the chances of making a really substantial catch are considerably reduced. I know only too well that one can never carry enough ground bait to hold a shoal of feeding bream, nevertheless one can carry quite an amount, and if it is carried dry and mixed by the river this gives the angler an advantage. And remember what you don't use you can always take home.

The second point which emerges concerns bait. Never be afraid to change from worm to paste, or vice versa, or for that matter to any other suitable bait, when the fish seem to go off feed.

My third point concerns the actual strike. Unless lobworms are being used, strike at the first indication of a bite. Sometimes you will miss, and if you continually miss the fish then wait a little longer. But at the outset strike on the first knock.

Golden days seldom come, but I have sometimes known what has started as a really black one suddenly turn silver and finally end on a high golden note.

Frequently fortune is more easily reversed than the angler may imagine, the point being that if the fish are there and they are feeding, it is up to the angler to present his bait in a manner which attracts them. If, however, the angler persists in legering a static bait, when for some delicious whim known only to themselves the bream have decided that they will feed higher in the water, then the angler can only blame himself if he fails to change his tactics.

I well remember one particular occasion when after a morning's fishing I had not even seen one roll on the surface, let alone hooked one, I joined up with a friend after lunch and we decided that we would leger a swim where several days previously I had taken a good bag. The afternoon was boiling hot, and completely airless.

After half an hour without a bite I decided to move a few yards upstream. If possible keep doing this until sport improves. I moved some ten yards and fished each swim for approximately half an hour. After four moves I had a bite but it came whilst I was waiting for the line to sink. The line which was still mostly on the surface began to move towards me. I struck and missed, and virtually the same thing happened on the following cast. I decided that a change in tactics was long overdue.

This indication, a fairly common one, has in the past led me to believe that bream were feeding some distance off the bottom, and were intercepting the bait as it sank through the water. This meant that I must change to float tackle.

The fish were feeding about twenty yards out, this allied to the fact that I wished to see the float very clearly dictated that I selected one with a stout tip which would carry one swan shot plus one B.B. shot. These were clipped to the line 15 in. from the No. 10 hook. I set the float so that when the bait was cast in, it would just touch the bottom, although I was more than certain that a bite would be indicated long before the bait reached the river bed.

On the first cast the float travelled no more than a few inches when it sank. Slowly and sedately it slid away – the result was a four-pounder. The following cast produced a similar indication and a slightly larger fish.

My companion by this time had joined me, and sitting no more than two yards apart we began to share some really excellent sport. For two hours fish followed fish, but there was very little pattern to the way in which the float moved to indicate a bite. Sometimes it would sink slowly from view, and then it would behave with

an odd little jig. There were occasions when it would travel downstream for a foot or so slightly faster than the current. And then there were those maddening times when the float did no more than lift slightly or possibly hold back for just a second. All in all the fish were behaving in a capricious manner, but by taking advantage of a change in tactics and by using a float which I could see most clearly and thus strike at the most opportune moment, a day which could have been blank was turned into one I shall long remember.

Throughout this two-hour period we both used brandlings, and once a bite was seen we both allowed two or three seconds before striking. Occasionally a fish was lost, but not often. The total bag weighed 90 lb, with the best fish a shade under 6 lb.

Only comparatively recently have anglers seriously fished for bream during the winter months. Our forefathers and angling writers of the day believed that bream overwintered in the slacker parts of the river and in eddies. This is not strictly true, in fact on occasions it can be far from correct. Broadly speaking, during the winter months bream can be found in many areas and types of swim varying from weirpools and lock-cuttings to the swims which harboured lilies during the summer; they may be lying in holes where the water 'boils' gently, and in gravelly runs alongside dead rushes. They can be found almost anywhere, some of the swims which I have found most productive have been the most unlikely-looking ones of the lot.

However, in time of flood, when a torrent of highly-coloured water surges down the river, the bream, in company with most other coarse fish, will seek calmer water. Lock cuttings, particularly on the downstream side of the lock, frequently harbour large stocks of fish when the main river is in flood. However, I do know at least two swims which are in the main river on a completely straight stretch which during the summer months are no more than 18 in. in depth, and which do not hold fish until the winter floods raise the level; then vast numbers of bream are to be caught there.

During the winter months bream tend to forget their roaming habits and are more likely to take up residence in particular swims. Despite the fact that they may not always be ready to accept a baited hook, once a shoal takes up its winter position it will normally remain there (except for floods, etc.) until the end of the season.

When bream fishing in winter my preference is for float fishing. But here I must explain that my methods are adjusted to suit the particular rivers I fish. Elsewhere in the country, paternostering and legering tactics are most successful, but as I said earlier in this chapter the methods that you use must be suitable to the place you are fishing. Two waters seldom react in a similar manner to any given set of circumstances, there are usually differences – perhaps merely an alteration in bait or the depth at which the fish are feeding.

I have found that the rivers I fish during the winter months tend to react more favourably to float-fishing techniques than to leger tactics. And of all the float techniques, 'stret-pegging' is my favourite method. For this I use a 12 ft rod, allied to a 5 lb b.s. line. Although I use as little weight as possible, I am not a light-tackle fanatic. To fish in this manner one must present the bait in as natural a manner as possible, therefore choose a float and a weight which, when the line is taut from float to rod tip, will remain in position but will move quite dramatically when the bait is taken. To achieve this, I adjust the float so that the distance between weight and float is approximately 12 in more than the actual depth. When the tackle has been cast in, hold the float back against the stream with the line taut to the rod tip. If you want the bait to roll towards the bank, then lift the rod slightly.

Bites are detected relatively simply: the float will normally either travel towards midstream, sinking as it goes, or it will dip quite sharply. If using brandlings, allow a few seconds before striking, but with other baits strike immediately.

Good catches are always possible during the winter months, but I have found that they tend to be more the exception than the rule, and I have also found that even a moderate-sized bag may take some time to compile, as the fish seem to come more slowly throughout a longer period, rather than in a fast and furious short spell. Despite this, however, it is essential to keep a supply of ground bait going continuously through the swim, although this need not be quite so heavily done as through the summer.

When large shoals of bream have been driven into fairly confined quarters by flood conditions, they can always be found reasonably simply. But

having found them, hooking them can be decidedly difficult. With perseverance a few will usually be caught, and it often happens that when the fish are herded together the bigger ones will be the first to the bait.

Eddies that contain too much movement are extremely difficult to fish. I have a feeling that there are frequently good fish lying in these quarters but getting at them is particularly difficult.

On one occasion when I attempted to fish an eddy which had a really disturbed or 'boiling' surface I used a 12 ft rod, a 5 lb b.s. line, one of Peter Drennan's special floats, which carried two swan shot nipped on to a sliding link and stopped 12 in from a No. 10 hook tied directly to the main line. I fished close to the rushes, right over the spot where I had previously placed a handful of a heavy mix of ground bait.

On the hook there were two brandlings and the float was set so that it fished at half-cock.

It was half an hour before the float dipped, righted itself and then slowly disappeared. After a short but very determined fight, a 5 lb 2 oz bream was lifted from the water.

I placed another handful of ground bait and once again the hook baited with brandlings was lowered into the water. During the waiting period the 'boil' would occasionally increase and then the float was pulled out of position. This meant re-casting, for the bait had to be in the correct position.

Suddenly the float moved out towards the main current and began to sink slowly, I struck and missed, and on the hook there was about half-inch of brandling. In these conditions and when using worm as bait one must give them plenty of time to take.

I ended this particular spell of fishing with seven fish, two over 5 lb, and the remainder between 1 and 2 lb. This was for me a rather typical winter day's sport, just a few fish, but included were a couple of really good ones.

In winter, as in summer, never be afraid to change baits. Maggots of many colours can be tried, and of course bread flake, bread cube or crust. By ringing the changes, your chances of a fair bag of fish can be greatly enhanced. Occasions do arise, when fishing disturbed water, when better results are obtained if the float is allowed to carry the bait round and round the eddy with the baited hook a few inches off the bottom. When fishing this method I would suggest that several feet of line are allowed to lie on the surface of the water, so that the terminal tackle can be carried at an even speed by the current. But make sure that although there are several feet of line lying loose on the surface, you can very quickly pick it up as you strike.

Always watch your float most carefully – a bite may be signalled by its rapid disappearance, or possibly no more than a slight lift. This is a first-class method of fishing, but conditions must be about right, 'boiling' very gently and the water reasonably warm; in other words, not at a time when large quantities of snow water have suddenly rushed into the river.

Over the years I have spent many happy hours hunting the bream. Sometimes the bag has been just a few pounds, and on other occasions nothing at all. But every so often there is a golden day, when a 100 lb or more of these challenging fish fill my keep net. On days like this I have felt that all the time spent in careful observation and in developing my own special technique has been more than worthwhile.

CARP

by

ERIC J. TAYLOR

Carp have fired the imagination of anglers for centuries, and there is no other freshwater fish that grows with such rapidity when introduced into enclosed waters of almost any size.

Small carp, e.g. 4- to 5-inch fish, can be purchased from reputable fish farms for about £20 per 100, and although carriage may be extra, the cost is still low enough to enable clubs to restock where carp do not breed naturally.

They will only breed in waters that are eminently suitable for this purpose, and in my experience one of the greatest hazards to successful breeding is the presence of other fish, especially perch, as they consume large quantities of spawn as soon as it is shed.

My preference is for a lake containing both deep and shallow sections, with the deeper parts not exceeding much over 12 ft and the shallows being of a greater, or at any rate equal, surface area to that of the deep section.

In such a water, especially if no natural breeding or possibly only very spasmodic spawnings take place, carp will grow at a fantastic rate, always assuming that there is an abundant food supply.

A winter stocking with small fingerling carp in a water which is well known to me found the same fish making 4 to 5 lb in about 18 months, although this growth rate dropped somewhat after 12 to 15 lb had been reached. These same carp are now well into the 20 lb class and a few exceptional fish turn the scales at 30 lb and more. A significant fact is that a subsequent re-stocking of small yearlings failed to reach anything like the growth rate of the original stock.

For the dedicated carp angler the introduction of small carp to a water that already holds large carp can be something of a mixed blessing, for the small fish are more inclined to take a bait, especially if they have never been hooked, and this fact considerably reduces the chances of taking one of the larger fish.

Much has been written in the past about the difficulties of inducing carp to take a bait, and this problem of suitable bait is something that takes pre-eminence with all carp anglers, for much of the natural food of the carp is of such microscopic proportions that anything else is viewed with the utmost suspicion. Only after prolonged pre-baiting will the carp be weaned away from the algae, laevae and daphnia, etc. which forms their normal diet, and in a virgin water this will take far longer than in one that is fished for other species.

Carp undoubtedly clear up much of the ground bait that has been deposited in the water by anglers in pursuit of other species. If you intend fishing throughout the night, it is always worth while moving into a swim that has been well baited by an angler who has left the water after fishing all day.

I am rather undecided as to whether ground baiting for carp at the time of fishing is of any value, for the carp that are in the habit of searching well-fished swims for food when bankside activity is at a minimum are just as likely to take a single piece of bait concealing a hook as when there are many free offerings scattered around. Less frequented swims will benefit for being baited over a period of several days before fishing, but I would still rather not risk scaring any carp that happened to be in the vicinity, by introducing ground bait at the time of fishing.

No matter how effective a particular bait, its value is limited by the number of carp it takes, for any bait will lose much of its attraction once several have been caught, and its usefulness will go on steadily declining. It is always worth taking different types of bait to a water, and introducing samples of it when one has finished fishing, this will help to get the carp used to various tastes.

Ordinary breadpaste, or breadpaste with additives, accounts for many carp, and if this is to be the chosen bait it should be made from bread not less than three days old. I prefer a loaf of the unsliced type, and it should be prepared by removing the crust with a sharp knife and after cutting into thick slices, should be placed in a clean container. The paste should be made up at the waterside, for I am inclined to think that the chlorination of our domestic supplies rules out the use of tap water when making paste for carp fishing. You may think that this is being over cautious, but when carp are the quarry nothing is too much trouble. Before kneading the bread into a soft lump-free paste, rub your hands well with either grass or water weeds to remove

as much 'human taint' as possible. If the paste is made up from no more than one slice of bread at a time, its texture is easily controlled, and a product which is neither too soft nor too hard is obtained. A soft paste will fly off the hook if a long cast has to be made, and a hard paste may well be rejected by the fish.

If various flavourings are to be added to the breadpaste, remember to include some in your pre-baiting offerings, otherwise you will be wasting your time. If you have been unable to obtain bread of the age which is required, a newer loaf may be prepared by removing the crust and after slicing placing the slices in an upright position to allow air to circulate. The drying out process may be accelerated by placing the slices in the open air, but protected from birds.

Do not be afraid to use a large piece of paste – golf-ball size is not too large, and it need not always be the conventional round or pear shape. A flat disc shaped piece will often rest on the top of soft weeds or mud when the more rounded pieces would sink out of sight. The best way to beat soft weed or mud is by using a balanced bait, one made up by impaling a piece of crust onto the bend of the hook, and moulding paste around the shank. The paste causes the whole to slowly sink to the bottom where it will rest on the top of the mud or weed. An experienced carp angler should be able to attach a correctly balanced bait in the dark without resorting to a light. This should be the aim of all carp anglers.

Bread crust is a first-rate carp bait and can be prepared by tearing or cutting a section from a loaf, but leave a fair amount of flake adhering to the outside.

From the fish-catching point of view, I do not think that it matters very much what shape the crust should be. However, from the casting standpoint my choice would be for a larger piece, and one which was rounded.

The presence of small fish in a water can be something of a mixed blessing for although they will whittle away a lump of paste or crust that is being fished on the bottom, their activity around a floating crust can be a definite attraction. A sudden cessation of this activity often means that a carp has moved into the vicinity. At times, carp will swirl around a floating crust without actually taking it, and will even break it up with their tail as they pass. To combat these tactics, pass the hook and line through a large crust twice, and

*This bream caught by the angler has been well played-out **and** he is using his keep net as a sea angler's drop net. It is below the level of the water and the angler has dropped his rod to guide the fish to the net by holding the line. The float is **in** his hand.*

Where possible it is better to land the fish in a landing net rather than use a gaff. This fish was hooked by the tail and put up a great fight as it was drawn over the landing net.

When fishing a water which is known to hold good shoals of big bream it does pay dividends to have another keep net available. This picture of a matchman was taken when two keep nets were essential – the angler landed over 75 lb of bream and won the match.

then slide it a few inches up the line, and place a small piece of crust on the hook. The big crust will attract the carp as usual, and after swirling around it and knocking it about a few times, the fish may well take the small piece with the hook in it in mistake for a fragment that has broken off the main crust.

I seldom offer carp a free meal, except when baiting with crust and fishing on the surface. When fishing in this manner and reaching the conclusion that it may be beneficial to offer them a tempting morsel 'with no strings attached', there is one point that has to be carefully watched. There is no sense in distributing pieces of crust on to the surface if it is to be rapidly swept away by the wind, therefore be guided by the prevailing weather conditions and decide at the time of fishing whether or not your best purpose will be served by trying to tempt the carp in this way.

If the fish appear to be in a capricious mood and merely attack a floating bait with their tails and keep knocking until all the bread has been cleared, it will sometimes pay to change your tactics in a manner that will take advantage of the carp's behaviour.

More often than not other fish have been eating the bread as it sank to the bottom after being knocked from your hook. Therefore, squeeze a piece of bread taken from the centre of a new loaf round your hook, cast in and let it slowly sink to the bottom. It is quite possible that you will fool one of the waiting fish into thinking that this is another free offering from above.

Bread in this last-mentioned form is worth using in deep water, or indeed anywhere that crusts have not been used to attract carp. There are many occasions when they have preferred a bait of this type to the more orthodox bread paste, and the number of times that large carp have been taken by anglers who have been baiting with flake while fishing for tench are too numerous to mention.

A crust bait may be successfully offered if fished just below the surface. The method to use is legering and by allowing the buoyancy of the crust to lift the hook and trace off the bottom; thus the bait can be fished at whatever depth

the angler desires. I would not recommend a stop shot when fishing in this way.

Carp often have a habit of patrolling mid-water beats between lily-pads where it is a relatively simple matter to place a crust fished on leger tackle. If, after the cast, the rod is placed in a suitable rod-rest with the rod butt tucked well under the arm, bites can be detected by holding a loop of line between thumb and forefinger. This is a rather unorthodox method, but it is essential to strike the fish on the first indication of a bite. If a definite carp 'run' is waited for, a dangerous situation will develop, as the fish will immediately run into the thick tangle of lily roots.

Potatoes as a bait have a limited use. In some waters the carp will totally reject them, no matter how much prebaiting has taken place, although in waters that contain a large head of bream they may well be one of the few bottom baits that give the carp a chance.

Small potatoes should be cooked in their skins until they are soft enough to be dented by the light pressure of thumb and finger. At that point, remove them from the water. On no account leave them in the saucepan once they have reached the correct stage, otherwise they will continue to cook, and become too soft. The line is passed through the potato on a baiting needle (a large darning needle is ideal) and the hook tied to the line before being drawn back into the potato. Then remove the potato skin, and all is ready. If the potatoes are over cooked, they will not stay on the hook when a normal cast is made. If this mistake has been made, open the bale arm on the reel, place the rod in the rests and gently throw the potato out by hand.

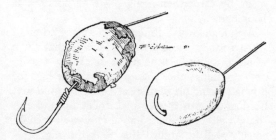

Once several carp have been caught on potatoes I have found that they lose their efficiency, and it is advisable to change to another bait form. The Peterborough Cut is a fine example of a water where the rejection of established baits takes place. The carp having changed their taste from floating crust to paste, flake and potatoes, are now at the time of writing back on floating crust once again.

Freshwater mussels are a natural item of the carp's diet, and this bait is naturally present in many waters – an advantage. If they can be obtained in quantity a period of pre-baiting can be carried out with confidence. Very big carp will consume mussels whole, the shell being dealt with by their digestive organs. For hook and ground bait they should be removed from the shell.

A bait which I find most efficient during the autumn is lob worm, for at this time of the year many carp feed during the hours of daylight, and a large worm cast to a fish that is grubbing in the bottom mud is almost certain to be taken.

There is, however, one interesting fact regarding lobworms. Many years ago, while fishing a lake where the shallows were full of underwater snags, my rather excessively lively worms continually hung onto, or became ensnared in, the underwater growth. I decided that the only way to overcome this hazard was by drowning my baits before they were used. I did this in a small can of water prior to use. Once worms are dead they deteriorate very rapidly, and become difficult to keep on a hook when cast. A freshly drowned worm makes an ideal bait and stays on the hook even when cast most vigorously.

When using this bait form it has been my experience that the bites which eventually materialise are slow and deliberate, the cruising fish pauses to pick up the bait before carrying on its patrol at its usual speed.

This is so unlike the fast and powerful runs made by carp when using paste or potatoes as hook bait.

A thought which immediately spring to mind when relating these last two facts is that there would seem to be little point in baiting a swim with anything other than a natural offering, for if potatoes and bread paste are used, it could well be that the fish merely pick them up and run straight out of the baited area. However, it could equally well be argued that it is the slight resistance offered by the line, or the feel of the trace as it passes over their lip which causes the carp to panic. If this last fact is true then one would naturally assume that the fish would run hard and fast when a worm was taken, but I have not found this to be so.

Small red worms are another extremely good bait form, and on a number of occasions while baiting with them and fishing for tench, I have taken really large carp. Here again, worm bait has induced the carp to take with a slow confident bite, once again proving their lack of suspicion when faced with these creatures on a hook.

I well remember that the downfall of a 13 lb 8 oz mirror carp was brought about by small red worms. Some years ago I had attempted to catch this fish for several hours. It had been feeding in the shallows of a lake on which I was fishing, and it refused crust, ignored paste, and shied away from flake. Finally, I offered it worm which it accepted almost at once.

I am almost certain that the fish had been preoccupied with feeding on blood worms, and as I was able to present a few small worms on weightless tackle the fish merely seized them as an unexpected bounty brought about by its own rooting in the mud.

It is well known that potatoes make successful carp bait, but there are many other fruits and vegetables which on occasions are equally efficient, I have known boiled turnip to lure carp of 11 lb 8 oz.

Bananas have taken some very big carp, and are one of those commodities ideal for an extensive pre-baiting programme. This is occasioned by the fact that other fish seem to be completely indifferent to its edible qualities. Banana can be used in large pieces or in the form of a paste, and it is a bait which is well worth using when fishing in a water in which carp have become wary of the more conventional offerings.

One aspect of carp fishing about which little is known is that these fish do on certain occasions show a marked tendency towards cannibalism.

During the early part of the season I have noticed that carp have distinctly predatory instincts, and several large ones have been taken on both dead and live small fish. Some eel fishers have for some time been convinced that the long runs they have experienced when fishing a dead bait have, in fact, been the result of carp picking up the bait, running, and then dropping it after some 20, 30 or more yards. These thoughts are often strengthened by the fact that the baits are frequently found to be unmarked.

This is a side of carp fishing that could well be worth considerably more research, which could well be undertaken by the many dedicated groups of specimen carp hunters that are now active throughout the country.

Probably the bait that has brought about the biggest surprise in recent years is the maggot chrysalis or, as it is now termed, the caster. On an almost snag-free North Midland water which is well-known to me several fish, averaging 20 lb, have taken casters. But, and this is the interesting point, these fish seem to prefer a single caster presented on a small hook, rather than a more substantial offering on a larger hook.

Carp are a species which react very rapidly to a change in water temperature. This being so, a thermometer is an indispensable item of the carp angler's tackle.

They seem to feed most readily during a relatively narrow temperature range which extends from 58 degrees to 68 degrees Fahrenheit. Anything much over 68°F. will find the carp more inclined to bask in the shallows and just lie among the weed. Once the temperature falls below 58°F., then the fish will once again become less and less interested in feeding.

One other weather factor which much affects the carp is wind. A fresh breeze will soon cause the upper layers of water to begin moving, and as these layers build up at one end of the lake, so there is a rapid increase in the oxygen content in the water.

Climatic conditions are a feature of carp fishing which the angler must consider most carefully, and he must also relate these conditions and how they vary to the water in which he is fishing. Shallow water will react to warming sunshine far more rapidly than deep water; of course it will also cool fairly rapidly once the sun has gone. Deep water will remain at a constant temperature for a longer period and will be less liable to the almost violent changes which can be experienced in the shallows.

These facts lead to a number of permutations; for example, the shallows which may have been too hot during daylight hours may be just right in the last two or three hours of darkness, or a sudden rainstorm may alter a favourable temperature in the shallows to one which is too cold. Frequent use of the thermometer should be made during a session of carp fishing to make sure that your bait is being presented in an area where temperature conditions favour your chances.

In the waters of the northern counties of England, where most of my carp fishing is done, the years have proved beyond argument that ideal conditions for me most often prevail during the late afternoon and evening. Therefore, these are the periods of the day into which I concentrate my carp fishing. My fishing diary has long confirmed this fact. Nevertheless, I would never forsake night fishing completely, for there are times when the early hours of the morning produce fish that are long remembered. Anyway, fishing throughout the night holds a fascination which is worth experiencing for its own sake.

The falling temperatures of late October usually bring to an end the still-water carp fishing season, but the fully-scaled wild carp and the partially-scaled king carp will, I have found, continue feeding well into early December. But, of course, much of this depends upon the overall standard of the average temperature. In severe conditions there is virtual cessation of sport much earlier.

There are waters where the onset of winter means very little to the carp fishing enthusiast. Where electricity power stations or industrial undertakings discharge clean warm water, carp fishing can be pursued even when there are several inches of snow.

The Peterborough Cut is one of the best-known waters of this type, and I have spent many a night by it, with steam rising from the surface and carp rolling close to the water's edge, while at the same time frost was forming on my hat. Unfortunately, due to the publicity that this water has received and the increase in the popularity of carp angling, each year it has become more and more difficult to pursue serious carp fishing here.

But despite the ever-increasing attentions paid by the angler to the Peterborough Cut, it is an interesting water to fish.

The carp move into the Cut during the late autumn or early winter from the River Nene, to which the Cut is joined. There are many who think that once the carp have taken up residence in the warm water it is a simple matter to catch them. This may have been so at one time, although I never found this the case. To-day there is very little that one can teach these carp about the cunning methods used by anglers. They are not shy in the accepted sense, for the number of people that fish this water has to be seen to be believed, consequently the carp are used to bank-side activity, but they are very loth to take a bait.

I have never ceased to be amazed by the fact

that carp not only live but seem to thrive in a water where the temperature fluctuates greatly between the periods when the water is being pumped from the station and when it has stopped.

During recent years carp fishing enthusiasts have demanded, and received, the sympathetic attention of tackle makers. There are several extremely efficient carp rods on the market, some constructed from glass fibre, and others of built cane. Although I prefer the action of cane I am the first to admit that much of this material offered to-day falls short of the quality required.

However, whichever you choose there are certain points which must be remembered. The rod must be capable of handling a line of up to 12 lb b.s., for this will be found to be adequate for almost any size of carp and/or situation.

To a large extent the maximum power that needs to be exerted by the rod and line is, I have found, related to the strength of the tissue of the carp's mouth. There is very little point in having a rod and line which is so powerful that the angler is able to exert an amount of power which does no more than tear the hook from the fish's mouth. My experience has been that a pressure of more than 10 lb will invariably tear the hook from the creature's mouth.

The lines used for carp fishing must be in first-class condition—the power that can be exerted by a heavy fish is so great that the slightest weakness will often result in breakage. No-one should attempt carp fishing with less than 100 yd of suitable line on the reel, and although the finer the line the less likely it is to be seen (a fact which results in more fish actually taking the bait) it is asking for trouble to use a line with a breaking strain of less than 6 lb.

I know perfectly well that on many occasions heavy carp are caught on fine tackle, and I have taken fish of 12 lb and more on 3 lb b.s. line, but these have been sheer chances and on occasions when I have been seeking other species.

Under certain conditions monofilament is certainly far less visible than braided line, but there are times when I prefer a braided line, mainly because it is considerably more limp and will follow the contours of the lake bed far better than the stiffer monofilament. This fact makes it far less likely to be observed by the carp.

However, monofilament line scores heavily when long-distance casting is required or when floating crust techniques are being used; it also has the advantage of being available in colourings which tend to make it almost invisible under certain light conditions.

Possibly one of the greatest aids to successful carp fishing has been the efficient state to which the fixed spool reel has been developed. With a reel of this type it is a simple matter to cast a crust of bread to a fish that at one time would have been considered out of range. There is also the added advantage that with the bale arm open, a fish can be allowed to run for some distance, yet feel virtually no resistance.

If the slipping clutch has been set correctly, then it is possible to strike at and hook a heavy fish at long range. The clutch is an adequate safeguard when striking hard over a long distance, particularly so if the fish is running at full power.

Many ardent carp fishermen have long held that much could be done to improve the hooks used when carp fishing. Many a good fish has been lost by hook failures when fish were being held hard. Repeated representations to tackle manufacturers are meeting with success, but in attempting to keep the price down, it is my opinion that they are not giving the very fine and extremely sharp hook that is needed.

The carp's mouth is large, consequently a large hook should be used, and it is a fact that a large bait cannot be cast efficiently on a small hook. Sizes 2, 4 and 6 are those which are normally used, and my advice regarding hooks to anyone who intends to become a carp angler is quite simply this: test your hooks often and rigorously and discard any that you find below standard, and be equally ruthless with a hook that shows the slightest signs of rust.

There is little point in using any other than an eyed hook which has been tied directly to the main line by a half blood knot, for the whole aim when carp fishing should be to keep the tackle as simple and straightforward as possible.

Rod rests should be of a type that allows the

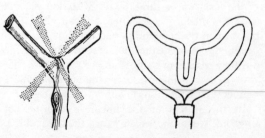

line free passage when the rod is in the rest. Landing and keep nets must be as large as possible, and some manufacturers specialise in the manufacture of equipment which has been specially designed for the carp enthusiast.

It is not unknown for anglers to keep large carp in a sack which has been sunk below the surface. This may be all right in an emergency and for a very short period, but it is not a method that I recommend, as a fish will rapidly avail itself of all the oxygen in the water within the sack, and as the very nature of the receptacle precludes an adequate water circulation, confinement for any great period will surely bring death or unnecessary suffering.

When arranging your tackle and selecting the area over which you intend fishing there are several points which, if remembered, will make success more likely.

The area which you have pre-baited should have been carefully noted. This can be achieved by lining up the area with a landmark on the opposite bank. The rod rests should be positioned so that the one at the rear is higher than the other. This will enable the rod to be pointed in a direct line to the bait. If this is done, the rod rings will offer far less resistance to the line as the fish takes the bait and begins to move.

After the cast has been made, carefully reel in any excessive slack line and place the rod in the rests and open the bale arm.

When legering there are several ways in which a bite may be detected, but I have yet to find a more efficient method than silver paper on the line. A small piece of this may be folded over a loop of line which has been drawn down between the butt and second ring. If there is a stiff breeze the silver paper may be pressed gently into the ground.

Often the first indication of a bite is the sudden movement of the line between the rod tip and the surface of the water which is followed almost immediately by the silver paper lifting towards the rod as the line is drawn out by the fish. This usually takes place at a fair speed, and as the fish is running, lift the rod and strike at your fish firmly.

Occasionally a bite will resemble a minor explosion, and for the inexperienced carp angler this can be rather unnerving. A fish will sometimes take with such power that the rod tip literally trembles and the silver paper indicator is thrown several feet up into the air.

During hours of darkness the strain of sitting and watching a piece of silver paper for hour after hour can be a very tiring business. After a while one can imagine that the paper has moved, when in fact it may only be the flickering of your tired eyes and the sagging of your head.

At times like this I favour one of the several excellent bite alarms which are operated by a torch battery. Although these alarms cut out much of the strain associated with carp fishing, they certainly do not make their capture any easier.

The section of the alarm that carries the antenna should be positioned just in front of a rod ring (on the side furthest away from the butt) and an additional rod rest placed at the rod butt to raise it higher than the tip.

As soon as line begins to run out in response to the demands of a fish, the line moves the antenna slightly to one side, the contacts close and the alarm begins to buzz.

One of the drawbacks of this type of alarm is that it will only work when the fish is going away, or in other words drawing line from the reel. There must be many occasions when carp pick up the bait and swim directly towards the rod tip. On such occasions the alarm would not register.

I well remember watching a carp that must have been some 20 lb in weight, pick up a large piece of flake in shallow water and swim leisurely close to the surface with the flake held just within its lips. The fish came within six feet of the bank before sheering off and all in all it must have covered about 30 yd before it ejected the bait and disappeared. At no time did that fish take the bait far enough into its mouth to warrant a strike, nor was there any movement on the line at its point of entry into the water. There was nothing whatever to show that a carp had taken the bait and if I had not seen the fish for myself I would have never known that the bait had been moved, that is until I came to retrieve my tackle.

Occasionally carp develop a habit of giving what I call 'twitch' bites, and when they are in this mood the silver paper will give little more than a slight shiver, or the electric alarm a momentary bleep. Little can be done to hook fish that persist in this behaviour, except striking at the slightest indication of a bite. Let me say at once you will rarely hook a fish that is acting in this manner, and after several hours of it you will be most frustrated.

Most waters that hold a mixed population are hard-fished during daylight hours. This being so, it is usual for the carp to keep well away from the banks during daylight. However, once darkness has fallen they will frequently come closer in to search for food and this is a movement of which the angler can take advantage. As it grows dark it is well worth while scattering a few crusts along the margin of a lake in readiness for the carp that make a habit of patrolling close to the bank when darkness has fallen.

Fishing with a floating crust at night can be a nerve-racking and exhausting business. Set the rod up so that the tip juts out over the surface like a crane's jib, with the crust already impaled on the hook and dangling a foot or so above the water.

The angler must remain absolutely silent, but be ever-alert for the sight or sound of a carp feeding. As it sucks the pieces of bread from the surface there is a most distinctive 'slooping'

sound. There will also be the soft lap of the water as the fish disturbs the otherwise silent surface. As the fish's approach is sensed then lower the crust gently on to the water, and the waiting begins all over again.

The dedicated carp angler soon realises that there is no short cut to becoming a successful carp fisherman, and he will come to appreciate that it is only by an intensive study of both the waters in which he fishes and the habits of his quarry that he will be able to reach his ultimate target.

CRUCIAN CARP

by

David Carl Forbes

The traditional crucian carp water is comparatively small, shallow and well weeded. However, very deep gravel pits sometimes yield fish whose presence was not suspected. In recent years several surprisingly large crucians have been taken from deep-water swims. Regardless of depth, it is invariably the more expansive waters which produce the larger fish, although occasionally small farm ponds offer surprises.

Only relatively can the crucian be considered big, for the other carps are great, ponderous fish reaching weights in excess of 40 lb, while the barbel-less crucian can be considered large if it exceeds 3 lb. The trend towards specimen-hunting has set 2 lb as a standard, but crucian carp can provide enjoyable sport, and some frustration, at much lower weights.

As with many other species the essential problem is locating them, for although many other species inhabit what we term as typical swims,

alas, crucians do not. They are still-water nomads, inconsistent in their habits, and often extremely difficult to find in a large water. A shoal may stay in one spot for days, and then

apparently disappear, turn up in another spot for a day and then move off again. Spasmodic catches result from contacting a moving shoal, but once they have settled down to feed in one spot the angler can anticipate almost non-stop action. Ground bait does not solve the problem for it seems to achieve no more than a concentration of the small fry of many species. These compete with the crucians to the detriment of your sport for usually the small fry are first to the bait.

Tiny bubbles rising to the surface over a large area, needle bubbles reminiscent of tench, may indicate feeding fish, and sometimes one may spot the fish rolling just beneath the surface or priming on it. This can be an introduction to good fishing, for when the crucians are rolling, they are generally feeding. When fish show high in the water, the angler must be very cautious in his approach.

Without visual indication the angler has to work to find his fish, and obviously is rewarded more quickly on the smaller water. I suggest a methodical approach, allow fifteen minutes for a section of approximately 20 square yards of water, and pay particular attention to beds of soft weed, e.g. Canadian pondweed, etc., and banks of sedge or reed. If one round of the water produces nothing, settle down to long range fishing, covering as much water as possible from one position, and if an hour of this produces nothing, start to work the section routine once again.

Crucians offer sport throughout the summer months, and often well into October if the weather does not become too severe. Surprisingly, night fishing is not particularly productive, and, in my experience, the best sport is usually to be had during the hour following dawn.

When conditions suit, the fish will continue to feed through the day, and sultry afternoons often promote a frenzy of surface feeding.

Like other carp, the crucian is a finicky and discerning feeder, but unlike its kin it has a small mouth. Through necessity one fishes with a small bait, and in this instance there is no strength in the old adage, 'Big bait, big fish'.

I find the most effective bait to be bread in paste form, with maggots coming a poor second. Red worms, while having some effect on certain waters that I fish, do not seem to be particularly popular with crucians.

To achieve a compromise between good bait presentation and effective holding power, I would suggest a size 10 hook, and would refrain from using one smaller than size 12. The crucian has a tough, leathery mouth which is so typical of the carp, and my experience has been that a small hook requires almost a minor operation to remove it. Far better a hook of sufficient size to allow one to remove it without causing too much discomfort to the fish.

While it is recognised that crucians attain no great size, they are frequently encountered in close proximity to clumps of tough lilies or reed stalks, and for this reason I use a 4 lb breaking strain line. Do not be misled by the angler who talks of the skill inherent in using an ultra-fine line. This is all very well in open water, and then only providing one does not have to strike a fish at long range, but ultra-light line causes the loss of many fish when they are hooked close to an underwater obstruction. A crucian will build up quite a good speed over a distance of six feet, and often they will be much closer to weeds than that, and in the short space and time involved one must check the fish and turn it. Skill has nothing to do with the breaking strain of the line. A forceful side-strain must be applied, a really fine line will not stand up to it. Consider a $1\frac{1}{2}$ lb fish moving in one direction at speed and a rod striking against it. The shock imposed is quite sufficient to part a 4 lb b.s. line. A line should be chosen as much to overcome the obstacles inherent in our fishing as to compete with the size of fish we expect to catch, and remember, it often pays to hustle a fish quickly out of the shoal before the commotion causes fright to the remainder.

Delicately balanced float tackle is my choice of method for detecting the subtle bite of the crucian. A slender 4 in porcupine quill should be shotted so that no more than a $\frac{1}{4}$ in of the tip is exposed above the water. Use dust shot and space them out at intervals on the line. Start 9 in from the hook and distribute the shot right up to the float ring. This will cause less commotion on impact with the water than several closely bunched larger shot. The slowly sinking bait will often tempt a fish.

A bite will register in a most distinctive manner, the float twitches slightly and then disappears almost immediately. If too much float is exposed above the surface it will dither, and the chances are that the fish will have taken the bait and ejected it half a dozen times while the angler is still waiting for the float to go under. Rig the tackle to give sensitive reaction and strike at the first indication of a bite.

The bait should rest just on the bottom, and therefore plumb the depth of the water carefully before fishing. It is often best to determine depth by trial and error, for a plumb lead may serve no other purpose than to frighten away the fish.

The art of fishing for crucian carp does not call for a specialised rod, that used for roach or dace fishing should be ideal. However, where the crucians grow big it is better to use a rod having a progressive rather than a tip action, for a rod which curves throughout its length will more than prove its worth when a good fish tries to get into reed stalks. If the fish wants to run into soft weed and you cannot stop it, there is seldom much to worry about. The fight is soon terminated, and the fish almost assured as it comes to net draped in a cluster of weed.

CHUB

by

PETER WHEAT

I had spent a long, hard day by the waterside. Fishing is never very easy in winter, and for one unused to the freezing conditions, and the high dirty torrent of water – from which I had almost lost hope of taking fish – it had been very much a time of tribulation.

The big, cork-bodied float, hung motionless in the slack at the tail of a fallen tree. Not once during the day had it dipped, and it was only the faint optimism of the embryo angler that made me think it might.

When the bite did come, just as light was fading, it was not the gentle knock I expected, but a deep plunging dive bending the rod even before I could lift it from the rest. How that rod bent! The unseen adversary tried again and again to bury itself in the submerged branches of the dead tree.

I suppose I was lucky to even hook that fish, yet as is the way of angling, it was to be my day. The fish made a last run before the float came smoothly from the surface, and over the net came the quarry; a lift, and the big bronzy form of a chub came dripping to the bank.

My heart beat fast, my first chub and a veritable giant! The scale needle stopped at 4 lb 8 oz and all thoughts of the elements were forgotten in the happiness of angling success. Since that day I have always held a soft spot for the chub – indeed for many years I fished for little else, and although I have caught many bigger chub, that very first held a magic which will stay with me throughout my angling life.

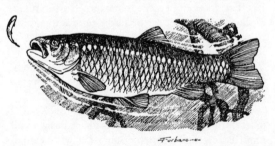

The Chub (*Squalius cephalus*) is a fish common to the majority of streams and rivers in this country. It is absent from most of Wales, Devon and Cornwall, but otherwise it is, I imagine, the most common of our 'bigger' coarse fish.

Mature chub, once seen, are very hard to mistake for any other fish. In shape they are well proportioned, strongly built, with big thick scales, blunt heads and thick white lips. The back is a bronzy green, shading bronze or silver along the sides, into a white or yellowy belly. The thick powerful fins vary in colour from each other, and from fish of different waters. Pectoral, ventral and anal fins are mainly orange red, but I have taken specimens with blood red fins, and others with no colouring at all. The dorsal is a greyish brown, while the caudal fin may, in some cases, have a distinct black fringe. Scales along the lateral line vary between 42 and 48.

As I said earlier there is very little chance of mistaking a mature chub, say over 2 lb, for any other fish. However, small chub and big dace are mistaken quite often, a number of record dace have been identified as small chub.

This confusion can be eliminated by simple observation. The main difference between chub and dace is the shape of the fins. In dace, the trailing edge of the dorsal and anal fins are concave, that is to say bent in. The corresponding fins on chub are convex or rounded outwards. If these checks are made, you will not mistake the two species. A glance will tell you what you have caught, be it small chub or record dace!

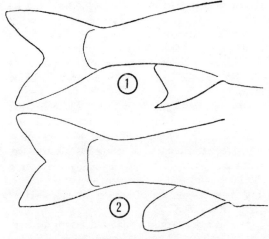

1. The concave anal fin of the dace
2. The convex anal fin of the chub

Spawning time varies a great deal from water to water, influenced to a large extent by weather conditions. Under suitable conditions it can take place as early as April, or in adverse years may be as late as July. The chub, congregated in the weedy, gravel shallows, lay and fertilise the eggs before moving to the faster runs for cleaning purposes. They will remain in the vicinity of such areas for the majority of the summer, only seeking deeper water during long periods of cold weather.

It has been said many many times that the chub is the most catholic of fish, quite prepared to gulp down anything at any time. While it is quite true that they have a very wide feeding range, being both predatory and vegetarian, it is not correct to assume they will take any bait you care to put on your hook. Chub can be fickle creatures, and I have known times when they will look at only one bait, and can be caught on no other.

The natural food of chub varies, depending on the feed available in the different waters. It can safely be said that chub will settle in nearly all rivers or streams, at least to some extent. This is made possible by the powerful throat teeth, digestive organs and juices, which enable the species to eat a very varied selection of water creatures.

The chub will feed quite happily on any of the following: bread, maggots, worms, cheese, wasp grub, caddis grub, silkweed, minnows and other small fish; elvers, lampreys, crayfish, snails, frogs, insects, slugs, freshwater mussels, cherries, bananas, elderberries, hempseed, and so on – the list is really quite endless.

From the angler's point of view the chub, as a quarry, has other advantages. It will feed at every hour of the day and night, quite often under bad conditions. The water temperature factor, so important when considering other species, has less influence on chub. I have taken them in low, clear water, after long periods of hot, dry weather, and I have taken them in winter when the cold has been so intense that fishing for more than a couple of hours has been too much for personal comfort.

Below about 40 degrees Fahrenheit feeding becomes much reduced, but they can still be caught, although tactics must be changed, and one must be prepared to sit for long periods between bites, remaining on the alert for the slightest movement of the rod tip.

Chub inhabit all types of waters, from small streams which are little more than a collection of pools joined by a thin trickle, to full-size rivers like the Hampshire Avon and the River Severn. As a rule the fast, well-oxygenated waters, produce the biggest chub, but there are exceptions to every rule, and waters of all shapes and sizes contain truly monstrous specimens.

The Hampshire Avon, home of record breakers, and a mecca for coarse anglers, dominates the list of chub which have weighed more than 7 lb, a list which is crowned by a specimen of 8 lb 4 oz. This fish taken at Christchurch held the British record from 1913 to 1951 when it was bettered by only 4 oz by a fish from the River Rother in Sussex. Only a few years later, in 1955, a 10 lb 8 oz chub was reported caught from the River Annan in Dumfriesshire by Dr. J. A. Cameron. This fish was accepted by the British Record Rod-Caught Fish Committee as a British record.

Shoal chub are very much the same size and it is not unusual to get a netful varying by little more than a few ounces. The bigger and older chub are either solitary fish, or in small shoals of two or three. Your approach to chub will depend on your approach to fishing. You can catch a lot of chub, or search out the very big solitary fish, depending on the type of sport which gives you satisfaction.

A 4 lb chub from any water is a big fish, a 5 lb exceptional, while those over 6 lb are monstrous and are fish of a lifetime. Some anglers have managed to capture a handful of such specimens after a great number of years, but as the result of a great deal of effort dedicated to the art of catching big chub. For the most part the average fish will weigh between 2 and 3 lb 8 oz; not monsters, but big enough to give plenty of satisfaction if you have your standards in the right place.

Tackle for chub fishing is standard big fish equipment. My own favourite rod is 11 ft 6 in long, hollow glass with a fairly firm action. It would not be in place to raise the question of glass versus split cane; my own opinion being that both materials have advantages, and it must be the individual who makes the final choice. I have used split cane rods from 10 to 12 ft and glass fibre ones of the same lengths for chub fishing, all have been perfectly suitable – the decision is yours! But bear in mind that the chub is a hardy fighter and lives close to snags and weed-beds. Quite often he will need stopping quickly and efficiently to avoid tree roots and the like, so choose a rod with a bit of power and an all-through action.

For trotting, I prefer to use a centrepin reel, loaded with 5-lb b.s. nylon line. In windy weather, or for legering and other methods I choose the more versatile fixed-spool reel loaded with 5-lb b.s. nylon which is suitable for a great deal of chub fishing. But, on waters containing many snags, I prefer something a little heavier -- 7 or 8 lb b.s. Once a big chub snapped my 7-lb b.s. line while fighting hard to reach the roots of a nearby tree, this gives you a measure of their power.

No matter whether I am float fishing, legering or loose lining, I always tie my hooks direct to the reel line. Both eyed hooks and spade ends are, in my opinion, excellent, but I choose to tie my own so that if the knot should give . . . I only have myself to blame.

Other important items of equipment include a big landing net, and the largest keepnet you can buy.

Chub baits can be divided into two main sections: those which cater for its vegetarian taste, and those which favour its often predatory nature. Perhaps the most common of the vegetarian baits is cheese, either in cubes or paste form. Many chub are taken by anglers who use this one bait to the exclusion of all others. My choice is for an English Cheddar. It moulds well and its texture is soft enough to allow the hook point to penetrate as the strike is made, yet firm enough to stay on the hook even in the fastest flow.

Another useful bait is bread, cheap and versatile. Paste, flake and crust are all good baits for chub.

During the summer months silkweed, that soft green weed found on weir aprons and stonework is an excellent bait, and is often most effective just after weed-cutting has taken place. It is easy to use, just drape a small amount over the hook, and trot it downstream at mid-water. Try it on a summer afternoon when the river seems lifeless.

Many anglers confine silkweed fishing to weir runs, but I have found it almost as good in the slower stretches of the main river. During weed-cutting, chub quite often become pre-occupied with this food, and at such times it is well worth the trouble of presenting your bait between the large islands of cut weed, as they are swept downstream on the current.

Other vegetarian baits I feel are less important than those just mentioned, although occasionally it is worth trying one of those listed earlier in the chapter.

The chub's predatory nature can be tempted

with a lobworm, an offering which, as far as I am concerned, must have pride of place. It is an excellent bait, one which chub love and often take fiercely. Despite the successes achieved by brandlings and other worms, I am convinced that lobworms are by far the best of the lot. In winter they can be most useful, staying soft in the icy water, and the smell given off encourages the chub to take, at a time when fish are in a very lethargic mood.

Needless to say maggot is also a good chub bait, but I feel that the average size of chub caught on maggot is never as large as those taken on cheese and lob worm. The fact that so many specimen fish are caught on maggot each year is probably due to the number of anglers using this bait, rather than any magical qualities.

Bluebottles, beetles, caterpillars, butterflies – the chub enjoys them all. To dap these live offerings use a loose line with a single swan shot placed 18 in up the line as steadying weight. When using this method try the bushy overgrown areas, but approach the water's edge carefully. Dapping for chub is one of the most exciting ways to take them.

Slugs fished on the bottom on a loose line can be deadly. I have used them a lot in the clear waters of the Dorset Stour. In such a river, where the fish are visible, it is possible to place the bait almost on the chub's nose, and if the fish is in the right mood, he will, after a little investigation, make off with it at top speed.

In the early part of the season chub will often be found cleaning themselves on gravel. At this time they are intensely predatory, they dash around making raids on the shoals of minnow, behaving very much like the perch. To a lesser degree this instinct appears to remain with them at least until the end of autumn. During the period of active hunting, minnows make excellent bait if trotted down through the shallows on float tackle.

A small grayling bob is my choice, with the depth set at 18 in. A single shot is set about 6 in above the hook to cock the float and the bait, a minnow, is hooked through the top lip only. When the float dives, delay the strike for a second or two to give the chub time to turn the bait and get it inside its mouth.

One can study and experiment with baits for a whole lifetime and still have things to learn. My own approach is to carry bread, cheese and

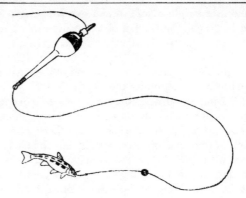

Live minnow trotting tackle

worms, plus a net and box to hold whatever insects I might find. A minnow trap and bait can for minnows is also essential. During the day I experiment, ringing the changes many times on both baits and methods. It all goes to make an interesting and varied day, which is preferable to sitting stolidly and using the same bait form and method, just hoping that something might turn up.

Legering, float fishing, loose lining and surface fishing methods will all take chub. Legering is probably the most common and popular method, and particularly so with keen chub hunters. During the summer I fish a rolling leger. This method keeps the bait on the move, for to be successful you must search all the likely swims. As the strength of the current varies, so you must alter the amount of weight your leger is carrying. This problem is best handled by using the nylon link leger, a style developed by Fred J. Taylor. This consists of a short length of nylon looped over the main line and then held together with swan shot. The leger is stopped from sliding down to the hook in the normal way. By adding to or subtracting shot from the link, the leger can be adjusted to a very fine degree.

Cast across and slightly downstream and pay out some line so that the bait comes to rest on the bottom. With the aid of the current and by gently lifting the rod tip, the bait can be trundled downstream and around under your own bank. Any suspicious 'knock' or 'pluck' should be struck immediately. When fishing in this manner bites can vary from a gentle touch to a violent snatch which can pull the rod from your hands!

Static legering is another method which is often successful if carried out in the correct way and in the right place – under overhanging trees or bushes and in the tail of a streamy run where the end of a weedbed will often contain chub. Fish with a long trail between hook and leger weight so the bait can swing round in the current and find the fish under the weeds.

During winter when the chub move into deeper quieter water, a static leger with a much shortened trail will often take fish when other methods fail. At this time bites are very shy, much in keeping with the slower movements of the chub during winter. Providing you are quick with the strike, these bites can be turned into fish on the hook, but to be successful hold the rod the whole time.

Float fishing is always a satisfying way to take fish no matter which species you seek. For normal trotting I use a float which cocks with the addition of only one swan shot; this I place 9 in from the hook. This rig will be adequate for quite a wide range of chub fishing, although obviously this will have to be changed to suit conditions. For example, when fishing a small stream both the float and shot can be much lighter.

When float fishing I normally begin by trotting a large piece of flake down through the swim at mid-water. If I have guessed right and the fish are there and the flake is successful, then one or two fish should be taken. Now is the time to move further along the swim and try again, gradually working down the river, taking fish as you go. If, for one of many reasons, it is impossible to be continually moving, try introducing a little ground bait. There are many different ground bait mixtures, but I think that one of the best mixtures for river fishing is sausage rusk and chicken meal. The chicken meal serves to bind the rusk so that it all sinks rapidly.

A few trial casts will help you to find the correct depth. After using ground bait, concentrate on working your hook bait slowly through the swim close to the bottom. Samples of the hook bait should be introduced with each ball of ground bait. When fishing with maggot I often throw the occasional dozen or so in. Do not, however, overfeed.

Where possible try dispensing with the float or leger completely and utilise the bait to give sufficient weight for casting. Lob worms and slugs are excellent for this mode of fishing which is called 'loose lining'. When employing this style it is essential that the rod is held continually, so that there can be immediate reaction to a 'take'. A large piece of crust can be fished on the surface by the same method. Try a piece about the size of a matchbox on a No. 4 hook. Good places for crust fishing are narrow overgrown streams. Lay the bait on the surface, and let the current take it away.

One other surface bait that is important to the chub fisher is a large bushy dry fly. These should be used in conjunction with a controller which can be either a bubble float or a short length of quill, balsa or wood. The controller is fixed about 18 in above the fly, in a similar manner to a float, but the line between fly and controller should be lightly greased so that it floats. Ordinary coarse fishing tackle is perfectly suitable for this operation.

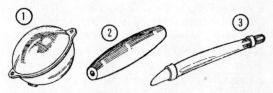

Controllers: 1. bubble float; 2. shaped wood; 3. small quill

The controller is floated downstream with the fly preceding it. The fly must behave in a natural manner, and on no account must it be allowed to drag across the surface. This is a method which works extremely well from a boat, although I have used it to good account while bank fishing. 'Poor man's fly fishing' it may be, but done well it is a skilled art, and it catches chub!

Orthodox fly fishing, both wet and dry, has been the downfall of many big chub. The late evening is a much favoured time for this style of fishing, and working down through the shallows in a river that holds a good head of chub, presenting both wet and dry flies, can be both exciting and rewarding. I would choose large bushy flies for an operation of this nature.

Chub can also be taken on spinning tackle. This is not really a popular method, despite the fact that a number are caught each year by anglers who are spinning for pike or perch.

Without a shadow of a doubt, the chub is a worthy quarry. In most waters it gives a good account of itself, and it can be taken on almost every method and it will move to a wide variety of baits. Perhaps it can justly be called the angler's 'all purpose fish'.

DACE

by

Colin R. Gamble

Judged purely on a basis of size the dace may appear to be a rather insignificant little fish, and few anglers can boast that they have caught, or even seen, a dace of a pound. Its colouring, as well as its size, is modest, lacking the flamboyance of the perch or the richness of a well-coloured roach or rudd; it is just a slim, bright, lively little fish.

Nevertheless, there are very many anglers who rely on the dace for the bulk of their sport, and there are others who find in the search for the larger dace a fascination which leads them to specialise in hunting for these fish.

For most anglers, though, the dace is just a shoal fish whose preferences in types of water bring it into competition with roach, and often with chub too, so that often the dace which are caught form part of a mixed bag.

These fish are very widely distributed in all kinds of rivers and streams, abounding in most of the major rivers, particularly in the higher reaches, but a great deal of the best in dace fishing will be found in quite small waters.

Perhaps the type of river which is ideal both for the welfare of the dace and for the sport of catching them is that which would be thought of as a typical trout water, where there is a good clean flow of varying depth, having a prolific weed growth and a rich crop of fly and larvae. There are many such waters where, to put it mildly, dace are regarded as regrettable in-

truders, but which, if seriously fished, could soon make one-pounders much less notable.

Anyone who fishes for roach in any of the normal styles, or even fishes for whatever may chance to come along, will surely catch some dace. They will feed on just about any bait whose size is within their capacity, paste, flake, crust, hemp, elderberries, small worms, wheat, and, probably the most popular dace baits of all, maggots and chrysalides.

There are not many occasions when one can confidently anticipate catching dace only; it is likely that there will come to the same baits and methods whatever other species are present and that they will be considerably larger than the dace. One must, therefore, decide beforehand whether to make any concession to this fact in the choice of tackle.

My own feeling is that to compromise must involve some loss of both efficiency and fun, and that it is preferable, when the nature of the swim and the methods in use make dace much the likeliest catch, to tackle up with only the dace in mind even though this may mean the loss of some other, larger fish.

In much dace fishing a quick strike will be needed to match the sharp, plucking bites, and a light, tip-actioned rod of 11–12 ft will be found both pleasant and effective in use when matched with a line of 1½–2-lb breaking strain.

Dace fishing is a light and delicate sport, and this should be reflected in the float and weight used, bearing in mind that the weight should be chosen first to present the bait properly in whatever current exists. A common error is to use a very small float carrying a shot load so light that the bait streams out in the current instead of being carried at the depth as set on the tackle. A more adequate weight, with a float accurately adjusted, will not only present the bait more effectively but will also give better bite registration.

I do not think any particular pattern of hook gives any advantage so far as hooking fish is concerned. I have never found reason to change from my usual round bend, medium length shank, eyed hooks of a size to suit the bait in use. A range from size 10 to size 16 will meet every need likely to arise in dace fishing.

Dace shoals usually respond well to careful ground baiting with conventional meal mixtures of finely ground bread crumb. The important point is to maintain a supply in the swim, giving only a little at a time but giving it often, and to introduce it well upstream of the fishing position. Once fish have been drawn into the swim it is often quite enough to give bait samples in small numbers every few minutes.

As already mentioned, dace are fairly well omnivorous and will be caught on just about every conventional bait. There is no doubt, however, that maggots, sometimes single, sometimes two or more on the hook, are not only the most popular bait but are also the most consistently effective. They are certainly the most convenient. I would always start by trying maggots and change only when they failed to interest fish which I knew to be present. There are times when more fish, or better fish, will come to pinches of flake, fragments of crust or to chrysalides.

During the first quarter of the season, dace, in common with other species, can often be found in quite shallow water, perhaps no more than a foot or so in depth, which runs at a brisk pace. Such runs do not occur on all good dace rivers, of course, but where they are found one can often locate very large shoals of dace attracted there by the fact that the shallows are the earliest areas to benefit from increasing light and warmth and consequently provide the richest feeding early in the year.

These swims can sometimes be fished with a float, though it will often be found that the flow is rather too irregular for this method. It may help to use a float which is shorter than usual, having a streamlined body with the bulk low down, attached by the bottom end only.

Dace, especially in fast water, will usually give a short, sharp plucking bite which needs to be struck smartly. Not all bites will draw the float below the surface; the float may appear merely to deviate in its course, rise a little in the water or just to be held back a little. Any of these movements should be struck at once.

In fast water it is often better to use a light leger to roll the bait along the bed. To rig this tackle attach the necessary weight in the form of

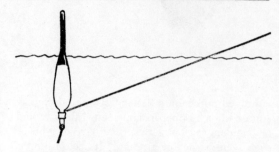

Float for use in fast rippling shallows

split shot nipped on to a short length of nylon doubled over the line, so that the line may slide freely through the loop formed by the shot holding the line together, thus minimising the drag felt by the fish. A small shot on the line will allow the bait a predetermined degree of free movement and this, although at times it may appear to be of no importance at all, can at others be a crucial factor. If bites do not come, it is always worth while to experiment and change the position of the shot from between an inch to a foot from the hook.

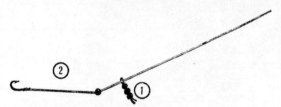

How to rig a rolling leger. 1. Split shot on nylon loop; 2. Hook link

A rolling leger tackle can be fished from a variety of positions, although the usual approach is to fish down and across the stream rolling the leger in an arc back to the near bank. Ideally it should trundle along, holding for a moment here and there, until the pressure of water on the line lifts it a little further. Sometimes it may be necessary to lift the rod to encourage the rolling but if this need is very apparent it is likely that a little weight should be removed.

I prefer to keep the line a little less than tight between rod tip and weight and, drawing a loop of line from the reel, hold it lightly between finger and thumb of the left hand. One is then able both to watch for lifting of the line and to feel bites through the fingers, both of which are superior methods to waiting for a pluck on the rod tip.

It may be that the bites will be such sharp

little plucks that they defeat the strike. A frequent answer to this problem is to leger upstream. The amount of weight is now absolutely crucial: it must be just enough to hold bottom after the cast, with the line falling fairly slack from the rod. When the line is tightened against the weight, the weight is dislodged to roll down the current a little to slacken the line again.

Thus a biting fish will feel only a very slight resistance as the weight is dislodged and there is a better chance of the bait being held long enough for a successful strike.

The usual indication of a bite comes when the line falls slacker or moves down the stream, and the reaction to this needs to be a strike sweeping enough to take up the slack line which is inevitable when using method. Occasionally, when a fish moves upstream with the bait, the bow of line will tighten, and then the strike must be made before the line is tightened against the rod or the fish will surely be missed.

During most of the season dace fishing is perfectly conventional in method, consisting of swimming the stream or trotting over fairly short distances in swims of moderate depth using tackle and technique very much as is normally used by the majority of match anglers.

The bait should normally be offered within the bottom quarter of the depth and it may sometimes be necessary to experiment very carefully with this detail. Initially, I would set the bait to trip the bottom, intending it to look to the fish as did the preceding samples of bait.

It is not uncommon for fish to come at first to baits which trip the bottom and then, as time passes, to move up in the water. There are two common reasons for this and both concern ground bait and samples of hook bait. If these are not thrown well upstream of the swim, at least some of them will pass through the swim before they have reached the bed; this will inevitably encourage the fish to move up in the water so that they may intercept them.

Occasionally it will be found that dace are so shy that the only way of taking them is to dispense with both float and shot. Tie a 14 or 16 hook direct to your line, bait with a single maggot, and strike as you see the fish turn as it flashes at the bait.

Where there is a good depth of water and a considerable current it may be more effective to enclose ground bait and samples within a paper bag.

Weight this with a stone to ensure that it gets to the bottom quickly; there it will break up and the bait will roll down the swim.

The second reason is not due to any fault on the part of the angler. A shoal of fish, intercepting food, tends to move slowly upstream to meet it earlier; this leads to the same situation – the fish are meeting food items as they sink.

Provided one is aware of the possibility, and is ready to lift the bait a little when it seems that bites are getting fewer, this is not a serious difficulty. It may be enough to check the float for a few seconds on its travel down the current, to cause the bait to swing up in the water, and it is always worth holding the float for a little time at the end of the swim down so that the bait streams out in the current, and then to begin the retrieve with a strike. Many a dace will be caught at this point even though a bite has not been seen.

As the season advances through Autumn, and mornings and evenings begin to bring a nip to the air, the dace will have forsaken their more shallow and rapid Summer haunts to congregate in deeper, gliding swims, and here they are likely to stay until the weather turns really cold.

They can be fished for here perfectly well by the methods and with the baits used earlier in the year although, as with all fish, because their need for food is diminishing, they may often be found to be more fickle.

It is important at this time not to give too generously of either ground bait or samples of hook bait; to overdo either will ensure an early end to feeding.

It may be found later in the year that better results will come to a bait which pauses now and then in its passage through the swim. This can best be achieved, provided the swim is one which can be fished directly down the current, by stret-pegging rather than long trotting. The bait can then be closely controlled, so as to roll down a foot or two, then pause for as long as seems desirable, perhaps stationary on the bed, perhaps waving about within the radius of the hook link, before it is allowed to travel a little farther down the swim.

When it is really cold, with water temperatures falling towards the lower thirties, dace may well leave the currents entirely and move into slack, or very nearly slack, water. Here it is generally best to fish a stationary bait and use laying-on methods.

The usual baits may still bring results but at this time there is much to commend small cubes of crust fished just an inch or so below the bunched shot. This bait, being buoyant, will rise clear of the bed and it seems that this fact is responsible for its success when the fish are somewhat less than eager to feed.

At times of high water expect dace to have moved away from the main press of water. This move, perhaps of no more than a few feet, will generally bring the dace bankwards so that they lie on the edge of the current, but where, as on a bend, the main flow sweeps along the bank, the fish may have moved out towards the centre of the river.

Although not much fished for by this method, dace are very willing to take a fly, either wet or dry, fished in a perfectly conventional manner. As good a fly as any, and better than some, is a small black gnat. Do not despise this fishing, even though the dace be of very modest size, for their rise to a fly, and their rejection of it, can be fast enough to test the reaction of any angler and to defeat many.

EEL

by

COLIN R. GAMBLE

The eel is perhaps our most controversial fish: there are anglers who regard eels with loathing and there are others who seek them with dedication. They occur in every river, most streams, some ditches; they abound in many lakes, most pools and some duck ponds, indeed it is safe to say that anywhere that an inch or two of water accumulates there may be eels.

They have been the subject of learned treatises yet gaps remain in our knowledge of them and there is plenty of folk-lore which has yet to be proved – or for that matter disproved.

They would perhaps be more popular if the best time to catch them did not coincide with the most popular time to fish for most other species. Although some eels are caught at less favourable times there is no doubt that they are at their most active from the opening of the season to about the end of September. In some areas it is permitted to fish for them, with limitations as to tackle, during the normal close season for coarse fish.

I have not, from personal observation, found anything to support the belief that close, thundery weather is a specially good time for eel fishing, though I am sure that warm, settled weather is.

Certainly eels offer a challenging field to the angler who is prepared to fish for them seriously, for there are many who believe that they are relatively common at weights far above the present record. I am utterly convinced that I have seen an eel of double the present record weight in a small Cambridgeshire drain, and there have been reports of eels captured by means other than fair angling which certainly make the record weight appear quite modest.

However, even in very ordinary, run-of-the-mill sizes, say between one and three pounds, the eel will give a fight out of comparison with its weight, a fight which has initially convinced many an angler that he had hooked something outstanding.

It would be a mistake to be too dogmatic about the most effective methods and time for catching eels; the fact is that one simply has to find out by experiment how to get the best results in individual waters, but one can be quite specific about tackle.

Notwithstanding that quite large eels are landed from time to time on light tackle, there is no point in setting out to catch eels on tackle which will not handle them effectively.

Not the easiest way to land a pike, but the angler here had brought his fish up the side of a concrete bank in an effort to 'beach' the fish without using a gaff. The pike did not bite the captor!

Experience and years of fish catching lie in the hands that hold this rod and the angler knows every move of his float as it is guided downstream to where the fish are waiting.

This 8-year-old boy knows little of the ways of fish – but he has lots of hope that one (even a small fish) will take his bait.

When fishing a tidal river the nests of water birds always give a good indication where the high tide will reach. These are the eggs of an oyster catcher, left in the sun to hatch. The birds know that the tide will not flood the nest and the angler will know the 'safe' mark to fish.

Any fish is more difficult to control on a short rod, and an eel needs to be forcefully controlled right from the moment of hooking. An ideal rod for this job would be not less than 10 ft in length, would have a progressive action, with enough power to allow one to haul hard when necessary.

The choice of reel can be a personal one, but there may be some value in the suggestion that a simple centrepin reel is less likely to produce tangles in the dark.

In any water where large eels are possible, and there are not many which fall outside this category, I see little point in using a line of less than 7–8 lb breaking strain and if there is reason to expect eels of the huge size which is not impossible, there would be no shame at all in doubling this strength.

I believe that it is no more than commonsense to use a short wire trace, about a foot in length, when dealing with a fish which has fearsome dental armament. No doubt many eels are landed without a trace being used, but more are lost; therefore when I hook an eel, especially a large one, I want every advantage that I can obtain.

I know of nothing more reliable for this purpose than a short length of banjo first string. Some may see a snag in its stiffness, but if this is a valid objection I think it is offset by the enormous strength-to-thickness ratio and the freedom from kinking. Certainly there is nothing which will give the same strength without being very much heavier.

A link-spring swivel, or a split ring, on the end of the line provides the safest and most convenient method of attaching the trace.

Eels can be caught on a wide variety of baits. I have had them on bread, cheese, maggots, live fish, mussels, bits of meat, kipper, liver, and so on, but most of these were either isolated or accidental catches. When fishing specifically for eels one need only consider two baits – dead fish, either a whole one or part of a larger one, and lobworms, for it is certain that no bait will catch more eels than these. However, on some fisheries there may be a marked advantage in one or the other of these baits.

I believe that, by and large, a dead fish is the more effective in heavily fished waters, because, as a side result of the heavy fishing the eels are more used to finding dead fish on the bottom. The incidence of other species may also have a bearing on bait choice. It may happen, for instance, that to use lobworms results in an unacceptable number of bites from small perch. The only thing to do is to use both baits and find out which brings the better results in a particular fishery.

Although there is no compelling reason why a float should not be used, there is no particular advantage in it either. It may be that in some situations a float will be called for to carry the bait to a difficult position, but the bait should always be presented stationary on the bed and legering is the best way to achieve this.

Of course, legering does not necessarily demand the use of a weight, and unless it is called for, either to achieve a long cast or to hold the bait in a current, weight is better omitted. Eels can be far more sensitive to drag than is commonly accepted and the weight is one possible cause of drag which can often be eliminated. If a weight must be used, ensure that it is absolutely free-running on the line or it will inevitably cause the baits to be dropped.

When baiting with lobworms a high quality, eyed, single hook is all that is needed, and if you choose between a size 4 and a size 6 you will not go wrong. One worm or several can be used; in either case the hook needs to be passed through the worm only once, some preferring to hook the worms about their middles, others choosing to hook through the heads.

How to hook a double lobworm bait

A dead fish bait can be of just about any species which will provide the size required. I have caught eels, or seen them caught, on roach, perch, rudd, gudgeon, bleak, ruffe, sprat and trout, also on pieces of herring and mackerel.

There is no doubt in my mind that the sense of scent is very important in the feeding of eels, and there may be real value in the suggestion that the bait, if whole, should be cut several times to release body juices.

Eels can undoubtedly be attracted by ground baiting with minced or chopped fish. Although I do not entirely discount the idea, I am less confident that there is value in the use of animal blood, eggs and offal, etc. which some favour for this purpose.

The method of hooking a fish bait is a subject on which there are different schools of thought. I believe that one large single hook gives as much certainty of hooking the eel as does a treble, perhaps even more. It also provides the eel with less chance of leverage to free itself, as a treble hook is often engaged by one point only, therefore offering the other two for the eel to bite against. It is quite common to see a treble hook flattened by this bite (however, I am probably in a minority on this point).

The hook should be baited before attaching the trace to the line. A baiting needle is used to thread the trace from mouth to vent so that the hook can be drawn back to sit in the corner of the bait's mouth. Some anglers prefer to drag the hook, bend first, from vent to mouth, before positioning it as before: this is done to mutilate the bait internally, the belief being that this makes it more readily detectable by scent.

There are several methods of placing treble hooks. If one treble is used it can be sited at the angle of the jaw; however, if two trebles are used their traces can be threaded separately from mouth and gills, so that the hooks come to rest on opposite sides of the bait with the traces emerging at or below the vent, where they are clipped on to a link-spring or split ring. Alter-

Dead bait with one single hook

natively, the two trebles can be stuck into the bait, one into the mouth and the other into the flank, leaving the traces outside the fish, and using a turn or two of thin, soft wire to bind them close to the bait.

When fishing at night with fish baits it is advisable to have a number of baits ready mounted,

so that having landed an eel one need only slip one trace and fix the next.

There is rarely any need for a specialised method of bite detection. If a little slack line is left after the bait has settled, one can, by day,

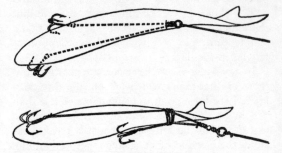

Alternative methods of using two treble hooks in a dead bait

watch for tightening of the line and drawing out of the slack. By night a slip of metal foil looped over the slack line will give both audible and visible warning of any movement of the line.

At this point, the first sign of a bite, one often meets another conflict of beliefs. Many anglers maintain that one should allow the eel to run with the bait, pause to swallow it, and begin to run again, before striking.

It must be accepted though, that this initial run is unpredictable in duration. I have known it to be of no more than a yard or two and as far as fifty yards, its length perhaps being decided by the distance to the eel's lair.

The subsequent pause may last no more than a second or two or it may last as many minutes, its duration being decided by the eel's eagerness or ability to swallow the bait. Nor can it be denied that not infrequently the pause which separates the two runs extends indefinitely because the eel has either dropped the bait and departed or has taken a bite from the bait and is apparently satisfied with that.

Whatever the causes may be I find that the traditional pattern of an eel's take fails to materialise frequently enough to warrant my preference not to look for it at all.

I use a bait which is perhaps smaller than is usual, certainly not more than four inches long. This I think increases the chances that an eel will take it well into the mouth at the first grab. I then strike as soon as line is being drawn steadily and I do not think that I lose a higher proportion of bites than do most eel fishers.

A larger bait does nothing to increase the chances of larger eels, and it does not bring any immunity from the attention of very small eels.

The first few seconds after hooking can often decide the outcome. Once the hook is driven home a heave at maximum strength should be made to lift the eel from the bottom. Failure to do this, even for a few seconds, will give time for the eel to lock itself into a hole or to burrow deep into such snags as it can find.

Once the eel is up to mid-water the battle is half-won: one must simply keep it moving towards the bank, for it is pointless to attempt to play out an eel to the point of exhaustion where it can be drawn in quietly – this point never seems to arrive.

Most eels are best landed by being drawn up the bank. When it has been brought within about a rod's length one simply stops reeling in and walks smoothly backwards until the eel is safely grounded. If a landing net is to be used it needs to be a really large one for there is nothing more hopeless than to steer a large eel into a small net and keep it there.

If it is to be killed, pin the 'neck' of the eel beneath the arch of the boot, and whilst pulling on the trace, place a sharp-pointed knife at the base of the skull, and push hard. The eel is then dead, but beware of the bite for some hours after this. Unhooking can sensibly be long deferred and I can show a scarred thumb as evidence that an eel can give trouble four hours after death.

If the eel is to be returned, a bit of dry sacking gives as good a grip as anything, and use forceps to remove the hook.

Generally, one should fish the deep water during daylight and fairly shallow water during darkness. However, in well-coloured water or among dense weeds eels may be found in shallow water at any time.

Some waters fish better by night and some are better by day, and in some there appears to be little difference. I used to think that deep mud on the bed meant that daytime fishing was likely to be fruitful and that a firm bed was a hint to fish by night, but more recent experience has not borne this out and I am now frankly undecided. One must set out to find the best times in one's own fisheries.

Long casting is very rarely needed by night. A bait which is laid a yard or two along the bank is as well-placed as any in most waters, especially if a trail of mashed fish has been placed so as to point the way to the bait.

I do not think it is possible to define a typical or ideal swim for eel fishing. If one tries to do this it is likely that whatever is said will apply only to one or two particular fisheries. It may not be very much help, but all that can confidently be said is that one is usually safe in avoiding the absolute extremes of depth and of current. Eels feed where food is most easily found and that is not often in the extremes of deep or shallow or in really fast water. The answer is mainly one of experience.

My final point is concerned not with the catching of eels but with their treatment after capture. Many people like to eat eels – I do myself – and I have no argument whatever with those who kill eels for this purpose. However, I am sure that the majority of eels are killed solely because they are eels and for no other reason. I make a plea for this fish – and don't forget that it is a fish – which deserves the same consideration as any other species.

It can offer splendid sport, it can be fished for almost anywhere that there is water and it probably offers a more realistic challenge to the hunter of specimens than do most other species.

GRAYLING

by

CHARLES DERRICK

The credit for bestowing on the Grayling (*Thymallus thymallus*) the title 'The Lady of the Stream' is attributed to Francis Francis, when he wrote in his delightful and gallant style 'If the trout be the gentlemen of the streams, the grayling is certainly the lady'.

Since then generations of anglers and angling writers who appreciate this delightful resident of the cool clear streams, have referred to it as Her Ladyship. No fish which ever swam is more fitted to bear the title.

Although the grayling is included with coarse fish and is governed by the same close season, it is a little out of place, for this lovely creature has the distinction of being a true member of the blue-blooded Salmonidae clan, and despite its likeness to a coarse fish, is a first cousin to the lordly Salmon, the Trout, Whitefish and the Char.

In common with the rest of the members of this aristocratic family, the grayling carries for all to see the unmistakable badge which identifies them, the small leathery adipose fin.

Perhaps the most outstanding and noticeable feature about the grayling is the outsize dorsal fin, a lofty sail-like appendage which when fully erect gives the fish a top-heavy and unbalanced appearance. For what purpose nature endowed the grayling with such an outsize piece of equipment, no one will ever know.

The eyes of the grayling are both distinctive and unusual, the pupils are pear-shaped and rich blue in colour, and the long shapely body varies in colour in keeping with the environment in which it lives, and to a large extent according to its sex and age. The colour range can vary from

bright silver to almost black. Mature cock fish show against light chalk gravel as black shadows, while the hen fish are much lighter and less easily seen.

The grayling's back shades from a deep green to black, while the underparts range from off-white to light grey. In the case of the mature male fish a broad streak of purest gold runs along each side of the belly, a point which many anglers miss and one which is well worth a second look.

Walton's view that the grayling had a soft and tender mouth was certainly never gained from experience. Unless they have changed a great deal since his day, and contrary to popular belief, few fish have a tougher or more leathery mouth. Indeed, once your grayling is properly hooked there is very little chance of losing it. For its size the mouth is quite large, and in the case of a fish of 3 lb, I have found no difficulty in putting in a penny on its edge.

The pelvic and dorsal fins of the older fish are mottled with a mixture of purple and chestnut in a most attractive and unusual tortoise-shell pattern, indeed a freshly-caught grayling reflects so many colours, tones and hues that it would be a sheer impossibility for anyone to give it an accurate description. No artist has yet succeeded in doing justice to this lovely creature, and I very much doubt if one ever will.

Grayling are distributed in the rivers of southern Scotland down to the south of England, wherever the water is pure enough to suit them. Some believed that prior to the grayling restocking fever of the 19th Century, the species was mainly confined to those rivers which flow in an easterly direction. The view is held that the species is indigenous to certain of our rivers, while others say that they were introduced by monks. It is certain that the grayling is found in many waters where the monks built their monasteries, and undoubtedly the monks were responsible for a great deal of restocking, particularly in the case of tench and carp, but the grayling theory is most unlikely. Anyone who has had any experience in moving them from one water to another even for short distances, will know only too well how soon they die without proper attention, the slow-moving monks would I fear have found the task impossible.

Grayling have a decided preference for fast-moving and well-oxygenated waters, favouring those with gravelly bottoms. For that reason they are found in nearly all trout waters, the few exceptions being those preserves where mill dams, weirs and the like prevent their upstream migration.

In waters where grayling and trout are fellow residents, the grayling are not always looked on as welcome guests. They multiply at a phenomenal rate and soon become a real threat where food supplies are limited. This applies more perhaps to the rain-fed rivers than to the chalk streams, but in both cases only by constant netting and fishing for them throughout the winter months can a reasonable balance be maintained in favour of the trout.

Some of my purist and fly-only friends have little to say in favour of the grayling, and think still less of their sporting qualities. Invariably their assessment is based on summer encounters when one has taken an offering intended for their speckled cousins. During the warmer months as a sporting fish they can be disappointing, but let the same fish be hooked after a few keen frosts have sharpened their fight, and the conceit will soon be knocked out of the critics.

With the onset of winter a remarkable change takes place, Her Ladyship is now in the prime of condition, a sinuous and agile creature that uses every ounce of its new-found strength to fight and then fight again a superb rear-guard action.

In the fast-running water the huge dorsal fin is used to much purpose, held erect it makes a very effective brake and often the first sighting the angler has of his quarry is the huge fin breaking the surface. The wise angler will lose no time in coaxing his fish in to the quieter water as soon as possible. A big grayling will make full use of the faster midstream run just as soon as it feels the hook, and even though it may disturb the other residents in the swim it pays to get downstream of your fish and make it fight the rod and current.

Usually a grayling fights to the very last ounce of its strength and when it does come to the net is quite exhausted. But beware the one which still has some spirit left – many a good grayling

has been lost at this critical moment and the angler has been left wondering what happened.

These days most of my grayling fishing is confined to the rivers of Yorkshire where the species is well established, and where they have been a part of the piscatorial scene for longer than anyone can remember. In all the waters which combine to form the Humber Estuary, the Aire, Derwent, Nidd, Swale, Ure, Wharfe, and all their tributaries, there are thriving stocks. The upper Hull, and its main tributary the Driffield Beck as far as Bell Mills is another fine grayling water.

As long as there is a hatch of natural flies on the water, my preference is for fishing with the artificial fly, and even when the trout season is over I still look forward to several months of good sport with the fly. Throughout October, November and often until well into December, grayling will continue to rise and give first-class sport on a dry fly.

During summer trout fishing the more splashy rises in midstream are often ignored, the angler tends to concentrate on the tiny dimples close to the bank where the trout are lying in wait. But now it is time to change our tactics, the more obvious rises of the grayling are quite easy to distinguish and the rise form is often followed by one or two bubbles, all in all far more of a disturbance than that made by the trout.

When the natural fly is on the water, one offers the appropriate artificial. It may call for a Dark Olive, or an Iron Blue, or perhaps during a late evening hatch of Sedges, you will be well suited with a John Storey or some other bushy offering, e.g. the Red Tag, a well-tried and proved pattern, which has a reputation for taking grayling. There are many artificials that are capable of interesting these sporting fish, indeed, almost any offering with a touch of red, yellow, silver or gold in its make up holds an attraction for the Lady of the Stream. From October onwards the hours around noon are the ones which are most likely to produce a hatch of natural insects, and so sport at this time of the year is almost certain to be of short duration, but it can be fast and furious.

Although I prefer to take my grayling on the artificial fly, and consider it to be the most sporting of all methods, a day or two bait fishing at the back end of the season makes a welcome break. I must admit that I thoroughly enjoy a lazy day or so by a nice deep pool, or trotting a succulent worm or a couple of maggots down a long gentle glide. One of my favourite spots is a small backwater which doubles back under a leaning willow. The swirling current brings a constant supply of tit-bits in its wake and the grayling are forever on the look-out for tiny morsels of food. These are the places much favoured by the grayling, and once they have been located one can fish them time and time again, and over the years much good sport will be enjoyed.

In the matter of tackle for bait fishing for grayling there is no need for anything elaborate. My personal preference is a light short rod of 8–10 ft (my own favourite is a ferruleless 9 ft 6 in Spanish reed, with built cane top). Although I was brought up on the old-fashioned Nottingham reel, and still use one on occasions, I find the fixed spool reel a decided advantage when fishing for her Ladyship. They are a great help when casting against the wind, and a blessing when trotting distances of up to 60 yd and more.

I favour a monofilament line of 3 to 4 lb breaking strain, greased for a few yards back from the business end. My floats are in the main home-made from Balsa wood and piano wire, and are self-cocking. I also use a variety of bob floats of varying sizes, to suit a variety of conditions. To give me greater casting distance or to put my float deeper in the water, a length of lead wire wound round the stem of the float is in my opinion, far better than added lead shot. Grayling look for food which is swinging along with the current, and swirling along the bottom in a natural manner. Lead shot on the cast below the float tends to keep the bait at a constant level and makes it perform in a most unnatural way.

In the choice of hooks opinions differ, but I lean toward the larger sizes, e.g. Nos. 12 and 14 old Redditch scale, with a round bend and made from fine wire are ideal. More grayling have been lost through using hooks that were too small than for any other reason. A grayling's mouth is big and tough enough to warrant a good healthy strike to drive home the point and set the hook.

Grayling are extremely catholic in their taste, and will readily accept a worm, caddis grubs either in singles or doubles, as well as maggot. The grayling of our Yorkshire streams seem to have a decided preference for a maggot that has been dyed a rose pink and will often refuse those of any other colour.

Finding your grayling is never a certainty,

sometimes one is lucky and locates a shoal with the first cast, on another day several hours may be spent in fishless searching. Once a shoal has been found it pays to keep a gentle trickle of maggots and a few broken worms going down through the swim. Set the float so that the bait is held just clear of the bottom, and I have usually found that success comes more readily when the bait is fished in the following manner. Slight finger pressure will help to retard the flow of line, this in turn tends to hold back the float, causing the bait to be presented to the fish in the most natural manner possible. When the bait precedes the trace and float, it is sent trundling along the bottom in a manner that attracts the interest of the grayling, and the signal that a fish is interested may come as suddenly as a flash of lightning. Without any warning the float may dip in a manner reminiscent of a dace bite, or on the other hand it may be a sideways swing or a sudden check in the downstream run as if the hook had suddenly caught on a snag on the bottom.

Any of these variations should be read as an offer and the response should be an immediate firm sweeping strike.

At times I find the grayling in my local waters in a fickle mood, playing hard to get and turning their noses up at all the usual baits. When this mood is upon them there is nothing for it but to try different tactics. I would suggest that the angler moves well upstream of the shoal that he is attempting to fish, and after disturbing the river bed, follow the cloud back downstream and as it reaches the locality of the finicky shoal place a generous amount of ground bait and a goodly helping of maggots into the water. If this fails rest the swim for an hour or so, and then come back to it very quietly. You may well have disturbed the fish on your first approach.

When baiting with worms, I find that the smaller and brighter ones bring the best results, lively little gilt tails, brandlings and marsh worms hooked well up towards the head, leaving plenty of the worm to wriggle are a most attractive offering. If the quarry is in the mood a tit-bit of this nature will not pass unnoticed.

It is seldom that the weather is too bad for grayling to feed, some of my most rewarding outings have been when all other self-respecting fish have seen fit to retire to the bottom of the deepest pools. When ice fringes the margins of the stream and your breath goes out in puffs of grey mist they will still feed, in my book 'The Lady of the Stream' is the most accommodating of all the fish that swim; if I had to make a choice of one fish to angle for, it would without any doubt be the grayling.

GUDGEON

by

COLIN R. GAMBLE

There are probably not very many adult anglers who get enthralled or even excited by the capture of a gudgeon, except perhaps when these are the only fish to be caught. They are, even when full-grown, of no more than a few insignificant ounces and once a good spot is found there is often no difficulty at all in catching them to the point of boredom.

Nevertheless, I am sure I am not alone in having a regard for this little fish which stems from the days when a gudgeon was a big fish by comparison with the more usual minnows; no one can deny that for its small size a gudgeon is a doughty little fighter – or that most of us know times when a few humble gudgeon are welcomed.

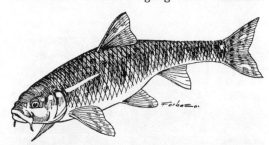

The conformation of the body and the position and shape of the mouth show that the gudgeon is essentially a fish of the stream and a bottom feeder. It is, of course, in many respects a miniature barbel, both in habits and appearance.

It is very widely distributed, being found in all kinds of waters from tiny trickles to major rivers, and it also thrives in some still waters.

A swim which could be expected to produce gudgeon in numbers will usually be a shallow reach, very often quite close to the bank, with a clean bottom of gravel and a moderate flow. In cold weather gudgeon follow most other species, moving to deeper water where the current is steady.

The fact that the great majority of gudgeon are caught accidentally by anglers using baits and styles intended to appeal to more imposing species, in swims where other species are expected to be, is indicative both of the gudgeon's catholic tastes in food and of its wide distribution. You can catch gudgeon on wheat, bloodworms, maggots, hemp, worms, bread, in fact just about any bait that you care to name; you can catch them by trotting, laying on, legering, in fact if you wish to catch other species in a water where there are gudgeon you may come to bemoan the ease with which they can sometimes be caught.

Even a fairly large bait is no real insurance against them: that sad-looking mouth can open to a sizeable gape, and many a chub and barbel angler has had his hopes falsely raised by the attention of an ambitious gudgeon.

In the last century, when the gudgeon was esteemed both for the pot and as the victim of a horribly cruel 'sport' which involved fixing a cork to the dorsal fin, the favoured method of ensuring a good bag was to first rake the bed some distance upstream, thus sending down a stream of fine bottom debris with the larvae, etc. which were thus stirred up.

If you really mean to catch gudgeon this is still a rewarding preparation, the value of which I have seen many times whilst wading, when gudgeon have come exploring up the trail of silt which was flowing from my feet.

Choose a swim which starts as rippling shallows and then deepens gradually into a smoothly flowing pool, scuffle the feet thoroughly around the shallows, put in a little fine groundbait and a few hook-bait samples as well, then fish the pool with the bait set to trip along the bottom.

Naturally, with so small a fish there is no need for other than very light tackle, although as there is always a real chance of larger species falling for the same bait and since gudgeon are not likely to be tackle-shy, there is no point in scaling down the tackle to a point where it will cope only with gudgeon. I see little advantage in using lines finer than 2 lb breaking strain in any circumstances.

The hook needs only to suit the bait: a very small, fine wire hook will be needed for blood-worms but sizes 14 and 16 will cope with all other baits.

The choice of float and the shotting will depend only on the current, the depth and the distance over which you are fishing.

If there is one bait which can be said to be better than any other it is a very small red worm, not more than an inch long, but it is certainly much less trouble and usually no less effective to use maggots which are more readily obtainable in quantity. Keep a trickle of samples rolling down with the silt cloud and you can almost guarantee to keep fish coming.

I cannot pretend that I find any great fascination in seeking gudgeon, for one cannot, as when catching equally small fish of other species, anticipate a better specimen coming amongst them. Nevertheless, they do provide a little interest when times are difficult, and they are worthwhile, if for no other reason than that they make most excellent live or dead baits for perch, chub or pike.

In any case, since they thrive in most of our fisheries, we shall go on catching them either by accident or design, and if they provide no great interest for most of us they will provide the encouragement for many youngsters to persevere and progress, as they did for me many years ago.

PERCH

by

DAVID CARL FORBES

I have long believed that there is no such thing as a typical perch swim, and I also think that a more general appreciation of this belief could lead to a greater chance of catching them, and particularly so the larger ones. It is said that perch may be found in the vicinity of camp sheathing, lilies and stone escarpments; we find this quoted throughout angling literature and, of course, one does find perch in such locations. However, this type of cut-and-dried ruling collapses when consideration is given to the nature of the water and the time of the year. Both are important, and indeed decisive, factors.

These traditional perch areas undoubtedly yield fish, but in my experience no more so than any other stretch of water. Mostly, perch from around lilies and stone escarpments, etc. are small, incautious creatures willing to engulf almost any bait. On many occasions I have used these spots to advantage on days when other fish are loth to feed. It is fun, but not serious perch fishing.

Real perch, those fish that have begun to put

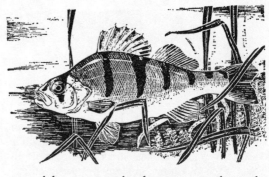

on weight, are nomads, almost constantly on the move, and content to stay in one place only so long as food stocks hold good. In rivers they are particularly hard to find. The shoal could consist of a dozen fish ranging from 12 oz to 2 lb, or could be a large gathering of fish ranging right up to 4 lb in weight. If so far you have caught only tiny, bait-robbing perch, such weights may seem huge, over-ambitious. But bear in mind that the record perch weight exceeds 5 lb, and while it is probable that you will never see such a fish, the species can be unpredictable. It is possible that a perch will be your first big fish. Whatever motivates our fishing we all like to think of big fish, and perch can be strangely accommodating.

I believe that the first essential is to consider the nature of the water to be fished in relation to the time of year. Perch in rivers showed marked contrast to their still-water kin, both in feeding and other habits. Weather conditions affect perch generally, but more so those in still waters.

During the summer months look for your fish in moving water. Most of our rivers and streams hold good stocks of perch, and the fact that we do not catch them as often as roach or dace can be attributed to their nomadic habits. Quite often a good catch of perch happens when a shoal is contacted by accident, and the fish fall for baits intended for chub or bream. On other occasions they may be attracted into the vicinity of the angler's bait, quite unintentionally, by the liberal use of cloud or ground bait. It is not the ground bait which serves as the attraction, but rather the hordes of small fry which gather to feed on the free meal.

The best rivers, or at least those which tend to offer good perch fishing, are those with wooded edges and a good depth of water right under the bank. You may encounter perch evenly distributed throughout every swim, even in the long, gently sloping gravel shallows, but such places are the very devil to fish. Our basic problem is essentially one of finding the quarry – they can be anywhere, and difficulties are reduced if we can reach the fish in a swim convenient to us.

To some extent chub holts are recognisable, and it is these spots the chub generally habitate. We soon learn to recognise the pools or glides which can be relied upon to produce roach and dace, but the lily patch or wooden piling that produced perch on one day will not necessarily harbour them on the next. The chances are high that the perch will have moved on to another spot. These areas which are traditionally considered perch swims, are not in fact true swims, but rather temporary holding points which break up an almost constant journeying. The time spent by the shoal in these holding points is determined solely by what it has to offer in the way of food.

Chub will sometimes find a suitable spot, one affording shelter from the current and predators, and offering easy access to food. There they may stay for the best part of their lives unless driven away by larger fish. Should this occur, the previous tenant finds a similar holt which he may defend against other, lesser fish. Not so the perch. The perch move into an area, deplete the caddis grubs and small fry, and then move on to other grounds. They stay just as long as the food lasts and seldom any longer. It is when the angler intercepts them in a bountiful, natural larder that most big perch catches come about. On such a day the angler might take anything up to 30 fish, and then not see perch again in that particular stretch of the river for many months. It has happened to me many times.

To contact a shoal of perch one can wander along the course seeking the holding points or try to discover the routes taken by the fish when they move. Both are lengthy propositions, and the former makes for more walking than fish. You may be assured that the river perch offers the least chance of a catch by intent, the best we can do is to lessen the odds against. This may sound rather depressing, but a constructive approach will, in the long run, produce more perch than fishing a spot once known to produce many fish, for a recurrence may never happen.

It is said that comparisons are odious, I think that examples are often equally as bad, but I do remember one particular day's perch fishing which does offer a lesson.

A friend had made several really large catches of perch over a period of three days from a side stream of the Hampshire Avon. This is a heavily fished river, and one which holds a large head of big perch, but strangely very few are ever caught. I went to Christchurch to fish this particular swim, but heavy rain had brought about almost flood conditions. The swim that had previously produced the fish must have been scoured clean of its upper layer of gravel and it seemed impossible to me that the fish had stayed in the spot. My companion had enjoyed three days of excellent perch fishing in a stream which does not normally produce them, and as far as he was concerned, he had found a perch bonanza, but he caught none that day.

I spent nearly two hours walking along the bank looking for the right place, and although the flood rushed right through to the main river

I eventually found an area that could contain the requirements of the perch shoal. It was a stretch of slack water in among sedge stalks, a mere ten feet by two feet of fishable water, but it was the only place that could hold food in some two miles of stream. Within the hour I took nine fish, before the activity frightened the shoal out into the fast water. I saw no more fish that day, and to my knowledge that ten feet by two feet stretch has never produced perch since.

On occasions I have enticed perch by putting small fish into keepnets, which have been pegged under under-cut banks. This idea is really no more than producing an artificial larder which attracts perch during their travels. This system

worked best for me on a trout stream which I know well, but from which I had only occasionally taken perch previous to using this decoy method. The stream complemented the method ideally, and provided the best perch fishing I have ever experienced, but it held no stretches that could even vaguely be likened to a traditional perch swim.

The smaller rivers, those with undercut banks, are, in my experience, the best perch rivers, and as the fish move they hug the banks. Such rivers invariably have currents which swing from bank to bank and wash cuts into the soil. In these cuts, right under the bank, not only is there comparative safety, but food is often abundant in these holes.

In the larger rivers the perch are extremely difficult to locate, for except in the very early hours they will be out in the dark water in the centre or travelling along channels between streamer weed or underwater lilies. Apart from the difficulties of actually finding the perch, there

are hazards of environment to contend with, and in such waters my perch seem to come more by accident than design. I understand what the many problems are, but I do not pretend to know the answers. I repeat, it is the smaller rivers that have given me my best sport with perch.

The perch is a lively fish and one of 4 lb caught in relatively confined waters will, in my opinion, put far too much strain on a match-type rod. I would recommend that for specialised perch-hunting a rod of 10 or 12 ft be used, and preferably one that has been constructed from split cane or hollow glass. I have found that a rod which gives tip action only is often not strong enough to control a large perch that is determined to break free.

In the smaller rivers most perch will be hooked close to trailing brambles, fibrous roots or submerged branches, and they will have to be played most of the time on the action of the rod alone. There will be very little room to allow them to run, therefore the action of the rod is very important.

The choice of reel depends to a large extent upon the ability of the individual to use a particular type, as well as upon the conditions under which he fishes. The fixed spool reel is the most efficient casting tool available, but quite often there will be no need to cast. Most of the fishing consists of trotting a bait as close to the bank as we can get it; and right under the bank when possible. One may find a fixed spool reel adequate, but for this style of fishing I prefer a good centrepin.

These are the simplest form of reel, and for this style they should have a diameter of at least 4 in to give speedy line recovery. When choosing your reel, ensure that the pillars holding the line are widely set. There is no point in having a wide diameter reel if the line winds on to a narrow core, and requires some 400 yd of line before an effective diameter is achieved; 150 yd of line will handle anything that the angler is likely to encounter in freshwater, but a line of this length can seem very little when wound on to the drum of a 4 in reel. Build up beneath the line with backing.

Avoid like the plague those reels with highly-chromed finishes, these reflect sunlight to the detriment of your fishing. Also beware of reels with many complicated fittings. These seldom do more than serve as an adornment, and provide traps upon which line will catch.

I use a line of 5 lb b.s. for this 'close-in' form of fishing. Bear in mind that your line has to take the strain of a rod flexing against a fish trying its utmost to gain the safety of nearby roots. The line must be complementary to the rod for often there is no relief for either until the fish is clear of snags, or in the net. Also, one must consider the floating debris that lodges in vegetation. I like to keep my floats and resent the time involved in tying on hooks – with a line of 5 lb b.s. one can often retrieve tackle that would otherwise be lost, and if done gently the fishing will not be spoilt.

I dislike lines which have a bright green or blue colouring – a personal fad, but one which I will never relinquish, so I choose my lines from those coloured in subtle tones of brown or green. Brittle line often parts as a knot is tied, so choose a really good supple line (but one that does not stretch or spring too much). Apart from its inherent qualities, the treatment you give to a line will greatly affect its performance. Check often for sign of wear, and, if you smoke, watch that you do not bring your cigarette too close to the line.

Hooks should be tied direct to the reel line, thus dispensing with weak hook lengths, and while it matters little whether the hooks be eyed or spade end, pay close regard to whipping spade end hooks to line.

While the pre-tied fine hook has its place in other aspects of angling, in my opinion there is no place for it here. Depending upon the bait which is being used, I would suggest that the choice of hooks be kept between sizes 6 and 10.

The perch has an extremely large mouth, but it is a sparsely fleshed one, and often the really large hook is made from wire which is too thick to penetrate and give a good purchase. As perch become larger, so they seem to become harder to hook. I have had more perch shed the hook before netting, than perch which have come to the net with the hook gorged.

The conventional perch float is round, cork-bodied and attractively painted. As far as I am concerned they may look well, but do they function well? My main disagreement with the use of a float of this type is that, even at close range, they cause a tremendous disturbance on impact with the water. I further believe that

they create too much resistance as a fish takes, although to some extent this should be overcome by correct shotting.

Large perch do not engulf the bait like their incautious smaller relations. Frequently they will move off with the bait held carefully in their lips, and experience has taught me that a badly shotted round-bodied float will cause the fish to eject the bait very quickly.

When live baiting these floats are at times ideal, and frequently a live bait will cause a large perch to take with great ferocity.

The main thing to remember is that the float should be chosen to suit both the conditions and the bait which is being used.

My own choice usually falls on a long porcupine quill, which is shotted so that with the addition of the bait, barely an inch of tip is showing above the surface. This is ideal under normal summer conditions.

Different days, different ways, and where a fairly turbulent current must work the tackle, and in so doing strip line from the reel, I would favour the use of a tapered float built of balsa or elder pith which has been built onto a quill stem. A float of this type will give you all the buoyancy of the round or bob-type float, but as the bulk is distributed all along the stem, it is in my opinion a more suitable item of equipment.

Maggots, grubs, worms, spinning lures, and small live fish all account for perch, but in the long run I have found that worm is the supreme bait. The others may have their moments of glory, but it is the worm, and in particular the lobworm, that consistently produces perch.

Small worms, brandlings or marsh worms, are very effective, but they do not last long enough in the water, and they are sometimes difficult to mount on a hook. The ideal creature is that which emerges at night and moves across a lawn. An angler once wrote in *Fishing Gazette* that if he could cultivate a lobworm that weighed half-a-pound, it would not be too large for perch. He was right, lobworms are never too big.

One point that must be remembered when

1. Porcupine quill float; 2. elder pith or balsa bodied float

baiting up is the distance you intend casting. When fishing fairly close to the rod tip no great force is needed, therefore it is normally sufficient to hook the worm lightly just once through the middle.

However, when distance casting is necessary place the worm on the hook as shown below. This method of hooking enables a long cast to be made, the force of which will not tear the bait from the hook.

Bait presentation is all-important, and to a large extent success depends upon the ingenuity shown by the individual in overcoming the varying conditions that prevail.

It is seldom that a situation can be correctly judged until one is at the waterside, and it is upon the angler's reading of the water and his ability to offer the bait to the fish in an attractive manner that gives success which is often out of the ordinary.

At this point I would impress upon you how important it is, particularly when fishing for big perch, to do the job thoroughly. In other words if you are attempting to take fish from a particular weedbed, then get your bait right into the centre of it; similarly, if trotting and attempting to search all those holes and nooks and crannies under the bank, make sure that your bait goes right in. By doing this you will, over a period of time, catch far more big perch, but you will also lose a lot of hooks. But that's an occupational hazard, and there is some compensation in the fact that hooks are much cheaper than golf balls.

Meet the perch on their own terms, and you will catch quite a few, but if you expect them to leave the easy pickings among the reed stalks to intercept something drifting past in the current you may well have to wait a long time for your fish.

There is an oft-repeated quotation: fish fine and far off, and while on occasions this is good advice there are many times when I feel that too many anglers neglect their own bank. Supposing that you were on the far bank to which you are casting it is an almost odds-on certainty that you

would be casting back to the spot where you are now in fact standing. So why not save the effort and disturbance of long casting and utilise the water immediately available; but remember, approach the edge quietly. This lack of extra noise will make your close-in fishing far more profitable.

The routine which I have explained above, will you will find be virtually the same during the winter months, but by now the plants in the river will have rotted and the fishing will be somewhat easier. Flood water and rain will invariably put a few extra feet of water into the river, and under these conditions, the perch will generally be found much closer to the bottom.

Small fish, mostly minnows and gudgeon, make good perch baits under certain conditions, but they do not, as is popularly supposed, control the size of perch you will catch. An 8 oz perch is just as likely to beat a larger fish to the bait, and is well equipped to take it. One can go to extremes by using 6 in roach or dace as bait, and although this will work, it is a lengthy process. The main drawback to using live baits is that they have a habit of getting themselves helplessly entangled with blanket weed or involved with fibrous roots, and once this has happened the angler may wait indefinitely for a bite. A bait which is not working effectively is almost as useless as no bait at all.

Live baits can be very effective in some waters, as extreme examples I would suggest the Thames weirpools, or close to reed margins on the Norfolk Broads. Unless one can readily control the bait – for example from a boat – small live fish by their mobility can be a hindrance to fishing.

When using a live bait, the fish should be hooked lightly through the upper lip with a single hook. I believe that the more traditional treble counteracts its hooking power by having disadvantages. The weight of this type of hook soon wears out a live bait, and renders it ineffective. One might as well start off with a dead fish. The two free points of the treble also provide the added risk of the bait tangling itself irretrievably in some underwater snag. Quite understandably, there are those who do not like to use a small fish as a bait, and completely ignore the method. For them there is spinning.

On small rivers where the banks are heavily wooded or where the watercourse is overhung by tall vegetation the angler of average skill will find that spinning is a hazardous business. With spinners and plugs at 3s or 5s a throw the losses that can be incurred during a day's fishing can rapidly become prohibitive. Under such conditions one learns very rapidly to become a good and efficient caster or goes bankrupt in the process!

But there is one consolation that I can offer. It has been my experience that these smaller, difficult-to-spin waters more often than not produce better results when fished with a natural bait. So often one finds when trying to spin on confined waters that as soon as the spinner has settled and the retrieve begun, one runs out of space or the hooks foul an underwater obstruction.

Generally speaking, spinning is best left for the open river where there are deep pools, or large still waters, for example reservoirs and gravel pits.

Spinning is a very active method of fishing, and on a fresh autumnal or winter morning this is one aspect well worth considering.

It is a method which without doubt produces its full share of perch, but it is not the simple method that many anglers imagine. True effectiveness lies not so much in the tackle that is used, but in the manner in which it is operated and controlled. If you cast as far as you can and

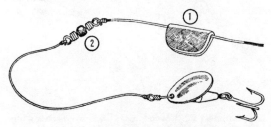

A basic spinning rig. The fold-over lead (1) always goes onto the line first. It activates the swivel (2) and thus prevents the line from kinking

retrieve the spinner by cranking the handle as rapidly as possible, you will certainly keep warm, but I very much doubt if you will catch any perch.

First, consider the type of rod that should be used. When spinning, my choice is for a rod with a long handle, in other words a double-hander which I can employ almost like an ultra-light beach caster. I like the rod to be at least

10 ft in length, this is a good and efficient length for playing and controlling a fish.

There are many shorter spinning rods which have a beautiful action, and with a weapon of this type an expert caster is able to drop a lure into a restricted area and fish most delightfully with it, but rods of this type are slightly restricting in that they are designed to cast only the lighter artificial baits. I have found that with my heavier double-handed caster I can not only spin quite efficiently with light-weight lures, but my rod has the additional power and strength necessary to be able to cast heavier baits with efficiency.

Whether one chooses a fixed spool or a light multiplying reel is a matter for the individual. My own thoughts are that while the fixed spool is an efficient reel and simple to use there is a great delight in being able to operate a multiplier efficiently. There is the additional fact that it is considerably easier to cast very light baits with a fixed spool reel, but fishing is such a personal sport that in matters like this much has to be left to the individual's choice.

Lures which are suitable for perch fishing come in many shapes, colours and sizes, and often the manufacturers give guidance on their use under specific conditions. My experience has been that although these formulae work for other predators, perch seem to be far more unpredictable. Frequently I have changed lures time and time again, and then suddenly the combination has fallen into place and I have begun to catch fish.

I would suggest, and this is based purely on past personal successes, that any small predominantly silver lure will tempt perch; this is

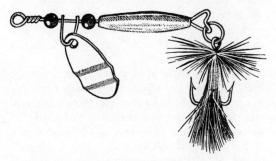

providing that it is retrieved correctly. If this fails then change to a wobbling spoon with black and gold colourings predominating. Finally, I would suggest that the lures to be used should be the smallest that can be obtained or the smallest that you can cast with efficiency.

Big lures which are retrieved slowly sometimes attract the attention of a perch and a violent take is felt, but for some unknown reason I have time and time again failed to hook such takes. Whilst I have no foundation for this, I am inclined to believe that this is caused by the perch striking at the lure from the side, instead of making the more orthodox tail attack.

During mild weather I have found that fly spoons have been particularly deadly. These I attach by the swivel and clip three or four split shot onto the line some 12 in up from the lure. The addition of the split shot helps to force the swivel to work. A bait of this type is difficult to cast very far but you can allow it to sink very deeply.

At one time it was suggested that a certain type of spoon was most effective when it was adorned with red tags, these tags were supposed to be tied to the treble hook. Although I have never added red tags, I do not think it has greatly affected my fishing successes.

One of the biggest mistakes made by the angler who spins for his fish is his constant and seemingly insatiable desire to get his bait from the water. In other words, he retrieves too quickly, and this in turn draws the lure too high in the water. For example, in 30 ft of water a lure which is worked 10 ft down will to a large extent be ineffective.

When commencing to spin over a water with which I am unfamiliar, I make my first cast with a pear-shaped leger lead in place of the spinner. I choose a lead which is comparable in weight to the spinner that I intend using, and by judging the time that the lead takes to strike bottom I have learned to be able to estimate the depth and also to judge fairly accurately when I should begin to retrieve line.

The action of the spinner whilst in the water is the real secret of effective spinning, a retrieve of equal speed and constant direction will rarely take fish. Continually alternate the speed of recovery from the first short quick burst to the almost lifeless fluttering as the bait is allowed to sink. By swinging the rod tip from side to side, make sudden changes of direction which add lifelike realism to the action.

When one begins spinning, the fear that the lure will become permanently attached to a snag

on the bed often inhibits the correct and most efficient action, but practice and the loss of a few lures help one to appreciate the killing properties of a slow retrieve.

There is one other important attribute that the angler must have, and that is his constant awareness of the efficiency of his method. This awareness gives him confidence, and confidence sharpens his appetite for a rapid strike. Spinning becomes less and less productive as the angler's

Regardless of the type of water, or the species sought, a lure should always travel in an erratic course it it is to be effective. Swing the rod tip slowly from left to right, and then back, again, while varying the speed of line retrieve – this should keep the lure moving attractively

anticipation wanes and the action becomes mechanical.

Lastly we turn to summer perch fishing in still waters. These fish do not seem to wander quite as far as their kith and kin of the river. Obviously there are restrictions which are

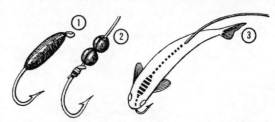

Drop minnow rig. Leaded hooks for convenient casting weight are shown in 1 and 2. The line is passed through the bait with a baiting needle, and mounted as in 3

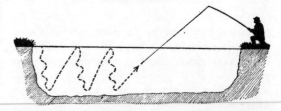

The minnow is dropped on a slack line so that it spirals down to the river bed. It is then drawn to the surface and the procedure is repeated until all of the water has been covered

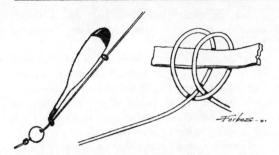

A sliding float rig for use in very deep waters, such as reservoirs and gravel pits. A rubber band, or heavy-guage nylon, is clove-hitched to the line as a float stop to set the tackle at the required depth

imposed by the topographical limits of the water, but over and above that they still do not seem to have such nomadic tendencies. Despite this fact, the problems brought about by their movement are still considerable, and particularly so when the lake is large.

I have found that perch in still waters tend to try and establish mastery over a certain territory. This may be a clump of weed, a cavity in a lake bed or a particular small bay, but whatever this area may be, they try to defend it against the intruder. In some situations a shoal of perch will deploy along a large bank of sedge and whilst each tends to guard its own little section against the other, they will occasionally sink their differences and join together and seek, as might a marauding army, the defenceless fry of roach or similar species.

This activity often takes place at first light and may last for no more than twenty minutes to half-an-hour, but during that time the angler can make an impression. After making their kill the platoons of foraging perch will retire once more to their territories, and for the most part they tend to be pike-like in their habits.

Secure behind their camouflage they become unwilling to wander far, and are content to use the vegetation as an ambush from which to launch themselves at an unwary prey.

During the months of high summer one will frequently discover big perch hiding among the lily stalks. Beneath the pads the vertical stripes of the perch blend admirably with the stems; hovering motionless except for the occasional tremor of a pectoral fin they are almost perfectly camouflaged.

At this time of year when the sedges are tall, fishing for big perch takes on almost a safari-

like quality. I like to wander around the margins of a lake, taking great care to remain hidden and to always approach the lakeside as quietly as possible. After a silent approach a worm dropped temptingly into a likely-looking hole between the pads or weedbeds, will often bring a great surge of activity.

The attributes of a good fixed spool reel under these fishing conditions are many, and the ways in which they can be used to the best advantage is well described by Barrie Welham in his chapter on Casting and Line Control (page 95). Here I will do no more than say that there is an enormous amount of fun and a great deal of excitement to be gained from fishing in this manner.

When the first perch has been caught I always assume there are more in the locality and will attempt to bring more to the net. Occasionally this approach brings good results, but when sport ceases I then start the second phase of my fishing activities.

During my original circuit of the lake, during the time I was actively hunting the fish, I would have decided upon two or three swims which I considered likely to warrant a more static form of fishing.

Assuming that these swims have a water-depth of up to 8 ft, I would be content to fish with a float. For the first few feet I would use normal float techniques, but once the regions of 8 ft are reached I would change to sliding float tackle. However, if the water should be more than 9 ft deep, I would leger.

When float fishing search the water thoroughly at all depths; for bait, I am still of the opinion that a lobworm is the 'bait supreme'.

When legering I would at first present a slowly sinking bait on an unweighted line. If that were not successful, I would change to more orthodox leger tackle and would do my best to present my bait well in under the lily pads. This method of fishing will inevitably result in the loss of a few hooks, but to be successful one must be prepared for this.

Invariably I would use the link leger arrangement and rely on a visual means of bite indication. By leaving the bale arm of the reel open one can spot the line peeling from the spool, but if your concentration is such that you can watch your line where it enters the water, then that makes an even more sensitive guide to the fact that a fish has taken.

One's chances of a successful day's perch fishing can often be enhanced by the correct use of ground bait. Not that the ground bait itself attracts the perch, it doesn't, but it does attract myriads of small fish which in turn entice a hungry perch. To achieve this end, I would suggest that a crumb is made by grinding very stale bread. This crumb can be moistened slightly and formed into a ball. As the ball hits the water, it will break up, some of it sinking very slowly and some remaining for a while upon the surface.

I believe that the smaller perch tend to stay and feed in the upper regions of the water where they feed voraciously upon the small fry. The really big perch will often tend to be lower down where they rely heavily upon the system of ambush or the finding of a sickly or wounded fish, and so, while there is great activity above, a leger placed below may well result in the capture of a large fish.

During the winter months the perch will have retired from their summer lies to the deepest parts of the lake, although occasionally they will be found in their summer haunts.

Attempts to locate perch during winter can be most frustrating. Increasing success will come as your knowledge of the water builds up. Once the deepest holes are known then legering is really the answer, but great accuracy is often needed to get the bait into exactly the right spot.

Live baits are really out of the question when one is considering long casting into deep water.

It may be possible to dead bait, but I always come down heavily on the side of a large lobworm for my perch fishing.

When fishing for perch in gravel pits and deep lakes during the winter, bites are invariably few and far between, and it becomes a pastime that calls for dedication, but it is my experience that when the fish do come they are often the big fish for which you have waited so long.

There is only so much that an angler can learn from an instruction manual, and remember that even the best manual is only a working guide. Success comes only when the instructions are applied and coupled with your own increasing experience and knowledge.

Contained in that knowledge there must be a fairly intimate grasp of the ways of the fish you seek. Regarding perch we still have a lot to learn and some of the points that I have made, for example those relating to the feeding habits and mobility of really large perch, are to some extent speculation. However, it is speculation that is born of much fishing practice, and after all, when delving into another element we are forced to a large extent to speculate. It is on the accuracy of our conjecture that much of our success in angling depends.

Without doubt, luck is always a commodity to have on our side, but one may wait a long time indeed for a big perch unless aided by more tangible qualities.

PIKE

by

HARRY TALLENT

Over the years pike fishing has been invested with a certain amount of mystery and a whole lot of lore. The tales of the strange happenings when big pike have been hooked are recounted wherever fishermen foregather.

Pike are hated, pike are cherished. On some waters they are hunted and killed mercilessly whenever they are encountered, and elsewhere it is the proud boast of the fishery owners that 'in this water there are giant pike'. You may love

them, you may hate them, but you cannot ignore them, for this species is the embodiment of all the primeval savagery of ages long gone.

The Irish waters and some of the Scottish lochs as well as the Norfolk Broads hold pike of almost legendary proportions. And for that matter there are many smaller waters which continually supply surprise catches which make headlines in the angling Press.

However, for a fish to grow to near record size

This barbel of 7 lb 5 oz fell to a single maggot float fished to a No 16 hook in the Thames near Maidenhead. It is gently introduced to its home again and held upright until it is ready to swim away under its own strength. Barbel are strong fighters but soon weaken after a time in a keep net; make sure all is well before you leave the fish in the water.

◄ This roach weighed 1 lb 14 oz and came from the Sussex Arun. It was gently returned to the river, to live and fight another day.

After the final whistle in a fishing match – and at times the prize can be really worth winning – the fish are brought to the scales for weighing. The scale pan in this picture was used five times before the final weight was added up!

Sometimes there is a good fishing spot within yards of heavy traffic. This picture was taken under a motor-way bridge –
and the boys were catching fish . . . educated-to-noise roach and dace!

Everything the angler needs during his day by the waterside – including his flask with a hot or cold drink – is within easy reach. The fish caught can be slipped quietly into the keep net close alongside.

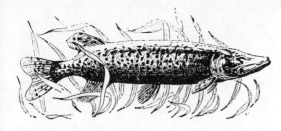

it must have a sufficiency of food and an environment which suits it, quite apart from the chance to grow. There are many anglers who, through force of circumstances, spend the majority of their pike fishing hours on waters which produce fish of the small to medium size quite regularly, but rarely if ever a fish which warrants a glass case.

There are methods which are suited to the varying types of water one finds throughout the British Isles, and while it is difficult, if not impossible, to generalise, by taking examples and following through a day's sport at each venue, much of interest can be learned.

We begin with a perfectly ordinary mill pool and the stretch below, typical of many similar venues which are to be found on quiet-flowing rivers, a location where both bait and quarry can be hunted.

Pike of these and similar waters feed to a large extent upon minnows and so it is with the bait that we will start.

A likely place to find these fish are the gravelly shallows which lie immediately downstream of the pool itself. The small depressions and hollows close to the bank are areas where large shoals will frequently be seen. All that is needed to catch them is a very light rod, 1 lb b.s. line and fine wire hooks size 16 or smaller. Two or three inches above the hook nip one small shot on to the line and bait with a piece of paste no larger than half a matchhead.

To facilitate the quick and easy removal of these small fish from the hook I always remove the barb with a pair of forceps or small pliers.

Lower the paste very quietly and gently down amongst the shoal and immediately it will be surrounded by the minnows who peck and pull the bait both this way and that. Eventually one will take the bait completely, and a preliminary sharp jerk of the rod, which is subsequently smoothed into a quick lift, will hook the fish and bring it quickly to hand.

As the minnows are caught, deposit them im-

mediately into a bait can. Providing that the light is good enough to see the minnows clearly, it will rarely take very long to catch a score or so, which is usually more than sufficient for a day's average sport.

Very often you will find that while fishing in this manner you will take several small dace and sometimes even a gudgeon or two. Keep them – both these species make excellent pike bait.

Knowing your tackle is as important as knowing the water in which you are going to fish, and for this style of fishing almost any light rod will be suitable. However, by 'almost any' I do not mean one of those lengthy stiff-stemmed, wandlike pieces of equipment which are the delight of the match-fisherman's heart.

For this form of fishing my first choice usually goes to an old light spinning rod which has become very pliable after years of hard fishing. My basic requirements for a rod used to fish a venue of this type is that it shall be pliable enough to give at least some fair play to even a small jack. To this rod I marry a fixed spool reel which is loaded with a 6 lb b.s. monofilament.

I would assemble the terminal tackle in the following way. First the small cork float which is bored through the centre is run onto the line, this is the pilot float and although not much larger than a marble it will be helpful in many ways. Beneath this goes the $1\frac{1}{2}$ in *Fishing Gazette* type float which is held in place by the central peg gripping the line. As a weight I would choose a small pierced bullet, and to the end of the line a small link swivel is tied.

For this class of fishing I would suggest that size 6 or 8 hooks would be adequate. Each hook is tied separately to a 12 in length of 5 lb b.s. Elasticum wire, which is terminated with a small loop.

When a pike is taken on tackle of this type it is simplicity itself to release the hook length, a fact which greatly facilitates the easy removal of the hook from the fish.

The baits are presented hooked through the upper lip, and are fished approximately one foot from the bottom. I suppose that this could well be described as 'mini' pike tackle, and it is eminently suitable for the size of pike which are more often than not found in this class of river.

Choosing the first position from which to fish is an exercise that can only be satisfactorily concluded when the conditions prevailing at the time have been looked at and thoroughly assessed. Usually, except when winter floods make it untenable, the mill pool is good for one or two fish. But first let us visualise the geography of a water of this kind. It is often roughly oblong in shape, possibly 40 yd in width and down the centre pours the millrace which gradually slackens in speed until, at the extreme end it fans out into a ripply bubble-topped area.

If there are any hungry pike in the pool, then more than likely they will be in that area, for experience has taught me that this is where they are most likely to wait for a sick, bemused or injured fish.

It is amazing how many small fish are injured as they are swept through a mill, and are taken with great ease by a pike which is patrolling the end of the run.

Beyond the bubble-topped area the true river channel will often narrow sharply to possibly 20 yd or less, and here the water will pick up speed again as it shoots away over the gravelly shallows. However, not all the water can get downstream at one time, the surplus returns back up the pool in the form of two quiet eddies, one up each side. In these eddies other pike may be found, although more often than not when they are lying to the side they will be resting. But if a minnow presented attractively within easy range they might well be tempted to 'have a go'. Usually the water in the quiet areas will be about 4 ft deep, and except for the one or two shoal patches the water in the eddies will be of a similar depth.

It is important to get the bait down to as near the pike as possible, but at the same time it must be kept above the debris and snags which are inevitably found on the bed of a mill pool.

To achieve this correct bait presentation, make sure of the depth and then adjust the large float to a position that will bring the bait to rest approximately a foot from the bottom; once the large float has been set, peg the pilot float 18 in further up the line.

Select the bait and having opened its mouth pass the point and barb of the hook up through the skin behind the top lip. By hooking the bait in this manner it will be able to breathe easily and consequently, it will remain lively (this is most important).

The method of fishing should be related, as far as possible, to the position in which you think the pike is lying. Remember that it is ex-

pecting fish to be brought down to it by the stream, and so lower the bait into the mill race and let it be borne downstream into the bubble-topped area at the tail of the pool. Once it has reached this, let off one or two more yards of slack, trip the bale arm, and let the bait wander for a few minutes, just to see if anything will happen.

The tackle can be made to wander by laying the line across the main race. The flow will catch it, and will eventually pull the large float from one side to another.

Assuming that one or two fish are taken from the pool and sport then goes quiet, it would be advisable to start searching the side eddies.

When pike fishing and using a minnow as bait, it will usually be found that the pike will take very decisively and suddenly. The minnow is of a size that allows the hunter to take it in one gulp and therefore there will rarely be the period of agitation and indecision which sometimes precedes the take of a much larger fish when it has been tempted by a live bait of $\frac{1}{2}$–1 lb in weight.

As soon as the main float has gone, the direction of the run can be followed by watching the pilot float, and when the strike is made it should be sideways and at the same time away from the direction taken by the fish.

The sideways strike will help to set the hook into the more fleshy corners of the mouth, rather than trying to drive the hook into the hard bony roof of its mouth, when it may even lodge between its sharp teeth.

Whilst exploring the side-ebbs of the mill pool, search them thoroughly, for the pike which are lying there may well have had their fill and be loth to chase far for a meal, but a minnow placed enticingly within range may just be sufficient to encourage them.

Remember, check the depth every time you change your area of fishing, and make sure that the bait is approximately a foot from the bottom.

Having searched the sides of the pool, the next area to fish is that section where the gravel shallows give way to deeper water.

Choose if possible a nice streamy run, varying possibly from 3–4 ft all the way down. But again do not forget to adjust your floats slightly, and in so doing keep the bait roughly a foot from the bottom.

When fishing a run such as I have just described, approach the edge carefully and quietly, keeping, as far as possible, at least a rod's length from the edge. Cast the bait out no more than a couple of yards, and as the current takes it downstream follow it quietly but still keep well back from the edge.

As the float dips from sight, watch the run of the pilot float, move quickly and quietly to a spot a yard or so below where the pilot float betrays the presence of the pike, and then strike. Having fished the run, then return once more and search the opposite side of the pool and river in similar fashion.

At this point I think a word about the minnow bait would be helpful. Do not try to take the minnow that you are using all the way back up to the pool on the hook, it will inevitably be dead by the time you get there. At the same time little good will be done to it if it is continually being unhooked and rehooked. My tip is to unclip the hook length and drop the fish on a slack wire back into the bait can. Failing that, merely put the bait back into the can on a slack line and carry rod and bait can in the same hand.

When using live bait, remember that a fish that has been cast many yards through the air to hit the water with a resounding thud, will hardly feel like moving. If it is not killed or stunned on impact, it will more than likely merely lie completely doggo refusing to move at all. Therefore always treat your bait with the utmost respect, cast it gently and use the current to take it to the area you want to fish.

Playing a pike, no matter whether it be a relatively small jack or the monster for which you have waited a lifetime, is always a matter of give and take. If you keep the rod tip well up and force the fish to exhaust itself against the spring of the rod, and the give and take of line from the reel, you will be able to dictate the course of the battle rather than have the pike beat you and finally snap your line like burnt cotton.

I feel very sorry for those who catch pike on short powerful sea rods, and 20 and 30 lb b.s. line, for they will never know the thrill of catching these sporting fish on tackle which is matched to the strength of their quarry. To merely drag a 5 lb or even 10 lb fish from the river on such tackle is not to my mind angling, nor is it sporting.

I well remember one glorious September afternoon when fishing a pool in the manner I have just described. I ended up with 13 pike, maybe not all monsters, but each one a delight to catch and a challenge to my skill.

Frequently on waters of this type there is one special holt where a big solitary pike will lie. Often this will be a cavity under a bank, a cavity that has been scoured out by the winter floods. Often the spot you are seeking will be found on the inside edge of a bend where the river current seems to draw back on itself, giving a stretch of water with hardly any movement at all. If there is a heavy fish then more often than not it will be found just here.

Take off the size 8 hook and put on the 6. Remove the minnow and bait up with a small dace.

Cast out into the stream just above the bend, let the flow carry it around, and draw it carefully into the quieter water. So often these tactics will be rewarded, and the dace will begin an agitated death dance on the hook, which just precedes to the surging rush of the pike which will carry the float down.

Watch the direction in which the pike is running; this will be betrayed by the pilot float, and then strike.

It might well be that a fish of 8 lb or even 10 lb can be taken from a stretch such as this, but as I said much earlier in this chapter, so often waters of this type will only produce fish of the 4–7 lb class.

LIGHT SPINNING

Spinning is an activity which I reserve for the colder months; what better than an October day when just sufficient breeze puts a ripple on the water, the temperature is steady and a fairly thick canopy of cloud obscures the sun? These are the conditions which have always prevailed when I have been most successful. A calm bright clear day with plenty of sunshine is not the weather I choose for spinning, but the diffused light which penetrates through a ripple tends to mask whatever there may be unnatural about a spinning bait. October is a month when the weeds have begun to die back, and therefore the rotting stems afford scant hold for the hooks which arm a spinner.

In preceding chapters there is much good advice regarding tackle, so here I will do no more than say that for this type of fishing I would choose a light spinning rod of approximately 7 ft in length and would use it in conjunction with a fixed spool reel and a 6 or 7 lb b.s. line. Remember that when using a reel of this type it is most important that the spool be correctly filled with line.

The arrangement of the terminal tackle is relatively simple, but the greatest enemy of all anglers who spin for their fish is line twist. There are many ways in which this hazard can be overcome, and who can say which is best when many operate efficiently. My own choice is a $\frac{1}{2}$ in diameter half-circle of transparent plastic with a built-in swivel, which is known as a spinning vane. This is attached to a link swivel which in turn is tied to the end of the line coming from the reel. The 18 in trace is 5 lb b.s. Elasticum wire, which is so important when pike fishing. A material of this type will take the rough and tumble of being within a pike's maw.

The small link swivel at the far end of the trace is placed so that spinners and plugs can be clipped on or changed easily and rapidly.

There is a further reason why I favour the

Light spinning trace, incorporating 5 lb b.s. Elasticum wire

small plastic vane; I find that its very light air drag saves much of the annoyance caused by lures turning over in flight, and thus catching the cast in their hooks.

My lures I keep in a box, about a score of them, each in a separate partition, all different and not one weighing more than a quarter of an ounce. When spinning, the correct balancing or grading of your tackle is most important. One cannot, or at least should not, try to use heavy lures armed with big hooks on light rods and lines, or for that matter vice versa.

A bait which I will amost inevitably take out first is a Devon. This compact little lure casts well against the wind, and it is a bait which in one of its many colour combinations I have found to be consistently successful.

For this exercise let us once again imagine a situation that can so easily be typical of many waters. A bank which is relatively clear, with shallows close in, but deeper runs in the middle, overall a small river of some 20 yd in width with variable depths.

I would make my first cast upstream, fairly

close in to the side on which I was standing. The retrieve would have to be fast, and the rod tip must be kept high, so that the bait is kept up off the bottom.

The bait is sent flighting some 30 yd upstream, to a point some 6 ft out from the bank. Remember to make allowances for both wind and the time it takes for you to trip the bale arm and begin recovery of line. While working the bait through the water, alternate the speed of recovery as well as the direction. After searching the particular stretch two or three times, begin to widen your field of activity and fish the deeper runs way out in the main channel.

When fishing the deeper water, give the bait a moment or two to settle before beginning the retrieve. The rod tip which was held high while fishing the shallows is now well down but still almost at right angles to the run of the line. Never point a rod directly at the lure. Despite the fact that a fixed spool reel has a slipping clutch, it is much better to fish in a manner that allows the rod to take the initial shock of a fish taking the bait, also the rod is already in a position to begin playing the fish correctly and to keep it on a tight line.

My experience has been that big fish as well as relatively small ones, will take small baits. I have taken pike of 9 lb or more on a 1 in Devon minnow, but no matter whatever the size your bait may be, remember to keep the hooks clean and sharp. If you do this, most pike, in their enthusiasm to seize a meal, will hook themselves.

Continuing now with the business of casting, I would suggest that after searching the deeper runs upstreams of where you are standing, then turn your attentions to the shallows on the op-

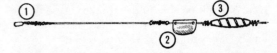

Heavy spinning tackle, incorporating 10–15 lb b.s. Elasticum wire. 1. link swivel; 2. anti-kink vane; 3. spiral lead (optional)

posite bank. Throughout October and November, and on occasions until almost the turn of the year, the sedges and reeds will still be in evidence, and so this casting operation needs an amount of care and skill. An over-cast and your spinner could well be lost, an under-cast and the fish will be disinterested. As with all sport, the aptitude to cast correctly and accurately is not only a joy in itself, but it is in the final analysis the only sure way of catching fish.

The main problem associated with fishing a location where shallows run into deep, and then back to shallow water, is that the bait must be retrieved quickly with the rod held high whilst searching the shallow water, then slowly and with the rod tip lower while coming through the deep, and finally quickly again as the last few yards are fished. If circumstances permit, I would carry the rod point round a little further, so that I am able to fish out to the very last each cast I make.

Having fished the area forward of my stance I would then search the waters opposite it and then gradually begin casting to cover the down-stream area in a similar manner.

While retrieving against the flow, one can do so at a slower rate, for even whilst fishing the shallows, the force of the stream will tend to not only operate the spinner, but it will hold the bait off the bottom.

While pike fishing in this manner, it is almost inevitable that you will hook or at least see some evidence of perch.

It has been said many times in the past, and it will be said many times in the future, but it is well worth while, in fact vital, to stress that there are many many occasions when a pike will follow the bait for many yards and will only strike at it in that last second or two before the spinner is lifted from the water.

Having fished the area and maybe taken a fish or two, move up- or downstream approximately 15 yd, and repeat the process, and continue moving and fishing until you have achieved an intensive criss-cross coverage of the whole stretch of river you are able to fish. Thus there will be very few pike that are in a feeding mood that will not at least have had a chance to see your lures.

The various spinners that one can use all have particular merits of their own. For example, a 1 in Devon if retrieved fairly fast can be used in water barely a foot deep .The small French Celta with a spinning blade not much larger than a silver threepenny piece can be used in similar waters, but can be fished at a slower rate.

I have found that the smaller-sized Voblex is ideal in water some four foot deep, for with a medium rate of recovery it will work extremely well about 2½–3 ft down.

A spinner of the Lill Atom type, one with a large single hook and a thin wire spring guarding the point, is ideal in weedy areas. A ¼ oz Toby is a lure which I use quite often when fishing sink and draw style, the Toby spins as well on the free fall as it does on the upward draw. And while talking about equipment, do not forget to keep your landing-net with you all the time!

Temperature is as important when pike fishing as it is when hunting any other species. My experience has been that when the temperature is falling, pike are not all that interested in feeding. They always seem to be more interested when the thermometer is rising, particularly after it has been doing so for two or three days after a cold spell.

When fishing in waters where it is known that big pike are to be taken, then it is courting disaster to use light spinning rods and small lures. Although the fishing techniques are basically the same, one must match the strength of the tackle to the probable weight of the fish you will catch.

On a river similar to that which I have been describing then fish of 10 lb will be exceptional, and a 12 or even 14 pounder is one that will be remembered and spoken about for years. On the Norfolk Broads, however, a 10 or 12 lb pike could well be described as a very average fish; in waters such as these there are sufficient large fish, up to and no doubt beyond the current British record, to warrant the continual use of big fish tackle and tactics.

For sport of that kind I would recommend a high quality heavy spinning rod, a reel capable of carrying at least 100 yd of 11 lb b.s. monofilament, plus an amount of backing. The traces must be correspondingly stronger, and the anti-kink vane of at least 1 in diameter. The plugs and lures will weigh about an ounce and sometimes more.

Although the basic techniques are similar, the stance from which they are carried out could well be completely different. On the Broads, where much of the surrounding land is marshy, a boat is normally used for fishing. By drifting into un-frequented bays where thick margins of reed afford plenty of cover, and presenting plugs and spinners, many great hauls of pike are taken. And for these very large fish it will be found that gaffing is the most efficient method of removal.

Referring back to live baiting with minnows, the principle of larger baits for larger fish which I have just related to spinning, also applies when live baiting. In the small river where pike up to

7 or 10 lb may be expected to be the largest fish that you will catch, then minnows and small dace make excellent bait. However, on the Broads or similar big-fish waters then live roach of 6, 8 or even 12 oz can be used to great effect. Fish of this size should be mounted on two big trebles, with a 3 in float to support them, two 1½ in pilot floats, a 15 lb b.s. line and matching trace, plus a rod that is strong enough to drive the hooks home into the sinewy bony jaws of a large pike.

There is always the chance that the unexpected will happen, and that a really large fish will take a small lure. Sometimes you will be unable to land it, but there is always consolation in the thought that at least you know a big fish exists, and by marking the spot, albeit mentally, you will be able to return with stronger tackle, and once again try conclusions with a fish of challenging proportions.

DEAD-BAIT FISHING

As pike get older and bigger they tend, like humans, to slow down a bit, and give up chasing small fish; they become more selective in their kills. Water fowl, voles, frogs, as well as fish that have died or are in the process of so doing, all are much easier, as well as more filling, prey for a big pike.

It is the bigger class of fish which frequently fall victim to a legered dead bait, often a herring.

This is neither an involved nor particularly difficult form of fishing. The main problems lie in the choice of a suitable rod and in the selection of an area likely to hold a fish that will move to a bait presented in this manner. The terminal tackle is simplicity itself, the main line ends with the link swivel, onto which is clipped the eyed trace which carries the three sets of trebles.

When choosing a rod for this type of fishing, several points must be considered. It has to be strong enough to cast a bait of herring size, and yet it must not be so stiff that it breaks the line when the strike is made. A stiff rod striking a

Dead herring prepared for legering. 1. cotton binding; 2. trace

25 or maybe 30 lb pike which is running hard will place a great strain upon a line, particularly so when a strike of some force has to be made in order to set the hooks.

My own favourite for this form of fishing is a 9 ft rod with a butt and middle joints of whole cane and a greenheart top. My rod is 25 years old, and has had a surfeit of fishing duties, which have all combined to give it a certain flexibility which I find just right.

There are several schools of thought regarding reels and line. There are those which favour a centrepin, and those who stick to a fixed spool reel. In the matter of line, whilst most use monofilament there are many who say a braided line not only lies more naturally on the bottom, but its lack of elasticity helps set the hooks more firmly when the strike is made. My choice falls on a fixed spool reel and monofilament line. I feel that the elasticity in nylon helps to counteract the movements of a heavy fish, and in this way it offsets whatever advantages there may be in having a non-extensible line.

It is rare that much lead is needed. In still water none need be added to the line, and even in rivers, large pike tend to stay in sections which are relatively slack, therefore the matter of lead weight rarely arises. Where it does, the terminal tackle should be made up in normal leger form.

When the bait is mounted on hooks, it is often an advantage to add a few turns of cotton just for extra security, but before you do this, puncture the bait several times with a penknife along its belly and back. This will not only ensure that the bait sinks, but it will also release oils and juices which will help to attract a hungry pike.

This style of fishing can be carried out from boats as well as from the bank. Cast in and if using a fixed spool reel, make sure that the bale arm is left open and draw a loop of line from between two adjacent rings and lay it once or twice around a box of matches. This is a first-class method of bite indication. As the pike takes the bait and begins to run, the box will soon fall clear and the matches will rattle.

In my opinion a dead bait is fished more effectively if it is moved every ten or twenty minutes, rather than casting out and waiting for the rest of the day.

Although this is a waiting game, and one that

is played very slowly, your casting has to be planned intelligently, so that all the likely holts are searched.

Normally I would cast a bait and allow it to settle in one position for possibly fifteen minutes; I would then lift the rod tip and in so doing draw the bait towards me, let it settle once again, and then reel in the slack line.

When a pike takes a live bait it is almost an odds-on-certainty that it will do so cross-wise and then turn it head-first before gorging. Unfortunately I do not think anyone is absolutely sure how a pike picks up a dead bait. This being so, there are various ideas regarding the method of hooking the bait.

My suggestions are fully illustrated, but there are those who mount their baits the other way round, i.e. with the bottom treble near the head and the top one close to the tail, and while both methods bring success, I think that the ultimate choice is largely a matter of personal preference.

While waiting for a take, it sometimes pays to stir things up a bit by spinning through the area in which your bait is lying. The extra activity and 'buzz' may just draw the fish to your bait.

When the fish for which you have been waiting does decide to take, do not be in too much of a hurry to strike. Give it time to take the bait properly; only when you feel that the fish is running strongly should you lift the rod and drive the hooks home firmly. Hooking a really big pike is in some ways rather like striking at a log. On so many occasions, for a split second that seems ages, you have that horrible fear that you have snagged the bottom; if you have never caught a really large pike you will hardly believe the resistance that it can offer.

Of course there are always those fish of almost every species that decide to give up the fight as soon as the hooks are in, but a pike is a fierce creature who hates the restrictions imposed by a determined angler. Once hooked, it will run for the reeds or similar cover, and will frequently rush towards the boat and after leaping may dive deep beneath it. You have to be ready to counter these tactics by passing the rod tip round and under the stern so that the line is kept clear. That is why when pike fishing from a boat you never anchor both fore and aft.

When the fish is beaten, and with a big pike this can take some time, bring it gently to the side of the boat and be very careful with the creature as you land it. Use a large net where possible, but if a gaff is employed insert it at the tip, under the lower jaw, and never into the fish's body.

Pike, whether the fish be 2 lb or 20 lb, have to be handled with care, but at the same time firmly. Its mouth consists of hard bone, sharp teeth and a grisly membraneous substance which does duty as lips and cheek, hardly a place for the soft skin of your hand. In other words, never try conclusions with a pike's mouth, it is an odds-on certainty that you will come off second best.

I never favour killing big fish, unless the rules of the water demand it, and so, assuming that this creature that you have just beaten is to be returned to the water, hold it firmly across its shoulders, and after having unclipped the trace from the main line, remove the hooks with a pair of thin-nosed electrician's pliers. It will frequently be found that if a pike gag is used, the removal of the hooks will be much easier. A gag can be one of several things, there are the custom-built jobs which are sold by tackle dealers and home-made items which are often similar, while some anglers will often stick an old pike float firmly into the corner of its mouth. The point to remember is that some device must be used to prevent these vicious teeth clamping home onto your hand. A small pike can cause wounds which need multiple stitches, a large one disfigurement and maybe maiming for life.

Having removed the hooks, then slip the creature back into the water as soon as possible.

The killing of pike is something which often brings out the worst in an angler. I have seen them literally battered to death, stabbed unmercifully, or sometimes discarded onto the bank with almost a shudder of revulsion. These creatures do seem to excite the worst and the best in some fishermen. Maybe it's the glassy unblinking eye, which to some seems full of malevolence and hate, but whatever it is pike have a way of attracting violent feelings.

For my part they are a sporting fish which have a place in the scheme of things, and I tend to favour returning them wherever possible. However, there are times when they have to be killed, and this should be done quickly and as humanely as possible.

The fish should be struck firmly on the top of the head with a weighted stick which is usually called a priest, an instrument which no doubt owes its name to the fact that it is used to administer the last rites.

A dead pike, and particularly one of reasonable size and from a clean water, can be eaten, they make a good meal if roasted; or if boiled in salted water the flesh can be used in fish cakes. These are not the only methods of cooking, the French have a great way with these fish.

TROLLING

This is a method of fishing which is closely akin to spinning, the main difference being that instead of the lure being drawn through the water by the action of the reel, it is towed by a moving boat.

The boat I use is an orthodox dinghy and although I like to have an engine with me for emergency or going to and from venues a mile or so away, the actual business of fishing can only be performed when your craft is being rowed. A slow and rhythmical dip of the oars will drive the craft at a very moderate pace (in fact if it is too fast, trolling will not be possible). The oars must be dipped carefully, without undue fuss and splashing, and when under way at a steady pace the lure is paid out slowly over the stern by the fisher until possibly thirty yards of line are out. The exact amount is dependent upon the depth of the water, if it is very shallow, then obviously less is needed than if it is deep.

Trolling is really a job for two, one rows and the other fishes, but make sure that your friends are able to row, otherwise you will find yourself doing all the hard work!

Apart from the conventional spoons and various spinners, plug baits are frequently used for trolling.

Floating plugs are particularly useful for this method of fishing, for they will only dive deep when you raise the rate of strike, and should you have to stop rowing then you need not fear that the hooks are going to become entangled with underwater growth.

From the lure point of view, trolling is a curious business. I have never been able to offer any explanation why 12 lb fish will sometimes accept a 1½ in spoon, while on the other hand the very first pike I ever caught on a Norwich

spoon, which had an overall length from swivel eye to hook bend of 8 in, was a fish of only 3 lb plus. On occasions kidney spoons have taken fish when big jointed, floating plugs have been ignored. Therefore, take my advice and always be prepared to change your lures as often as it seems necessary.

It is a relatively simple method of fishing, but there are certain things that, if remembered, will enhance your prospects. Never leave a rod unattended while the bait is working. A heavy fish will soon have the lot into the water; and if you troll while rowing, wedge the rod within reach, always have a lanyard attached to the oars, and make sure that the gaff or landing net is to hand. There's nothing worse than having to scramble for your rod while the reel is screaming, when at the same time your oars are drifting away on the current.

Tidiness in a boat is all-important, and I would seriously suggest that, when engaging in this type of sport and particularly so when alone, a life jacket be worn.

The tackle needed for trolling must of necessity be that much heavier, and therefore stronger, than for some other forms of pike fishing. I would suggest that the rod you use for dead baiting will prove adequate, but if a sturdy centrepin is not used, then the fixed spool reel must be much stronger than that used for light spinning. The main line and trace on my trolling equipment are both approximately 20 lb b.s.

This is a great method of fishing during the winter months when the weeds have died back and the chill in the air encourages you to keep moving. It is, of course, a method which has many limitations, some waters are of a type and so snag-filled that it is impossible to fish in this manner. The great Irish loughs yield many huge pike to this method of fishing and I well remember a companion of mine taking three large pike in one short run of 200 yd at the end of a day that had to that point been fishless.

This is one of the great joys of pike fishing. You just never know what will happen next. They are a species which offer a constant challenge to the thinking angler, as well as offering the average fisherman a chance to catch a really big fish on what are often known as small fish waters.

ROACH

by

PETER WHEAT

Few anglers pass through their first angling season without taking roach at one time or another, for these are one of the most widely-distributed fresh water species in the British Isles.

From tiny village ponds to expansive reservoirs, small streams to our largest rivers, roach are taken in sizes varying from stunted midgets to handsome fish of 2 lb and more.

I well remember one of my most successful evening sessions of roach fishing. The water was a smooth fast glide running alongside a reed-fringed bank on a most beautiful southern chalk stream. After introducing a few balls of ground bait into the head of the swim I began to trot the stream with my float running parallel with, and possibly a foot out from, the reeds. The hook, which was baited with maggot, was going through the swim a few inches above the bottom, and it wasn't long before the bait attracted the first fish. Away went the float, and, as I struck, I could feel a powerful creature struggling furiously to rid itself of the hook.

A roach will often fight in a rather typical manner, the sharp pulls giving a jag, jag sensation as the fish bores for the deeper water. They seldom seem to head immediately for the reeds as do chub and perch.

Finally the fish came to the net, and there was 1 lb 4 oz of red and silver beauty, a loveliness which to my eyes cannot be matched by any other species. That was the first fish of many which I took that evening, the best weighed 1 lb 12 oz and the smallest 15 oz. This was a red-letter day and one which I shall never forget.

Roach fishing on a fast-flowing river is seldom easy, and in fact there are often many blanks for every success. One of the essential qualities an angler who specialises in roach must possess is the ability to approach his fishing with an open mind and be prepared to change tactics and swims over and over again.

It has been said that roach are easy fish to catch, stupid brutes that are ready to bite at anything they see. In waters which contain large shoals of stunted fish, as a consequence of lack of food, this statement could well be true, but in fast rivers where there is an abundance of natural feed the roach grow big and fat and are wary, shy creatures, which are likely to eye with the utmost suspicion any badly-presented bait. Such roach can hardly be called 'stupid brutes'.

There are many who specialise in fishing for roach, and therefore it is only natural that there should be many thoughts regarding the tackle and methods which are the most efficient. Angling, being the very personal sport that it is, is full of ideas which spring from the eternal search for the perfection which we shall never attain.

My choice of tackle and methods is the result of many years' experience on varying types of water, tackle and methods which have served me well and have brought great reward in both fish and enjoyment. With experience you also will develop a technique of your own, but for your help and guidance this is how I hunt the roach.

For bank fishing where weed beds and sedges, etc. sometimes extend for several feet, I like to use a 12 ft glass fibre rod which has a very fast springy action. This is ideal for long trotting and at a pinch it can be used for legering, although for this style of fishing I much prefer a heavier split cane rod, one with an all-through action.

I find that a good fixed spool reel serves me well for both float and leger fishing, and there is one advantage which I find particularly useful: by carrying a selection of spare spools one can easily change to a heavier or lighter line. However, despite the many advantages offered by these reels, there is still a great amount of pleasure to be obtained by being able to fish correctly and well with a centrepin. The final choice is yours.

When long trotting or legering, a line which is less than 5 lb b.s. is in my opinion a liability. The power which is put into a hard fast strike which is necessary when possibly 30 yd of line has to be picked up and the hook set into a fish, will frequently snap a line with a lower breaking strain. This difficulty is magnified when the fish you strike is a heavy one. It is pointless to handicap yourself with a very light line, and it is also most unsporting to fish in a manner which is likely to leave a fish swimming about with a hook in its jaw and yards of line trailing from its mouth.

There are occasions, for example when laying-on close to the rod tip, a method which I find very effective during the winter months, when a 3 or 4 lb b.s. line can be used; but always select your line to suit your method of fishing.

Many floats have proved themselves excellent supporters of vast amounts of shot, etc., but this is not the criterion by which a float should be chosen. It should be remembered that a float has two jobs to do, one is to register a bite and give the angler warning that a fish has taken, and the other is to support the bait at the depth selected by the fisherman. Having agreed these two basic facts, one has to find the successful permutation which will then indicate the float you should use. It is impossible to be dogmatic about the calculations which have to be made, but they must include: the depth at which the bait is to be presented, the speed of the water, the depth of the water, whether one is fishing the far or near bank, wind direction, distance to be cast, and any other features which has a bearing which may be apparent at the time of fishing. These basic facts have to be considered before your float is chosen, but remember, a roach will rapidly eject a bait if it feels much resistance. The float you use must be only just sufficiently buoyant to overcome the weight of the shot.

I cannot overstress that the way in which your bait is presented is absolutely vital to your subsequent success, and the way in which the bait goes down to the fish is so often influenced by the float you choose.

Generally speaking, quill floats will prove excellent for roach fishing, but where the current is

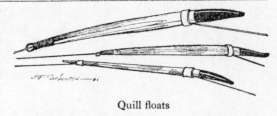

Quill floats

fast and the water deep, a cork-bodied float must be considered.

I would suggest that a fluted pith float would serve you well when fishing a centre run or the far bank, and also in areas where conflicting currents make for disturbed conditions.

It is my opinion that the distance between the hook and the shot is a vital factor. Correctly spaced it will enable the bait to behave in quite an attractive manner as it is trundled along by the current. When using maggot or the tail of a lob-worm I would place the shot 12–18 in up from the hook, but when using bread crust or flake then the distance between the hook and the first shot is decreased to about 3–6 in.

The broad principle to which I work is this. If the bait is what I term 'non-floating', e.g. maggot or worm, then the shot is placed further away from the hook. However, if it is a bait which is buoyant and tends to rise in the water, as does crust or flake, then the shot is dropped closer to the hook so that it keeps the bait down. It will frequently happen that incorrect shotting will result in the bait being presented above the shoal and in consequence one will spend a completely fish-less day. It is always worth spending a while getting your shot positioning right.

Flake bait (top) with shot placed close to hook to keep the bait down. Non-floating worm bait (bottom) with the shot placed further away from the hook

In common with most varieties of fish, roach in a feeding mood will normally accept one or other of the standard baits.

Maggots and chrysalis are most effective, they are an easy bait to use, and this being so it is very easy to fall into a rut and use them to the exclusion of all others. Bread paste or flake taken from the centre of a new loaf is attractive, as is a piece of crust about the size of a shilling.

I favour these bread baits, as I have found that the small fish ignore a larger bait whilst the roach of about 1 lb come forward to take them quite freely – indeed, I have seen this happening.

It is a fact that when maggots are being used and the swim is being constantly fed by the handful many small fish will move into and take over a swim, in other words the small dace and roach will snap and take the bait more rapidly and with less fear than the larger fish will do. Therefore, the bigger, older and more wary fish do not get a look-in.

During the winter months the tail of a lobworm, or brandlings, make attractive baits. These can be legered or fished in a laying-on style in what are suspected or known to be roach swims.

Hempseed, elderberries and wheat are three more baits on which you can take large bags of roach, but remember on some waters hempseed is banned, so make sure that it is allowed before you attempt to use it.

It is often thought that hempseed has magical qualities; this is pure nonsense. There can be no denying that it is an attractive bait, and as a food it is enjoyed by fish. But it is a bait which needs considerable skill to use correctly, the angler must have lightning reaction to a bite and if a water is heavily fished and fed with hemp, then this seed tends to become the fish's staple diet and other baits will be ignored.

Ground baiting can be accomplished in several ways. Done well, it can be the factor which leads to a record bag; badly carried out it can mean a blank day. I prefer a feed made from stale bread. Collect as much as you can, and keep it dry by hanging it in a string bag away from the possible attentions of mice. To make the feed, chop or break up the amount you intend using and soak it in a bucket of water, after a while drain off the surplus liquid and knead the pulpy mass into a soft paste to which is added dry sausage rusk. Make sure that the correct consistency is obtained, too much rusk and the ball of ground bait will lie on the bottom like so much undercooked plum duff. It will just lie there for hours in one solid piece, and therefore will not be the slightest use to your fishing. On the other hand, if the mixture is too soft it will be washed quickly out of the swim and be of limited value as an attraction.

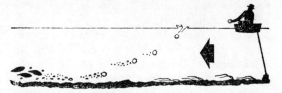

Correctly mixed ground bait will sink to the bottom and give out a constant flow of particles which will hold the interest of the fish

The correct mixture when introduced into flowing water will give out a steady cloud of white particles which in passing through the swim will hold the interest of the fish.

Other ground baits can be made from chicken meal or possibly a mixture of chicken meal and sausage rusk. But in my opinion these are not as efficient as the mixture which uses stale bread as a base.

The time of year and light intensity are two more factors which have a great bearing upon your success as a roach fisherman. These fish, particularly the larger ones, do not like bright conditions, therefore during the summer months your chances of taking a really good bag of these fish from relatively clear water on a bright day are small indeed. The best time under these conditions would be the early morning or the cool of the evening when the sun has left the water, and my experience has been that it is the latter time when the roach feed best of all.

When the fish are likely to be shy and difficult to catch I begin preparing during the late afternoon. After choosing a suitable swim I would slip the first of the ground bait in as quietly as possible. Because the fish may be lying in a fast

Roach love to lie in the streamy runs between reed clumps

shallow run between the weed beds or a deep glide close to the bank, locating the shoal is to a large extent a matter of trial and error. Once the ground bait is in, I assemble two rods, one for float fishing and the other for light legering, and having checked the water for depth I will sit back and wait until the sun has left the water before attempting to fish.

As soon as conditions are suitable I begin searching the swim in a systematic fashion. By careful control the float can be sent down the swim, each time on a slightly different path. The depth at which the bait is being presented is changed until the time arrives when the first fish is taken. Make sure that your next trot down follows the same path, and if once again a fish shows interest or is hooked, then it is reasonable to assume that you have made contact with a shoal and by careful fishing you should be able to take advantage of your good fortune.

If by the time darkness arrives sport is good and you feel reluctant to leave, then change to leger tackle and try for the really big fish that will often take a static bait at this time.

During the winter months the pattern which summer has set changes completely. Once the first cold snap has occurred and the river approaches its winter level, the roach will begin to form into larger shoals and seek quieter water. This can be a backwater or a slacker run, in fact anywhere they can shelter from the main thrust of the stream.

This shoaling instinct, which is always strong in roach, increases as the year comes to an end, and is probably influenced by the spawning which takes place in late spring. I have found that it is always more difficult to locate roach during the winter months than during the summer, and it has also been my experience that the winter sun has little or no effect upon them and they will often feed at any time from early morning until dark.

Although the deeper quieter swims are more likely to hold roach during the winter, there are occasions when the shallows around the silted bends on the edge of fast water will hold fish, I have known roach up to 1 lb to lie there in water which is no more than 18 in deep.

The question of trotting or legering is sometimes settled for you by the water conditions, but my own experience has been that legering tends to give overall better results during the winter months, and for bait I would suggest bread flake, the tail of a lobworm, or maggot.

I would tend to be more sparing with ground bait during the winter months, but I would stick to the same overall principles that I applied when summer fishing.

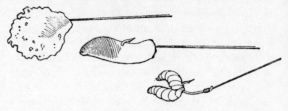

Leger baits for the winter – bread flake, lob tail and maggots

On certain rivers boat fishing is a very popular and worthwhile sport. In fact, fishing for roach from a punt is a most enjoyable experience. You can anchor above the swim and trot your float tackle down on the current, judging to a nicety the path that it is taking.

The tackle and tactics that I would use from a boat are very similar to those I adopt when bank fishing. The main difference in my tackle is in the length of the rod. Whilst on the shore I would use one of 12 ft, from a boat I find a 10 ft rod more adaptable.

Boat fishing can be fraught with difficulties unless you set about it in a workmanlike and efficient manner. Always assemble your tackle before going on board, and stow your tackle box, landing net and other items of tackle in a neat and orderly fashion, and most important of all make sure that the mooring ropes or chains are clear and ready to be paid out when the moment arrives.

Assuming that there are two of you in the boat, moor across the current; from this position you can trot the stream to perfection – long trotting can be judged accurately and the presentation of both hook and ground bait can be achieved efficiently.

One thing which is most important when boat fishing – noise. Equipment dropped on the bottom boards will make a great booming sound which will be carried to the fish. I have known a feeding shoal to be put to flight by the clatter of a landing net as it was laid down in the boat.

Finally, a reminder about ground bait. In my opinion it is far better to ground bait so that it does not reach the river bed until it has gone downstream for some yards. If the fish are drawn too close to the boat the shoal can so easily take fright and will not return to the swim. It is, I think, much better to fish for roach from some distance upstream of them, and draw the hooked fish from the shoal with the minimum amount of disturbance.

Although roach, through their habits of browsing on and through the weed beds, are sometimes called freshwater sheep, they are a species that gives sport and pleasure to many, and the fascination of hunting these fish in our rivers and streams is a pastime which never fails to absorb me completely.

Editor's Note:

The techniques which one can adopt for roach fishing in still waters, for example canals, are described in the chapter on Match Fishing by Billy Lane, page 181.

RUDD

by

COLIN R. GAMBLE

The very name 'rudd' conjures up a summer picture of broads, meres and quiet pools, fringed with reed and rush with rafts of lily pads spreading here and there. There are plenty of streams and drains and some major rivers which do hold rudd, some of them very good fish, but the cream of rudd fishing is usually to be found in still waters where there is a rich marginal plant growth; the Norfolk Broads are probably supreme.

The rudd's liking for reeds and weed can be both an aid and a problem; an aid because it tells of the likeliest spots, and a problem because the proximity of plant growth can be a considerable impediment to catching them.

If these are the ideal situations in which to look for rudd, the ideal conditions are those of high summer, with warm water, good light, a gentle onshore breeze and complete freedom from any kind of disturbance. Having said that, I must now confess that the two best rudd I have ever caught came in very different conditions: one took a large knob of paste which was being legered for carp at four o'clock in the morning, while the other took bread flake, intended for bream, and both fish came during a violent thunderstorm which included sleet and hail. These, and similar unexpected catches, I regard merely as indicating that rudd are as unpredictable as most other species and can sometimes be caught in conditions which might fairly be regarded as unfavourable.

However, if one is setting out specifically to catch rudd there is little point in doing so in other than favourable conditions, and for me this means choosing a fairly warm day.

One very serious snag with many of the better rudd waters is that it is practically impossible to approach the fish other than by boat, and even where the marginal weed or reed growth is narrow enough to allow a bait to be placed over it from the bank, the shyness of worthwhile rudd inevitably means that the catch is restricted to very small numbers.

Ideally, on a water of any size, one should row along very quietly and slowly, some thirty or more yards out from the reeds, watching for signs of fish. They may be showing fins and tails as they roll, they may be rising to feed, or they may be making audible splashes as they indulge in what looks very like light-hearted play.

It is important to look into the reed beds as well as along their outer edges, for rudd shoals will sometimes remain deep within the reeds for a very long time. It is just possible to fish for them within the reeds but this entails using a bait which will blanket the hook completely, otherwise you will inevitably hook a reed stem and once you have to pull to retrieve tackle you can say goodbye to the shoal.

If rudd are active among reeds it is better to attempt to draw them out to a point where they can be more effectively fished for. This can be done in a number of ways, all essentially a form of ground baiting; but normal ground baiting, such as throwing in balls of solidly formed food, is certainly not recommended, nor is any other activity which creates splash or noise.

It is far better, when the breeze is favourable, to float one's offerings down to the fish so that they drift in among the reeds, where some will lodge against the outer stems, and then wait for signs that the fish have moved outside the reeds to feed.

If you scatter broken, but not soaked, bread or maggot chrysalids there will be no doubt when the rudd have been tempted out. Large pieces of bread will be pushed about and sucked at until they disappear, small pieces will be sucked straight in, and no one will misinterpret the rises to floating chrysalids.

One method of attracting and detecting rudd

It has often been recommended that large slices of bread, tethered by a thread and anchored by a stone, should be placed along a likely margin so that one can observe from a safe distance when one of the pieces becomes the centre of a disturbance. This may work very well for some, but whenever I have tried it I have discovered that rats and water fowl are quicker to move in than rudd.

One can, of course, sometimes catch them by casting hopefully into spots which appear to be likely, but this can mean a great deal of wasted time. The rudd is a shoal fish and they often give their presence away to the patient and observant.

The tackle needed for catching rudd gives plenty of scope for personal choice. My own preference is for a rod of about $11\frac{1}{2}$ ft in length, with a supple casting action which will deliver light baits to a good distance, and which has enough backbone in the middle section to bully a fish quickly away from the shoal. My rod must also be light enough to be hand-held all the time, for rudd can take a bait decidedly quickly, and any delay in striking can mean that the fish has gone into the reeds.

The need to get a fish quickly away from both the reeds and the shoal rules out the use of really fine lines: something between 3 and 4 lb b.s. will meet most situations, though where there are lily pads nearby this could sensibly be increased a little, for there is no virtue in losing fish so that it swims off with line attached.

For rudd fishing, as for practically all other types, I much prefer eyed hooks which have been tied direct to the reel line. Matching the size of hook to the bait is important, a size 16 for chrysalis, size 12 for maggots, size 10 or 8 for flake, paste and crust.

As a close approach is usually out of the question there are few anglers who will not feel the need of a fixed spool reel to achieve the length of casts needed. It is possible to drift a bait downwind, feeding out line as in long-trotting, but this is a slow process which contradicts the customary need to take fish quickly before the shoal moves on.

If the bait is to be paste, flake or maggots, all of which are good rudd baits, or for that matter is any other bait that will sink, a float must be used. The depth to which the bait is allowed to sink may be a matter for some experiment, and can be anywhere from within 6 in of the surface to just off the bottom, but in either case, the weight should be either incorporated in the float or attached immediately below it so that the bait may sink quite naturally through the water.

I cannot agree with the idea that a well-filled bubble float is suitable for this fishing, although admittedly it makes casting very easy. Sizeable rudd, even though feeding eagerly, are sensitive both to the splash which this float must make on arrival and to the drag which it offers to a taking fish.

I prefer a float about 6 in long made of two fat goose quills joined centrally by a wooden plug with one end holding sufficient cemented-in shot to cock it.

This float makes far less disturbance, offers less drag to a biting fish and reacts more decisively to a bite.

When using a floating bait a float can be dispensed with, unless the distance between rod and bait is so great that rises are difficult to identify,

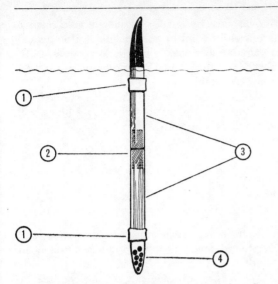

A self-cocking float: 1. rubber rings; 2. wooden plug; 3. goose quill tips; 4. shot (cemented in)

and there are occasions when the extra weight of a float is essential to enable light baits to be cast, particularly so when one must keep away to avoid alarming the shoal.

For this style of fishing I would suggest a slim float, attached by a ring at each end and used without additional weight. One made from oak, ash, greenheart, or a similar dense wood gives a good casting weight. It will float horizontally in the water, and will react to a bite either by shooting along the surface or by lifting to a vertical position.

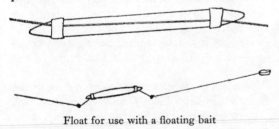

Float for use with a floating bait

It may be that even though one exercises the utmost caution the shoal will begin to drift away; should this happen, watch the surface along by the reeds, for unless you have been guilty of causing a major alarm, it may well be that the shoal will not travel far. It is not impossible to follow a shoal for half a day or so, taking fish at intervals.

I have seldom caught rudd while river fishing. When I have, the picture has been much the

same as that in still waters. The prime consideration is still to locate the shoals, and though it may sometimes happen that you find them by accident, it is usually essential to be prepared for a protracted search.

My successes have invariably come in the less streamy swims, as, for example on the inside of a bend where shallow, slack water has permitted the growth of lilies and other weeds, or sometimes from the stretch immediately below the confluence of a feeder stream, where an area of slacker water exists near the bank. I have never encountered rudd in the main stream of a river where there is power in the flow.

When river fishing, no matter what technique is being used, there is much to commend an upstream approach. There is less chance of alarming the fish by sight or sound, and, with the current acting in one's favour, one can more quickly draw a hooked fish away from the shoal, a point which must be borne in mind if you hope to take more than one or two from the shoal.

Provided one is prepared to take the trouble to move with infinite caution and take advantage of every possibility of concealment, it is possible on bright summer days to watch rudd cruising in clear water and to cast to individual fish.

Fish which appear to be just wandering aimlessly are often free risers to floating baits, and will take a dapped natural fly of the blue-bottle type or will follow a bunch of maggots or a pinch of flake which has been dropped in front of them.

The angler who is willing to try a somewhat unconventional approach will find that fly fishing for rudd is a very rewarding exercise. The approach work is basically the same as for any other method, the accent being on finding the fish without first alarming them.

Ordinary fly fishing tackle is used with an 8 ft tapered cast carrying a single fly. To use a team of three or more flies, as is popular in some districts, is to invite trouble when fishing within a foot or so of reeds, rushes or lilies; it is easy to find oneself attached to a fish by one hook and to a plant by another. This is a situation which is rarely resolved in favour of the angler.

Rudd will take many flies, but I doubt if anything will be more successful than a small, sparsely-dressed nymph of brown or greenish shade, a fly which might well be tied with odds and ends of silk and feather.

The fly should be dropped as close as possible

to the reeds; after a pause of few seconds, during which time the fly will sink a little, give the smallest possible twitches with a pause between each. The fly is retrieved very slowly.

By their habit of swooping up from below, taking the fly and swinging down again all in one movement, rudd will often hook themselves.

There are other methods which will take rudd, for instance they will occasionally take a small artificial lure, but to catch them consistently and in any number usually means that one must fish for them deliberately when conditions are at their most favourable.

There is one certainty, whichever method you use, this colourful fighter from the reed beds will never disappoint you.

RUFFE

This species is of no sporting consequence, as it seldom attains a size of more than 2, possibly 3, oz. In many ways they resemble small perch, but where these have two dorsal fins, the ruffe has only one which is spiked in the front section, but not at the rear.

Ruffe have a rather limited distribution, and are found predominantly in sluggish waters in southern, central and Midland areas.

When they are caught it is usually more by accident than design; an angler fishing for perch will sometimes find that he has hooked a ruffe.

TENCH

by

FRED TAYLOR (Oxford)

June, the month in which coarse fishing opens, is to my mind one of the most glorious periods of the year. The forget-me-nots and moon-daisies add colour to the bankside, and the hum of the bees gives music to a fine day.

Along the stream the last of the mayflies dance over their stretch of water before a fish rises to take them as they touch the surface.

In the early days of the coarse fishing season it is good to fish for tench, and thoughts come of early mornings in June with mist gently lifting from the water and of late evenings when the float has long since mingled with the shadows.

What a fascinating creature the tench is: small red eyes, large tail and beautifully iridescent olive skin. Izaak Walton referred to the tench as the 'doctor fish', pointing out that 'tyrant pike will not be wolf to his physician'. This I have proved wrong many times, having seen tench attacked by pike, leaving them badly mauled and bleeding.

Much of my tench fishing has been done on the famous Blenheim Lake, near Woodstock. I well remember one particular day which I spent on this water, when, after leaving the boat house at dawn, we settled to fish a particular swim. Evening came much too soon, for when darkness forced us ashore we counted the fish as we returned them, and the total was a fantastic 88.

Tench are found mostly in lakes and ponds, terms which, as far as I am concerned, include gravel pits (which are frequently stocked with tench by the angling societies and clubs).

I have found that during June and July tench tend to seek the shallow ends of lakes and ponds,

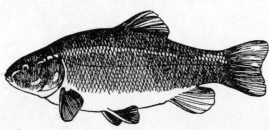

Pliers or forceps are both useful tools for the angler when removing a stubborn hook from the mouth of a bream. They are essential when taking that same hook from the mouth of a pike!

Autumn – and peace and quiet return to the river. The 'butterfly anglers' have all left by this time and real fishermen are left to continue their sport alone. 'The fishing always seems better when the crowds have gone' said the angler in our picture.

and can often be located by watching for the movement of the reeds as the fish push their way through the underwater jungle. Later in the year they move into deeper sections, and during the winter months they hardly, if ever, feed at all. This is a pattern which I have found to operate every season.

Without doubt, tench love weed, and apart from the movement of the above-water stems, one can frequently locate these fish by watching for the bubbles which rise to the surface which are caused by its pig-like method of rooting for food in the mud.

Early mornings before the sun is on the water and in the evening when it has gone can normally be reckoned the best times for tench fishing. But there are days when an overcast sky and a steady temperature encourage the fish to feed all day long.

Occasionally one will hear or read the term 'tench hole'. I doubt very much if tench do actually occupy a particular hole in the lake bed; I tend to believe that they frequent certain depths of water according to the time of year. In other words they follow the pattern which I described earlier.

Tench fishing is a peaceful sport, the cast having been made, one settles back on a box or chair and waits for that peculiar tell-tale waggle of the float which is so distinctive of this species. As the float glides away, that is the moment to strike.

Opinion may be divided as to the best method to fish for this species, but when I consider float or leger fishing, I must admit that the fascination of the float brings me down firmly on that side every time.

The depth of water to be fished will influence to some extent the choice of rod, and although many advocate the use of an 11 ft Avon type rod, a rod of this type can in my opinion be bettered by using a 12 or 13 ft tubular glass rod.

I have found that when fishing in a depth of 12 ft, as one occasionally has to in waters such as Blenheim, 12 and 13 ft tubular glass rods make grand tools. Glass will take great strain without showing signs of a set; unfortunately after a season's heavy use, many cane rods will frequently begin to show signs of wear.

Over the years I have used both centrepin and fixed spool reels, and whilst I agree that the centrepin gives one a great sense of being in direct contact with the fish, there being no mechanical aids to the successful playing of the fish. I feel that if one requires to cast a long distance with relatively light terminal tackle, then the fixed spool reel is the better choice. Recently, the 'closed face reel' has been introduced; as soon as the release button is pressed with the forefinger, the line is disconnected from the pickup and is automatically picked up again as soon as the crank handle is turned. With it I have found it impossible to get line twist, or for that matter to get the monofilament at the back of the spool.

My choice of line depends on whether I am using a centrepin or a fixed spool. On the former I prefer braided nylon as this holds to the drum more efficiently. On a fixed spool or closed face reel I use monofilament.

Remembering that tench live and feed among the weeds, and also that they have great power, I never use a line which has a breaking strain of less than 5 lb.

Many stories have been written regarding catching tench on 2 lb b.s. lines. I would challenge any angler to hold the tench on such light equipment in many of the waters that I fish. These fish are very strong creatures, and the tremendous dive that they so often take when being drawn towards the landing net has to be experienced to be believed. I remember an angler once saying to a very famous fisherman: 'The reason I fish light is to give the fish a chance'. My friend's reply was: 'Yes, a chance to swim around with yards of gut hanging from its mouth'.

Much has been written regarding the shape and colour of hooks. My choice has always been gilt crystal. Forged hooks will certainly hold a fish well, but I have found that on so many occasions once a fish has taken a hook of this type it almost needs an operation to remove it.

Argument also arises regarding the merits of hooks which have already been tied to nylon prior to buying, and their relative values when compared with the eyed or spade and hooks which you tie yourself. I favour the pre-tied variety and have rarely been let down by them.

When maggot fishing I use a size 12, 14 or 16, depending on how shy the fish are, and when using worm or flake, I would change to a 6, 8 or 10. One golden rule I always adopt is: never use a small hook if the fish can be caught on a large one.

Floats, like flies, appear to catch the eye of

most anglers, and as a result of hours spent browsing in tackle shops many of us have hundreds of floats of all shapes, sizes and colours.

I frequently use the French Mady float with great success. In this type the line passes through the body and it can be efficiently prevented from slipping. How often one gains the impression that the fish have gone off feed, and yet when the plummet has been used it is discovered that the float has slipped, thus bringing the bait away from where the fish are feeding.

The importance of having the float set so that the bait is being fished at the correct depth cannot be over-emphasised. On the bottom of many lakes and ponds there is a blanket of weed, and success will frequently only come to the angler who can lay his bait just, and I mean only just, on the top of this covering. When several of us are fishing together, we make it a common practice to set our floats in a similar manner to the one who catches the first fish. On many occasions this has brought good results.

The positioning of the shot on the line is to some extent the result of experiments carried out by yourself. However, normally, when fishing a still water, I would place a A.A.A. shot immediately below the float and a B.B. shot about 12 in from the hook. This method allows the bait to sink slowly so that master tench can watch it coming down. When fishing with flake, you may find that you need slightly more weight near the bait, this will help to overcome its extra buoyancy.

When tench are being very finicky, the movement of the float may be almost negligible. I remember one evening, when I was baiting with flake, I noticed the float give the merest flicker, and while I watched it carefully nothing else happened. I reeled in, re-baited, cast out and waited until there was a similar happening, when I struck immediately. To my delight I hooked a fair-sized fish.

When the fish are difficult to hook, the 'lift' method can be used to great effect. Use an ordinary peacock quill float, and attach the line only to the bottom of it. Squeeze a swan shot onto the trace just 2 in from the hook and make sure that you set the float so that when it is cast in, only the tip is showing. When the fish picks up the bait, the float will rise and fall flat on the water.

There are occasions when a bait presented on

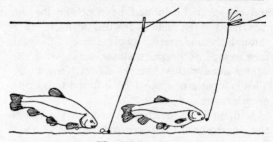

The 'lift' method

leger tackle will take more fish than that which is offered under a float.

In recent years a number of anglers have made large contributions from their skills to this method of fishing. Rods have altered greatly, as have the types of lead that are used.

When legering for tench, I would use either an Arlesey bomb or swan shot attached to a short nylon link which in turn is attached to a split ring.

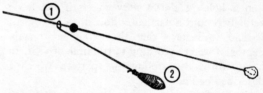

Legering with an Arlesey bomb (2) and using a split ring (1) stopped by a shot or piece of rubber

When using paste as a hook bait, I will frequently dispense with all other weight. This method is most efficient when fishing at night, and many a specimen fish has been fooled by its simplicity.

There are occasions when it is necessary to cast a long distance, much further than it would be possible to throw ground bait, and then I use a swim feeder which acts as the leger weight and will also carry ground bait to the area being fished.

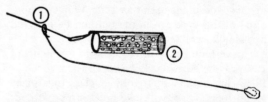

Swim feeder (2) attached by a split ring (1) stopped by a shot or piece of rubber

Great skill is needed to pack a swim feeder correctly, the point being that if the feed is too stodgy it will never leave the container, and if it is too soft it will fall out before it reaches the desired spot. I would suggest that one end of the container is plugged with dampened rusk or a similar material, the centre filled with maggots or chopped worm, and then the other end sealed with some more rusk or crumb.

Leger fishermen use many methods to detect bites. There are indicators that fit to different parts of the rod, for example the swing tip. There are the electrically-operated bite indicators which are so popular with carp fishermen, and of course the many visual aids, e.g. pieces of paste or silver paper, etc. which are squeezed or clipped onto the line.

Where the swims are accessible ground bait can be introduced by hand, and I would suggest that an ordinary loaf that has been soaked in a bucket of water until it is pulp is a very satisfactory feed. This mixture can be scooped up in a cup and thrown into the swim, but remember that little and often is the most effective. It sometimes helps if chopped worm or maggot is added to a mixture of this kind.

Regarding the suggestion that it pays to prebait a swim, my answer to that is it depends to a large extent on where you are fishing. If it is a club or day ticket water, it could well be that the swim you bait will be occupied by someone else when you arrive to fish, and therefore all your efforts will have been in vain. But if there is a reasonable amount of certainty that you will be the only one to fish the swim that you have baited, then I would recommend that the area to be fished be treated on several occasions before actually fishing. When ground baiting in this manner, remember to add to the mixture a quantity of the bait you intend using on the hook.

Whilst discussing ground baiting, one must include the technique of raking, or in other words dragging the lake bed to attract the fish into the swim. This is a very simple but widely used method, and it can be likened to a farmer ploughing the land, an act which attracts birds to feed on the life in the upturned soil.

A drag can be made by placing two rake heads together, so that the points face in opposite directions. Bolt or wire them securely and attach them to a line. Dragging can be done either before or at intervals whilst fishing. One thing is certain: the splash of the drag will not frighten the fish away. One tip regarding dragging that I would pass on is the result of bitter and costly experience – always secure the end of your drag

line before making herculean efforts to cast the drag well out!

The tench has a most catholic taste and when it is feeding will accept maggot, worm, bread crust, flake, boiled wheat, crayfish, caddis and other freshwater insects. When fishing with maggot, I would suggest that you bait with only one for a start; if this does not bring success, then gradually increase your offering until maybe four of five are on the hook.

When fishing deep water, I favour the use of yellow maggots, but even more important than that is the fact that your maggots should be large. Be careful not to pierce the bait, only nip the skin so that the creature can twist and turn whilst on the hook. In my opinion it is this movement that attracts the fish. I do not think that it makes any difference whatsoever that the hook is showing. However, one can camouflage the shank with a piece of paste, and place a maggot on the point.

As with all fish, there are times when they appear to be completely disinterested. On occasions such as this, try changing to a smaller hook which has been baited with a single grain of wheat or possibly a very small red worm.

Although worm will frequently attract eels, I am still of the opinion that it is a bait well worth using. I think that its advantages far outweigh its disadvantages. However, remember that mid-June is a time of the year when it can be very difficult to collect a sufficient number of these creatures. I collect a supply of large lobworms earlier in the year when they are easy to find and keep them in a container which has been packed with old turves.

There are many good tench waters in this country, and they are not all lakes and gravel pits. Many of our rivers hold good stocks of them, and I know several places in the Thames where tench can be found. They frequent the mouths of small ditches and feeder streams, their reason for choosing such quarters is no doubt that, apart from being normally quiet areas, they always have a backwater into which they can retreat when the river is in flood.

I have found that relatively small waters will frequently produce excellent tench fishing, and many clubs have created such fisheries in a relatively short time. But to save disappointment and frustration, before you embark on any ambitious schemes take the advice of a good fishery consultant and make sure that you have got a long lease on the water you intend improving. Many clubs and syndicates have suffered bitter disappointment through not taking these precautions.

There is, however, one point about which I am certain. No matter where and how you fish for tench, you will always find them worthy opponents, and, what is more, you will be fishing during the loveliest time of the year.

MATCH FISHING

by

BILLY LANE

My formative years, from the fishing point of view, were the rather lean early thirties. It was a time when youngsters who were interested in fishing found that garden canes and linen thread scrounged from Mum was the extent to which their demands for tackle could run. In those days even a manufactured hook was a highly-prized item of equipment for youngsters of my age. As for split shot and swivels, etc., well, to own these put you among the angling aristocracy.

Although the garden cane and bent pin is often referred to, I am sure that to-day there are few youngsters who really believe that this sort of equipment was used, was much-prized, and caught fish. But I can assure them that it was, and did.

Going back to the mid-twenties and early thirties, organised angling as we know it to-day was in its infancy. Clubs were relatively few in number, and even associations such as the Coventry Association could only boast of some 1,000 to 1,200 members.

One of the interesting features regarding the membership of those days was the high percentage that were concerned with competitive fishing.

There was, I suppose, little point in joining a Club or Association unless one was so minded, for relatively, and this is of course a broad picture, there was plenty of coarse angling to be had, some often had it within walking distance, while those with a cycle had far wider horizons open to them.

In my young days coach trips were sometimes arranged, but more often than not, it was a case of cycling to the venue to fish for a first prize that might have been as much as a pound, if the Club had 30 or possibly 40 members.

The bigger competitions, those organised by Associations, usually attracted a much larger entry and so naturally the top prize was more attractive. For a premier open competition the prize-money could be as much as £10.

During the nineteen-thirties the Annual Open Competition organised by the Coventry Association used to attract up to 1,000 anglers. As you can well imagine, to attract that number the top prize was well worth while, in fact it was £20. These matches were fished on the Oxford Canal, and even in those days competing anglers came from a radius of well over 100 miles.

As I said earlier, this was a time when the vast majority of Club and Association members were keen competition fishermen, and it would be a very fair comment to say that the vast majority of them were of comparable skill. The day of the dedicated match fisherman had not yet arrived.

Another interesting feature of the thirties was the sudden increase in the interest in match fishing that was shown by bookmakers. From the middle years of that decade money began to play an increasingly important part in this branch of coarse angling, so much so that by the late thirties it had become apparent that match fishing was fast developing into an art.

With increasing financial incentives being offered to the winners, new skills and techniques began to be developed and many experiments were carried out to determine the efficiency of various hook and ground baits. I first became involved in match fishing at the age of twelve, and by fourteen I was a match-fishing enthusiast who was fast learning the craft.

During this period there was a most fascinating development in the knowledge concerning the types of food which fish would readily accept, although at the time it was not readily appreciated and in fact many years passed before one could discern the changing pattern. In short, as the anglers developed their skills, so the fish rapidly became more choosey regarding their diet.

At one time bread paste was an almost universal panacea, but as maggot became more and more widely used, the types of baits used by the angler began to change. I found that if I were using paste, but those in the swims adjoining mine began baiting with maggot, the fish would soon move. They found maggot a more acceptable food.

During the period of competitive fishing bait development, when I was fishing on a local canal, I would bait with paste and feed very carefully with feeder maggots. By so doing I was attempting not to upset the pattern, for in those days we were afraid to change baits in case we put the fish right off feed and thus failed to take any more. Little did we realise that maggot would, in fact, have been far more successful.

Eventually maggot became the accepted bait and anglers realised that there was far more to a maggot than one would imagine. To some it rapidly became apparent that maggots were very involved creatures, that reacted in a variety of

ways to whatever initial feeding they were given, and that the maggot from various flies brought different responses from the fish.

The story of the development of this type of bait is in its way one of the most interesting in modern fishing. Originally the angler used any form of fly maggot, in his bait can there would be the grub of bluebottle, greenbottle, and the ordinary house fly, etc. At this point I must make it clear that the names I use for the various species of fly are those of the layman, I am not a biologist nor do I lay claim to any specialised knowledge other than that which I have acquired as a fisherman and one who annually breeds millions upon millions of maggots.

From the hard back or ordinary house fly, a maggot with a very hard skin is bred. By altering the diet and by careful temperature control it was found that these could be turned into very soft-skinned creatures, which became known in the Midlands as squats, or in the North Country as feeder maggots.

The main use to which this last type of maggot is put is to some extent explained by its name, 'feeder' – a maggot which is introduced into the swim to encourage the fish to congregate and feed.

Throughout the country the names given to maggots vary considerably. The small soft maggot which in the North is termed a feeder, is a squat in the Midlands, while a feeder maggot to the Midland angler is a half-grown bluebottle maggot.

During the early days of maggot fishing a definite pattern began to emerge, anglers using the small maggots for feeding the swim, in other words as ground bait, and placing the larger maggots on the hook.

Normally, to breed feeder maggots they are underfed so that their growth is stunted; you just let them 'scrat' around until they grow to the size you think they should be, then take them off their feed for two days. The maggots can then be re-fed with a small amount of liver. The added weight will cause them to sink immediately they are thrown in. Therefore, by adopting this technique the angler is in possession of a small but heavy maggot, one that is just right for the job.

From the greenbottle fly yet another maggot was developed, this one was called a 'pinky'. These, as it soon became very apparent, were more effective when fishing on canals, and they were not only an excellent feeder maggot, but also an invaluable stand-by as a hook bait for roach.

Greenbottle flies will lay eggs on virtually any type of offal, but experience has led me to believe that fish is the most efficient base. However, the problem is not so much a matter of getting the flies to lay their eggs, as containing the maggot when it hatches. They have to be carefully controlled in traps, for the maggot from this type of fly will crawl anywhere. Originally, it was extremely difficult to get greenbottles to lay eggs at any other time than during the summer and very early autumn, but by careful temperature control and the correct amount of lighting, it is possible under 'factory' conditions to get them to breed during any season.

Experience is a hard school, but what you learn through it is learned well, and it is in this way that I have discovered that one of the most important factors in the breeding of maggots is the base material on which the eggs are laid, for it is upon its quality that the ultimate success of the maggots depends.

From the North we have acquired another type of maggot, namely a 'special'. These can be likened to an over-grown squat, and make an excellent hook bait on hard-fished waters. Specials are bred on a mixture of bone meal and bran which has been moistened with cabbage water.

The modern match fisherman has a further valuable aid to catching fish in what is called the 'gozzer'. This is a maggot specially bred to be used as a hook bait. Gozzers are reared on a freshly killed meat base (preference from a woodpigeon or similar creature). They are a very soft-skinned maggot, and are slightly smaller than the normal commercially-bred variety.

During the past ten years the caster or sinking chrysalis has become a most popular bait form, one which will frequently produce results when all other baits fail. But one important fact regarding casters must not be overlooked – for these to be really successful they must be heavy enough to sink immediately. Before using, check your casters and reject any that do not sink.

While these developments in bait techniques were taking place, the competitive side of coarse angling was growing apace. Angling was coming of age and my own Association, Coventry, was growing by leaps and bounds. By the mid-nineteen-sixties there were some 13,000 members, out of which number approximately 3,000 would take part in competitive angling. In this 3,000 are a hard core of some 150 to 200, who are the really dedicated match fishermen.

As the types of bait altered and fashions changed, so did angling techniques and tackle. We have travelled from cane and greenheart rods to the highly-sophisticated ferrule-less tubular glass rods weighing a mere 8 oz or even less. In my opinion much of the development in rods, reels and ancillary equipment is a direct result of the growth in competitive fishing, for as the rewards grew larger, so the effort that went into the winning of them increased. Manufacturers were continually being bombarded with requests for rods that were lighter yet more powerful, reels that were more efficient, and for lines that were more reliable, e.g. lighter and yet having a relatively high breaking strain.

By the mid-sixties match fishing was a booming sport, with the big open competitions attracting a thousand or more competitors. The Thames Angling Championship had an attendance of well over 1,000, as did the Trent Championship Competition. The Birmingham Angling Association Annual Members' Match had to cater for an entry of some 6,000, a number which made it necessary to split the competitors into three groups, one section fishing on the Severn, the others going to the Avon and the Worcester Canal. Large firms and industrial organisations have now entered the field of competitive fishing and sponsor well-organised competitions which attract a thousand or more entrants to a particular event.

Surprisingly, though, the top prizes have not increased to any great extent. In the thirties it was possible to win as much as £20, and this sum is still considered a reasonably good first prize. No, the big money in match fishing is not in the prize-money itself, but in what the individual can win by backing himself with a bookmaker, or by winning the pool or sweepstake money. It is certainly not impossible for an angler to win as much as £200 on a Sunday in a five-hour competition.

One may well ask how and where all this began. Without doubt, the roots of match fishing are in the Midlands and North Country, for it was here that industrial workers seeking relaxation from their arduous and often dangerous jobs would go down to the local canal and fish. All too often the sport that was available consisted mainly of small fish which, although skill was needed to capture them, gave little really worth-while fight. It was natural that eventually the 'I bet I'll catch more than you' attitude prevailed. To encourage sales, as the barge traffic declined, waterside innkeepers began offering prizes and organising competitions.

But all this is history, and from a dozen or so bikes leaning against a canal rail we have now reached the era of fleets of luxury coaches and cars by the hundred. On occasions the Police are involved in controlling the traffic arriving at, or dispersing from, big competitions. As air travel becomes more convenient and relatively cheaper, so it is that this form of transport is gradually attracting the match fishing enthusiasts. It is not uncommon to find that several aircraft have been chartered, so that anglers from the Midlands and the North can go to Ireland for a day's competitive fishing. We have come a long way from bread-paste and bicycles!

To be successful in any sport or pastime you must have more than just natural ability, and despite what the non-fishing fraternity may say or think, in no sport is this more true than in fishing.

The modern match angler must possess certain qualities and powers that are not demanded of the angler who seeks his sport in a more leisurely manner. This is not to decry the other style of fishing, it is merely that one is fiercely competitive and gets more so, whilst the other tends to be more contemplative and relaxing. Believe me, there is little relaxation in a keenly-fought contest.

No-one enjoys a spell of solitary fishing more than I, but for all that, the excitement and tension that are generated in a big match is for many of us equivalent to Wimbledon to the tennis player.

The mental approach to match fishing is most important. The angler must be confident and willing to concentrate – under no circumstances must attention wander. If asked to name the greatest asset that a match angler can have, I would say that it is confidence; confidence in one's own ability to out-fish all rivals, as well as confidence in method, tackle and bait.

The match angler must be fit in both mind and body, for this is not a 'chuck it and chance it' business, and the effort demanded by continually casting and recovering, as well as the

concentration that has to be exercised, can be most exhausting. Not the least consideration is the amount of tackle that has to be carried; on occasions I have walked four miles to my peg carrying up to 1 cwt. of tackle and ground bait. I can assure you that when faced with a round walk of some eight miles, I have been extremely pleased to think that on the return trip there will be some 40 or 50 lb less to carry (this is the amount of ground bait that I sometimes use).

If he hopes for success, the matchman's equipment must be as complete as possible. He needs at least three rods, a conventional bottom-fishing rod of some 13 or 14 ft in length, and a lighter edition of this, say 12 ft in length, and a rod for leger style fishing.

His 13 to 14 ft bottom-fishing rod should be of tubular glass, and while I prefer one which is ferrule-less, this is to some extent a matter of personal choice. A rod of this type which has been built by a good manufacturer will have all the necessary refinements, e.g. stand-off rings, good quality cork handle, and a sliding winch fitting. The second rod should again be of tubular glass and ferrule-less. The rod for leger fishing must not be longer than 11 ft, in fact a good leger rod for match fishing can be 8 or 9 ft in length. Once again, a rod built by a good manufacturer will have all the fittings that are necessary.

The basic tenet that decides my choice of reel is the type of fishing which I am about to undertake. Quite simply, choose your reel for the job that it has to do.

Basically, I would divide into three the types of waters on which I fish, and in broad terms the, equipment I use is as follows: On still waters, e.g. canals, I favour a 12 ft rod with a centre-pin reel, but if the canal were particularly wide, then for ease of casting I would change to a fixed-spool reel. When fishing moderate rivers, e.g. the Upper Nene, and even wide streamy waters such as parts of the Trent, my normal choice would be again the 12 ft rod and centrepin reel, but on occasions a fixed-spool reel would be used. For wider deeper rivers, e.g. the Welland, Witham, and Great Ouse Relief Channel, I would plump for the 13 to 14 ft rod and a fixed-spool reel, unless I were forced to fish close in to the bank for smaller species, and then I would choose the centrepin reel.

When fishing on parts of the Witham or Welland or for that matter on any good bream water it is more than likely that leger tackle and tactics would be called for.

Over the years there has been much controversy about the strength of line that should be used. Broadly speaking, my advice is this: Relate the breaking strain of the line to the type of fishing you are about to undertake. On canals, and in particular on those where big fish are not to be expected, I think that a 2·5 lb b.s. line is sufficient. However, when long casting on wide rivers, light lines often break as the fish is struck, therefore, use a line which has a minimum breaking strain of 3·5 lb, and on occasions a 5 lb b.s. line will be suitable. When choosing a line, consider the following points most carefully. It must be soft and very flexible and have an even diameter throughout its length as well as a reasonable amount of elasticity. I would also choose a line which tends to become invisible in water.

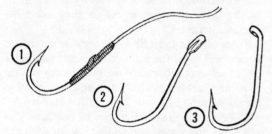

Hook choices: 1. Serrated shank, McKenzie bend; 2. Spade end, 'Crystal' bend; 3. Eyed, forged

The importance of the correct choice of hook cannot be over-emphasized. Bascially I would recommend a forged hook when using one of a size 16 or larger. Whether your choice be for eyed or spade end. I do not think matters overmuch. But when choosing hooks of size 16 and smaller, I would recommend one having a serrated shank and the hook length whipped on.

However, there is one most important point that must not be overlooked – the nylon length should be laid on the inside of the shank and the whipping be carried down to the end of the shank, otherwise as the strike is made the hook will not penetrate correctly.

In my opinion gilt hooks should be used when maggot or paste fishing, and black hooks when baiting with casters, hemp or similar small grains. Overall, I would suggest that for brightly coloured baits, gilt hooks should be used, and for those having a darker colour, black hooks should be chosen.

The day of the big hook in match fishing is over, except when baiting with flake or lobworm, when a size 10 or 8 or even a 6 can be effective. Apart from this, a hook no larger than a 16 should be used, with 18s and 20s for maggot fishing. Even on good bream waters, these hooks will prove to be more than adequate.

So often too little attention is given to the correct choice of float. Broadly speaking, for still water a crow quill is ideal, but it must be at least 6 in long. Regarding colour, the bottom section should always be green or brown but the tip may be any colour just so long as it is readily discernible to your own eyes.

When a ripple on the water is making the detection of a bite difficult, attach your float by the bottom ring only. This ring should be attached to the thick end of your float, and under these conditions sink your line, if necessary putting a dust or No. 6 shot on to the line 12–18 in from the float. When fishing on still water, you will find a Zoomer, a self-cocking antenna float, most useful. These can be cast a long distance, and require but a small amount of shot.

Moderate rivers suggest the use of a float which has the cork body positioned approximately two-

Canal rigs: (left) Inverted crow quill; (centre) porcupine or crow quill; (right) Small zoomer

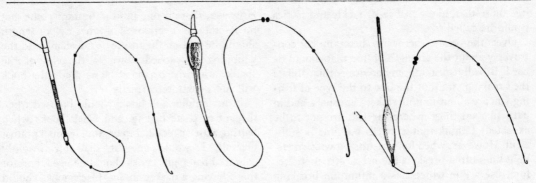

River terminal rigs: (left) Stick float; (centre) Avon 'trotter'; (right) Welland antenna

thirds of the way to the top. Never forget when fishing with the wind against the flow, attach both ends. However, when the wind is with the flow, or into your face, I would recommend a Ducker style float. These have the cork almost at the bottom, and are connected by the bottom ring only. Here again, never be afraid to install a fairly large shot at a minimum distance of one foot up from the float, a B.B. or No. 3 shot will get your line down under the water and will help to slow down the rate of travel, thus presenting the bait more naturally.

The size of the float must be judged against the conditions ruling at the time, viz. distance to be cast, depth of water, and the strength of flow.

Whenever the depth exceeds 8 ft, I use a sliding float, for these are indispensable when fishing on wide and deep waters. Unfortunately, to many anglers sliding floats are a dreaded curse, but, believe me, if used properly then can be a great asset. On streamy water, always fish with the slider in the orthodox manner, and shot down until the top ring is level with the surface,

but when fishing in still or deep water, run the line through the bottom ring only.

The species mainly sought by the match angler are, for all practical purposes, bream, roach, dace, chub, bleak, gudgeon and perch. I feel that it is easiest to deal with these species by allying them to the various waters in which they are most commonly found.

In canals it is most likely that roach, perch and bream will form the bulk of catches, therefore I would select the shorter of the two bottom-fishing rods, and tackle up with a reel and line suitable for the occasion.

Prior to the match, find out as much as you can about the water, and equip yourself with the baits that are normally successful. You will find that on some still waters, particularly canals, ground bait is sudden death to sport, particularly if the waterway is rarely if ever used. However, if it is a working canal, you will normally find that ground bait can be used with success. But there is a right way to approach this technique.

First plumb the depth, then introduce a few balls of ground bait during the first few minutes (these balls should be no larger than walnuts). Use paste bait and fish in the deepest section of water you can reach, and set your depth so that the bait is just off the bottom. When paste fishing there is often a short time-lapse before the fish begin taking, but if this method is going to prove successful, you should be taking a fish on each cast for the first ten to fifteen minutes.

On the other hand, if you do not get a bite within five minutes, change to another bait; I would suggest a pinky or gozzer on the hook and feed the swim with a few squats. Although you have changed your bait, it will not necessarily follow that you will immediately begin to catch

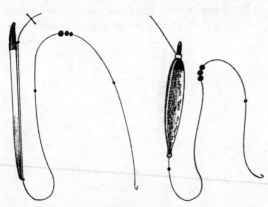

Top sliders: (left) porcupine; (right) Severn trotter

fish, for the ground bait must be given a chance to work. Remember one most important fact – do not over-feed.

During a three-hour match under these conditions, I would not expect to use any more than four pints of ground bait which would include one pint of squats. In addition, I would not expect to loose-feed into the swim more than a half-pint of pinkies.

Naturally, these tactics will not work on every water on every day, but here it is only possible to give an indication of broad principles. Experience and practice will give you many answers to the multitude of problems that you will face during competition fishing.

Assuming that the fish are moving to paste, then obviously one does not want to hastily change to another bait. Under these conditions, ground baiting must be very carefully carried out, and the amount being put in should be gradually reduced until you are doing no more than merely keeping the fish interested.

If the water on which you are competing is heavily fished with casters one must be very careful with ground bait. Never feed with more than six casters at a time – in fact, two or three at a time should be adequate. If you over-feed, you will find that sport will rapidly die off.

I never alternate casters with maggot, I would recommend that you make your choice at the start and stick to it. (See note on p. 188.)

On moderate rivers, where roach, dace, bream, gudgeon and chub can be expected, I would choose my longest bottom rod and match it with a reel and line to suit conditions. Here again your first job must be to plumb the depth, for this will not only tell you where the deep holes are, if any, but whether the bottom is mud or gravel.

In waters of this type the ground bait should be a heavier mix, completely different from the rather light fluffy mixture used when fishing in canals. The heavier consistency is a vital factor in getting the balls of ground bait down to the fish and therefore not being swept immediately out of the swim (this would only benefit your competitors).

If it is a good roach water, then you can begin using casters or maggots from the outset. My first choice would be casters, for you will find that on the majority of rivers it is possible to successfully change to maggots, if necessary, but if the fish are taking casters, why change?

It is impossible to generalise on the amount of ground bait that one should use on a river of this type. Normally there is a generally-accepted level, and this can be found out by prior investigation, or, as time progresses and your experience widens, you will come to know the potential of the various rivers and canals that you are likely to fish. If casters are the accepted bait on a particular water, you will often find that little or no ground bait is required.

A streamy water will not usually react favourably to squats, except when there are bream in the swim. Get the squats down to the bottom by adding them to a heavy mix of ground bait; they will lie among the stones or in the mud, thus encouraging the bream to stay and feed. On this type of water I like to introduce all my feeder maggots by this method.

On waters where hemp, wheat or any similar bait is regularly used, it is up to you to go to the match fully equipped and prepared to use whatever bait is called for.

On certain wide and deep rivers during the mid-sixties, there was a tendency for the pattern of fishing to change. For example, on parts of the Welland roach used to predominate and therefore it was reasonable to assume that one could fish for roach and bream at one and the same time. One could feed continually to hold the shoals of fish in your swim, the ground bait that fell away as it went down through the water attracted the roach, and that which went to the bottom held the interest of the bream. One would use a heavy mixture of ground bait, which held feeder maggots, and again some of the maggots went to the roach, and the rest to the bream.

The important point to remember is that the fish were held in the swim not by the total quantity of ground bait but by the fact that it was regularly and freely put in. To deposit 40 or 50 lb of feed in the water at the start of the match would produce little result, the secret was – and is – fair quantities and often.

The changing pattern of fishing on some rivers has meant that now the angler will be better employed in searching for and holding the interest of the bream from the very outset, for these fish that provide the bulk of the sport and certainly the bulk of the weights. But if the former pattern should emerge once again, then by all means fish for both species.

Ground baiting for bream is quite an art. One

should use a heavy mixture of a bread-based ground bait, and for a five-hour match 28 lb (dry-weight), plus one gallon of squats, should be allowed. When mixed, the ground bait is used as a vehicle to carry the squats down to the fish.

During the summer months I find that the addition of a few pinkies and maggots of whichever type I am using as hook bait is particularly valuable, and certainly adds interest to the ground bait. At this time of the year I have found that gozzers are more effective than by any other type of maggot, despite the fact that occasionally flake proves to be a match-winner.

As the season progresses, so the bait pattern changes, and despite the fact that maggot is still the predominant bait for bream, the complete matchman will include worms in his array of baits. In my opinion a size 14 hook baited with a red marsh worm is one of the most effective baits of this type, particularly during the colder months of the year.

It is on the wide and deep rivers, when the sliding float for one reason or another is impracticable, that I occasionally turn to leger fishing. Allied to my leger rod, I use a fixed-spool reel, loaded with a line having a 3·5 lb minimum breaking strain. When leger fishing is discussed, it is inevitable that methods of bite-indication will be well to the fore. My own choice is the swing-tip. It is easily fixed, it offers no disadvantage that I can think of, and most important of all, it is positive.

When employing this method, use just enough weight to hold bottom, but, remember, not so much that the bait is prevented from moving occasionally and fractionally. The Thames is a river which frequently pays big dividends when fished in this manner.

There is another method that one can adopt when leger fishing, and that is to use a heavy lead. By 'heavy' I do not mean a lead which is heavy by sea-angling standards – I would choose a half or three-quarter ounce Arlesey bomb and having cast in, would tighten up and leave for a few moments. Then tighten the line and move the bait a few inches, and once against let it rest. This should be repeated over and over again, searching the river bed for a fish that is interested in what I have to offer.

Always remember that the swing tip must be heavy enough to compensate the slack line and register a bite effectively.

Practice makes perfect. This is an old but very very true saying, and in no type of fishing is it more true than when fishing in a competitive manner. For no matter how much you read, in the final analysis success will go to the man who perfects his style by constant usage. This means quite simply, compete as often as possible on as many varying types of water as it is your good fortune to be able to travel to. And above all think constantly and exercise your brain to see if it is not possible to add just one more trick to your repertoire, for this may be factor that swings a match in your favour.

NOTE: It is impossible to over-emphasise the importance of using fresh casters. If they are stale and sour-smelling the fish will often reject them completely. It is also important—indeed vital—that the casters you use sink immediately and are not carried away on the surface.

BOATS AND ENGINES FOR RIVER
AND LAKE FISHING

by

R. H. WARRING

Literally anything in the way of a boat that floats *can* be used for fishing, but not necessarily with safety, even on sheltered inland waters. And whilst safety is an obvious requirement, comfort should also be put high on the list in deciding on a suitable size – and type – of boat. To a large extent the two go together.

If the boat has to be transported to the water rather than left on moorings, then size and weight are important factors. For convenience of handling both need to be kept to a minimum, but for safety and comfort just the opposite applies.

Regarding *size*, it is possible to be fairly specific. For safety *and* comfort the hull volume should allow 12 cubic feet or more per person carried. You only need to work out hull volume approximately to apply this formula, e.g. estimating the dimensions of an equivalent 'box' shape. Equivalent volume, expressed by multiplying length, breadth and depth all in feet and dividing by 12 will give the safe carrying capacity, in number of persons, and ensure space enough for gear and reasonable comfort. If it is to be used for long periods, a bigger boat is to be preferred, but this will put the cost up and increase the

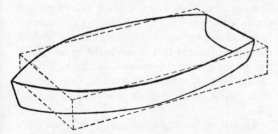

Calculate hull volume on 'equivalent box' size

difficulties of manhandling in and out of the water, and overland transportation.

This formula also indicates the best type of hull shape for minimum size (and minimum cost) – a square-ended, flat-bottomed punt. This should be entirely adequate for really sheltered waters, but could prove a bit of a handful at times on a tidal river; it would be decidedly uncomfortable on a larger lake where the surface can rough up quite considerably in a wind. The sea-sledge shape with its more seakindly characteristics would be a much better proposition under such circumstances, but such hulls are usually moulded in glass fibre and tend to be expensive. The flat bottomed hull with a pointed bow is a simpler alternative, and can be built cheaply in marine ply. The conventional hard chine hull with 'veed' forward sections is an unnecessary luxury for sheltered water operation, although it may be preferred because it looks more like a real boat! It will also be an easier and better boat to handle against strong currents.

The conventional round bilge dinghy we put bottom of the list mainly because in small sizes and light construction (which is almost universal with glass fibre construction) they are very 'tippy' craft. It is only safe – and then not always safe! – for one person to stand up or move about at a time. Where we are not concerned with a boat which has soft riding qualities on choppy waters we prefer something that sits down flat and solidly in the water – and has enough beam to allow you to stand on the gunwale without it tipping dangerously (below). Use this as a test, though, not something to make a practice of!

A broad hull beam and hard chine or flat bottom reduce 'tipping'

A round bilge dinghy may still be attractive because of its price. In that case its stability will almost certainly be improved with ballast in the bottom of the hull. Many a fisherman has found his light glass fibre dinghy far more stable and safe to move around in when wear on the outer skin has allowed water to seep in and fill the space between the two skins forming the hull bottom, or what were hitherto air-filled buoyancy compartments! A few light hulls are, in fact, deliberately made with hollow compartments in the bottom which automatically fill with water to increase stability when afloat. These compartments drain dry again when the hull is pulled ashore, reducing the hull weight to a minimum for handling.

Balance size and weight requirements against *how* you are going to operate. If you can leave the boat on moorings or pulled ashore during the season that question need not arise. You can always hire a trailer or arrange towage home for winter storage. If you have to take the boat with you each time, however, it must either be of suitable size and weight to carry on the roof of a car; or you will have to go to the additional expense of a trailer to tow it behind a car. That can cost as much as the boat itself.

Where 'portability' presents a critical problem, do not overlook the possibilities of an inflatable craft. Numerous models are nowadays available, and the leading types are extremely stable and utterly reliable – as well as being seaworthy enough for use in really choppy waters, if necessary. They can be fitted with a bracket to take an outboard motor and, although perhaps not as comfortable as a conventional dinghy, at least they can be deflated and folded into a 'kitbag' size package for transport. They do, however, tend to work out more costly than an ordinary dinghy. Low price inflatables may be all right for certain purposes, but not for continuous and long term use.

Inflation at the water's edge can be a bit of a snag. With a large (four or six man) dinghy this can take a quarter of an hour or more, and using a hand pump it is quite hard work. I have never quite liked the idea of inflating via a special valve replacing a sparking plug on a car engine and then running the car engine as this charges the inflatable with a highly explosive petrol/air mixture on which to sit and smoke – although I have never heard of any explosions resulting from this cause!

The main snag with inflatables, however, is that the bottom comprises merely a sheet of rubberised fabric which is literally resting on the water and moves under the feet. You soon get used to this, but it can be cold to the feet. Also any rain collects in the bottom and immediately runs to the point where feet are resting. Floorboards, usually available as an extra, are well worth the price for the additional comfort they give on inflatables, as well as providing stiffening for the whole craft.

The same comment also applies to a lot of conventional dinghies (particularly small glass fibre dinghies) which are produced without floorboards. The added comfort of floorboards to keep feet out of bilge water is worth ten times the cost of fitting them – and seaboots or Wellingtons are *not* the sort of footwear for small craft in case you do fall overboard. (Nor, incidentally, are Wellingtons good for walking ashore through thick mud; they are liable to be sucked down and trapped – which means wriggling out of them before you can proceed any further.)

If you are buying a secondhand boat, be suspicious of ply hulls that are quite old. Ply gets brittle with age and joints become suspect. Ten years is a good life for a ply hull, although complete renovation is possible (for example, with nylon sheathing). However, a proper renovation may cost more than the difference between hulls in 'fair' and 'good' condition to start with.

With secondhand glass fibre boats, look for signs of rubbing wear on the hull bottom which can cause leaks. Once the gel coat has been worn away the exposed glass fibres will mop up water and the only cure is to recoat the damaged area. Crazing of the gel coat – i.e. a series of surface cracks – is an indication of poor initial construction, and also old age. It is not significant on deck mouldings (except that it spoils the appearance), but needs covering treatment on the hull itself. Minor damage, such as chipped edges to mouldings, can be repaired quite easily with resin and filler.

Repairs which have been made to glass fibre hulls are usually quite obvious on inspection. If they have been well made, then the hull is still sound – but patched areas which show signs of lifting or poor workmanship are suspect.

As for secondhand inflatables – well, personally I would not consider anything more than about four or five years old – and nothing younger that showed signs of extensive puncture repairs!

Functional features which may well be added to a standard hull include simple lockers or 'pocket' spaces for loose gear, tailored to suit the specific gear likely to be carried and accommodate it tidily and yet readily accessible instead of it having to be scattered about the boat. This is largely a matter of individual ideas as to what can be done, and what will serve as *useful* purpose. There is no point in adding fittings which are not directly useful.

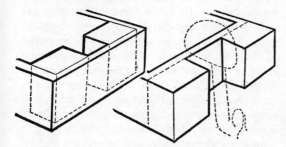

Built-in bait boxes can easily be fitted to the transom

Watertight compartments for carrying live bait or fish are held to be highly desirable by many anglers. These can be quite simply made as marine plywood boxes attached either to the front or rear of the transom (above). If assembled on a simple framework and screwed and glued up with Cascamite or Aerolite and the interior painted with standard marine paint (undercoat will do), these can be fully watertight. Drain plugs can then be fitted for emptying when not in use – draining through the transom in the case of inboard fitted tanks or directly through the bottom in the case of outboard fitted tanks. A point to bear in mind with outboard fitted tanks is that they are likely to be subject to lifting loads when handling the boat, so they need to be more robustly constructed and *firmly* screwed to the transom.

Another addition well worth considering is a

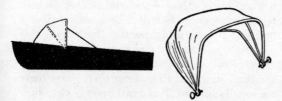

simple 'dodger' comprising a couple of hoops in aluminium alloy tubing with a canvas covering which can be lifted and held erect by tapes, as shown (above). The comfort this can provide on a wet and windy day is considerable!

An outboard motor is the logical power unit for all small craft which have to be handled in and out of the water. The motor can be removed completely to lighten the craft for lifting, and taken home in the boot of the car after each session. Regardless of the type, and to a large extent the size, of the boat, the power required is quite modest and thus a suitable outboard is not necessarily an expensive proposition. Yet another advantage of an outboard for river and lake work, of course, is that should the propeller get fouled with weed the whole unit can readily be tilted and the prop cleared. The fact that an outboard will tilt also means that you can operate in shallow water without danger of damage to the propeller, and even continue running in very shallow water with the outboard partly tilted forward. In the latter case always run at reduced throttle and support the outboard in the tilted position rather than let the skeg drag along the bottom.

The maximum speed of a non-planing hull is directly related to its waterline length. As a rough rule, this maximum speed is equal to about 4/3 times the square root of the waterline length. Adding more power than is required to reach this particular speed will not necessarily result in any increase in speed. Rather, the stern of the boat will 'squat' in the water and all the extra power will be used up in creating a bigger wake. The boat is also likely to be more unstable when 'squatting'.

Basically, therefore, there is no point in fitting a motor more powerful than that necessary to produce the craft's *optimum maximum speed*. Fig. 5 gives close approximate figures for optimum maximum speed and power required for different lengths. From this it will be seen that six horsepower is about the most that will be required for typical fishing boats. Besides saving in size, weight and cost of outboard this will also give all the realisable performance that a larger outboard would give.

This size-speed-power relationship is also important when considering a suitable combination for operating on tidal rivers. The only way to gain speed against the tide is to have a boat that is long enough to produce a suitable speed difference.

Thus driving against a 4 knot tide, an 8 ft boat would have scarcely any margin of speed, whereas a 16 footer should be able to make about 3 knots headway. This is a question of hull length and *not* power. Increasing power would have no affect at all, unless the hull was of planing type.

Actually most people like a little power in hand and there is some advantage in this in that the motor can be run at a reduced throttle setting. This is usually more economical in terms of fuel consumption – and a relatively high fuel consumption is the main disadvantage of outboards. Thus, for example, if we are considering a 14 ft craft where the optimum maximum speed is about 6½ knots, the power required will be of the order of 3 h.p. Instead of a 3 h.p. outboard we can fit a 5 h.p. unit. Whereas the 3 h.p. motor would have to run flat out to give the full optimum maximum speed, the 5 h.p. motor would give this speed on perhaps two-thirds throttle opening. Although a larger motor, its fuel consumption at this speed (developing the same actual power output) would probably be less than that of the smaller outboard.

Fuel consumption varies considerably with different types of outboards but, as a general rule, is approximately of the order of $\frac{1}{8}$ gallon per hour per horsepower developed. That is to say, a typical outboard developing, say, 4 h.p. can be anticipated to consume about $\frac{1}{2}$ gallon per hour.

As we have said, though, this can vary so one of the most important things with a new outboard is to make a check of the fuel actually used on a typical run of a certain duration at the throttle setting you would normally use. You can then work out a true figure for 'gallons per hour' and, on non-tidal waters, 'miles per gallon'. It is important to know these figures as this determines the amount of fuel you need for a day's outing. Before starting, check that you have this amount of fuel in the tank, or aboard, and in addition *carry a spare can of fuel as a safety measure.*

Provided you give it reasonable care an outboard should give entirely reliable service through a complete season. The most likely source of trouble is a fouled sparking plug, so a clean plug should always be carried as a spare (not forgetting a spark plug spanner). For inland water and river operation that is about all you need to worry about as regards tools to carry. It is still a wise precaution to carry an alternative form

of 'power' however – which means paddles or oars.

Unless laid out for rowing, i.e. with rowlocks, paddles are probably the best choice. They are shorter than oars and more easily stowed out of the way. But it really takes two people to make good progress with paddles (paddling one each side). For the lone hand, therefore, oars are a better proposition.

Finally – since the object is to get to a certain spot and stop there – a word about anchors. On non-tidal waters a dead weight is as good an anchor as anything and is unlikely to get snagged on the bottom. Its holding power, however, will only be about two-thirds of its own weight. A grapnel or stock anchor will have a holding power of about three to ten times its weight (more on a rocky bottom) and so can be very much smaller in weight than a dead weight. Plough type anchors have a holding power from twenty to one hundred times their weight and quite a tiny size is adequate for small craft. They are excellent for holding in mud or a soft bottom in tidal or exposed waters.

Remember, though, the holding power of any anchor will also be affected by its scope or the ratio of the length of line let out to the depth of water. A scope of about 7 or 8 to 1 is necessary to realise the full holding power of the anchor – so if a wind comes up and you start to drift, let out more line to increase the scope.

On tidal rivers remember, too, that the scope will change with a rising tide and the holding power of your anchor will decrease unless you have let out enough line initially. Also the strongest currents and greatest change of water level will occur during the third and fourth hours before and after high (or low) water.

Maintenance should not be a major problem provided you start right – i.e. with a good sound hull and an engine in good condition (preferably a brand new one). If the craft is left out of water, turn it upside down if it is light enough to manhandle so that it will not fill with rain water; or at least fit it with a canvas cover for the same purpose. This can save a lot of unnecessary strain being put on the hull. At the end of a season plan to scrub and clean the hull right down, inside and out, and repaint straight away. Don't leave this job until the start of the next season. Glass fibre hulls, of course, do not need painting when they are fairly new, but after about three years there are usually scars to fill and make good, when they will benefit from painting just like any other hull.

As for outboard maintenance, provided you can take the engine home after each session and keep it in the garage, you need not bother about anything other than an occasional check on the lubricant level in the lower gearcase until the winter. Then it needs preparing for winter storage – unless you are one of those hardy types who operate regularly all the year round. For winter storage requirements, follow the specific instructions given in the maker's manual. If you do not have an instruction manual, get one from the local agent for that model or by writing direct to the manufacturer. Then follow what the makers have found through years of experience to be the best treatment for their engine.

BOAT FISHING

by

ALAN WRANGLES

I seriously doubt whether there is another sport which is affected by so many rules and regulations, which in fact have little to do with the sport itself, as angling. The coarse angler must face problems that are posed by rights of access, riparian ownership, and the general shortage of available fishing water.

Unfortunately, despite the very great appeal that boat fishing has, once the coarse angler decides to follow his sport in this manner, his difficulties multiply.

The ordinary rule of law is that all Her Majesty's subjects have the right to pass and re-pass, in other words to row up and down, on all tidal water. Having said that, I must point out at once that there are exceptions to this rule which are usually occasioned by a particular landowner's ancient rights.

But assuming that one is on a river, that it is tidal, and there are no peculiarities regarding riparian ownership, one is then faced with the problem of getting a boat into the water, embarking and disembarking, and also mooring at any given spot.

In broad terms one must assume that the only right that you have is that which entitles you to pass and re-pass on tidal waters. All the other necessary actions, embarking, mooring, and so on, are subject to whatever restrictions are imposed by riparian ownership and rights of access, etc., the one big exception being where there is a public hard or landing stage.

On non-tidal waters there are no rights regarding passing and re-passing and, strictly speaking, to use à boat on such waters it is necessary to obtain the permission of whoever owns both banks. However, if the river is wide enough to allow a boat to be navigated using one-half of the river only, then all that need be obtained is the permission of the owner of that particular bank.

Inevitably there are exceptions, and one of the most interesting of these is the River Thames.

Basically, one Authority has the responsibility for the regulation of boating on this river, the Thames Conservancy, whose authority stretches from Cricklade downstream to Teddington. From Teddington downstream the river comes under the control of the Port of London Authority, but this is not an area in which the boating fisherman is likely to be greatly interested. Therefore, we will consider the situation upstream of Teddington.

From Staines to Cricklade it is safest to assume that all the fisheries are controlled in one way or another. The right may be leased by clubs or hotels, or they may be in the hands of private individuals, and it is from these various sources that the angler must obtain permission to fish.

From Staines downstream to Teddington the fishing is open (this is known as the London Free Fishery) but the angler must pay due regard to private property and rights of access, etc.

We now come to the nub of the matter. Every boat used on the part of the Thames which is controlled by the Thames Conservancy, viz. Cricklade down to Teddington, must be registered with the Conservancy Board before it is used. The owner must also have paid the appropriate fee and obtained a licence plate which must be fixed to the boat in a prominent position before the vessel is used.

There is one further point which must be remembered. If occasionally the boat owner intends to use an outboard engine on his craft then the boat must be registered as a launch.

Actually getting the boat into the water may seem a comparatively simple job, but this is not necessarily so. On the Thames there is a relatively small number of officially designated launching positions, and even where they exist you will more than likely find that parking facilities for your car and trailer are non-existent.

All in all it would seem that the man who wants to enjoy his fishing from a boat is up against almost insuperable odds, but these in fact are not as bad as they may seem to be. The many rules and regulations exist mainly to bring some sort of order to a situation that could otherwise become completely and utterly chaotic, where other people's rights might be totally disregarded.

My advice to the angler who wishes to own a boat and indulge his sport under slightly different conditions is: decide where the majority of your boating is going to be done, and then write to the local River Authority or Conservancy Board, asking for as much help and advice as they are able to give. By making a few local enquiries the angler will soon be able to discover if and where he can fish.

It may appear from all this that the problems associated with boat fishing mean that it is hardly worthwhile. Let me assure you that this is not so. Most of the problems can be overcome quite easily; the others sometimes take a little longer, but just so long as you play the game according to the rules you will find that fishing from a boat opens a whole new world of excitement and adventure.

The advantages of boat fishing are many, but in my opinion the following are the most important. The areas which were previously unfishable from the bank can now become your own secluded fisheries, and moving does not present the problem that it does when you are landbound – with a paddle, a pair of oars or an outboard, a move of a mile or more presents hardly any problems at all. On the other hand, when fishing from a bank, to pack up all the many bits and pieces and begin a mile walk along a bank which could easily resemble a commando battle training course is an operation which has on many occasions deterred me from moving on. And of course, apart from the facts than one is more mobile and able to fish otherwise inaccessible parts, there is another great asset – the ability to be able to position yourself to take the fullest advantage of whatever physical features the water may offer.

The type of boat, fixtures and fittings suitable for the angler has been thoroughly discussed in Chapter 11. So here I will deal only with the mechanics of angling from a boat, which has many facets which do not concern the angler who fishes from the bank.

The two greatest enemies of successful fishing are noise and movement. By noise I mean the vibrations set up by movement in the boat: a leger weight dropped on the bottom boards must sound to the fish much as a kettle drum does to a human ear. This sort of incident can be ignored by the bank fisherman, for a half-ounce bullet dropped into the mud will not affect his fishing one iota. Even the laying of a rod on a boat gunwale can send fish flashing away from the vicinity of the craft. This again is not a problem that affects the bank angler!

Movement mainly concerns the sudden intrusion into a quiet stretch of water of the large solid floating mass of a hull. Its attendant shadow has quite an effect upon fish life.

These points must be borne in mind and sensibly related to the water on which you are fishing.

Fish of busy waterways pay little attention to boat traffic, in fact they will frequently take more readily when a powered craft has gone through, for they are used to the sudden disturbance of the river bed and the consequent sudden eruption of food.

A commonsense approach and a fair amount of reasoned thinking will solve many of the problems which the boat angler will face when he comes to consider the limiting factors which are imposed by boat movement.

Ideally, and assuming that there is a season's fishing in front of one, I would recommend that the area to be fished by boat should be thoroughly surveyed before any fishing is undertaken. Draw a plan of the area, and mark in all the important features, e.g. compass directions, the direction of the prevailing wind, weed beds, and relative depths, paying particular attention to any holes or deep channels. Keep plumbing the depth as you move on and build up a store of knowledge – it will prove invaluable. If the stretch of river that you are attempting to chart is not too wide nor the current too swift, then I would suggest that, if possible, the boat be allowed to drift downstream on the flow. This will give an accurate indication of the course the main current takes. All these facts, and many others that may strike you as important, outfalls and feeder streams, etc., should be noted on your chart, as well as the areas you really favour for your fishing.

To get to know a water really well, one has to spend many years of close acquaintanceship. A water is like a woman – you have to live with her a long time before you have some of the answers, and even then surprises can come when you least expect them.

Having decided the area that you are going to fish, then plan your campaign. It will be relatively easy to discover the types of fish that are in the water, and your main job will be to ally your knowledge of fish and their movement to the plan which you have made.

Having decided upon the section you are going to fish, think carefully regarding the approach. If the chosen section is secluded and one which is normally by-passed by boat traffic, do not send your craft straight through the swim with engine roaring or the oars flaying.

Get upstream of the swim, moor yourself conveniently so that you can cast to or allow the current to take your baited hook to whichever section of the swim you might desire to fish. This initial mooring is most important, for the less you move, the better.

A small craft can be successfully moored in several ways. Poles can be driven into the bed at the bow and stern, and lines passed around; weights can be dropped, or when lying parallel with, and close to a bank, a small mooring anchor rather like a single-pointed pick may be driven into the bank and will hold you securely.

The way in which you moor will to a large extent depend upon where you are fishing, the depth of water, and the composition of the bed; it is impossible to drive a pole into hard gravel or a rocky bed. Mooring across a stream can be dangerous. For example, in the excitement of playing a fish you may forget that stability is an important safety factor and throw too much weight on to the upstream side of your boat. Should this happen and the gunwale dip below the level of a fast-running stream, your boat will be swamped in a matter of seconds. Remember, when mooring, whether it be with poles or weights or an anchor, that this is not an act of final union with bed or bank, you must be able to get under way again quite easily. Driving a pole into soft mud is considerably easier than retrieving it, it is quite surprising the small amount of penetration that effectively holds a pole in position, thus giving adequate mooring.

The fish you hook may be very large and extremely lively; I can assure you that should a large carp decide to run straight under the boat and between the mooring poles, then you have a problem which can only be solved by being able to release one of the mooring lines rapidly.

The tackle and tactics that the boat angler uses are in many ways closely allied to those used by the bank fisher. However there are several variations which make for interesting comparison.

Fishing from a boat rarely calls for long casting. Therefore one is often able to fish with lighter, and consequently more sensitive, floats, but apart from this float fishing techniques are very similar.

It is when one comes to legering that difficulties arise. The bank angler is able to set his rod very carefully upon rests, but however carefully you moor it is virtually impossible to completely obviate boat movement. It therefore follows that certain styles of legering are difficult because of the problem of detecting a shy bite.

When leger fishing for carp I would choose a centrepin reel. The rod can be laid across the boat and a good reel will spin quite freely, allowing the fish to take line and yet feel no resistance. With a fixed spool reel, I have found that if coils of line slip from the spool in the relatively confined space of a boat one can easily get into a mess.

Where the river or lake bed is relatively hard sand or gravel, I have found that leger style fishing has been successful only when I have continually held the rod and felt the bites.

Ground-baiting techniques are similar, whether boat or bank fishing, but the boat angler will find that he has one big advantage. To get the bait in the exact position that he has chosen, often he need do no more than just gently drop it over the side, the current will do the rest.

Maggots can be simply, but effectively, distributed from a paper bag. Fill this with maggots and weight with a stone, twist the corners at the 'open' end, thus expelling some of the air, tear one of the bottom corners off, and slip it gently over the side. The stone will carry it to the bottom where the maggots will soon begin to find their way out of the hole. The bag will eventually disintegrate and will not cause any nuisance.

There is one other method which can be tried, although it is only successful when there is a fair amount of stream and the bottom is relatively hard. A fine mesh bag or similar receptacle can be loaded with ground-bait, including maggots, with the open end tied and the other weighted. This can be lowered to the river-bed – the current to do the rest.

In certain waters trolling, trailing a spinner or

similar bait behind a moving boat, is a highly effective method of fishing for pike. It is a relatively simple operation, but unless it is gone about in a systematic fashion one can end up in the most appalling mess.

If one trolls alone, several precautions must be taken. While rowing, the rod must be within easy reach, and if the angler is wise he will attach a lanyard to the butt. The rowlocks must be tied or fixed in position with whatever device is supplied, and the oars should also be secured to the boat by lanyards. The gaff or landing net should be stowed within easy reach and no loose items of equipment should be allowed to impede them. In a boat, tidiness, efficient angling, and safety go hand in hand.

Safety must be paramount. Only a fool or somebody very inexperienced ignores the dangers inherent in boat fishing. Never stand up to play a fish, and in fact try never to stand at all unless the boat is so stable that it is virtually impossible to capsize it. Always have a suitable baler in the craft, and make sure that your mooring lines, etc. are in good order. Always keep clear of powered craft and adopt the attitude that discretion is the better part of valour – keep clear of craft larger than yourself! Never venture into the upstream approaches to a weir.

On large expanses of water, e.g. Irish loughs and some of the larger English lakes, a sudden wind can rapidly whip the surface into a fury and generate surprisingly large waves. So, when fishing an exposed stretch of water, watch the weather most carefully and at the first sign of deteriorating conditions seek shelter, particularly if you know that you have a fairly long row home against the wind.

Boat fishing offers a challenge which, if met properly and with a reasonable amount of forethought and planning, is well worth accepting. It is a pastime which glass fibre boats and car-top transportation has brought within the reach of thousands who, a decade ago, would not have dreamed of such an activity.

THE CARE AND MAINTENANCE OF TACKLE

by

TERRY THOMAS

The modern angler has many fewer problems to face in maintaining his tackle than he did even twenty years ago. The new tackle materials – glass, nylon, Terylene, none of which is affected by damp – have obviated the need for the care once essential to the keeping of equipment in reliable condition. Nevertheless the wise angler still lavishes attention on his tackle.

RODS

Coarse fishing rods may be made entirely of split cane, of whole cane or reed with a split cane top, of hollow glass, solid glass, tubular aluminium and tubular steel.

Any rod in any material can be broken easily. A rod is a delicate instrument often used in a rough way. Lateral pressure, usually in the form of a foot or a car door, is the most common cause of fracture. Vertical pressure, mostly caused by the rod tip being pushed against some object, will break any kind of top. The first priority then, in looking after a rod is *care*. Do not lay rods down where they can be trodden on. Treat car doors like fierce bulls. When you carry a mounted rod, carry it with the tip to the rear. Never leave a rod where curious cattle can nibble the top.

Rods in natural materials need more attention than those in glass and metals. Modern varnishes give the different woods a very high degree of protection, but care must still be taken not only to protect the basic material but also the rings, fittings and whippings.

The old axiom: 'Never put a rod away wet or in a wet bag' still applies. Damp not only affects all types of cane and metal; equally it rusts rings, rots whippings and causes mildew. Every angler should carry a dry cloth with which to dry off his rod at the end of the day. The rod bag should never be allowed to get wet.

When not in use, the rod should be hung up vertically in its bag. It should never be left leaning against a wall. In such a position it is easily knocked over and trodden on. Cane rods stored in this way can easily become distorted. It is very common for a rod to be returned to the maker with the complaint that it has a 'set'. The wise maker takes a look at all three sections. If the 'set' occurs at the same point in each, he knows that the rod became distorted in its bag either by being left against a wall, by a weighty object being placed on top of it, or, not infrequently, by the rod being carried over a shoulder with a basket on the end.

Wooden rods should never be kept close to any form of heat as this can also cause distortion. Cane consists of a large number of fibres contained in pectin. Heat softens pectin. Indeed it is by the skilled and judicious use of heat that the cane is straightened in the first place. Unwise storing close to a radiator can undo this.

After several seasons' use, most cane and split cane rods will require some attention. There will probably be minor distortions and the finish may need renewing. Some skilled amateurs and some skilled tackle dealers are capable of making a good job of this sort of overhaul but in most cases the rod is best sent back to the firm which made it. This should be done immediately at the end of the season, or, better still, if the rod can be spared, in November. If you start thinking about having a rod overhauled at the beginning of June, you are likely to have to wait some time for this work to be done; tackle makers are at their busiest at this time of year and all receive a large number of rods for repair and overhaul at the last possible moment.

FERRULES

The ferrules of a rod can give a great deal of trouble unless properly looked after. It is essential that they be kept clean, for the tiniest piece of dirt or grit can prevent a ferrule being pushed home, or much worse, being withdrawn. The female ferrule can and should be cleaned by rotating a slightly oiled piece of rag inside it. The male can likewise be cleaned with rag and a little oil. Some anglers like to lubricate ferrules. Provided the lubricant is kept to a minimum this helps good fitting. Too much oil or grease, however, attracts dirt!

'Built-in' ferrules on glass rods must also be kept clean, although the fit here is always easier than with metal ferrules. When separating ferrules always grip the metal, or as close to the metal as possible. Rods are easily distorted and ferrules loosened by twisting the cane or glass.

Joints which have 'stuck' can generally be freed by two pairs of hands. The important thing is to have one of your hands and one of your partner's on each side of the ferrule. In this way the maximum freeing pressure can be applied. Failing this, a little heat from a match will often do the trick.

ROD RINGS

Rings should be frequently checked for damage. Modern lines have considerable cutting power and easily groove intermediate rings. A cracked agate end ring can weaken a line very quickly. Whippings, too, should be regularly inspected to make sure they are holding the rings firmly.

A cork handle looks and feels all the better for a wash. A little soap, warm water and a nail-brush work wonders. Metal fittings should be kept clean and a wipe with an oily rag does no harm from time to time.

THE ROD BAG

Finally, that much misunderstood item of equipment, the rod bag. The purpose of the bag is to contain the rod, to make it easily transportable, to allow it to be hung up and to afford it some degree of protection. Its purpose is not to give weather protection. The rod bag should never be allowed to become wet or covered in mud, which is the fate of probably three out of four.

REELS

Most reels now sold are accompanied by some form of maintenance instructions. These should be adhered to. Unless you are a good engineer, do not take your reel to pieces just to see how it works. You would be surprised how many brand-new reels are returned to the makers to be re-assembled because the owner took his to bits and was unable to put it together again.

As with a rod, so even more importantly, with a reel. Keep it clean. Fifty per cent of reels returned for after-sales service are dirty and some of them are filthy and covered in old ground bait. The fact they still function is tribute to their design.

Where the instructions state to lightly oil, oil lightly. Do *not* smother the reel in oil which will only attract dirt. If the reel is 'pre-lubricated', leave well alone. Remember that fresh water reels are not generally protected against salt water corrosion. If you wish to use your reel in or close to the sea, wash it thoroughly after use, oil it and give the exterior a wipe over with an oily rag.

Care is most important. A reel can be broken, or damaged in other ways, if dropped. Some form of reel case or bag is always worthwhile; these keep reels clean and protect them against damage. Reel handles and bale arms are easily distorted and this damage can stop their functioning or lead to failure at a crucial moment.

When buying a reel, make sure it is supported by a proper guarantee and by an after-sales and repair service. The service given on British reels is quite exceptional, usually 'by return'. Good service too, is given on some imported reels but on others the opposite is true.

LINES

Time was, and not so long ago at that, when lines needed a great deal of after-care. Modern synthetic lines require little if any.

The modern coarse angler uses either nylon monofilament or braided nylon or Terylene. None of these lines rot, so the old bugbear of drying the line after each use is eliminated. Nevertheless, particularly in the case of braided lines, it pays to strip the line from the reel for a short while to allow it to dry; a wet line cannot do the reel any good.

The last couple of yards of line should be cut off after each day's fishing. The act of casting, particularly when spinning or live baiting, imposes a very considerable loading on the line end which drops the breaking strain rapidly. The end of the line is also weakened by contact with rough surfaces on the river bottom.

Damage to a monofil line is very hard to detect but braided lines usually fray out and the point of weakness is easily seen. On multiplying reels a loop of line often works loose on the drum and protrudes through the upper loops so that it can continually foul the pillars and even worse the level wind. Lines can be easily damaged in this way. Monofil lines which have penetrated into the 'works' of a reel should be very carefully checked.

It is most important to load a reel properly and the line should be wound off the packaging spool by allowing it to revolve on a pencil. On fixed spool reels the line should be wound on to about $\frac{1}{8}$ in from the drum lip.

Kink is another factor which weakens lines. A line can be easily unkinked by allowing it to stream out in a strong current.

HOOKS

The most important fact about a hook is that it is sharp. A small carborundum stone should always be carried and the hook point touched up with this. Always test the spring of the hook against the thumb nail to ensure that it is neither too soft nor too brittle.

Hooks, either loose or fixed to nylon, are now so cheap that they should be looked upon as ex-pendable. It is folly to use a mounted hook for more than one day's fishing. Equally any suspect hook should never be used.

SWIVELS

A touch of oil greatly increases efficiency.

NETS

As with every other item of tackle, keep clean. Mice like eating dirty slimy nets.

SPINNERS, SPOONS, ETC.

For obvious reasons they should be put away dry and the hooks checked for sharpness.

BAGS, BASKETS, ETC.

A good scrub gets rid of dirt, fish scales, and old ground-bait.

WADERS

Keep clean, and hang up by the feet so that the stocking part is uncreased and the whole of the inside is exposed to the air.

To sum up, KEEP THINGS CLEAN. In angling, cleanliness is next to 'rodliness' . . .

ABOUT NYLON AND KNOTS

by

ALAN WRANGLES

A knot can be one of several things: a measurement of speed, a hard mass in a tree trunk, or even a group of people. However, from the angler's point of view a knot is an inter-twining of line which enables two separate pieces to be joined together; or, so that a line may be formed in such a manner that it will help to assemble his tackle in the correct manner.

The art of knot-tying is as old as the history of man. Most of the knots in current use to-day stem from the seafaring profession, many and wonderful are the knots that come from the days of sail. The names given to them are as fascinating as the methods used to tie them: turk's head, sheet bend, bowline, and reef knot are but a few.

These knots, and many others, were developed for use with ropes and lines that had been constructed in the conventional manner, but with the coming of nylon monofilament a whole new range of knots had to be invented. Originally when a knot was tied in rope much of its efficiency was based upon the fact that as one section of the line crossed the other, so the texture and general physical characteristics could be used to the advantage of the knot-tyer. When the knot was correctly constructed and under strain, one section bit home hard on the other, but the hard polished surface of nylon monofilament does not give much assistance in this manner.

All lines, no matter what material is used in their construction, lose some of their strength as soon as they are formed into a knot, or run over or laid around a sharp bend. Just how much efficiency is lost depends mainly upon the severity of the bend.

Monofilament lines are no exception, and in some ways they are more prone to damage than braided lines constructed from natural fibres.

This can be demonstrated quite easily by taking hold of a piece of ordinary string made from cotton or hemp. Squeeze a fold of the line between thumb and forefinger, and it will be seen

that it will straighten out quite easily, and it will soon be impossible to see where the line was folded. If a similar test were carried out on a piece of nylon monofilament, the bend would be far more permanent.

Synthetic fishing lines have certain peculiarities, and to understand them it is necessary to have an insight into their beginnings. It is an interesting story and once understood, the reasons for the advice given regarding usage can be readily appreciated.

The origin of nylon lies in the coal mines and oil reserves of the world, and it is from these fundamental materials that tar is extracted. The tar is then converted to benzine from which phenol is obtained, a material which after a further manufacturing process is turned into caprolactam.

Continuing the manufacturing process, caprolactam is further treated until there emerges a plastic-like material called Type 6 Nylon, which is only one of five basic types.

The Type 6 Nylon in chip form then enters a manufacturing process during which the chemists build into it the various properties which the angler demands. In other words, it is possible to make the final product either very stiff or extremely limp. At both ends of the scale there are problems. The very stiff line becomes unmanageable and will fracture extremely easily, and the very soft line may have excessive stretch or other characteristics which the angler does not want. But, and this is the important point to remember, nylon monofilament is a man-made fibre which has a set pattern in its molecular construction.

This pattern is to a large extent 'placed in order' during the stretching process. This is the point at which the line is placed under tension and is stretched to approximately four times its original length (and is reduced to half its original diameter).

This is done to increase its breaking strain in

relation to its diameter, and to decrease its tendency to stretch under the pull of a heavy fish.

When a knot is tied the pattern becomes disturbed and a weakness appears. This weakening can result in a loss of efficiency which can mean a reduction in the strength of the line of up to 30 per cent. If then, it is possible for the line to lose as much as 30 per cent of its efficiency when a specially designed knot is used, the result of using a non-approved knot can easily be imagined. Of course, the 30 per cent loss is at the extreme range. There are many knots which have the strength of 80–90 per cent, but if one is using a line of 2 lb breaking strain, a 25 per cent loss in efficiency could result in the loss of many good fish, unless this fact is realised and allowed for.

There is one other important fact regarding nylon monofilament line which concerns the seldom fully-appreciated fact that nylon does absorb water and when it has done so its strength is reduced. For example, a line which was rated as having a 4 lb b.s. when dry, could be 'reduced' to a 3·5 b.s. line when completely saturated. Nylon will absorb as much as 11 per cent of its own weight of water, the smaller diameter lines absorbing water far more rapidly than the thicker ones.

All these factors, although in themselves possibly marginal, as a whole can have great bearing on the angler's chances, particularly when he is using lines of a relatively low breaking strain.

Assume that an angler buys a line of 2 lb b.s. (which has been calculated when the line was dry) after several hours' use it will have absorbed much water, sufficient to mean that the breaking strain may be reduced to 1¾ lb. Next, take into consideration a perfectly simple knot, the double overhand loop knot, which has a strength of approximately 75 per cent. This further reduces the strength of the line so that its effective breaking strain is about 1¼ lb.

These figures are obviously an approximation, for there are several other factors which could have a bearing on the final strength. The line could have been in use for some time, and may already have been weakened by excessive strain. Cracked or badly-scored rod rings may have begun to fray the line or wear it in places. All these factors have a great bearing on the efficiency of the angler's line.

A term which is often used but frequently misunderstood is 'balanced tackle'. Whilst this may on occasions refer to a rod's point of balance, it frequently relates to the balance between rod and line.

Imagine a 10 ft beach fishing rod, one capable of casting a 6 oz lead, being used in conjunction with a 2 lb b.s. line. Striking at a fish with a rod of this power would snap the line like a piece of burnt string, for there would be insufficient 'give' in the rod and the sudden shock on the line would prove too much. However, if a 2 lb b.s. nylon were matched with a rod with a wand-like tip, e.g. one specially built for roach fishing, the shock would be cushioned by the flexing of the rod.

I am grateful to Messrs. Noris Shakespeare for permission to reproduce a few of their recommendations regarding rods and matching lines:

It is suggested that a 30 lb b.s. line would be suitable for use with a 12 ft Superfulmar beach caster. This rod is capable of casting 8 oz leads.

A 7 ft Superdynamic medium spinning rod, weighing 8 oz, is capable of delivering 1 oz weights, and it is recommended that 4 to 8 lb b.s. lines be used.

The 13 ft Golden Jubilee match rod weighs 14 oz and can cast ½ oz leads. For this rod, the recommended lines range between 2 and 4 lb b.s.

It can easily be seen that there is not a strict mathematical relationship between these examples, for many factors have to be taken into consideration. For example, the material from which the rod is made and the shape of the curve that the rod assumes when under stress have a bearing on both minimum and maximum line strengths. The versatility of the rod in terms of its capacity to handle the range of line sizes and casting weights is yet another factor which must be borne in mind.

The majority of manufacturers issue or will supply on request all the necessary data regarding their product; so when you buy a new rod, request all the relevant information and use a line which has a breaking strain suited to it.

Apart from nylon, other materials are used in lines for the coarse angler, for example, terylene. Lines of this material are popular with some float fishermen. Match anglers in particular find that its propensity to sink just below the surface

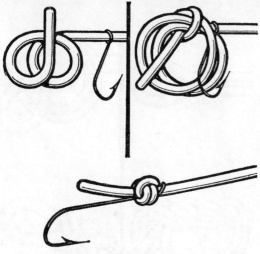

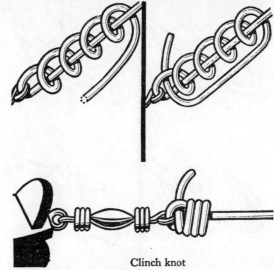

Two-circle turle knot

1. Thread hook or fly, and slide up cast out of the way. Make first circle 6–8 in from this point; overlay the second circle
2. Holding the circles with the thumb and forefinger, tie a slip knot as shown. Tighten the slip knot and push the end of the monofil, and then the hook or fly, through the two circles
3. Pull on standing part, and circles – close one after the other. See that circles close round neck of hook or fly.
Knot strength 88%

Clinch knot

1. Thread the end through the eye of the swivel and twist four times round the shaft.
2. Pass the end through and over the loop next to the eye.
3. Hold the end and pull shaft to tighten knot.
Knot strength 85%

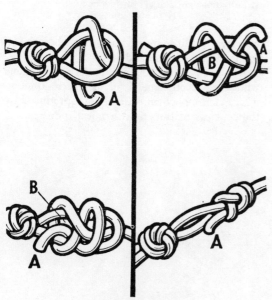

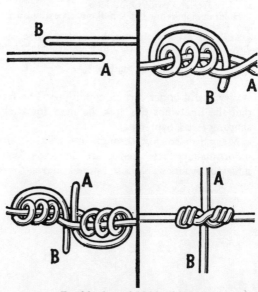

Tucked sheet bend

1. Pass line A through, over and under the cast loop as shown.
2. Pass line A under itself to form loop B.
3. Pass line A over itself and through loop B.
4. Pull line A tight, holding its other end firm.
Knot strength 69%

Double three-fold blood knot

1. Place the two ends to be joined, A and B, alongside each other.
2. Twist the end B three times round the shaft of A, then pass B through the space formed where the ends just cross.
3. Twist the end A three times round the shaft of B, then pass A, in the opposite direction to B, through the space formed where the ends just cross.
4. Pull knot tight and cut off ends A and B (unless you want to catch a dropper, in which case one end can be left long).

Knot strength 80%

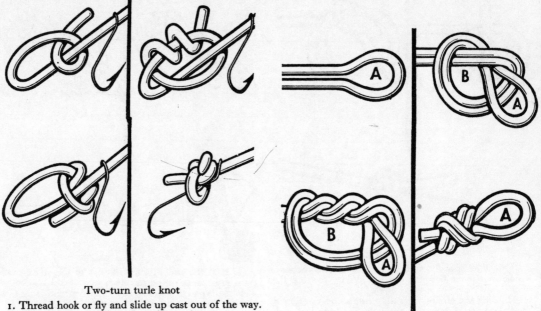

Two-turn turle knot

1. Thread hook or fly and slide up cast out of the way. Pass free end round the cast to form a loop.
2. Twist free end twice round loop.
3. Holding loop in one hand, pull on free end until the knot is tight.
4. Push the hook or fly, together with the free end, through loop and pull on cast until knot is tightly held round hook or fly.

Knot strength 83%

Double overhand loop knot

1. Bend end of cast back on itself to form loop A.
2. Twist loop A round cast to form loop B.
3. Twist loop A once more round.
4. Pull knot tight and cut off free end.

Knot strength 74%

is very useful under certain conditions. The fact that the line sinks obviates the need for back-shotting (see Chapter 10).

Many fish are lost through line failures, and unfortunately these losses are so often 'self-inflicted wounds'. These would never have occurred if a little more thought had been given to the subject of knots and lines.

Above and on p. 203 are a selection of knots which are recommended for use in conjunction with nylon monofilament and are reproduced by the courtesy of Imperial Chemical Industries.

FLY FISHING FOR COARSE FISH

by

BARRIE WELHAM

Bickerdyke wrote at length about catching pike on salmon flies, and most years the occasional eel is

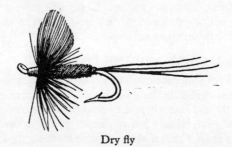

Wet fly

caught by a sea-trout fisher. There are also rather special conditions, such as in a heavy fall of flying ants, when all manner of coarse fish will turn their attention upwards to the food on the surface and so could, for a short time, be taken on a fly rod. In fact during these times their pre-occupation with surface feed may mean that the fly rod would be the most efficient and effective way of taking fish, but these are obviously rather rare occasions.

Dry fly

The scarcity of fly fishing within reasonable distance of our larger cities has, in recent years, been slightly alleviated by the new reservoirs which have been stocked with trout. These artificial lakes certainly provide some very excellent fly fishing, but unfortunately it is all of one type – still water, whereas access to river fly fishing is getting more and more difficult.

Running water, where a fish can take up a station and wait for its food to be carried to him by the current, has additional appeal plus the fact that in running water a dry fly, or a nymph fished high in the water so that the take is visible, can often account for a high percentage of fish.

Admitting to the appeal and excitement of running water, and at the same time making the point that river trout fishing is either difficult to obtain, very expensive or both, leads us quite naturally to Fly Fishing for Coarse Fish.

At certain times during the season all manner of coarse fish can be taken on the fly. John

The coarse fish species that fall regularly to the fly rod are bleak, dace, rudd, chub and slightly less often roach and perch.

Of these the bleak is so small that while encouraging to the young angler, it is hardly worthy of serious specialisation. Coming to the dace we have an unfortunate contradiction. Game in spirit it certainly is but being generally small, and often in a shoal, its sporting properties are diminished. Even worse, its very speed of rise is a distraction from the pleasure of a visible take.

The rudd is not subject to the same shortcomings as either of the species so far considered but as rudd are more often found in still water than in rivers, this is its own deficiency.

We come now to roach but these are only occasional risers and while perch will certainly take a wet fly, they do not rise well to surface food.

That leaves just chub and here we have a quarry that fills the bill perfectly, for not only is it capable of growing to great weight, it is cautious and almost cunning, and strong and powerful into the bargain. The chub, and here I can only judge from my own experience, does not deserve the reputation of being a sluggard and a bonehead, for when a good chub is hooked on normal fly tackle he will give an excellent account of himself.

There is only one thing wrong with fly fishing for chub – it has not become as fashionable as fly fishing for trout. But it is high time that fly fishers woke up to the fact that the chub offers good sport and more fun than some of the trout to be found in many places nowadays. Remember there are no hatchery, hand-fed chub, they are all wild native fish and on average they are also much larger than most river-caught trout. Even more important – almost everyone can find good chub fishing whether it be in the Thames, the Ouse, the Severn or any one of many rivers all over the country. There is also one last and not unimportant plus feature. Chub will take a fly right through a summer's day, even when most other fishing is in a slump.

THE PLACES AND THE TECHNIQUE

Fly fishing for chub does not really start until about mid-July. By then the fish have moved out of the shallows where they cleaned after spawning and have taken up a station over deeper water where they can, if alarmed, sink from sight. The point about sinking is worth remembering for chub will rarely cause a commotion by rushing off if alarmed. Hence they do not give their position away – they just sink from sight and are gone. Because of this preference for the safety of deep water, do not waste time casting up to the gentle shelving edges. Fish up to clean-cut banks, search every pocket in marginal weeds, around lily beds, along walls and camp sheathing, by the sides of bushes and under overhanging trees.

The amount of chub fishing that I have done on small rivers has been very limited and not always successful. Most of my time has been concentrated on the bigger rivers and in these a boat is necessary. In fact this is a two-man team job with one person at the oars while the other fishes. The oarsman's job is to put the fisher quietly and carefully within range of every likely fish holding spot, and to hold the boat there while his partner covers the area. As fishing is done from the sitting position it is possible to get quite close, therefore long casting is not necessary. The angler nets his own fish so the boat is never allowed to swing out of control to possibly spoil other water as yet unfished.

The spell at the paddle will not be found monotonous as there is a very real satisfaction in putting your companion quietly and cautiously within casting range for the fish he then catches are as much through your own efforts as his own.

FISH REACTION

Although most of the fishing will be with a dry fly, there will rarely be a sufficient rise to allow the fish's position to be positively pinpointed. This being so, one usually fishes the stream rather than the rise but do not think that the best fish shoot up immediately to engulf every morsel that drops into their field of vision. I have had many opportunities to see fish in the water and to watch their reaction as both natural and artificial flies came over. Often as the fly drops, the best fish back away a few inches and lie watching. Sometimes they sidle forward, coming up as much as a minute or more later to sip the fly quietly from the surface. Other fish just lie inert as if the tasty morsel so close above them did not exist,

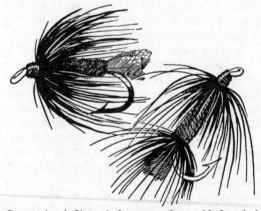

Conventional flies of the type often sold for chub fishing

but let the fly fidget and struggle and they sometimes rush to take it.

All of these observations led me a long time ago to largely abandon the big bushy palmer type fly normally sold for chub. I did this for several reasons. The first being that however well hackled or carefully oiled, it was not long before they got so wet as to necessitate continual false casting. Secondly the conventional fly needs washing, drying and re-oiling after every fish and the frustration that this causes when the fish is small, can be greater than you might think. Finally and most important of all, if you try to work a heavily hackled fly in an endeavour to imitate a struggling insect, it just tends to drown it.

For these reasons I now almost always use lures (you can hardly call them flies) that are natural floaters through being made of either cork or wood or some other buoyant material. Such things require no oiling and float perfectly.

The assortment of suitable commercially-made lures is not large, but some small wooden grass-hoppers are available and at times these can be very successful (see below). Some of the floating lures popular in America for black bass can also be excellent but unfortunately many of these are too large.

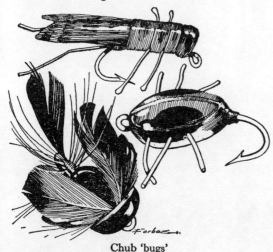

Chub 'bugs'

AMPLE SCOPE FOR EXPERIMENT

From this it is obvious that the room for improvisation is large. Just as great in fact as the ceaseless experiments which go on in an endeavour to find more effective trout and salmon flies. The wide scope can cover little ladybird-like animals (column 1) made from cork or balsa wood down through bugs made from the end of a large quill with the cut end plugged with cork and the whole threaded on to the shank of a hook (column 1). It is a sound plan to paint the top surface in a bright colour, orange or yellow, for example. Anything you can see easily will cut down eye strain. Remember, the fish cannot see the top surface, however garish it may be, and the bottom side can be coloured more appropriately.

BUG TACKLE

The use of buoyant bugs has all the advantages of the dry fly in that the take is excitingly visible. The only disadvantage is that they are heavier than a normal fly, so a very light rod is not suitable and you need a rod which will carry a line of sufficient weight to turn over this rather bulky bait. The point of the cast must not be too fine either, for the extra weight of the bug will soon fatigue fine nylon. Monofilament of ·010 in or even ·011 in is not too heavy and will ensure a clean delivery; it is also useful when a good chub makes its first powerful lunge for underwater tree roots, at which point it is very much a question of hook and hold hard.

The last advantage of the bug is that it can really be moved and so lure a fish into taking. To do this, lower the point of the rod as the cast is completed. Recover any slack and after the ripples have died away snap the rod tip up about six inches. Really make the lure 'pop' and then watch out for fireworks.

Bug fishing is exciting and particularly so when you have induced the take. It also gives variety, with the many types of 'take' that range from the gentle, timid, sippy rise to the full blooded rush that pushes a wave of water before it.

OTHER WAYS

There are of course ways other than dry fly.

Sinking nymph

The sinking nymph is certainly effective, and probably more so than the surface fly. Also it is

207

very exciting to see the tell-tale draw of the cast, but in the broken light under bushes this is sometimes difficult and without this visual thrill the excitement is largely lost.

Although, as I have explained, there are many species of coarse fish that will rise to a fly, in my opinion only the chub really justifies the effort that must be expended when fishing in this manner—but a big chub on a fly between July and September can be both thrilling and worthwhile.

BRITISH RECORD FISH

		lb	*oz*	*dm*		
Barbel	*Barbus barbus*	13	12	0	J. Day	Royalty Fishery, Hants, 1962
Bleak	*Alburnus alburnus*		3	15½	D. Pollard	Staythorpe Pond, nr. Newark, 1971
Bream Common Bronze	*Abramis brama*	12	14	0	G. J. Harper	R. Stour, Suffolk, 1971
Carp	*Cyprinus carpio*	44	0	0	R. Walker	Redmire Pool, 1952
Crucian Carp	*Carassius carassius*	4	6	4	P. H. Oliver	Private lake, Surrey, 1970
Catfish (Wels)	*Silurus glanis*	43	8	0	R. J. Bray	Wilstone Reservoir, Tring, Herts, 1970
Char	*Salvelinus alpinus*	1	1	4	J. K. Hargreaves	Carn Tarsuinn, Inverness-shire, 1971
Dace	*Leuciscus leucisus*	1	4	4	J. L. Gasson	Little Ouse, Thetford, 1960
Eel	*Anguilla anguilla*	8	10	0	A. Dart	Hunstrete Lake, 1969
Gudgeon	*Gobio gobio*		4	0	M. Morris	Susworth Roach Ponds, Lincs., 1971
Gwyniad (Whitefish)	*Coregonus lavaretus*	1	4	0	J. R. Williams	Llyn Tegid, 1965
Loch Lomond powan	*Coregonus albula*	1	5	12	D. J. Warren	Loch Lomond, 1970
Perch	*Perca fluviatilis*	4	12	0	S. F. Baker	Oulton Broad, 1962
Pike-perch Walleye	*Stizostedion vitreum*	11	12	0	F. Adams	The Delph, Welney, 1934
Pike-perch Zander	*Stizostedion lucioperca*	15	5	0	W. G. Chilling-worth	Gt. Ouse Relief Chnl.
Roach	*Rutilus rutilus*	3 / 3	14 / 14	0 / 0	W. Penney / A. Brown	Lambeth Reservoir, 1938 / Stamford, 1964
Rudd	*Scardinius*	4	8	0	Rev. E. C. Alston	Thetford, 1933
Ruffe	*Acerina cernua*		4	0	B. B. Poyner	R. Stour, 1969
Trout (Brown)	*Salmo trutta*	18	2	0	K. J. Grant	Loch Garry, 1965
Trout (Rainbow)	*Salmo gairdneri*	10	0	4	M. Parker	King's Lynn, 1970
Salmon	*Salmo salar*	64	0	0	Miss G. W. Ballantyne	River Tay, 1922
Schelly Skelly	*Coregonus lavaretus*	1	1	0	P. F. White	R. Eden, Cumberland, 1969
Tench	*Tinca tinca*	9	1	0	J. Salisbury	Hemingford Grey, 1963

INDEX